ACROSS THE GAP

FRAGMENTS OF HISTORY FROM WIDNES AND RUNCORN

Jean M. Morris

First published in Great Britain in 2016

Copyright © Jean M. Morris - 2016

SPRINGFIELD-FARRIHY PUBLISHING

CONTENTS

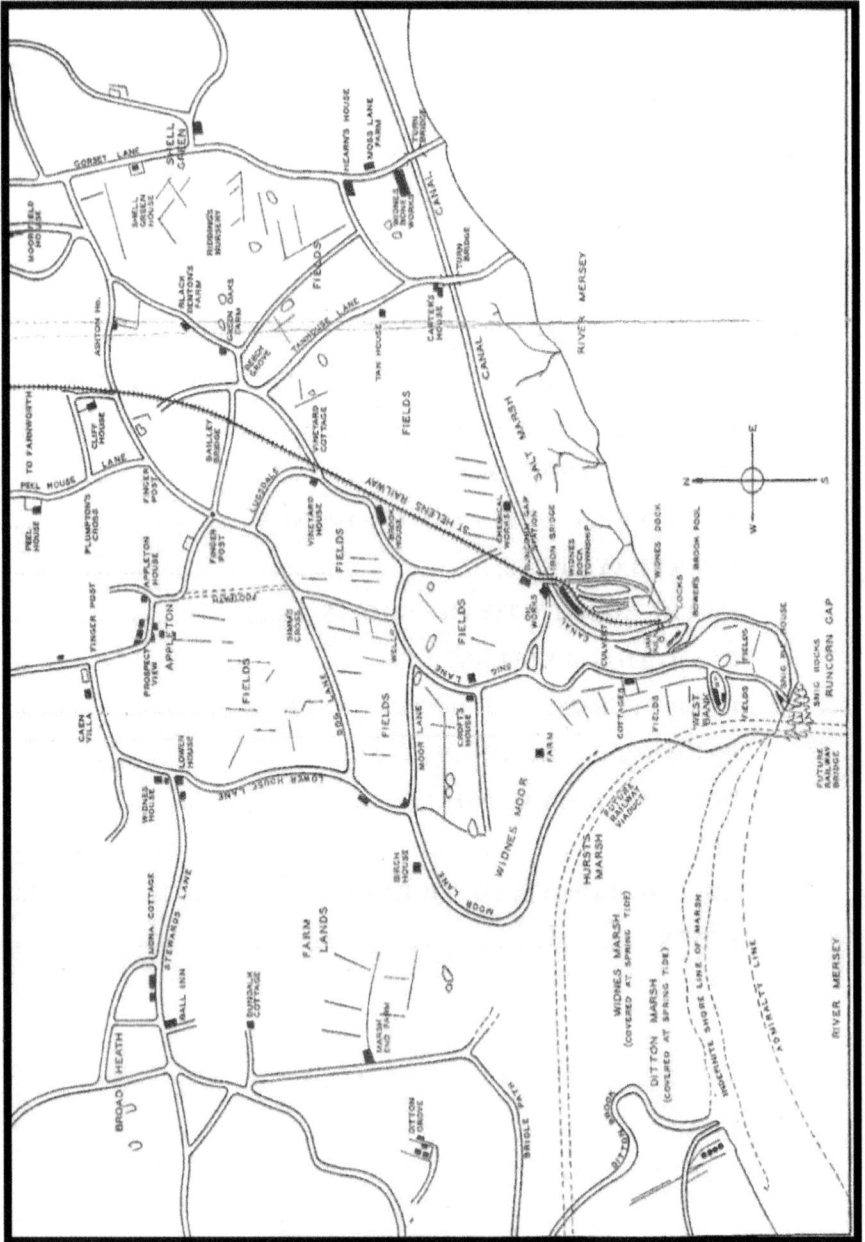

WIDNES 1845

INTRODUCTION

I have always found historical research a fascinating and rewarding activity, as not only does it provide a window on our past it also allows us to view and evaluate important events from a critical distance. By sampling just a small amount of the hundreds of thousands of original documents available in Public Record Offices and other official repositories we are able to mull over contemporary comments and opinions on past events and people. Although the internet is available to everyone now, and it can certainly be a useful tool, I much prefer to work with original material whenever possible. I do this because the internet presents numerous problems for historians, not because of the volume of information available, but because of the quality and accuracy of some material. There is no guarantee that the mound of historical data posted on a plethora of websites is correct, as internet information can only be as good as the work which goes into preparing and copying original documentation. In some cases personal opinions or suppositions have been quoted as fact and given credence because they have been published online. Furthermore, some of this *"history"* is un-supported by documentary evidence, sources are not always revealed, nor has the information been referenced or footnoted. But, apart from problems of inaccuracy which can sometimes occur, from a completely personal viewpoint, the internet does not provide the thrill of viewing and handling original documents. So, for those of you with a real thirst for history, I suggest a visit to our local Record Offices or a trip to the National Archives at Kew where even routine research tasks, though laborious, will give you a great deal of personal satisfaction.

Apart from original documentation, interpreting other historical material is never an easy task as, for obvious reasons, modern historians must generally refer to previously written works for information. With that in mind, we all know that there is probably no such thing as an unbiased history and therefore we cannot be sure that what we are reading has been presented in an objective manner. From time immemorial history has been written by the victors to the detriment of the losers, or written specifically for one section of society or another and, therefore, slanted in a favourable way for whichever group it was aimed at. Interpreting such material means reading history from all perspectives and recognising the partiality in each. The true story is often somewhere in the middle. Of course all human beings have some form of bias and it would be quite dishonest of me to say otherwise. However, this bias only becomes a problem when it prevents historians from being cautious, sensible and, above all, truthful in their representation of the facts. So, although in reality there is actually no such thing as an impartial history there is such a thing as a *"balanced history"*. With that in mind, and despite any personal bias, it has always been my intention to offer balanced historical accounts.

Over the past years I have written several books on the history of Widnes and its hinterlands. My main theme has been the social history of ordinary people, not just the social elites. I believe that the history of these non-elite groups is of particular interest and relevance to our modern communities because these countless generations of people, whose names have usually been buried in the mists of time and obscurity, represent the silent masses from which most of us descend. The study of their lived experiences and the relationships between people, no matter who they were or where they came from, should be explored as a way of commemorating and acknowledging their labours and achievements.

As we all know, the transformation of both towns, both physically and socially, was the direct result of the arrival of industry and its fairly rapid expansion. The swift and unprecedented scale of local trade and industry attracted whole groups of people from a variety of cultures and backgrounds into our two towns. As a consequence, there were marked differences of race, religion, culture and status among our evolving industrial populations. The subsequent interaction between all these groups of people in daily life forms an interesting and important part of our history. There is no doubt that the general vitality of local urban life in both towns in the 19th century was due to a new compound of many diverse experiences.

During the research processes for my previous books I came across numerous bits of information which at the time, though interesting, did not fall within the framework of a particular work. However, all history is valuable and relevant to someone and therefore historical research is never wasted. Much of this additional material was connected to Runcorn and its inhabitants. Despite the fact that this was outside my area of work, nevertheless, any items of information about our neighbouring town were kept for personal interest. Recently, when looking back through my research material I was struck by the variety and amount of information I had amassed about both towns. Naturally, being a Widnesian, my main concentration of historical and sociological research has always been associated with my hometown and for that reason the greater part of this work concerns Widnes. However, I do hope that Runcorn readers will also find this book of some interest as I include a significant amount of historical information relating to that town.

As you journey through this book I am sure that some readers will feel that I have placed undue emphasis on class divisions and social inequality. However I make no apologies for doing so as these two themes were recurring issues during the periods covered in this work. Both topics, along with politics and the law, affected all aspects of people's lives and none more so than the poor. It may also seem that I have included overly long accounts of general history, rather than devoting this book entirely to local matters. Once again, I make no apology for doing this as I feel it is important to provide the historical background to some of the events and viewpoints which influenced local matters and impacted on our residents. National actions, laws, and attitudes had a considerable bearing on the manners and conduct of our local populations so, because of this, I feel it is justifiable and constructive to include some wider historical information. It is often necessary to view a larger picture to appreciate the finer details in a smaller one, otherwise only half the picture is visible instead of the entire landscape.

Whilst looking through my collection of material it was difficult to decide what to include as determining what is relevant is never straightforward. Some of the pieces were interesting from a historical point of view whilst others were relatively inconsequential or simply amusing. However, I believe that even minor pieces of information are worthy of note as, when viewed from a modern perspective, they sometimes highlight the difference between the values and moral standards of those times with those of today. Nevertheless, whatever degree of importance this information may be, it serves to shed a ray of light into some hidden corners of our history. Unfortunately, space does not allow me to embrace all my material in one book, so I have tried to create a reasonable balance. Therefore, I offer this small collection of historical fragments to all Widnesians and Runcornians who share my appetite for history.

I would like to conclude by acknowledging the liberal assistance I have received from a variety of people during the writing of this book. The numerous members of staff at Public Archives, Record Offices, official repositories and libraries offered welcome help and guidance in my searches and often made my task much easier with their extensive knowledge. Paul Meara of The Catalyst was generous with his help and customary good humour and archivist John Blewett was patience personified. The Catalyst archives provided me with useful information about the Hutchinson Company and other chemical related material. However, in addition to this, John Blewett spent a great deal of time in finding supplementary Hutchinson material for me, which I hope may result in a book in the future. I thank John most sincerely for his copious help, kindness and tolerance. I also called upon my old friend, Dr. William Petrie, for assistance in gaining access to significant records and, as usual, he gave good advice and opened several doors for me. Despite extraordinarily high demands on his time he was extremely liberal with his help and guidance and I am greatly indebted to him and his army of history professionals. Thanks are also due to Frank Jones for providing the cover and other photographs as well as to my friend Marion Wilson who offered me photographs from the collection of her father, the late Gordon Howarth.

Lastly, but certainly by no means least, I would like to acknowledge the enormous personal gratitude I owe to the late, lovely, Joan Briscoe who bequeathed to me her collection of history books and history related documents. Joan loved history, especially the history of her beloved Farnworth. She was also passionately interested in education having many years ago, during her teaching career at The Wade Deacon School, written the history of The Widnes Education Board. I dedicate this book to Joan's memory and also to that of my dear friends the late Mary Riley and her brother Jack, the late Lord Ashley of Stoke. Over countless years Mary and Jack provided me with encouragement, inspiration and humour, as well as a myriad of interesting and entertaining conversations. They were both dear and much loved friends who are greatly missed.

Jean M. Morris

OUR TOWNS AND THE CHANGING FACE OF BRITAIN

In order to understand how and why our two towns developed and expanded we need to appreciate the origins of the changes which caused these things to happen. To identify the reasons we must look far beyond local events, as Runcorn and Widnes were only a minor part of a growing national movement of social and economic change. Our two towns, like countless other areas around Britain, were to experience the numerous influences of the progress and industrialisation which transformed the country after the Industrial Revolution. This revolution, which started in Britain around 1760, was to be the herald of enormous change. Not only did it bring great and positive developments in manufacturing methods it also had a major influence upon the traditional nature and structure of social order. Whilst historians may not entirely agree on the exact definition of the Industrial Revolution, it is a handy term used to describe the processes of industrialisation and change which occurred in Britain in the 18th and 19th centuries. The impact of these processes was wide ranging, severe and often very sudden. Obviously, industrialisation was bound to have radical consequences both socially and economically upon all levels of British society and there were few people who were unaffected. These sweeping effects were most acute in small areas like Widnes and Runcorn.

In the early 1800s Britain was primarily an agrarian country but by the middle of that century, having undergone a rapid industrialisation process, it had become known as the workshop of the world [1]. Employment opportunities with the prospect of regular wages meant that the lure of the towns was strong for agricultural workers whose rural employment was previously governed by the demands of season or weather. As a consequence, a large rural exodus meant that towns swiftly replaced villages and hamlets as the focal point of population. Unfortunately, this mass departure from the countryside outstripped the natural population growth which meant that village communities

---

[1] A term commonly used by historians when writing about that period.

diminished drastically. The spectacular and fairly rapid advance of industrial towns inevitably led to concerns by landowners and tenant farmers about the depopulation of rural areas. However, the wheels of industrialisation had been set in motion and change was unstoppable.

The effects of the Industrial Revolution and a subsequent population influx into towns were the key driving forces behind rapid urban expansion in Britain during the nineteenth century. This growth was also aided by improved roadways and increasing rail coverage which made distance travel more accessible and helped to keep migration costs low. There is no doubt that the rise of industry and urban growth, through internal and external migration, were inexorably linked to the development of our two towns. Of course Widnes and Runcorn were not unique in this respect as the spread of industry and economic modernisation created wage differentials which induced migration all around the country. This mass movement of workers contributed to unprecedented population growths in all the developing industrial areas in Britain, rapidly swelling towns and cities alike. In fact, the resultant high rate of internal mobility, particularly from the declining rural areas to the fast growing urban regions, was one of the most prevalent demographic features of nineteenth-century Britain.

Before the advent of significant industry the places we now know as Widnes and Runcorn were little more than a collection of scattered villages with small populations. In King's *"Vale Royal"*, Runcorn in the mid-17th century was described as *"nothing but a fair parish church, a parsonage and a few scattered tenements"*. Towards the end of the eighteenth century Runcorn had seen some minor development, although the area was still typical of many other parts of Britain in that the local economy was based mainly on agriculture, small cottage industries, quarrying or river related occupations. Things were far quieter on the other side of the river as, even as late as 1841, at least 80% of the land which comprised the rural township of Widnes was under cultivation and only 3.6% was occupied by buildings. In fact, throughout Britain prior to the Industrial Revolution the land was the greatest source of wealth in rents, profits and wages.

In the early 1800s almost all economic, social and political power was in the hands of those who owned or farmed land. At that time, and for countless generations before, the social and economic composition of Britain was based on a pyramid structure. At the apex were the great landowners, an aristocratic ruling class who completely monopolised economic and political power. This arrangement was unmistakably marked out with a tiny minority of the rich and powerful at the top, through even larger and wider layers of lesser wealth and power to the great mass of the poor and the powerless at the bottom. The extreme simplicity of this social and economic pyramid, from the wide spread at the base to the narrow point of the summit, demonstrates a clearly defined social structure of different strata with distinct measures of status, power and economic interests.

Even though the land had provided employment and wealth for centuries, the tide of innovation and enterprise which occurred in England, particularly during the Victorian era, brought about a fundamental change as industry developed at a rapid pace. The impact of this drastic change affected all aspects of life, particularly the lives of the working classes. As we have seen, the countryside became a reservoir of cheap labour as workers left in droves and travelled to new manufacturing towns like Widnes and other northern regions in search of work. For most people this new type of employment, though arduous, was more secure and reliable than agricultural work which was seasonally controlled and notoriously low paid. Of course, with the growth of industrial England, these migrant workers were simply reacting to a situation which was visibly changing all around them. This change, and the shift of focus from agriculture to industry, meant that both workers and employers were forced to adapt to new situations and difficulties. However, it should be pointed out that despite the fact that industrialisation had spread quite quickly; there were still many survivors from the older social and economic structure. Some types of employment remained an essential part of daily life. For instance, in 1847 there were still more shoemakers than factory workers and one in ten of all females over the age of 11 years was employed in domestic service of some sort.

It could be said that the Industrial Revolution was fairly late coming to places like Widnes and Runcorn, nevertheless, the changes that first took place in Britain during the late eighteenth century spread throughout the country like ripples on a pond. By the beginning of the nineteenth century the industrial and social transformation of Britain had made steady progress. The age of the factory had arrived and the decline of agriculture as the main source of employment was firmly underway. Therefore, it was inevitable that the ripples of change would eventually reach our area.

The great tide of optimism and modernisation that swept through the country at this time offered tremendous opportunities and rewards for enterprising men who possessed both courage and vision. As a result, new breeds of *"self-made men"* evolved. These men were active working capitalists who both owned and managed their own business ventures. They were the pioneers of a new industrial economy which replaced the land based economy of previous centuries. Naturally this economic change, and the new advances in industry and commerce, completely undermined the feudal system of labour that had previously existed and, as a result, landed and aristocratic privilege was challenged. This fairly radical change meant that the balance of power gradually tilted in favour of the new entrepreneurial middle classes to the detriment of the landed aristocracy.

Fellow students of the Victorian era and its culture will be familiar with a strain of literature, such as that of Thomas Carlyle and William Ruskin, which attacks the factory system for brutalising workers and destroying home life, and there is a lot to be said for that theory. However, some modern historians have based their own opinions of this period upon the traditional image of the nineteenth century as a period of great opportunity for men of energy and skill who strove to establish a society based on merit rather than on the circumstances of one's birth. Certainly, the development of our two towns can be attributed to the latter view. In fact, our local expansion was mainly due to the enterprising nature of a few far-sighted men who seized the unique opportunities available to them. As a result some individuals, through their own diligent enterprise, were able to accumulate spectacular wealth which subsequently led to the growth of a prosperous entrepreneurial middle-class society. Of course this wealth was due in no small way to the thousands of workers who contributed to this new industrial economy with their sweat and labour. I might add that many hundreds also contributed with their lives. It is also well worth saying that even though local industry brought benefits for many; we should remember that the benefits came first and in larger quantities to the entrepreneurial middle classes.

Whilst the Industrial Revolution was responsible for bringing about an alteration in the established social structure throughout Britain, it also drastically transformed the physical environment in those places where industry had developed. In fact, the rapid process of industrialisation completely changed the face of a large part of Britain's landscape. The damaging result of industry upon the countryside was the most obvious visual downside of progress. Although Runcorn and Widnes were once renowned as places of beauty, attracting visitors to their river banks in pursuit of relaxation and fresh air, both towns were to change radically with the growth of industrial development. The transformation which occurred was obviously a cause of great regret to those members of the indigenous populations who had known the areas prior to the arrival of industry. Although we modern readers are unable to appreciate their unique experiences, we are extremely fortunate to be able to draw upon numerous written accounts which provide glimpses of both towns prior to their industrialisation. These fascinating descriptions give contemporary versions of the sweeping changes which took place in the two towns. When reading them we are tempted to peep beyond the written word and create our own visions of what local places may have looked or felt like in those times.

Obviously, the development of industry with its new methods of production created a demand for heavy goods like iron and coal. These raw materials could not easily be transported by horses over inadequate roads, which in some cases were little more than dirt tracks. Besides the difficulties associated with the appalling state of the roads there was also the problem of only being able to move small amounts of material at one time. This made commercial transportation by road both hazardous and expensive. Therefore it became imperative to improve communications either by upgrading roadways or by developing some other form of transport so that industry could expand. Of course the sea and rivers provided an ancient form of access for mercantile transport but although the rivers, so far as they were navigable, were important distributing channels they could only serve part of the country. Digging new artificial waterways, canals, which could be constructed wherever they were needed, was the obvious answer. And so by the late eighteenth century these man-made waterways were being developed around the country to provide new transport links between places of industrial activity or trade.

Most of the early canals followed the contours of the land as this made construction easier and less locks were needed. However, this method of construction, where the canals curved around the lie of the land, meant that some canals were meandering over long distances and therefore used up more land and took longer to build. As a result they were lengthy and expensive projects. The later built canals, which cut through rocky landscapes or required large aqueducts, gave rise to whole new disciplines of civil engineering. In the 1790s canal building was at its height and a network of canals linking major rivers was constructed around the country. The first canal in our area was the Sankey Canal, later to be known as the St. Helens Canal. This was initially financed by local mine owners as the primarily purpose had been to provide an alternative way of transporting coal down to the Mersey and onward to Liverpool. This canal, which was built by a talented engineer called Henry Berry, had the first double locks in England, sited at Broad Oak, St. Helens.[2] Like the Sankey Canal, most of the early canals were privately funded enterprises and the owners merely provided the waterways as a facility for the transit of goods but the vessels used to transport the cargoes were usually owned by others.

As canals were cut through the countryside to transport the coal, salt, and the other raw materials needed to satisfy the demands of industry, the environment and topography around Britain was drastically altered. This transformation would have been particularly evident in small places like Runcorn where the nearby rivers and canal began to bring substantial commerce and labour into a once quiet locality. Obviously, one of the most important factors in Runcorn's development was the building of the Bridgewater Canal which was opened in 1761 but not fully completed until 1772. The Bridgewater was the first modern purpose built canal in Britain. James Brindley, the Duke of Bridgewater's foreman and one of the greatest canal builders of the age, was responsible for designing and overseeing this enormous project. It has been said that Brindley was rough mannered and virtually illiterate but we can see, from notebooks which have recently been displayed at the National Waterways Museum, that this was not the case. He was a pioneer and a visionary whose skill and experience in canal building was without equal. However, in spite of this brilliance, I am sure that Brindley's early working life had given his contemporaries no indication of the hidden talents which were to emerge. He started off as a ploughboy then became apprenticed to a millwright before eventually taking over the business. He obviously had an aptitude for engineering and began trying out early steam pumping engines for a variety of purposes. Surprisingly, he was in his mid-50s when his first attempt in water transport engineering, the Bridgewater Canal, was finally completed.

Although the building of the Bridgewater Canal brought enormous economic benefits to the area some local residents were extremely unhappy about the detrimental effect on the landscape. In June 1771, prior to the completion of the extended canal, a Runcorn correspondent wrote to *The Derby Mercury* stating that: *"You will have no cheers from this part of Cheshire for the Duke's men who, like locusts, devour the fruits of the earth."* A few months later, in October, another correspondent from Runcorn writing to *The Leeds Intelligencer* gave an

---

[2]The Sankey was later extended from Sankey Bridges down to Fidler's Ferry, then to St. Helens with a further extension down to Widnes Docks.

impression of the local attitude towards the Canal. The letter, which is reproduced here, also gives an idea of the scale of the work involved.

> *Extract of a letter from Runcorn in Chefhire*
> " If you were to fee this place, you would think the Duke of Bridgewater was going to build a town, with a church of ftone. He has made a million and a half of bricks, and brought fome ftones as large as thofe upon Salifbury-plain, which, with eafe, he weilds about by engines; thefe are to make his locks to defcend the banks of the Merfey; for though his navigation through Lancafhire and Chefhire is moftly level, yet here, as the river lies 28 yards below the level, and his fcheme of croffing the ftream by a navigation-bridge to Liverpoole is at prefent laid afide, his barges muft go down to the river by locks, which will be finifhed in this quarter, and he have a free courfe to Liverpoole in two years; this done, his workmen will cut a water carriage between the trading towns of Manchefter and Stockport, which will open another magazine of profit to the Duke. Many of the Gentlemen of this county met a fortnight ago to fix the price of the land belonging to Sir Richard Brookes, which his Grace is to cut through; after two days debate they fettled the fum laid for damage to be nine hundred and odd pounds."

THE LEEDS INTELLIGENCER – OCTOBER 1771

One can well imagine the feelings of local residents as the small town was inundated with noisy workers as they cut mercilessly through the local landscape. Obviously the volume of labour involved in this process would have been substantial. There were several hundred navvies whose only tools, apart from their brawn, were pick axes, shovels, buckets and wheelbarrows. These powerful workers were joined by teams of stonemasons and the poor puddlers who had the awful job of treading in the clay which lined the base of the canal to make it watertight. It was difficult, slow and extremely dangerous work and countless men were killed in the process. Of course the fact that it was not a quick job meant that disruption to life in the town and surrounding areas was probably a major and long term annoyance. However, besides the noise and interference caused to daily life, the influx of hundreds of canal workers would also have had a considerable impact on the social milieu of the town. On the other hand, some would have viewed the arrival of this huge stream of workers as a welcome benefit to the local economy.

Apart from the intrusion upon local life and the countryside, the Duke of Bridgewater's undertaking came at a huge financial cost. It is worth mentioning that the Duke did not use much of his personal money to fund this venture, instead, large sums of money were raised by borrowing and issuing bonds to the lenders. Although his Barton Aqueduct had proved to be a huge success, the Duke still found it difficult to find investors for his scheme and his debt steadily increased with every new addition or refinement to his plan. It was reported that by 1786 the Duke was in debt to the tune of £365,000 and had found it necessary to limit his personal spending to £400 per year; he even resorted to borrowing money from his employees. It is interesting to note, from the above letter, that Sir Richard Brooke apparently drove a hard bargain as it took two days of fierce negotiation to fix the price of compensation for his land which, when finally agreed, amounted to a figure in excess of £900.

The proposed Bridgewater Canal received a considerable amount of national publicity as it was a huge and important project as well as an enormous feat of engineering. Readers in various parts of the country were hungry for news and newspapers obliged by offering regular updates on its progress. In August 1772 another Runcorn resident wrote to *Drewry's Derby Mercury* to provide readers with the latest news about the canal. The letter, which is reproduced on another page, paints a vivid picture of the magnitude of the task and provides a fascinating and important historical account relating to several aspects of the building work. We are informed that in the region of 500 men were employed on the local part of the construction and, although James Brindley was the engineer in charge, it seems that the Duke of Bridgewater took a personal interest in overseeing the work on a daily basis. Of course this was an important financial project for the Duke as he had a large number of investors to satisfy, therefore, it was essential that the work progressed as planned.

We can see from this correspondence that its author appeared to be greatly impressed by the vast scale of work involved in building this new waterway communication. No doubt the writer also appreciated the fact that, when it was completed, the canal would bring enormous economic benefits to the town.

Extract of a Letter from Runcorn, *in* Cheſhire, *Auguſt* 19.

" Our Caſtle was famous in Cromwell's Time. Our Gap has ever been notorious for the Wreck of Coaſting Veſſels, but our Navigation Duke has now cut away ſome of the Rock, and when he cuts the reſt, it will probably lay many Miles of Land dry, which are now overflowed by every Tide, and it is expected this will reduce the Merſey to its proper Channel. At preſent we are famous for the Machines of the Duke of Bridgewater, who here employs 500 Men, and 700 in other Parts of his Works ; and it is reckoned that he has expended One Hundred Thouſand Pounds on his Inland Navigation. Mr. Brindley is our great Engineer, but the Duke is chief Director of the Works, and generally overlooks the Men from Morning to Night. The Locks are chiefly finiſhed, being Ten in Number, and are ſuppoſed to coſt on an Average, 200l. each. The lowermoſt Lock is 22 Feet and a Half in Depth, (which is about the Heighth of the higheſt Tides) and will diſcharge Veſſels at neap Tides. One Set of Men are here making Well-Brick and Culvert-Brick ; others are burning Lime in a Kiln whoſe Fire is never extinguiſhed, and ſeveral Engines are grinding Terras-Mortar by Mill-Stones drawn by Horſes.

" The Duke gets Stone in this Place, ſome of them weighing between five and ſix Tons, which are uſed in the Locks and Baſon.

" He has built a very large Houſe, to which it is ſuppoſed he will add ſome Baths to receive the Salt Water, and turn the whole into an Inn to accommodate Paſſengers going from Mancheſter to Liverpool.

" The Engines with which he moves the large Stones, ſtand on a Frame, and are moved from Lock to Lock as Occaſion requires, and ſo well conſtructed are they, that four Men will remove a Stone of ſix Tons.

" The Locks ſtand in P   s, each Lock falling ſeven Feet except the lowermoſt, which falls 22 Feet at low Water, emptying itſelf into the Merſey, where it is two Miles broad. Each Lock being 27 Feet wide, and 70 in Length, will receive Veſſels of 60 Tons Burthen. We often keep great Company, for many Peers of the Land viſit us."

On 22nd December 1772 all the locks at Runcorn were finished and the following day the Bridgewater Canal was officially opened for business. After the formal opening ceremony around 800 workmen were entertained to dinner and for that occasion a whole ox was roasted and generous amounts of ale provided. It was said that during the course of the canal's construction there had been several difficult problems to surmount. In December 1772 all that remained to be solved was the problem of cutting through a small section of land which had previously been the property of Sir Richard Brooke. One would presume that this was the land that had been purchased for around £900. At this time it was still uncertain how this tract of land would be cut and until it was done the Duke of Bridgewater was compelled to draw his materials in carts over fields. It was reported that: *"The gentlemen and tradesmen of this country wish to see this nook cut through, as the land carriage will annoy the Baronet, and bring an additional expense of eighteen pence per ton upon all the merchandise."*

Despite the long disruptions to local life, when the Bridgewater Canal was finally completed local residents were appreciative of the numerous commercial benefits the project had brought to the area. In fact, many viewed the canal as a thing of beauty rather than the destroyer of the local landscape. Several decades later, in 1813, one Runcorn resident described the local waterway in this manner:

"In an extent of a few miles, one can distinctly observe where five navigable rivers unite their waters with the Mersey, all of them contributing very essentially to the convenience and commercial prosperity of this enviable country. The principal of these inland navigations is that stupendous work known by the familiar appellation of "The Duke's Canal", undertaken and completed at the expense of the Duke of Bridgewater, and carried from Manchester to Runcorn, a distance of about thirty miles, without a single lock. On a fine summer's evening, when the beams of the setting sun play upon the surface of the magnificent sheet of water which appears before you, enlivened by so many passing sails, the prospect is inconceivably fine, and the beholder is tempted to exclaim, in the words of the sublime Architect of the Universe – "It is good."

Two years after the opening of the Bridgewater Canal, which now provided an industrial corridor between Manchester and Liverpool, an extension to the Mersey and Trent canals was completed. This project had been financed by the pottery and salt manufacturers of the Midlands. The extension, which was to form the system known as the

Grand Trunk Canal, had commenced in 1763 and took ten years to its completion in 1773. These new water highways now provided the area with great transportation links and bulky barges with their cargoes of coal, salt, stone, slate, pig iron, pottery and clay were soon taking full advantage. Along with these heavy loads other manufactured goods and commodities such as flour, corn and potatoes, which helped to supply the growing industrial populations, were also being transported along these busy routes. It has been estimated that between 1873 and 1884 the Bridgewater Navigation Company was handling an average of 489,758 tons of goods per year. Of course coastal shipping was also tied to river and canal borne traffic, meaning that the canals constructed in the Mersey estuary gave access to the Irish Sea and beyond, enabling local businesses to trade with world markets.

The opening of the Bridgewater Canal's Runcorn Docks in 1776 further enhanced Runcorn's status as an important canal port. This subsequently stimulated trade between Liverpool, Manchester and other northern towns such as Warrington, which was connected to Runcorn in 1804 by the opening of the Runcorn-Latchford Canal. Runcorn's transport communications were further improved in 1810 when the Weaver Canal Company opened their Weston Point Docks[3]. These first-rate water communications, created by a convergence of canals and superb dock facilities, provided Runcorn with excellent links between the salt producing districts of mid-Cheshire and the coal producing regions of Lancashire. All these benefits meant that Runcorn evolved into an important transport and shipment centre. Indeed, it was reported in December 1818 that *"upward of 500 vessels have discharged their loading in this little port during the last twelve months."* It should also be noted, that the superb transport facilities which were available at Runcorn also played a vital role in the economic success of Liverpool and Manchester, whose industries and trade relied heavily upon the shipment of raw materials such as coal, salt and clay.

Apart from the escalating trade stimulated by its excellent waterway communications, Runcorn's economy in the early nineteenth century also benefited from some significant industrial development. Soap manufacture in the town had started as early as 1803 when John Johnson opened his soapworks on the bank of the Bridgewater Canal.

---

3 In 1886 a tidal dock was constructed at Weston Point.

In the following years the manufacture of soap expanded considerably. Joseph Crosfield established a soapworks not too far away in Warrington in 1815. The following year, 1816, the Runcorn soap-making industry was increased when Thomas Hazlehurst opened his *Camden Soap Works* in the town. The Hazlehurst business had originally started out as a small resin and turpentine works but by 1850 this had grown into a substantial soap-making concern.

At that time soap-making, although a profitable industry, was heavily laden with taxation. This tax impacted not only on the soap-makers themselves but also on other industries who were great users of soap, such as the wool trade. Because of the heavy burden this tax imposed, there were countless illicit soap-making ventures hidden from the watchful eye of the excise men. In fact, the covert manufacture of soap was a significant industry in many parts of the country. Of course excise duties were an important part of the national economy and therefore the excise men were always on the lookout for contraventions. Nevertheless, legitimate businesses like the Johnson, Crosfield and Hazlehurst concerns managed to turn a healthy profit whilst acting within the law and meeting their legal obligations. The tax on soap was officially abolished in 1853.

In the years that followed, apart from the several soap manufacturing ventures and the existence of a brewery and tanning yard, Runcorn experienced further advancement with the arrival of other profitable industries. Alongside these new concerns the old traditional trades associated with the river and stone quarrying continued to offer employment to large numbers of local men. Nevertheless, despite growing industrial development in the town, even as late as the 1840s Runcorn was still considered to be a delightful place to visit. Over previous years summer visitors, and invalids seeking recuperation or respite from the hustle and bustle of the larger towns and cities, were attracted to the town in great numbers. Evidently there were several things to commend the area as, apart from its scenic riverside location and fresh air, it had the added attraction of a salt water baths which had been constructed in 1822. Because of its popular appeal, sometime around 1831 a row of boarding houses known as Belvedere Terrace was built to accommodate the crowds of summer visitors who came to the town. An article in *The Manchester Courier* in June 1842 gave a wonderful description of Runcorn. One would assume that the owners of the numerous inns and lodging houses in the town were delighted to have been given such a glowing endorsement. Long before the days of *"TripAdvisor"* this type of favourable publicity would have been invaluable to the town and its small businesses.

"We are right glad to observe that this lovely summer weather is tempting many people, who are pent up in towns, to refresh themselves by excursions into the country, where they can look upon green fields, and breathe fresh air; and while other places of resort present their attractions to visitors, we rejoice to find that our own favourite spot, Runcorn, which Doctor Percival styled "The Montpelier of England," is resorted to by many families from Manchester and the neighbourhood; and glad we are to find that Doctor Bardsley and other eminent medical practitioners, have lately recommended Runcorn for the salubrity of its air, and the romantic cheerfulness of its scenery. But besides its qualities so conducive to health, and its surrounding picturesque beauties, Runcorn possesses many objects of interest to the stranger. The rock, so bold and prominent, upon which stood the famous castle of "the martial lady and manly Ethelfleda," about 1000 years ago, the lover of antiquities will regard with affectionate curiosity; and the venerable parish church, of date as ancient as the castle, with its quiet and shady burial ground, "where the rude forefathers of the hamlet sleep," is surrounded with associations holy, deep and solemn. Norton Priory is a sweet, sequestered spot, and its beautiful grounds and woods present a pleasant and cool retreat to the visitor of Runcorn; and then the Mersey, with its flowing tide, upon the bosom of which, in boats and packets, many an invigorating trip may be taken, affords varied and continual objects of interest; and along the extensive piers of the spacious and elegant docks of the Mersey and Irwell Navigation, and the Bridgewater Canal, the visitor may take pleasant walks, or ramble over the fields to Rocksavage, Higher Runcorn, and around Beetle Hill, from the summit of which he commands a prospect at once beauteous and magnificent, which is only equalled by the rich and splendid view from Halton Castle, on the east of Runcorn. Along the shore to Weston Point is a favourite walk, and between this place and Runcorn the steamers "Tower" and "Blanche" make no charge for parties visiting Runcorn; and a nice little excursion it is from one place to the other. The baths at Runcorn have lately been repaired, and are now well-ordered, neat, and clean and the respectable inns and lodging houses of the town need no commendation of ours; families there are sure to be comfortable. Of the many other advantages of Runcorn, as a place of summer resort, we cannot now stay to speak. We only recommend our friends to go and judge for themselves."

The following year, 1843, another pleasant description of Runcorn appeared in a Cheshire newspaper. This narrative gives a wonderful picture of the town at that time and also provides some indication of the changes which had taken place in the area prior to that date. The numerous industrial developments and the physical and social transformations which had occurred in the town are laid out for us in this interesting account.

"Runcorn, this delightful little port is in a most thriving condition. On looking back a few years, that venerable looking pile of more than 1000 years old, the parish church, was surrounded with its yew trees and corn fields, and the township itself consisted of a population of somewhere about four or five thousand inhabitants, but now increased to near ten thousand. The land, formerly used as corn fields, is now covered with beautifully built houses, inhabited by families of the greatest respectability, a number of cottages, as well as a very large hall built by that respectable society of men The Foresters. We have our post office, stamp office, and gas-works; the streets are all lighted with gas; we have a Town Hall, as well as a Mechanics' Institution. At the present time there is in the course of erection, opposite to the Town Hall, six handsome shops, adding greatly to the appearance of the town. There is, also, a most splendid building, in the Elizabethan style, the residence of D. Brundrit, Esq., situate near the ferry. We have, also, the new church of The Holy Trinity; the splendid residence of James Loch, Esq., M.P., facing the river; together with the immense pier, lines of locks, basins, dry dock, warehouses etc., built by the trustees of the late Duke of Bridgewater; the Old Quay Company's large basins, etc.; the extensive soaperies of Messrs. Johnsons and Hazlehursts; one of the largest patent rope manufactories in England, now in the course of erection by Messrs. Johnson and Hayes; the large ship-building yards of Messrs. Brundrit and Whiteway, Anderton, Mason, and the Old Quay Companies; the large iron foundries of Messrs. Statter and Caldwell; together with numerous other establishments. Still we are short of something to find employment for the great number of young persons and children under sixteen years of age, and a factory would be of great utility to Runcorn, and would be a source of profit not only to the employer but the employed; everything is ready at hand for an undertaking of that description, which would be well worth the attempt of some influential and enterprising individual"

In 1843, when the above description was written, although Runcorn had become relatively busy Widnes had remained more or less untouched by industry. At that time the township of Widnes consisted of a few hamlets comprising of places such as Farnworth, Appleton,

Upton and Cronton. As well as these scattered rural communities there were also several wide expanses of open space consisting of farmland and some large barren areas which are signified on local maps by place-names which denote features such as Moor, Moss, Heath and Marsh. An advert from March 1820, placed by Joseph Gerrard the occupier of West Bank Farm, gives us an idea of the character of the land he offered for seasonal rental. He described his land as *"a ley for cattle which consists of the most excellent marshland and upland"*. Elsewhere, the small hamlets of pre-industrial Widnes were mainly a collection of unremarkable rural settlements where folk laboured in the fields or in the old established trades that had been performed by their families for generations. These traditional craftsmen were mainly engaged in producing parts for the watchmaking industry or in toolmaking, file cutting, wire-drawing or the production of canvas for the sails of ships. Most of these, apart from wire-drawing, were common domestic "cottage" crafts in several areas of South-West Lancashire at that time.

Early census data gives valuable information concerning the inhabitants of the township of Widnes and the occupational structure of its residents in pre-alkali times. Statistics tell us that in 1801 the population of the township was 1063 and of this figure 662 were workers. Thirty-eight percent of the workforce was involved in the old crafts of canvas making, watchmaking and toolmaking while sixty percent of the workers were in agricultural occupations[4]. The next census, providing data for Widnes with Appleton in 1811, gave a population figure of 1204 and tells us that there were 611 males and 593 females. There were 247 families occupying 246 houses. Their employment statistics at that time were especially interesting. The data shows that there were 100 families employed in agriculture, 126 in trade, light manufacturing or handicrafts and 21 unspecified.[5]

From early census records we can see that between 1801 and 1831 there had been a gradual growth in the local population. However this rise was in line with other areas in Britain where there had been a general increase in population. Despite the small local increase it would appear that up until 1830, apart from transient agricultural workers, very few new people or businesses had been permanently attracted to the area.[6] It is also clear that in spite of a large proportion

4 *"Into the Crucible"* – Jean M. Morris (2005), (2nd edition 2009)
5 Census Returns 1811 – Lancashire Record Office
6 Between 1851 and 1861 the population of Widnes doubled.

of the indigenous population being involved in light manufacturing and handicrafts, the area was more or less free of any significant industrial development. However, after this date things slowly began to change.

POPULATION RETURN FOR THE DIVISION OF PRESCOT, FOR 1811.			
	Males.	Females.	Total.	Total in 1801.
Allerton	154	124	258	178
Bold	372	401	773	713
Bootle & Linacre	324	286	610	537
Cronton	166	168	334	311
Cuerdley	112	136	248	251
Childwall	88	74	162	152
Ditton	219	203	422	401
Everton	328	585	913	499
Eccleston	803	781	1584	1362
Formby	555	546	1101	1045
Fazakerley	160	169	329	272
Great Sanki	219	247	466	431
Garston	299	298	597	458
Huyton and Roby	485	470	955	862
Hale	254	273	527	537
Halewood	464	439	903	777
Kirkdale	284	381	665	593
Knowsley	449	464	913	739
Kirkby	474	438	912	883
Liverpool	41296	53080	94376	77708
Little Woolton	249	279	528	419
Much Woolton	293	308	601	439
Penketh	690	715	1405	1181
Parr	170	171	341	326
Prescot	1747	1931	3678	3465
Rainhill	278	267	545	402
Rainford	643	672	1315	1185
Simonswood	194	170	364	274
Speke	223	186	409	374
Sutton	1065	1049	2114	1776
Torbock	276	258	534	412
Toxteth Park	2643	3221	5864	2069
West Derby	1639	2079	3718	2636
Widnes	611	593	1204	1063
Whiston	500	514	1015	1031
Walton	354	440	794	681
Windle	2114	2180	4294	3252
Wavertree	626	772	1398	860
Total	61800	75369	137169	110304

LOCAL POPULATION FIGURES - 6TH AUGUST 1811

At the beginning of 1830 several exciting plans were unveiled by the directors of *The Runcorn Gap Railway* and the owners of *The Sankey Navigational Canal*. The outcome of these schemes would eventually have a massive impact on the fortunes of the area. The plans were to extend the Sankey Navigational Canal and build a Dock[7] at Widnes Wharf. Adverts were placed in local and national newspapers requesting tenders from suitable contractors. One advert, which appeared in *The Liverpool Mercury* in February 1830, is reproduced here. This gave notice of intended work and invited bids from interested parties. Notification of a special meeting of the proprietors and shareholders of the Sankey Brook Navigation appeared in the same edition of this newspaper. The meeting, which was held in the offices of a solicitor in Exchange Street East, had been arranged for the purpose of submitting a draft to the shareholders of the proposed amendments to the Acts relating to the Sankey Navigational Canal.

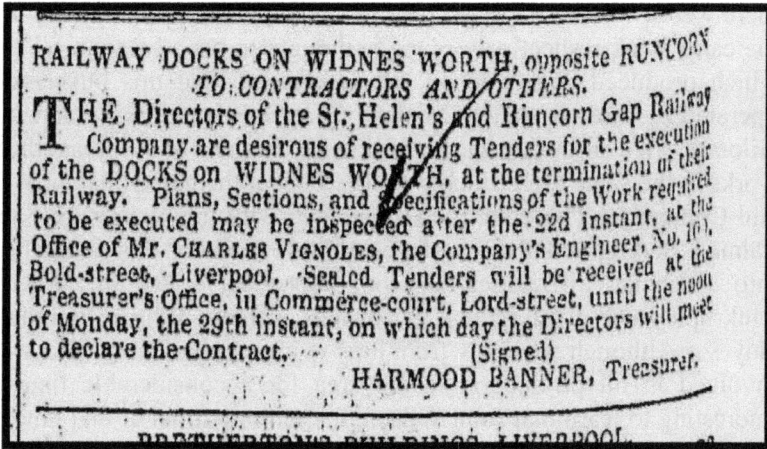

The subsequent completion of these impressive schemes, which included the extension of The Sankey Navigational Canal from Fidler's Ferry[8] to Widnes and the opening of The Runcorn Gap Railway in 1833, meant that some new employment opportunities were created in the vicinity. Consequently, these additional facilities brought a minor stream of new workers to the area around Widnes Dock. This additional workforce, though small, contributed to the development of a

---

7 This dock was completed in 1831 and the first man appointed as Dock Master was Mr. John Palin.

[8] A different spelling *(Fiddler's Ferry)* has been adopted in modern times.

small community and residential area in that locality. Later on, in addition to the workers associated with the railway and the dock, the area of Widnes Dock housed the earliest industrial workforce in the south end of the town. By 1841, even though the population had grown slightly, the overall figure for the township of Widnes was still relatively low with the census of that year listing just 2209 inhabitants. However, although heavy industry had not yet reached the area, and the population was still moderately small, the opening of the railway, canal and dock had laid the foundation for the change which was about to occur.

Although the census of 1841 shows that a small community had developed at Widnes Dock, consisting mainly of boatmen and dock and railway workers and their families, the rest of the south end of the town was then quite sparsely populated. However we can see from local maps that immediately prior to the arrival of the alkali industry in 1847 there were two works located near to Runcorn Gap Railway Station and the canal bank respectively. One is thought to have been an oil works which produced vegetable oil. It is believed that this business was operated by three Irishmen, Michael Carroll, Edward Scilly and James Giloran. We also find earlier evidence in the 1840s of another oil works in the same area which was listed under the name of John Wilson and Company. The other men associated with this firm were Samuel Salmon Berend and Patrick Hayes. Unfortunately this company got into financial difficulties and in September 1843 an order for bankruptcy was filed against the owners, namely Wilson, Berend and Hayes. Although we know from later evidence that Patrick Hayes was involved in oil production in the area for a considerable time it is interesting to learn that John Wilson, his senior partner at that time, was also the manager of the Holden and McLellan chemical works based in Liverpool.

Despite the fact that all the men named in the above case were declared bankrupt it did not stop them from carrying on business with other people. During this period it was common practice for businessmen to file for bankruptcy and then start up again almost immediately with other partners. Neither was it unusual for men to be involved in several businesses in addition to their own major concerns. During my research I found that Patrick Hayes operated his Widnes oil works over a long period with a number of different partners. In November 1843, shortly after the firm of John Wilson and Company filed for bankruptcy, we find evidence of a partnership being dissolved between Patrick Hayes and a Liverpool man called Thomas Urquhart.

In the dissolution notice both men were described as Widnes based oil manufacturers.

Despite having previously had several partners in oil manufacturing concerns at Widnes Dock, by the late 1840s it would seem that Mr. Hayes had become the sole owner of an oil works in that area. A newspaper report of October 1848 gives details of a fire occurring at his factory. Unfortunately, the poor quality of the original report prevents me from including it here but I provide a full transcript:

"Fire at Widnes – On Friday last, considerable alarm prevailed in the neighbourhood of Widnes Locks, owing to a fire having broken out on the premises of Mr. Patrick Hayes, oil merchant. It appears that, about noon on Friday, the men were employed in melting some pitch in a large pan, when the bottom, which was much worn, suddenly dropped out, and, as a natural consequence, the pitch created an immense mass of flame, which was seen at a great distance. Fortunately, the building in which the burning pan was situated, lay at some distance from the rest of the works, or the consequences might have been very serious. We are sorry to add that two of the workmen were very much burned on the occasion."

Some four years later, early in 1852, Mr. Hayes was in serious financial difficulty. It is possible that loss and unexpected expenditure due to the fire may have contributed to his fiscal problems. By the summer of that year he was declared bankrupt once again. In August we find records of a number of sales relating to Mr. Hayes and his works at Widnes Dock. The sale notice provides us with interesting information regarding the size of the works, its equipment and other facilities on offer. We can see that, in addition to oil, Mr. Hayes was manufacturing soap at this time. It also tells us that most of the buildings were fire-proof which might indicate that he had lately invested money into making the works less flammable.

"All that extensive Soapery and Oil Works, situated at Widnes Dock, now in the occupation of Messrs. Patrick Hayes & Company, consisting of a soapery, newly fitted-up with Copper Vats and other Apparatus necessary for carrying on the business of a soft soap manufacturer. Also a Resin Oil Distillery, fitted-up on the newest and most improved principle, capable of making 40 tons of oil weekly, with Gas Works, to secure the Gas generated in the manufacture of Resin Oil. The premises comprises 2712 superficial square yards which adjoin the Sankey Canal, and communicate with the Runcorn Gap Railway by

means of a Branch passing through the centre of the works, and the proprietor has the right of taking water to an unlimited extent from the canal for the purpose of the works. There is also an Artesian Well of pure spring water.

To soapmakers, oil manufacturers, and parties desirous of entering into the chemical or any other business requiring easy communication with Liverpool and Manchester, this property affords an opportunity rarely to be met with. It is within six miles of St. Helens and Warrington, twelve from Liverpool, and eighteen from Manchester; and coals and every description of material can be laid down either by canal, railway, or the Mersey, on the premises. A great portion of the buildings are fire-proof. This Lot is held under the St. Helens and Runcorn Gap Railway Company for the term of 75 years, commencing on the last day of December 1849, subject to the annual rent of £30, payable half-yearly. Immediate possession may be had. Included in the sale will be a steam-engine, with all the apparatus and fixtures on the property."

Also offered for sale at the same time was Mr. Hayes` newly built residence, Highfield House, in Highfield Road. The house was offered for sale with its entire contents; the reason being that Mr. Hayes was about to leave the country and head off to Australia. John McLellan subsequently became the occupier of this house although it is not known if he purchased it at this time or later. It is interesting to note that the entire acreage of the house exceeds that of the oil works.

"The dwelling house, with the coach-house, stable and garden thereunto belonging, situate in the Hamlet of Appleton, within the township of Widnes aforesaid, on the north side the public highway leading from the village of Appleton, through Ditton and Hale, to Liverpool and now in the occupation of Mr. Patrick Hayes.

The house, which commands an extensive view of the River Mersey and surrounding country, has been newly erected by the present proprietor, regardless of expense, and is fitted for the immediate reception of a respectable family. The grounds are carefully laid out and planted. It comprises: Dining, Drawing and Breakfast Rooms, a Bathroom, Nursery and five sleeping apartments, besides Kitchen, Scullery, Butler's Pantry and Washhouse. The property altogether consists of 5275 superficial square yards and immediate possession may be had. The tenure is copy-held of inheritance, subject to the payment of the annual quit rent of 6d. to the Lords of the Manor of Widnes".

There was an additional twist to the failure of Patrick Hayes` business and his subsequent bankruptcy. Before his bankruptcy case came to court he had made a swift departure and was already on his way to Australia. However, there was a rather sadder end to this story. His wife, Martha, along with their young children, 6year old John and 3years old Mary Teresa, had left Widnes some weeks before in order to settle in Australia and await his arrival. Unfortunately the ship they were sailing in sunk in a shipping tragedy and all three were drowned.

In spite of the existence of a number of small industrial concerns at the south end of the town, it is evident that wildlife was still abundant and that stags and does roamed freely in areas around Widnes Marsh. Inland from the Marsh was Widnes Moor, a wide barren area, thought to be common land. Apart from West Bank House and the Boat House Inn there were just a few small cottages and two farms. One farm stood near to the site of the present day Hutchinson Street to the west of Snig Lane (Waterloo Road). Apart from these scattered dwellings, relatively short distances away were several larger private houses such as Lower House, Vineyard House, Carter House and Brook House. As we have seen, in 1841 the inhabitants of all the places within the township, to the north, south, east and west totalled just over two thousand people.

I am sure if we try really hard we can all imagine how tranquil and charming the area must have been. The river was a paradise for local fishermen and along its banks flora and fauna found a natural habitat in wide open spaces. The landscape was only interrupted now and again by a few scattered dwellings. In much the same way as Runcorn was described as a pleasant resort, Widnes too attracted numerous visitors to its shore. J. Fenwick Allen, in his book about the founders of the chemical industry, tells us that in pre-industrial times residence in Widnes *"was not only bearable but even inviting, bathers frequented the shores of the Mersey round about Woodend, and some of the young men kept their yachts there. Woodend was bright and sweet and salubrious"*. The same author, when describing the area at the time of William Gossage's arrival in Widnes, says:

"....fields with green hedge-rows and healthy trees still extended down from his house along the river past the old "Snig Pie House". This noted hostelry was still a favourite place for picnic parties. The Widnes Marsh was used by the neighbouring farmers to graze their cattle on. A prettily situated estate was the property of Mr. Wright, whose house, with its parklands, overlooked the river from behind the ferry".

Apart from attracting visitors to its shoreline, long before the river and streams were polluted and poisoned by effluvia from numerous

31

factories, the area was one of the best fishing localities on the banks of the Mersey. Eels, known locally as snigs, were in abundance and salmon was plentiful. As was the case with Runcorn, we can benefit from numerous written accounts which allow us to catch a reliable glimpse of pre-industrial Widnes. I think the most interesting descriptions are written in the years immediately following the arrival of the alkali industry, those in which the writer could call on his or her own personal experience and memories of times past. In most accounts the writers laments the damaging effects of the alkali industry upon the local environment. It is not hard to visualize how pleasant it must have been. The article below was written in 1889.

"One can hardly imagine that Widnes, seeing its present state, was once frequented by pleasure seekers and picnicers. Yet such was the fact. We need not now expect to see the gay devotees of pleasure come to Widnes and its shady pleasant walks by the Mersey. Yet time was when the gardens of Widnes were well known and the Lovers` Walk, shaded and arched over by green branches, was a sweet reality. When Snig Pie House ministered to a luxury of the epicure who delighted in the taste of snigs angled for and caught in the river hard by. Times are changed since the days when there was no house between Appleton Church and the Railway Station, with the sole exception of Solomon's Temple, the glory of which has also departed. The memory of these things is now fast dying out and instead of the pleasant odour of woodland we have the disagreeable smell of chemicals." 9

Whilst the manufacturing district in the southern part of the town became a hub of industrial activity, in the northern areas the villages of Upton, Cronton, Farnworth and Appleton were to remain relatively untouched by the arrival of the chemical trade. In these small rural districts change came so slow as to be almost imperceptible to the inhabitants. Indeed, for some considerable time after the arrival of industry into the area, the occupations and social routines of village life in these places must have seemed the same as they had always been. Apart from the sight of smoking chimneys which could be glimpsed from the heights of Appleton, now obscuring their view of Halton Castle, life in these pleasant villages continued at their own natural pace.

In the south of the town things were to change dramatically. The tree-lined landscape which had shielded West Bank House[10] and its

---

9"*Into the Crucible*" – Jean M. Morris (2005) re-prints (2009) (2011).
10 West Bank House built c.1820 by William Hurst for his own occupation.

occupant, Mr. Hurst, from the gaze of his neighbours was soon to fall victim to the effects of hydrochloric acid gas. So too were the leafy lanes which led to a few scattered cottages and farms. The Boat House Inn, which was commonly referred to as *"Snig Pie House"* because of its signature dish of eel-pie, had once entertained day-trippers seeking a pleasant retreat from the bustle of Liverpool and Manchester. Naturally, the arrival of the chemical industry and the detrimental effect it caused to the surrounding areas changed all that. No longer was this ancient hostelry, nor its epicurean delights, a draw for the day-tripper.

John Hutchinson opened his chemical factory in Widnes sometime around 1847. Although he did not know it at the time, he was to be the architect of a great transformation in the visual, environmental and social character of the whole district. His arrival and the establishment of his alkali factory placed Widnes on the threshold of great change. This change was to be extreme in every respect. The twin forces of industrialisation and population growth had a dramatic effect not only upon the landscape but also on local society and the economy. This unprecedented rise in population meant that the social fabric of the area was completely altered as old established social structures were steadily undermined. This extraordinary shift influenced all aspects of local life from working and living conditions to religious and class relationships.

By 1851 the Widnes population figure had risen to 3211. Of course it was not only in Widnes that things were changing, the arrival of the Industrial Revolution had meant that the lives of all of the nation's working population had been dramatically and irrevocably changed. Obviously, the Industrial Revolution was fairly late coming to Widnes but despite its tardiness the impact was no less dramatic. Within a relatively short space of time the alkali industry was well established in the town and was the most dominant employer in the area. The previously insignificant little township rapidly evolved into an important industrial area which was destined to be an intrinsic part of the world's heavy chemical industry. The census returns for 1851, which came only four years after the establishment of the first chemical factory, shows how the local population and the occupational configuration had changed.[11] The next census, taken in 1861, clearly shows the extent of the chemical industry's growth.

---

[11] *Population Survey* – Archives & Local Studies Service (Cheshire County Council)

When contemplating the development of Widnes and the subsequent transformation of this little-known corner of England into the centre of alkali manufacture, I never cease to be amazed by the comparative speed with which it all came about. In fact, it sometimes seems that Widnes came into being almost inadvertently; as it was merely a place where factories had been built and to which a new industrial population was attracted. Within a relatively short space of time factories and houses had sprung up on what were once green fields. The lovely streams and brooks that had formerly been renowned for their pastoral beauty became noxious sewers choked with the waste of countless factories. In addition to polluted watercourses, smoke, and pungent fumes, the alkali trade also generated mountains of deleterious waste, known locally as galligu. Unfortunately, as the tipping and dumping of industrial waste was completely uncontrolled at that time, this resulted in harmful chemical waste being deposited throughout the southern end of the town in huge heaps. Sometimes these waste heaps were dangerously near to residential districts. This foul waste, which was largely impregnated by sulphur, gave off strong fumes and an offensive smell of sulphuretted hydrogen in damp and foggy weather. This unpleasant odour supplemented the other noxious smells and fumes which emanated from the numerous chemical factories in the town.

In concluding this chapter on our towns and the changing face of Britain, we can see that the development of both Runcorn and Widnes as places of industrial trade was a direct consequence of the effects of the Industrial Revolution. The result was to be most conspicuous in Widnes, where the days of green meadows, crystal clear watercourses, leafy lanes and rustic charm became a thing of the past. The local population figures rocketed to an unprecedented level and local society became diverse both culturally and spiritually. In fact, the transformation brought about by industrialisation was radical on all levels. When the wind of change which had swept through the country eventually reached our own areas the process of change became both drastic and unstoppable.

URBANISATION AND SOCIETY

One of the main features of the Victorian era was that it was a period of enormous growth and expansion. Of all sectors to expand the alkali trade was one of the greatest, growing spectacularly in terms of manufacturing volume. The arrival of the alkali industry and an unparalleled increase in population were the two elements which shaped the town of Widnes. The introduction of industry into the area on a large scale was ultimately responsible for urban growth and the establishment of our first industrial society. It is obvious that whilst towns grow physically, as building work develops and extends, the make-up of the population plays an important role in forming the character of a place. In Widnes, as in most new industrial towns of that era, the population consisted of a multitude of people from a variety of places with different sets of values and beliefs. The structure of this new population was woven from a thick textured culture of many strands. It was initially an incongruent mix of people from numerous parts of mainland Britain and Ireland with different religious and social views and attitudes. Although most of the new population had shared a similar agricultural background, the diversity of their traditions and experiences meant that there was little common ground to unite them. The wide range of birthplaces, nationalities and cultural differences meant that this new society was a jumble of mismatched inhabitants. To repeat the term I used in an earlier book, Widnes ultimately became *"The Crucible"*[12] into which this sundry combination of people was received and moulded.

As Widnes and Runcorn were transformed by the arrival of industry and the formation of a new industrial society, the social and economic pyramid I described in an earlier chapter was evident in both towns. In order to build up a reasonable picture of our area and the populations on either side of the river, before and during industrial development, we should be aware of the deep gulfs which existed between the different

---

[12]*Into the Crucible* – Jean M. Morris (2005) and (2007)

layers of society. English society at that time was first of all a hierarchical society in which men took their places in an accepted order of precedence. In both towns there would have been an established and finely graded hierarchy of great subtlety and discrimination in which all elements of society were acutely aware of their exact relationship to those immediately above and below them. The disparity in lifestyle, both economically and socially, between those at the top of the pyramid and the larger poorer group at the bottom was vast. Nevertheless, despite its blatant inequalities and many injustices, this form of social organisation was generally accepted by most people, rich and poor alike. I presume that most poor people tolerated this situation because they believed that traditional social order and power was predestined and unchangeable.

Although civilisation has always had degrees of social order into which people have been categorised, from around the mid-eighteenth century the term *"middle-class"* came into common use. This term was used to describe those people whose status fell below the aristocracy but above the workers. The rise of a new entrepreneurial class after the Industrial Revolution, and the increased wealth of manufacturers, created a middle-class who made great fortunes and sometimes converted their economic success into political power. Regrettably, this political power was often used to ensure policy which reflected only middle-class interests. The division between the rich and poor members of society was heightened during this period and nowhere was this more keenly felt than in new industrial towns like Widnes. Unskilled labourers in their thousands were attracted to our new town in search of work and what they hoped would be a better standard of living. Unfortunately, although the new industries created wealth and employment, in some places the wages were so low they were barely above subsistence level.

The expanding gap between the classes was more pronounced in towns such as Widnes and Runcorn where local society was dominated by a minority who enjoyed a mixed pattern of economic, political and social influence. This domination was most notable in local government; although in many cases their power in this area was derived more from personal status and property than any official or personal attributes. It is interesting to see that when the Local Board of Health was formed in Widnes in 1865 six of the nine Board members were owners of local chemical factories. However, our area was no different to other new towns where similar hierarchical systems operated and manufacturers held positions of authority in local government. Unfortunately, as industry in Britain expanded at a rapid pace, class divisions became more clearly defined and the uneven distribution of wealth led to a widening gulf between rich and poor. The increasing chasm between the classes was even evident in places where one would expect a degree of parity, such as the Church. Despite a natural anticipation of equality in religious matters, the sad fact was that, even in this supposedly moral and fair institution, there was a marked element of division as demands for pew rents often excluded those on low incomes. The practice of renting out private pews in some churches meant that there was little or no space for ordinary people. In some churches this led to congregations comprising mainly of well-to-do parishioners.

In the years immediately after the Industrial Revolution the population surge into the new manufacturing districts and mercantile cities was astounding. Because of this unprecedented urban growth, most historians agree that the expanding towns and cities of nineteenth century England were the crucial agents of historical change. New urban neighbourhoods, which enveloped old rural settlements, became the centres of political change and conflict. They also became the point from which a new type of civilisation emerged. This new industrial society, created by the migration of masses of workers from the countryside into towns, was further augmented by an increase in the number of smaller entrepreneurs such as shopkeepers, publicans and other merchants who provided service to the new industries and growing populations. Understandably, the enormous changes which took place in such a moderately short space of time were heightened in small places like Widnes and Runcorn.

Of course, from time to time both Widnes and Runcorn had already experienced minor increases in populations. These relatively small rises had sometimes been connected to the arrival of transient agricultural workers or to the coming of the railways and the building of canals. However, the development of industry on a large scale, particularly in Widnes, created an unparalleled surge in population. Understandably, this extraordinary rise put great pressures on both the urban infrastructure and the long established social order. There is no denying that the Industrial Revolution brought great economic prosperity and enormous commercial benefits, however, for most people its impact was mainly felt through social transformation. One could say that as well as an industrial revolution there was also a social revolution which touched all levels of society.

Locally, the social effects of industrialisation were extreme. It should be remembered that while concentrated industrialisation was a new concept, so too was the type of society it created. The members of this new social order were faced with a social upheaval they did not understand. Unfortunately, this pioneering society had no natural model on which to base its conduct. It was deprived of guides to behaviour and consequently this produced some serious and unpleasant social difficulties. The masses of new town dwellers had experienced a radical change in their environment which, together with long hours and bad working and living conditions, brought about a huge change in their habits and behaviour. They were impoverished, exploited, and herded into slums which combined both wretchedness and squalor. It is not too surprising that many sank into demoralisation and found that alcohol was the easiest way to deal with their misery. However, it is very important to point out that Widnes was no different from most other industrial areas of that time. When one examines statistics relating to other developing Lancashire towns during this period it is quite clear that mass alcoholism and violent behaviour were invariable companions of rapid industrialisation and urbanisation.

History shows that the new urbanisation process in industrial towns and cities around the country developed into a gigantic system of class segregation which created its own unique problems. Apart from the obvious divisions in population, urbanisation, which was a necessary by-product of industrialisation, caused family structures to change radically. In pre-industrial times extended families lived and worked together in the same places for generations. However, as people moved to where work was available this meant that family bonds became fragmented. In their previous environments village life often consisted of living alongside people with shared bloodlines. There was also the close and familiar relationship with friends and neighbours that contributed to a time honoured communal behaviour. All these reassuring elements of rural life offered a natural protection in times of distress or economic difficulties. The loss of these social roots and stable family structures was keenly felt in all new industrial towns, especially as the new population was a mixture of people with little or no common bonds or shared history to unite them.

When studying historical writings and public records it is possible to see that the introduction of the new factory system into our area, and the rapid development of our two towns, brought some men fortunes while for others it brought only debt and bankruptcy. Some industrialists experienced great financial rewards for their efforts and were able to amass vast fortunes. However, it is interesting to see that whilst some of our local entrepreneurs, both in Runcorn and Widnes, had undergone periods of great economic success some ended up in the bankruptcy courts. The high level of economic failure, among alkali producers especially, was often due to the fact that many had borrowed heavily to finance their ventures and overstretched themselves. Although the alkali trade had developed rapidly, and there was a great demand both at home and abroad, the industry was aggressively competitive. There was also the problem of over production as new factories came on stream. This meant that sometimes availability exceeded demand. During these periods, although production costs remained the same, the selling price of alkali fell dramatically. This was often the reason why previously profitable alkali businesses went bust.

Unfortunately, for the thousands of labourers who swarmed to Widnes in search of a living, the alkali trade brought no riches — only misery, monotony and brutality. Despite the growing wealth from manufacturing and commerce, prosperity lay in the hands of a small elite group of residents. The working people who contributed to the production of this wealth usually lived and worked in conditions of the most desperate poverty and degradation. Furthermore, this new and inexperienced workforce soon discovered that a whole new lifestyle, far removed from their previous existence and customs, was being shaped for them. They learnt that factory labour imposed a routine and pace of life set by industrial processes rather than by the seasonal or climatic requirements they had experienced in their old way of life. The rhythms of life in an industrial town also forced an awareness of man-made timekeeping where clocks, timetables, and work schedules were an important part of daily life. In the alkali factories, human beings became integrated with chemicals, machines, and furnaces in a wearying process. Their pace of work and surroundings were no longer tied to the traditional tempo and conditions of nature but were determined by their employers and managers. Obviously, industry and its processes necessitated standardised and regular work patterns and therefore a strict communal work discipline had to be strenuously enforced by employers. Of course, we should also recognise the fact that imposing order and work discipline upon a novice workforce would not have been an easy task. Therefore both workers and employers were forced to get used to new situations and complications.

Despite its difficulties, the unfamiliar urban work patterns gradually constituted a new norm for the workforce. And as these rural workers progressively acquired new industrial skills, completely divorced from the traditional routines of the countryside, they were also slowly adjusting to new urban habits and values. Most found the change very difficult to deal with especially as the environment in which they lived also presented its own dismal challenges. Years ago, when I read *"Hard Times"* by Charles Dickens, I was particularly struck by some of his descriptions of the fictitious *"Coketown"*, which was supposedly an archetypical industrial town of that era. I thought immediately of Widnes and wondered if this was a fair representation of the lives of our early industrial workers. Dickens said of Coketown:

"It contained several large streets still more like one another, inhabited by people equally like one another, who all went in and out at the same hours, with the same sound on the pavements, to do the same work, and to whom every day was the same as yesterday and tomorrow, and every year the counterpart of the last and the next".

It could not have been an easy transition for the new inhabitants of Widnes and it was probably not viewed by them as a change for the better. They were now forced to learn how to live a new urban way of life and in the process they had lost the local attachments and peculiarities which had held strong for generations. Over the coming years the thousands of labouring men and their families who made up this new urban society were to be debased by intolerable living and working conditions. Although they now had reasonably steady work, most men found themselves at the lower end of the occupational and wage earning scale. Work in the alkali trade, although dangerous and gruelling, was very poorly paid and men were required to work long hours in arduous conditions in order to generate a less than adequate income. Most were unable to earn enough to cover more than the bare essentials and, sadly, sometimes not even that. They soon found that living expenses in the town were far higher than those in the countryside. This meant that, generally, working men and their families were extremely poor and often found themselves on the margins of subsistence as their incomes were usually absorbed in paying for the necessities of daily life. It was not unusual for families to be compelled to pawn their clothes and bedding each week in order to survive until pay day.

Of course, as I have continually pointed out, our area was no different to other places where industrialisation had occurred. There were innumerable reports and surveys carried out in the nineteenth century into working and living conditions and unfortunately all these investigations told the same story. The reports show that low wages, long working hours, dangerous and unhealthy working conditions, insanitary dwellings, short life expectancy and high infant mortality were the norm among the working classes. Amid these numerous reports and publications one piece gave a particularly graphic account of the lives of ordinary working men in Lancashire. This publication, by Frederic Engels, entitled *"Condition of the Working Classes in England"* gave a flavour of the environments and attitudes of those times. In one section Engels gave a personal account of meeting a businessman in Manchester. He said:

"One day I walked with one of these middle-class gentlemen into Manchester. I spoke to him about the disgraceful unhealthy slums and drew his attention to the disgusting condition of that part of the town in which the factory workers lived. I declared that I had never seen so badly built a town in my life. He listened patiently and at the corner of the street at which we parted company, he remarked: "And yet there is a great deal of money made here. Good morning Sir".

The majority of our new workforce had previously come from small rural areas where in times of need they had been able to rely on the good neighbourliness of village life. In the countryside, to some extent, the old or the sick and the destitute had usually been cared for by the community. In new factory towns like Widnes things were vastly different and ties of kinship and neighbourhood had been left far behind. Therefore our urban poor had to fend for themselves. At that time there was no concept of social security to help them and the existing Poor Law system was inadequate and humiliating. This meant that our new inhabitants had no natural protection to turn to in times of distress or fluctuations in employment. Consequently, the immediate needs of the urban poor were often abandoned or ignored.

Although the process of urbanisation inevitably created class segregation, even at the commencement of our area's development there were considerable differences in the social milieu of each of our two towns. Even in relatively small industrial towns like Widnes and Runcorn human societies were variegated and complex. Nevertheless, despite a hotchpotch mix of people, these early urban societies gradually became knitted together by a variety of social bonds and networks. These social networks were built upon status and were formed on the basis of those who shared similar social prestige, religions or lifestyles; therefore there was usually a clearly defined class structure which was made up of unified and socially conscious groups. However, for the working class population there were less status divisions at that time as most manual workers shared similar living and working arrangements. In later times a more complicated social gradient developed with a multitude of intermediate positions between the working classes. These newer ranks were created as craftsmen, semi-skilled workers and foremen took on higher status positions. However, in the early days there were very little marked divisions within the working class and any differentiations that did exist were usually based on religion or nationality. Unskilled work was often casual and there was little opportunity for occupational or social upward mobility. Of course, literacy levels at that time were very poor, with most working people having only a rudimentary knowledge of literacy and numeracy. This meant that the majority of working people were *"in the same boat"* so there was little competition in social status. Although, having said that, there will always be some form of pecking order in any society.

For the working class population their main social networks were based on kinship ties or nationality and religion. In fact religion was an important social unit for all sections of our local society as it played an essential part in the assimilation of new arrivals into the town. This was beneficial to all members of our local society as institutions and church groups could often transcend any class or social barriers that existed. Naturally, in our new town wealth and poverty also provided a dramatic and contrasting image. For the poor there was little interest in social standing but, for the better off, there were those people who were sensitive about their status and anxious to emphasise their claim in the urban ranking. Unfortunately, in those days social standing was often valued merely by property and wealth rather than by merit, intellect or character. Today we have a slightly more democratic society but one can see that in nineteenth century Widnes and Runcorn society was dominated by a select and wealthy minority. Furthermore, these privileged minorities, in both towns, wielded an enormous degree of political and social influence.

When assessing the social changes which occurred in Widnes during the nineteenth century we should not forget that Runcorn had undergone similar changes earlier on. However, the scale of population and social change in Widnes far exceeded that of Runcorn. Nevertheless the initial impact of population growth would have had a comparable effect upon their indigenous societies. The valuable information contained in nineteenth century census records give an indication of how the populations of each town increased. Runcorn showed a slow but steady growth rising from 2060 in 1811 to 6950 in 1841. Interestingly, it is noticeable that in the 1841 census for

Runcorn, although there had been an increase in population, only around 28% of the inhabitants had been born outside of Cheshire. This means that the increase had been mainly due to natural growth and short distance migration rather than long distance movement. The occupations listed on that census give us an indication of the trade structure of that time. They include flatmen; shipwrights; sailmakers; ship's carpenters; ship's chandlers; labourers; quarrymen and rope-makers.

The census figures relating to Widnes show how quickly the town and its population expanded and the occupations listed show the rapidity with which industry developed. The census information also reveals a gradual decline of old traditional crafts and occupations as chemical manufacturing increased. We are also able to see that among this unprecedented surge in population a large number of single people came into the town. Consequently, there seemed to be an above average proportion of young people who were at the height of their working and reproductive capacities. Many of them became lodgers in the homes of others so, in fact, there developed an element of the population with a kind of sub-status, neither heads of households nor legitimate family members. This meant that this section of society had no real family base to return to at the end of a long working day and as a result the pub became their regular habitat.

The rapid growth in population, which was inexorably linked to industrialisation, brought people into the area from the length and breadth of Britain and from the island of Ireland. In later times there was also an influx of labour from the Baltic States, particularly Lithuania and Poland. In addition to these, there were also people from Belgium, France, Sweden and other places. Almost all the internal migrants who came to Widnes were country people who viewed the new industrial towns as places where employment opportunities and higher wages could be had. This movement from country to town had been facilitated by the coming of the railways which made travel to further parts of the county more viable. Prior to this time most migration had been short-distance movement as most people went on foot. Of course there had always been a regular volume of this type of mobility among rural workers as they travelled to work in nearby villages and small towns, usually after an annual hiring fair. This form of work was notoriously low-paid and usually seasonal, so the prospect of long-term employment with higher wages was a great incentive for them to travel further afield. Certainly, one of the most obvious downsides of the new freedom offered by the railways was that it dispersed and fractured families as their more enterprising members sought new opportunities further away.

It is evident that in all new industrial areas the working population was generally mobile. Widnes was no different as, apart from those who settled permanently, there was also a highly transient working population. Some people left a single imprint on census records and then vanished completely from the area. This was most noticeable among the Lithuanian workers who arrived here later in the century. Although a significant number of Lithuanians settled here there were, nevertheless, a high proportion of transitory workers among this group. Chain migration was also a contributory factor whereby workers moved on to other places where friends or relatives had found work opportunities. As a result, many Lithuanians moved onwards to America or other places in Britain where Lithuanian communities had been set up. However, it was not only this ethnic group who featured in this type of transitory process, from the inception of the alkali trade in Widnes we can see that people from all ethnic categories moved fluidly from one industrial area to another. Although this mobility meant that the turnover of inhabitants fluctuated, nonetheless, the permanent population figure in Widnes increased at a startling pace.

The continued increase in population meant that there was a regular stream of newcomers to amalgamate into local society. This in itself presented huge difficulties as a whole host of people were presented with unfamiliar and hostile living and working arrangements. In addition, in practical terms, there were inadequate provisions in place to deal with this surge in population. At that time the local governing body was the Highways Committee which was the sole body for overseeing the limited services in the township. With the unprecedented surge in population the Committee was ill-equipped to handle the demands placed upon it. Apart from the general practicalities of dealing with a dramatic increase in population and rapid urban expansion, there was a sharp alteration in social relations and routine for everyone. This was particularly relevant among the indigenous population who faced great changes to their established way of life. In fact, to reiterate, a whole new and previously unimagined type of urban civilisation came into being. Naturally this affected all levels of society, rich and poor, young and old, and involved both newcomers and native inhabitants alike.

One can only speculate about the difficulties of adjustment experienced by the wave of workers who came into Widnes at that time. The change in their lifestyle was extreme. They had left behind a rural society which was solidly entrenched in habits of thought and social relations, as well as the comforting links of family and friendship. Despite its semi-feudal conditions and an age-old acceptance of those traditions, one of the main characteristics of rural life had been a reassuring unity of interests among those who shared life in contact with nature and the land. Therefore, it was some time before this new urban society was able to replicate a similar sense of belonging or community to that they had left behind. Whilst in this book we are mainly looking at the growth of Widnes or Runcorn, it is important to remember that during this period similar transformations were taking place all around the country. Once this pattern was underway a steady rhythm of progress meant that there was an unstoppable surge in urbanisation in many parts of the country.

The first significant wave of migrants into Widnes was primarily from the mainland of Britain and their arrival was connected to the development of the dock and railways. Later, as industry developed and rail travel became more accessible, people arrived from all parts of this island including a substantial number from Wales and Cornwall. The men from these two communities were often involved with work in local copper related industry as well as alkali manufacture. It is also worth mentioning that prior to the arrival of the chemical industry there were a small number of migrants from Scotland resident in the area of Lunt's Heath and Farnworth. This group mainly comprised of weavers who were employed in the sailcloth industry in that locality.

In the years following the famines of the 1840s large numbers of Irish workers also came into Widnes and their presence in the town was considerable. However the arrival of Irish in Runcorn preceded this, as there had always been a small transient Irish agricultural workforce present in parts of Lancashire and Cheshire. In addition to these transitory farm workers, the construction of the canals, docks, and waterways in the district also attracted substantial Irish labour. There are also records of long-standing maritime trade between Runcorn and Ireland, even as far back as the 13th century[13], so it is perhaps not too surprising that there was always a minor Irish presence in that town. In the mid nineteenth century the main concentration of Irish in Runcorn was in the area bounded by Church Street, Brunswick Street and Mersey Street. There were several Irish lodging houses located in The Rookery and Mersey Street.

---

[13] *"Medieval Cheshire"* – H. Hewitt (Manchester University Press 1929)

The Irish were generally unskilled labourers and we can see that in the census of 1851 there were 665 men classed as labourers in Runcorn; of this number 162 were Irish. Although the Irish presence in Runcorn in 1851 was less than 25% of the working population, this number increased considerably later in the century during the building of the Manchester Ship Canal[14]. Needless to say, the Irish in Widnes were a far more significant group. At one point in time there were more Irish workers in the town than English. If you collate this data with family units it is quite obvious that they had a tremendous presence in the area. Their main residential concentrations in Widnes were in the districts of Newtown, Lugsdale, Moss Bank and upper West Bank.

The major flood of Irish into Widnes and other parts of England during the mid-nineteenth century was a result of the terrible famines which took place in Ireland during the 1840s. However, there is also an earlier history of substantial Irish migration into the north of England after the 1800 Act of Union. This Act had numerous political, economic and social consequences in Ireland. By 1830 many of the Irish industries, particularly the woollen trade, had been crushed out of existence by the unequal competition created by the Act. This meant that Irish handloom weavers and others in occupations associated with that trade were forced out of work. As a consequence, whole families moved to England where their services were in demand in the cotton and woollen districts of Lancashire and Yorkshire. In fact, in times of high demand, Irish weavers were regularly recruited and brought over to England by cotton and silk manufacturers and, because they had been obliged to leave their own declining industries, they were often used as a source of cheap labour. Although this particular migration of Irish labour into the north of England was not insignificant, it paled in comparison to the numbers who arrived during the famine years.

The Irish Famine was responsible for the huge and overwhelming migration of masses of Irish people into both England and North America. This dreadful catastrophe meant that hundreds of thousands of starving men, women and children were forced to flee from Ireland in order to survive. Although this book cannot be a vehicle for re-telling the story of this terrible event, nevertheless, the Irish Famine had an important bearing on our own local histories. Both towns nineteenth century populations, especially the populace of Widnes, comprised of

---

[14] The construction of the Manchester Ship Canal led to a marked increase in population (20,050 in 1891) but this was only a temporary condition and the figure decreased considerably after its completion.

substantial numbers of Irish people who came here as migrants during or immediately after the famine. Although it is obviously outside the scope of this present work to expand on the subject, I believe it is appropriate that some reference should be made to that event because the Irish Famine, and its aftermath, had a major impact upon the composition of our local societies. Background information helps us to appreciate why Irish migration into England reached such high levels during this time. It also allows us to put into perspective the reasons why the native English population had such a negative attitude towards these newcomers.

The complete failure of the potato crop in Ireland during the 1840s led to a nationwide famine. As most families at that time relied upon this crop for sustenance and income this meant that many tenants were obliged to surrender their small cottages and patches of land in order to qualify for relief. However, in most cases relief was not forthcoming as the authorities were swamped by the sheer scale of need and the workhouses were full to capacity. Those tenants who tried to hold out found they were unable to pay their rents and they were subsequently evicted. In fact, this suited most landlords as it gave them an opportunity to clear their estates of tenants in order to put their land to more profitable use. Indeed, many unscrupulous landlords used the law mercilessly at this time and evictions became a common scene all around the country. The cottages of evicted tenants were usually burned to the ground immediately to prevent them from returning. This meant that whole areas were cleared of housing and a means of earning a living.

Some people ask why the Irish were so reliant upon the potato crop and why didn't they hunt for other sources of food? The reason was that the landowners, many of whom lived abroad, imposed stringent laws against the native Irish which prevented from them from hunting or fishing on their land. In fact, the Irish had little rights apart from being allowed to cultivate their small patch of rented land. They could not cut or prune trees or remove fruit and those who trespassed on private land in pursuit of food faced severe punishment. This meant that after the failure of the potato crop, and the subsequent evictions, huge numbers of homeless, weak, starving people were wandering around the countryside in search of food and shelter. The Poor Law system could not deal with the volume and workhouses were overflowing with human misery. The result was that millions of people on our neighbouring isle literally died of starvation. The number of deaths was so large that mass graves had to be dug in almost every

47

village and town in the country. Many British newspapers of the time contained graphic reports of corpses of men, women and small children lying scattered along the roadsides. It is certainly hard to imagine such a devastating occurrence being allowed to happen so close to our shores, but it did.

When reading eye-witness accounts of events in Ireland during this black period one cannot fail to be horrified and incensed by the inhuman attitude of landowners and authorities alike. This heartless approach was compounded by the British Government who refused to relax their trade policies and continued to allow the export of food from Ireland to England. Furthermore, those desperate souls who stole food for their children were usually imprisoned or shot. These days there would be international outrage and condemnation of such actions. Interestingly, trade statistics show that by the late 1830s Ireland was routinely exporting around 80% of its grain production to England. Irish farmers were also exporting pigs, cattle and dairy produce and, in actual fact, half of Ireland's livestock production was exported to the industrial towns of northwest England as steamships facilitated direct transportation across the Irish Sea to our northern ports. This trade in grain and livestock continued almost uninterrupted throughout the whole period of the Irish famine.

Apart from the inhumanity associated with the export of food from a county whose population was starving, I think it is also important to point out that under *The Act of Union* Ireland was at that time an intrinsic part of Britain, therefore, the Irish were British citizens. However, they were treated somewhat differently than other citizens of Britain in that there were no great efforts on the part of the Government to alleviate the suffering caused by the famine. To our modern minds the behaviour of the British Government at that time was reprehensible and inexcusable. Most historians have classed this period as one of the most shameful episodes in British history. The census of 1851 shows that the population of Ireland was reduced by well over two million after the famine, this decrease was mainly due to death from starvation or forced migration.

Many migrant Irish were already on the verge of death when they arrived, and a large percentage of these poor souls died before they even reached our shores. It should be remembered that in those days the journey across the Irish Sea was both perilous and arduous, as the vessels they sailed in were often un-seaworthy as well as being unhygienic and overcrowded. Consequently, these congested ships were a breeding ground for all sorts of disease. Not surprisingly, for the majority of English inhabitants the arrival of these impoverished people was an undesirable occurrence. In many ways this attitude was understandable as the English Poor Law was already overstretched and the Irish placed an additional demand upon the system. Consequently, this abnormally heavy drain upon the Poor Law placed huge burdens upon local ratepayers. This meant that the arrival of Irish people into our towns and cities was not greeted with Christian compassion but with undisguised contempt. Furthermore, there were no local charitable organisations raising funds for their plight, instead, they were looked upon simply as an unwelcome weight on an already over-stretched economy. As a result, the Irish were reviled by the locals and, being Roman Catholic, this also promoted feelings of anti-Catholicism as well as anti-Irish prejudice among the general populations of the towns they inhabited.

Although the famine years brought a huge influx of Irish into the north-west of England there had been a minor scattering of Irish in Widnes and Runcorn in the years immediately preceding this. In Widnes these were mainly transient agricultural labourers who worked on local farms. Despite the nature of this work being seasonal, nevertheless, some Irish did settle here on a more permanent basis. There was a small group of Irish labourers residing in the Appleton area of the town as early as 1840. In the census of 1841 the returns for Appleton give details of a number of Irish born workers in that district. The surnames were Sweeney; O'Rourke; Boyle; Hanratty; Henry; Kinsdale; Byrne; Green; Devany; Hines; Murphy and Simmons. After the arrival of the chemical industry in the late 1840s the number of Irish in the town increased significantly.

Many of the early Irish workers in Widnes came here from St. Helens. Most of these were famine migrants who had arrived in Britain through the port of Liverpool. At the time of their arrival in England the town of St. Helens was already an established centre of industry. It had a number of thriving manufacturing concerns including glassmaking and alkali production as well as coal mining and pottery. The town was within easy walking distance of the port of Liverpool and, as it offered employment opportunities, it attracted those Irish who were fit or strong enough to work. However, once the chemical industry in Widnes began to develop on a large scale there was a substantial movement of these Irish workers from St. Helens to our town. The wave of *"St. Helens Irish"* who came to Widnes during the inception of the local chemical industry was supplemented with large numbers of new Irish arrivals in the following decades. This meant that the Irish population in Widnes expanded significantly.

Whilst there is no clear evidence to suggest that the Irish and other ethnic communities had a definite wish to isolate themselves from other groups, the desire to live near to people of a similar and familiar culture was natural. In some ways, retaining cultural identity as a group went a long way in re-creating some of the lost bonds of their previous life. This meant that communal and social organisations and relationships were instrumental in developing individual ethnic localities in the town. The area around Newtown was predominantly Irish in character, as was Lugsdale and Moss Bank. There were several Irish social organisations such as *The Irish National League* which was a strictly male organisation with a strong political ethos. *The Irish Foresters*` was another all male society but *The Irish Social Club,* which was located in Victoria Road, was a mixed club where both men and women could attend. This club was managed by Daniel Lowry who was an insurance agent based in Lugsdale Road. It is believed that Mr. Lowry also had a link with a Music Hall in Liverpool and later, after migrating to America, became a famous musical entrepreneur and the owner of a large theatre in New York.

The Irish were by far the largest ethnic group in Widnes; in fact they became the largest immigrant group in England during the nineteenth and early twentieth century. In addition to the huge Irish presence in the town there was also a substantial immigrant Welsh community. Interestingly, although the Irish were classed as the *"outsiders"*, the Welsh could be accused of deliberately creating their own separation from the English communities. Whilst the Irish generally used the English language, the Welsh population in the town spoke Welsh on a daily basis and conducted all their religious services in the mother tongue. The preservation of the Welsh language and its regular use within the community was an important element in maintaining a strong cultural identity; but it also served to disconnect this group from their neighbours. Several visitors to the town drew attention to the fact that the Welsh language was quite widespread in the district. It was said that when passing through the main thoroughfares in the town, or visiting shops, it was quite common to hear everyday conversations being conducted entirely in Welsh. Interestingly, despite their initial detachment, in later times the Welsh group was the first to integrate and become absorbed into general society. This assimilation has usually been attributed to a religious compatibility with the native English population.

Even though the chemical industry was mainly responsible for bringing the Welsh into Widnes, historically, there had nearly always been some movement of workers from Wales to parts of Lancashire and Cheshire. There was an enormous Welsh community in nineteenth century Liverpool. Some of the most beautiful old churches and buildings in and around that city were the creations of talented Welsh born builders and architects. Of course, we should remember that our sister town, Runcorn, also had a sizeable Welsh community. Because of Runcorn's numerous stone quarrying concerns it is usually supposed that many of the early Runcorn Welsh were originally quarrymen from North Wales who came to the area to work in local quarries. A Welsh church was first established in Runcorn when Welsh Calvinist Methodists opened their chapel in (Back) King Street in 1829. The Rev. John Jones served this congregation as their minister for around 7 years from 1837. As the Welsh parishioners in the town increased another Chapel was erected in Rutland Street in 1856.

It should be said that the Welsh also had a significant presence in our neighbouring towns of St. Helens and Warrington. The Welsh populations in both these towns were associated with the presence of the copper industry in these localities. Since the discovery of copper at Parys Mountain in Anglesey in 1768[15] there had been a significant increase in copper mining on the island. Subsequently, in the latter years of the 18th century, copper ore was shipped in considerable quantities to both St. Helens and Warrington. In Warrington it was destined for the Warrington Copper & Brass Company which gave employment to a significant number of Welsh workers. These workers and other Welsh incomers were housed in a district that took on an overwhelmingly Welsh character. In later times several Welsh churches were established in the town to cater for the religious needs of this growing community.

St. Helens had also been receiving Welsh incomers since the mid-1700s and by the late 1770s there were a considerable number of Welsh workers in that town. Most of these were employed in local copper smelting works which had strong links to Welsh copper mines. The connection of Welsh mines with the St. Helens area had been made possible by the construction of the Sankey Brook Navigation[16] and its opening up of the local coalfield. Initially, coal had been transported

[15] Copper was also discovered in the lead mine of *Penryn Du* on the Lleyn peninsular in 1764.

[16] The Sankey Brook Navigation was the first true canal in Britain.

from St. Helens to Anglesey for copper smelting but in later times some mine owners decided to establish smelting works in Lancashire and ship the ore to the coal instead. Most of the early Welsh workers in St. Helens were employed by an enterprising Welshman called Thomas Williams who had a controlling interest in several ventures related to copper and brass in Cornwall, Lancashire, Anglesey and Flintshire. Williams, who was financially involved in two St. Helens copper works, The Stanley Works and The Ravenhead Works, was also the exclusive proprietor of Anglesey's copper mining interests. In order to transport his large consignments of copper ore from Amlwch in Anglesey to his two St. Helens works the enterprising Mr. Williams acquired his own fleet of sailing vessels. He also resolved to make the transportation of raw materials between these two places more cost effective by ensuring that after his vessels had discharged their copper cargo at St. Helens, the empty ships were filled with coal from the Ravenhead and Thatto Heath coalmines. The ships then returned to Wales with a full cargo of coal for the Parys Mine Company on Anglesey. Obviously it was more profitable to have a full cargo in both directions rather than returning to Wales with an empty vessel.

Another Welshman who had an important influence on the Lancashire copper industry was Michael Hughes of Sherdley House in the township of Sutton, who became an eminent St. Helens magistrate. Born in Anglesey, and a member of the family who had originally owned the copper-rich Parys Mountain, he moved to St. Helens with the copper trade and established a long standing business association with Thomas Williams. In addition to copper, he had financial interests in coal mines and a number of ships. In partnership with the Clare family, who were boat builders at Sankey Bridges, he became part owner of several flats. He also held shares in the Sankey Navigation Company and, in a rather clever move, by purchasing the Penketh Hall Estate he was able to lease this land to the canal company for a healthy annual rent. Hughes put a good deal of his capital into local industry, especially the copper and coal mining industries and, together with his fellow Welshman, Williams, made an enormous contribution to the industrial and commercial life of St. Helens. In addition, they were both responsible for bringing countless Welsh workers into the town, housing them near to their copper works in the Ravenhead district. The infusion of Welsh into St. Helens obviously had a significant impact on the social composition of the area. The tremendous number of Welsh residing in the Ravenhead area gave the locality a distinctive Welsh ambience and resulted in the area acquiring the descriptive name of Welsh Row.

It is reasonable to say that most of the Welsh communities in our local towns were established because of some sort of trade association with Wales. In fact, a large number of the Widnes Welsh originated from Flintshire and it is generally believed that many of them came here as a result of Muspratt's industrial connections with that area. Like the Irish and other ethnic groups the Widnes Welsh also created their own distinct neighbourhoods. They were the dominant group in the vicinity of Moor Lane and the streets around Victoria Road. Some of the builders who erected property in this area were themselves Welsh, such as Mr. J. Griffiths, who named two of his streets Rhyl Street and Ellis Street[17]. There were also a considerable number of Welsh residents in West Bank.

The number of Welsh in Widnes was sufficient to require the provision of three Welsh chapels giving religious accommodation to Presbyterian, Congregational and Wesleyan worshippers. The Welsh Wesleyan congregation opened their first chapel in Cromwell Street in 1866 and it was said that at that time there were in excess of 400 Welsh people resident in the town. In that same year the Welsh Presbyterians laid the foundation stone for their chapel in Milton Street. This ceremony took place on 1st February 1866 and was performed by Mr. E.G. Salisbury who was the retired MP for the city of Chester. A glass bottle, containing copies of *The Liverpool Mercury*, *The Baner* and *Amserau Cymru* as well as the diary of the Welsh Presbyterian Churches for 1866, was placed under the foundation stone. To mark the occasion Mrs. Carey, the widow of the late Rev. Eustace Carey, presented Mr. Salisbury with a silver mallet and trowel. The celebrations continued in the evening with a meeting in the Public Hall during which the assembly was entertained by music from a Welsh choir. In addition to the Wesleyans and Presbyterians, there was also a substantial number of Welsh Congregationalists in the town and they established a chapel for their own flock in Moor Lane. As an indication of the expanding Welsh churchgoing community, in a little over twenty years the Welsh Wesleyan congregation had increased considerably. In 1887 this increase necessitated a move from Cromwell Street to a new larger building on the corner of Lacey Street and Luton Street[18].

As we know, the Welsh were extremely devout and were regular and pious churchgoers. The services in their chapels were conducted

---

[17] Located off Moor Lane

[18] In later years this building became the Widnes Spiritualist Chapel.

entirely in the Welsh language which, being their first language, was used not only in their religious worship but also in their daily life. From time to time, the Welsh chapels in Widnes entertained eminent Welsh preachers who came to spread the gospel to their exiled countrymen. Amongst the well-known Welsh preachers who came to the town was the famous Pedrog, a much admired Welsh cleric who had a large following throughout Wales as well as in Liverpool and all the northern towns where Welsh people had settled.

Apart from devotion to their chapels, we know that the Welsh were also extremely fond of music especially when sung in their native tongue. It is no coincidence that Wales is often referred to as *"The Land of Song"*. In modern times this reputation has been kept alive through numerous notable musical events such as the International Eisteddfod. For the Welsh community who had settled in Widnes in those early days music was also an important way of keeping their culture alive. The Widnes Welsh, in an effort to replicate the ancient musical traditions of their native place, established their own local Eisteddfod in Widnes. This event became an extremely important occurrence in the town and was enjoyed not only by the Welsh citizens of Widnes but by all sections of the local communities on both sides of the river. It became a prominent social occasion in the town's calendar and such was its importance that the local Education Committee made it a half-day holiday at all council schools. The event was renowned for the high standard of musical competition and entrants for the various categories came from far and wide. However in the latter years of its existence there was some reluctance on the part of male voice choirs from outside the area to enter the event. The reason being, that Runcorn's leading male choir usually carried away the trophy for this category. There was no suggestion that the Runcorn choir was favoured in any way, simply that they were so good they were considered to be unbeatable.

In addition to the Irish and Welsh, later in the century Widnes also attracted migrants from the Baltic States of Lithuania, Poland and Latvia as well as small numbers of people from other countries such as Belgium, France, Germany and Sweden. The Lithuanians were particularly prominent in Widnes and a major community developed in the Waterloo area of the town. As with many of the migrants who came into Widnes, the Lithuanians were a drifting workforce who had previously been in other parts of the country before settling here. In the case of the Lithuanians, many of these had previously worked in Scotland, particularly in areas of Lanarkshire, before moving south to Lancashire where settlements were established in parts of Manchester and Liverpool as well as in Earlestown and Widnes.

In much the same way as the Irish had been forced to abandon their homeland in order to survive, the Lithuanians too had been compelled to migrate for reasons which made life intolerable in their own land. In addition to severe economic depression, the political and religious oppression under the Tsarist regime made their existence unbearable. For many, the lure of guaranteed employment and accommodation in another country proved irresistible. The Baltic States and Lithuania in particular, were prime targets for the recruitment agents of Lanarkshire ironmasters and mine owners. Newspaper adverts described the great opportunities available in Scotland for those willing to work hard. For any decent family man, or single people with the spirit for survival, the prospect of living and working in Scotland was extremely appealing.

At that time the economic situation in Lithuania was extremely bleak and ordinary inhabitants of the country were suffering greatly. However, in addition to dire economic conditions there were other equally serious reasons for wishing to migrate. These mainly concerned the fact that towards the end of the 18th century both Lithuania and Poland had been annexed by Russia. Following this annexation a strict philosophy of Russification had been imposed on both counties. This meant that Lithuanian and Polish men were routinely conscripted into the Russian army. Naturally, for most young men with a sprinkling of patriotic pride this was an insufferable affront.

Conscription and the crushing poverty created by a desperate economic situation were cause enough to migrate. However, one of the most serious motives would have been the imposition of a Russian political and religious culture upon the native populations of these two proud nations. The repression and persecution experienced by both Lithuania and Poland was tyrannical and brutal. In both countries, religious anti-Catholic discrimination and harassment caused violent clashes between the native populations and the Russian government troops. There was a powerful attempt by the authorities to impose the orthodox Russian faith upon the populations and, as a consequence, Catholic churches were routinely closed and often burned down or desecrated. This provoked organised resistance by some members of the indigenous populations. Unfortunately this defiance usually resulted in arrests and floggings and sometimes the outcome was deportation to Siberia. Apart from the aggressive attempts to impose a religious philosophy upon the inhabitants, there was also a ban on their native language. All books and publications, other than those printed in the Russian Cyrillic alphabet, were prohibited. Lithuanian and Polish literature, including newspapers and journals, were outlawed and those printing or reading them faced severe penalties. In fact, the inhabitants of both countries were subjected to an unremitting and extremely ruthless and brutish form of religious and political oppression.

One can only imagine the hopelessness experienced by men with families to rear and young people who could see no positive future in their own homelands. The opportunity of creating a better life in another country would have been hard to resist for those young enough or fit enough to leave. In many ways these people were not only economic migrants they were also asylum seekers who were desperate to escape oppression as well as grinding poverty. Unfortunately, like many strangers arriving onto these shores, there was no great welcome awaiting them. They were treated with suspicion, hostility and loathing. The local populations in the areas they inhabited made nonsensical claims which suggested they were a danger to health and accused them of bringing in disease. Their customs and language isolated them and in the workplace their presence was blamed for creating unemployment among the local workforce. It was certainly not an easy transition, and not what they had been led to expect. The very act of migrating was a huge step both physically and emotionally. They had made a long and gruelling journey which involved travelling westward through East Prussia to Hamburg before taking a ship to Leith, Glasgow or Hull. Many sons and daughters left behind their parents, siblings and friends as they set out in search of a better life. Like the age old story of emigration, many families were separated and were never to be reunited. Most elderly parents reluctantly accepted the fact that emigration would rob them of their children and grandchildren forever.

Records show that a large proportion of the Lithuanians who passed through or settled in Widnes had previously worked in the coal mines and ironworks of Lanarkshire. This area of Scotland was host to one of the earliest Lithuanian settlements in Britain and had been receiving a steady stream of Lithuanians since the late 1870s. However it was the latter years of the nineteenth century and the early years of the twentieth century which saw the greatest number of Lithuanian arrivals. The main concentrations of Lithuanian communities in Lanarkshire were in the districts of Bellshill, Coatbridge, Carfin, Motherwell, Wishaw, Carluke and Larkhall. Incidentally, it is interesting to note that a sizeable proportion of the newcomers into Scotland, and later into Widnes, came from the southwest of Lithuania, mainly from small villages in the Sulvalkija region and districts of Kaunas. What is also interesting is the number of extended family connections there were among the new arrivals. These connections became broader as a result of many young single Lithuanians marrying fellow immigrants from their newly established communities. This was a natural occurrence in all ethnic groups as young immigrants usually married other young people from the same ethnic community. This meant that there was no significant Lithuanian integration into local Scottish or Widnes society for several generations.

The Lithuanians began arriving in Widnes during the 1880s and during this period many of them were members of a transient workforce who came into the town and then moved on to other places in Britain. In the north of England places like Manchester, Liverpool and Earlestown attracted substantial Lithuanian workers who were joining friends or relations who had settled in those areas. We can see from Widnes census records from the 1890s onwards that some Lithuanian and Polish names appear only once and are missing from subsequent lists. Many moved on to America, which was a magnet at that time for migrants of all nationalities. Despite the transitory nature of their employment habits a large number of Lithuanians remained in Widnes and raised their families here. Like other ethnic communities in the town the Lithuanians created their own distinct neighbourhood. They lived mainly apart from other groups, huddled together in a few streets in the Waterloo area of the town. The substantial Lithuanian presence in this district gave the area a marked ethnic identity. Census returns for this district show that Lithuanian surnames were numerous, although at that time these surnames were probably unpronounceable to the general population. This was another factor which meant that established locals saw them as a separate caste with their own alien culture

In the early days the hostility and discrimination which had been experienced by Lithuanians in Scotland recurred in Widnes. Part of this was due to conflict between immigrants and local workers over the distribution of jobs. This came about because of the ebb and flow of demand for labour in the local job market. The Lithuanians and Poles were singled out for particular criticism. In 1892 a man called Joseph Mott set in motion a chain of events which led to questions being raised in parliament by the local MP, Mr. Edwards-Moss. Mr. Mott's letter to the Prescot Guardians suggested that Lithuanian workers, who were always referred to as Poles or Russian Poles, were responsible for the chemical workers of Widnes being *"thrown out of employment"*. This letter was a response to the threatened discontinuation of relief work for the local unemployed. James Mott wrote:

"Widnes, March 10, 1892. Sir, I have been deputed by the relief-workers of Widnes to bring the following statement under the notice of your Board at their meeting today (Thursday): - At the present time, and for some considerable time, there have been employed in the Widnes Chemical Works a great number of Poles, whilst we, who are chiefly composed of householders and ratepayers, are compelled to walk to and from Whiston[19] daily for the purpose of keeping body and soul together. We should be very thankful to the Board if they would, through you, communicate with the authorities of the United Alkali Company, to see if they can do nothing in this matter, as we think it strange they should consent to assist in supporting us here and at the same time pay complete strangers to the country for work that we should now be doing. We would not have troubled you with this statement, only that we have been misled so often by reports that the Poles were to be discharged to make room for us. Finding that this was only imagination on the part of someone, we thought that we would see if the Board could do anything in the matter."

A few weeks later Mr. Edwards-Moss raised the matter in parliament. He asked the President of the Local Government Board whether his attention had been called to the application which had recently been made to the Prescot Board of Guardians by the chemical workers of Widnes. He claimed that:

"... the workers of Widnes had been thrown out of work and become dependent on the workhouse, owing to the employment in their place of foreign paupers at their works; whether he is aware that these pauper immigrants are Poles, 80% of whom arrive in this country quite destitute, and who, by working for starvation wages, are displacing the natural working population of the locality; and whether, in view of the fact that much distress is caused thereby, and an additional burden is being placed upon the rates of the district, the Government will consider the recommendation of the Select Committee on Emigration and Immigration of 1889, especially the last clause of their report and take some steps to put a stop to the immigration of paupers into this country."

The President of the Board of Trade, being duty bound to investigate this matter, immediately consulted local employers who assured him that this was certainly not the case. They certified, unequivocally, that the *"Poles"* were definitely not working for *"starvation wages"* which

---

[19] To petition the Prescot Guardians who were based at Whiston Workhouse (later Whiston Hospital).

would threaten the employment of the native population. The wages paid to them was calculated at the same rate as that of other workers, whether they be British or of any other nationality. In fact, the claim had no substance whatsoever but was merely indicative of the anti-immigrant attitude which existed at that time. In Scotland, there was also continuing complaints about the immigrants. Mr. Gilmour, the representative of the Lanarkshire miners, told the annual meeting of The Miners Federation of Great Britain, held in Leicester in January 1897, that 25% of the men employed in Lanarkshire coal mines were Russian Poles. He claimed they were a danger to all the other workers as they were unskilled, having come straight into the mines without any experience. It was suggested that immigrant workers should not be allowed to work on the coal face until they had three years' experience. Until that time their wages should be greatly reduced.

In addition to general prejudice among the population, there was a great deal of underlying anti-immigrant propaganda in the press. There were countless derogatory newspaper reports and in cases where Lithuanians were involved in crimes of drunkenness or fighting their nationality was always emphasised. Because of this emphasis one gets the desired impression that they were a major cause of crime. In earlier times the Irish had received the same treatment in newspapers. However, the undeniable fact is that English lawbreakers were more numerous in proportion to their presence in the town. It is also worth noting that long before any of the immigrant groups, either Irish or Eastern Europeans, arrived in the town the behaviour of the general population was no different. The carousing, drunkenness and fighting associated with the celebration of Farnworth Wakes bears testimony to this fact. However, the drastic increase in population only served to boost and highlight this type of behaviour among all elements of society. There were more people so more crime.

Despite the fact that all newspaper references describe this community as Poles, in fact there was only a relatively small number of Poles in our area[20]. The vast majority of the immigrants who came from the Baltic region into Widnes were Lithuanian. Although there were, indeed, a considerable number of Polish families in the district they were in the minority. Despite their lesser number in our particular area, the Poles were slightly earlier arrivals into Merseyside than the

---

[20]There were also a small number of Latvians.

Lithuanians. Most of the Poles who came into north-west England arrived through the Port of Liverpool having travelling there directly from German ports. Although the Baltic migrants did not arrive into our area in any significant number until the late 1880s and the 1890s, Poles began settling in Liverpool as early as the 1870s. At a Select Vestry Meeting held in Liverpool in 1876 it was claimed that there were 65 Poles housed at that time in the local workhouse. A report presented to the meeting by the workhouse supervisor said that there had been a recent outbreak of smallpox in the workhouse and the inference was that the Poles were responsible. During the course of the Vestry Meeting it emerged that prior to that date a number of Poles had been sent to the Cheshire salt-works. It was suggested that the remainder be sent back to Hamburg, the port they had sailed from.

Although Liverpool did receive a significant number of Polish immigrants, some of the Poles who eventually came to Widnes had previously lived and worked in the St. Helens area. Like earlier migrants of other ethnicities, many of these would have been attracted to St. Helens through a system of chain-migration. There were small Polish communities in the districts of Peasley Cross and nearby Sutton Manor, with most of the Polish menfolk being employed as miners at Sutton Manor Colliery. However, the growing alkali industry in Widnes proved to be a more attractive employment proposition for many of these men and a number of families moved to Widnes. As we have seen, other Poles who had arrived directly into the Port of Liverpool chose to stay in that area. A large number of these migrants found employment at Tate and Lyle`s Liverpool Sugar Works. There were also a number who headed to the salt areas of Cheshire in search of work. Unlike the Lithuanians, the Polish families who came to Widnes did not establish a distinct ethnic district as they were too small in number to do this. However, they were present in the Newtown area as well as parts of upper West Bank and they also co-existed alongside the larger Lithuanian community in the Waterloo area.

The blurring of nationalities between Poles and Lithuanians at that time is not too surprising. This misunderstanding came about because both countries had been annexed by Russia and thus both nationalities became Russian subjects. The Poles were commonly described as Russians or Russian Poles and it became convenient to put Lithuanian immigrants into the same category. For the ordinary Briton at that time it might have seemed that there was no real difference between them. They all had strange names, strange lifestyles whereby they dressed differently, spoke a different language and ate different types of food. To the ordinary Briton they appeared to be the same. However, for both of these distinct and proud ethnic groups the confusion must have been particularly irksome in view of their shared histories and the previous antagonisms between Lithuania and Poland. For a Lithuanian to be called a Pole and vice versa would have been like calling an Englishman a Scot or an Irishman a Welshman. However, it should be pointed out that it was not only the newspapers and the general public who made this glaring mistake. Government, local authorities and employers often made no distinction between these two separate nationalities. I have seen numerous official documents which describe people as Russian Poles when in actual fact their birth certificates and oral family history confirm that these people had been born and raised in Lithuania.

Obviously, the early Irish and Welsh incomers were set apart from the native English population by their marked cultural differences. Nevertheless, these two groups quickly established their own distinct and viable communities, as did the Lithuanian settlers who came later. However, there were additional problems to overcome for the Lithuanians and Poles. Whilst the Welsh had used their native language through choice, like the Irish they had a command of the English language. On the other hand, most of the immigrants from the Baltic were unable to speak English and were therefore unable to communicate with their fellow citizens and work colleagues. This lack of verbal interaction created a further barrier to acceptance by the general population. More importantly, fellow workmates claimed that their lack of English gave rise to fears that they were a serious danger in the workplace as they could not understand verbal instructions. To be perfectly honest, I suppose one can understand the trepidation of colleagues who were unable to communicate with them, especially as they were all working in a dangerous environment.

There is no doubt that their inability to understand or speak English was a major problem both in the workplace and socially. There were several unfortunate cases in Scotland where the language became a legal issue. One case involving a Lithuanian woman in Motherwell prompted an exasperated judge to remark: *"The Sheriff of Hamilton must have very hard work as there is a whole colony of Poles in the district and very few if any of them know much of the English language"*. The woman, Mrs Annie Wasebriski (*sic*) or Sreht (*sic*) of Carfin, asked the court to declare that she was the lawful wife of Francis Sreht who was accidentally killed while in the employment of William Dixon Limited at Motherwell. The woman had made a claim against the company for compensation for the death of her husband. The company refused to make payment until it was proved that she had been legally married to the deceased. A number of her friends and neighbours were called to bear witness to this fact; they all gave their evidence with the aid of an interpreter. Many years later this woman's daughter migrated to Widnes with her husband and they raised their family here.

In almost all cases it was the Lithuanian and Polish children who first mastered the language whilst attending local schools; they then taught their parents. However, this was not always the case as some of the older immigrants never completely got to grips with English. In these cases they relied on others to help them navigate the pitfalls which occurred in day to day situations. As well as the language problem, there were additional factors such as their dress, food and customs which set them apart from other incomers. The Irish and Welsh had blended more easily into society as their outward appearance and clothing was indistinguishable from other members of the working classes, whilst the Eastern Europeans, particularly the women, were more identifiable because of their unusual attire. It was extremely difficult on so many levels for this ethnic group to interact with other sections of society. Their difficulties were not lessened by the shameful intolerance and hostility which was directed towards them. In retrospect, one cannot fail to feel immense sympathy coupled with a great deal of admiration for their courage and perseverance in the face of so many problems and such widespread and undeserved enmity.

Undoubtedly the segregation of our urban society into specific geographical ethnic districts, whilst being a natural choice for those groups, further isolated communities. Separation, and the mutual ignorance, suspicion and misunderstanding that went with it, were a powerful factor in the rise of discord and distrust. Religion also became a barrier as church schools of varying denominations created *"differences"* from an early age. Although, generally, there was a certain degree of grudging tolerance towards people of different faiths there were several examples of discord involving members of the Protestant and Catholic populations. Most of these incidents involved Orange Lodge celebrations which, as one can imagine, created conflict with the Irish Catholic communities of the town. Naturally, disputes over religion were sources of strong feelings and heated controversy, especially when merged with other political or social grievances. However, despite the negativity of the social, ethnic or religious divisions which existed we must balance these with the achievements of creating viable and lasting communities and allegiances. The positive side of urbanisation was that it formed and strengthened bonds among incomers who lived in the same district. This led to a shared *"loyalty"* to a neighbourhood, a street, or a locality and this in turn produced a substitute for the old societies they had left behind.

As we have seen, when looking at the history of our two towns, the diverse composition of our early societies, particularly in Widnes, is remarkable. New industrial development imposed a drastic change in the structure of local society as the original communities were swamped by a multitude of incomers with unfamiliar lifestyles and work arrangements. In places like Widnes and Runcorn, where there had previously been only small indigenous populaces with established social arrangements, this influx of migrants completely altered the traditional fabric of local society. History shows that, due to the multifaceted composition of the new population, society in both towns became more complex and unstable. Of course Runcorn had experienced this change much earlier as the river and canals had brought construction and marine workers to the area, as well as small numbers of quarry workers and labourers from the surrounding counties and Wales. However, the change in Widnes was far more extreme and alarming as the numbers and rapidity with which the change occurred was overwhelming.

It could be said that the concentration of people within the two towns, from a variety of backgrounds, religions and cultures, offered a rich potential for different forms of communication. The opportunities to establish and create a unique cultural identity were also multiplied. These identities, I suppose, have developed into what is now known as the *"Widnesian"* and the *"Runcornian"*. It could be assumed that the characteristics which today's local born inhabitants possess are partly due to the rich amalgamation of inherited cultures from these early migrants. In both towns significant numbers of Welsh and Irish added to the existing cultural mix, which included rural migrants from neighbouring and far flung counties as well as the resident indigenous population. In Widnes this wide assortment of people was further enriched by the arrival of economic migrants from the Baltic States and several other countries.

In addition to the population increase and inevitable change in the structure of society, another obvious social outcome of our industrialisation, apart from pollution, was the resulting overcrowding. The rapid expansion of industry meant that there was an ongoing and urgent need for accommodation. As there was no local authority at that time to provide the necessary accommodation this void was filled by speculative builders who constructed streets of houses quickly and cheaply. This attracted numerous builders and *"buy to let"* investors to the area. Some builders constructed and let the houses themselves, while others just built the properties then quickly sold them on to property opportunists. These speculators would often buy up whole streets of houses and rent them out. In September 1856 a Runcorn builder, John White, offered a block of twenty-one houses and two shops for sale near Widnes Dock.

A GREAT BARGAIN – AN INCOME OF £115 PER YEAR FOR AN OUTLAY OF LITTLE MORE THAN £500.

On sale By Private Treaty: 21 four-roomed cottages, having separate back yard and petty to each. AND Two SHOPS, all new and well and substantially built, the whole respectably tenanted. The two shops are both doing an amount of ready-money trade; there is a good bake-house and oven to the grocer's shop. The property is situated in that well-known and very flourishing locality Widnes Docks, close upon the Runcorn Gap Station; it is subject to ground rent of £13 per annum on a lease for 1000 years. The rent produced amounts to £114.8s.8d yearly, and although recently valued by a respectable surveyor at £1500 will be sold for £1370, £850 of which will remain on mortgage at 5 per cent. For further particulars apply to Mr. John White, builder, Halton Road, Runcorn."

Despite an unparalleled spate of urban building, housing stock could not keep up with demand. This led to congestion and unwholesome living conditions, as most of the early housing lacked many of the basic amenities required to live a healthy life. In those days there were no planning regulations to adhere to and no rules regarding density levels or sanitary provisions. This allowed builders complete freedom to compress the largest number of homes onto the smallest parcel of land. We can see from early maps that the subsequent arrangement and widths of streets and back entries meant that there was a minimum amount of sunlight and air space. In addition to this, in most cases there was little spatial division between residential developments of tightly packed terraces and the polluting factories.

In retrospect one can see that this was an example of private enterprise at its worst. However, although we can now recognise the appalling lack of control relating to the Victorian housing boom in Widnes, in fact, at that time speculative private enterprise was seen as the most effective way of providing sufficient housing at a low cost. It might be argued that jerry-building was unavoidable because the demand for accommodation was immediate and builders were expected to provide houses rapidly and on the cheap. It is worth noting that, in spite of these houses being sub-standard, most of them stood and served as homes for almost a century or more.

Many of our early industrialists were involved in providing rented accommodation for their workers and some manufacturers built and owned streets of housing. John Hutchinson, mindful of a need to accommodate his new workforce, acquired some land to the north of the canal and developed it for housing. This area became known as Newtown and was the earliest significant residential district of its kind. Some streets in this neighbourhood, such as Elizabeth Street, Ann Street and Catherine Street [21] were named after members of the Hutchinson family. Earle Street was named after Hutchinson's brother-in-law, Oswald Earle, who was his early business partner. Records indicate that residential building in Newtown and parts of West Bank began as early as 1852. In that year William Hurst, who was the owner of both West Bank House and a considerable amount of acreage, decided to sell off part of his land in West Bank to builders for housing development.

Although Hutchinson had personally arranged to have some of the Newtown houses built, presumably those streets just named, he mainly leased or sub-leased plots of land to other builders who erected numerous streets of houses on them. One interesting feature of these leases was that when an occupant of a house wished to make or sell alcohol then the rent for the whole block was increased, usually doubled. This gave rise to the widely held belief that Hutchinson was strongly opposed to alcohol. However, it is more than likely that this may simply have been a reflection of Hutchinson's concern about the moral climate of the town. His own wine cellar at Appleton Lodge was quite extensive, so he was certainly not adverse to alcoholic refreshment himself. Naturally, the clause in the lease, relating to the making and selling of alcohol, did not discourage builders from providing pubs for the new residents nor did it deter landlords from renting them. By 1876 there was estimated to be over 50 pubs and inns in Widnes. Of course, Hutchinson was not alone in inserting clauses

---

[21] Elizabeth was the name of Hutchinson's wife and Catherine and Ann were the names of his sisters.

relating to "Public Houses" in his leases. Many landowners put conditions on the sale or lease of their lands. Both William Hurst and his son-in-law, William Wright, who administered the estate after Hurst's death, included similar "Public House" stipulations in their leases.

Some of the lessees of the Newtown area were named as John Bennett, William Palin, James Lea, Edmond Brereton, William Colquitt, Isaiah Sadler and W.H. Kershaw. All these men subsequently built streets of houses in the Newtown district. In addition to the land leased for residential building in Newtown, a parcel of land on the present day Lugsdale Road was leased for the construction of St. Mary's Roman Catholic Church[22]. Later on, after some persuasion from his close friend Father Fisher, the Parish Priest from St. Bede's, Hutchinson agreed to gift this land to the Church. In 1860, Hutchinson leased several other sections of land for residential building. This land lay to the West of Waterloo Road, between the original St. Mary's Church[23] and Hutchinson Street. Unlike the land in Newtown, which was freehold, these parcels of land were on lease from the trustees of the Wright Estate. Plots of this land were sub-leased to speculative house builders.

It is evident from his land leasing, house building and other lucrative ventures that Hutchinson was a farsighted and astute individual. However, all of these projects required a substantial amount of financial investment and his personal resources were extremely limited. The constant need for capital to fund his business schemes led to an early example of a *"sale and lease back"* system. This scheme involved approximately one acre of land in the area of Penn Street and Earle Street, in Newtown. This land, having had houses built upon it, was sold to Rev. B. Carr who was buying on behalf of *The Queen Anne Bounty*. The rentals of the houses were to be paid to the Vicar of Rainford. These houses were part of a number of similar housing acquisitions in the Widnes area purchased by *The Queen Anne Bounty*[24]. Of course, when this plot was originally purchased it was bought as agricultural land but now having had a total of 21 houses built upon it; the value of the plot had increased considerably.[25] One might wholeheartedly applaud and admire these examples of

---

[22] Later it became known as St. Marie's.

[23] St. Mary's (C of E) church, West Bank

[24] A charitable organisation set up by Queen Anne for the purpose of funding the established church.

[25] This plot and the houses built upon it were later made part of a post-nuptial agreement between John Hutchinson and his wife, Elizabeth.

Hutchinson's entrepreneurship but for several occurrences which reveal a ruthless and mean nature. The Newtown venture gave one insight into the danger of crossing him or of provoking his displeasure. The land to the east of the Newtown development was owned by a Mr. Bibby who had previously had a disagreement with Hutchinson over some land matter. In a rather spiteful move, a narrow strip of land along the eastern boundary, measuring about three feet in width, was deliberately left unleased by Hutchinson. He also gave specific instructions that there was to be no road or rail connection over it to Mr. Bibby's land then, or in the future. This had the effect of cutting off the Bibby land without means of access.

As industry expanded at a rapid pace, house building was equally prolific. Unfortunately, hardly any of these homes were of a good standard. The houses in all the hastily constructed residential areas were built of porous handmade bricks and the walls were solid with no cavity or damp-proof course. The accommodation was very small, usually consisting of two rooms downstairs with two bedrooms above. There were no drains or running water, the only provision for sanitary purposes being an earth-closet in an outside yard and a standpipe for water at the end of some streets or in nearby works. Consequently, these homes were damp, dingy and unhealthily crammed together into the smallest possible space. In fact, these early houses provided little more than a crude protection against the elements. They were built quickly and cheaply as it was considered that anything that was more than barely minimal would increase cost.

It goes without saying that overcrowding was a standard feature of these homes. Almost all the families were large and the homes provided for them were extremely small and certainly not of an adequate size to allow a healthy and comfortable existence. In the census of 1871 we can see that one small house in Elizabeth Street, Newtown, a two up and two down dwelling, was occupied by six adults and five small children. This cramming together of human beings, young and old, male and female, was obviously unhygienic and detrimental to physical and mental wellbeing. The lack of adequate sanitation facilities and the sheer density of the housing stock meant that these areas were also a breeding ground for diseases. The picture as a whole is a depressing one. It is impossible not to feel a sense of horror and outrage when we realise that employers considered this type of accommodation to be satisfactory for working men with large families. The very same working men who had to set out from these airless hovels at the crack of dawn; and who were expected to work long hours in hot dangerous chemical factories for a meagre wage.

As the housing stock generally lacked basic sanitation provisions and there was a high degree of overcrowding, it is not too surprising that fevers and contagious diseases were common. Smallpox epidemics recurred regularly in both towns throughout the nineteenth century, even though legislative Acts in 1853 and 1867 attempted to make vaccination mandatory. Typhus and cholera outbreaks were also frequent. Typhus was a particularly dangerous disease due to its high contagiousness and because people lived in cramped conditions this disease was often hard to contain. Cholera was also a killer disease and there were regular outbreaks. Unfortunately, the medical establishment of the day was completely unequipped to handle these particular outbreaks, primarily because the methods of disease transmission were not fully understood. It was some time before it was discovered that some infections were transmitted through contaminated water and at that time there were no proper purification systems in place. Of course, disease was a great leveller as epidemics affected all classes of society not just the poor.

The surge in population brought huge problems in the form of providing public facilities. In the early days, prior to the formation of an official Local Board of Health, the Highways Committee was solely responsible for providing and overseeing the limited services in the township of Widnes. In the mid-1850s John Hutchinson who, as we have seen, was in no small way responsible for the expansion of the town, was an influential member of this Committee. Fellow industrialist Henry Deacon was also a member. A report of the annual meeting of 1857 gives us an indication of the social composition of the Highways Committee. We can see that as well as those two alkali manufacturers other members included a sailcloth factory proprietor, a watchmaker, a local doctor and a landowner. A short account of that meeting included this information:

"The annual meeting of the township of Widnes, for the election of overseers and a surveyor of highways, was held on Tuesday in the large room belonging to Mr. Garton, In Farnworth. The room was crowded to suffocation, and the excitement was intense, owing to the strong party feeling with regard to the election of surveyor of highways. Mr. Henry Deacon, of the chemical works, Widnes, was called to the chair. Mr. John Lucas, Mr. Henry Doward, Mr. Frederick Beck, Mr. John Shepard, and Mr. John Hutchinson were chosen overseers for the ensuing year. Mr. John Shepard then proposed, and Mr. Henry

Doward seconded, that Mr. Moss be appointed highway surveyor, at a salary of £20 per year. Mr. John Hutchinson, alkali manufacturer, moved as an amendment, seconded by Mr. Samuel Shaw Brown, that Mr. Robert Barrow be appointed to that office, at the same salary. The amendment, on being put to the meeting, was declared to be carried by an overwhelming majority. The following gentlemen were afterwards elected as highway committee, under whom the surveyor should act: - Mr. John Hutchinson, Mr. Henry Deacon, Mr. Thomas Shaw, Mr. Samuel Shaw Brown, Dr. Greenup, and Mr. Samuel Whitfield. The meeting broke up amid considerable cheering from the friends of Mr. Robert Barrow."

Clearly, John Hutchinson wielded a great deal of power and influence in the town at that time. Evidence proves that he was both an astute businessman and an expert manipulator who had his finger in a number of pies. He was always on the lookout for new business opportunities and was prepared to take a risk, usually with borrowed money. Fortunately, he was endowed with exceptional resourcefulness and foresight as well as an ability to persuade banks to finance him. Apart from his alkali factory and the instigation of a number of house-building schemes, he started a company to provide piped water and gas. Initially, the provision of gas and water was mainly for his domestic benefit and that of his near neighbours in the area around Appleton Lodge. However, the enterprising Hutchinson saw an opportunity to expand this small concern into a more profitable undertaking. In 1856 he founded the Widnes Gas and Water Company with the intention of supplying water, gas and street lighting to the town.

The premises of the Widnes Gas and Water Company were located in Earle Street, Newtown. The newly formed Company held its first meeting on 24th November 1856. The members present on that occasion were: John Hutchinson, Chairman; James Trevelyan Raynes, Arthur Sinclair[26] and Oswald Earle. Shares in the new Company were taken by Robert Daglish (100), Edward Greenall (50), William Lupton (50), William Wright (100), William Gossage (50) and William Pennington (50). By November 1857 the Company had 180 street lamps. The lamps were paid for by individuals and companies at a rate of £2.12.6d per year. In addition there were 141 water tenants who paid 1d. per week. In 1859, in order to deal with the extra land work relating to both the Hutchinson works and the Gas and Water

---

[26] A friend and former business partner of James Cross.

Company, Hutchinson decided to employ a surveyor to oversee these operations. The man chosen as the new surveyor was Mr. Joseph Carruthers Routledge, who proved to be an exceptional and valuable employee. In fact, Mr. Routledge remained with the Hutchinson Company for almost forty years. After Hutchinson's death he was retained by the Hutchinson Trustees as Surveyor and Land Agent and it is believed that his employment with the Hutchinson Company continued until sometime around 1900.

Although the Widnes Gas and Water Company had been operating successfully and supplying residents for around four years, it wasn't until May 1860 that an Act of Parliament was applied for to enable the Company to officially provide the township of Widnes with gas and water. Royal assent was reported the following month when the Company was formally authorised by an Act of Parliament to provide the town with these services. At that point the Company was reformed with John Hutchinson as the Chairman. The other directors were Oswald Earle, Rev. E. Carr, Arthur Sinclair, James Trevelyan Raynes and Major James Cross.

Later that year Hutchinson agreed to supply the railway with water. A ten inch water main was laid along Ferry Road and a new gasholder was purchased. There were also numerous new street lamps erected in the area around West Bank. Seven additional lamps were installed on the Ferry Road between the Toll Bar and the Ferry; four of these were paid for by The Railway Company. Hutchinson & Earle paid for a lamp to be placed outside their new office building; John Wright paid for one opposite West Bank House and a further lamp, opposite The Snig Pie House, was to be paid for by John Wright or the tenant. Gas was also supplied to the Lambert Works, the Police Station, the Vineyard Public House, the Wesleyan Chapel and St. Mary's R.C. Church in Lugsdale Road. The gas supply to Gossage's Works was piped from Waterloo Road over the footbridge through Mr. Gossage's garden.[27] Muspratt's Works was supplied with gas through a meter, but they experienced several problems with leaking gas pipes. As a remedy, the leaking pipes were routinely plugged with wood.

By the mid-1860s the local inhabitants had come to realise that something major needed to be done to provide the essential infrastructure that was required for an evolving town. Apart from the relentless problems associated with industrial pollution, the insistent pace of urban growth brought new pressures for collective services to

---

[27] Publications of *The Lancashire & Cheshire Historical Society*.

provide at least the basic amenities for mass living. As multitudes of newcomers poured into the area the town was suddenly faced with great problems of housing, water supply, sanitation and drainage. It was quite clear to residents that the existing Highways Committee was ill-equipped to deal with the increased demands for these services. The Government, which had been faced by a new problem-ridden British urban society, was acutely aware of the necessity to assist and manage the growing towns and cities around the country. Therefore, in order to regulate these mounting problems, Public Health Acts were passed in 1848 and 1858. These Acts were introduced to encourage and permit town improvement schemes, including the creation of new administrative authorities or commissions.

The Public Health Act of 1858 had empowered ratepayers in urban districts to set up Local Boards of Health in order to oversee, improve and provide facilities for local citizens. In June 1865 the residents of Widnes held a meeting in the Public Hall in Hutchinson Street where a resolution was passed to set up a Local Board of Health. Following this, the Widnes Board of Health was constituted on 8th August 1865 and the first meeting was held on 3rd October 1865. It has been said that the chief motivation among upper and middle class ratepayers to tolerate the expenditure on new urban services was their own fear of exposure to infection. Where dirt was hard to control so too was disease.

One of the prime concerns for the new Local Board was the supply of decent water to the district. Although John Hutchinson's Gas and Water Company had been empowered by a Private Act of Parliament to supply these utilities to the town, the quality of the water was appalling. Hutchinson's water supply came from a well on Spike Island and was pumped to a tank on top of Tower Building which was located in Hutchinson's No.2 works. Unfortunately, the water supply was often contaminated and in one instance it was polluted by caustic soda which had leaked from a tank in the works. On another occasion Henry Deacon had a sample of the water analysed in his laboratory. He reported to the Local Board that it contained 171.5 grams per gallon of solid matter, mainly salt. Apart from contamination, there was also the additional problem of there not being enough water available to supply the township of Widnes. Henry Deacon offered to allow a pump to be put down in his own factory (Gaskell Deacon Works) to supply water to the public but the offer was not accepted.

In November 1865 the newly formed Local Board of Health wrote

71

to the Widnes Gas and Water Company to say that the quality of water was unacceptable. They also complained that, apart from the water being bad, there was also an insufficient amount to supply the township. It was pointed out to the Company that, under Clause 70 of the Public Health Act 1848, the Local Board could make a formal demand for The Widnes Gas and Water Company to improve the quality and supply of water. If the Company did not comply it would be obliged to surrender the right to provide this service or to give the Local Board the freedom to do so themselves. The Local Board indicated that they would be willing to purchase the Company's works and water mains. After a series of protracted negotiations an agreement was reached in 1867 when the Local Board of Health formally acquired the Company. This agreement allowed the Local Board to petition Parliament to supply the township with gas and water. The Bill was duly promoted and subsequently passed as *The Widnes Improvement Act 1867*.

Apart from providing a mandate to supply the town with water and gas, *The Widnes Improvement Act* also authorised the building of a Town Hall and the abolishment of the private tolls taken on Snig Lane (now Mersey Road). Implementing the latter part of the Act proved to be quite difficult as one of the shareholders of the Widnes Gas and Water Company was William Wright of West Bank. Mr. Wright had previously levied a toll on every vehicle passing along Snig Lane and on those people using the Ferry. Eventually, after some fierce negotiations, Mr. Wright's trustees agreed to sell the Snig Lane tolls to the Local Board for the sum of £50. Whilst the provisions of *The Widnes Improvement Bill* had allowed the Local Board to buy up the undertakings of the Widnes Gas and Water Company, it was recognised at the time that there was an insufficient supply of water for the township and that additional waterworks would be required. Fortunately, the Bill had also given the Local Board the power to borrow money to carry out necessary improvements for the town. One of the more pressing issues was the provision of an alternative source of water. After professional consultation it was decided that this supply would be provided by building a new waterworks at Pex Hill.

Once *The Widnes Improvement Act* had been formally passed by Parliament, the Local Board wasted no time in getting down to the business of building, organising and staffing the proposed new waterworks. On 27th May 1867 the following advertisement appeared in *The Times*.

"CIVIL ENGINEER AND SURVEYOR – The Widnes Local Board require a GENTLEMAN competent to prepare plans and specifications, and to lay out and superintend the execution of their new water works and to act as Surveyor to the Board. Experience as a water engineer indispensable, and some knowledge of gas engineering and the duties of a local surveyor desirable. Salary £300 per annum. Address (at once), to: T. Beasley, Solicitor, St. Helens."

Work on the new reservoir at Pex Hill commenced in May 1868 and the following year, on the last Saturday in July, the new waterworks were officially opened amid a great deal of pomp. Mrs. Knight, the wife of the Chairman of the Gas and Water Committee, was given the honour of performing the opening ceremony. The overall cost was estimated to be around £40,000 which was to be repaid by the Local Board over a period of thirty years. The magnitude of the occasion can be estimated by the following report which appeared in *The Liverpool Mercury*. Although the original report is overly long, I have included almost all of it as it gives us an idea of how important the new waterworks were to the townspeople of Widnes. It also gives a superb flavour of the communal atmosphere which existed at that time.

"By way of doing every honour to the opening ceremony, Saturday was set apart as an almost general holiday in the neighbourhood of Widnes – a privilege the more appreciated because the most agreeable of summer weather prevailed from morn till night. It was a little remarkable to notice – as few could fail to do – the effect in Widnes itself of many of the tall chimney stalks of the chemical works ceasing for the time to vomit forth their nasty smoke. For once the atmosphere became partially relieved from that "very ancient fish-like smell" which so often offends the nostrils of those even who are not used to the sweet perfumes of "Araby the blest". But very few of the Widnesians remained to enjoy this better odour, preferring to share in the "demonstrations". Of these latter the first feature was the procession of at least five thousand school children and adult clubs. In order that the weariness of a three mile walk might not prevent even the tiniest youngsters from assisting, commodious carts were pressed into service for their conveyance. Not only were the horses adorned with showy trappings, but the lorries they drew were also set out gaily with coloured calico and wild flowers. Decorated thus profusely, the carts with their joyous living freight assumed something like the appearance of triumphal chariots. Certainly, the children, whether driving in this manner or marching under the command of their teachers, seemed highly pleased to be allowed to take part in the celebrations. In the

73

course of their march they amused themselves by now and then singing snatches of cheerful songs, or giving forth ringing cheers. Occasionally, they appeared, and no wonder, to be greatly puzzled at the droll costume of the mystic brethren who took part along with them in the procession. There were nearly 300 of the ancient order of Oddfellows wearing, of course, aprons and sashes covered with the most mysterious hieroglyphics. The Company, likewise included about 150 of the Brotherhood of Shepherds, attired in equally curious fashion. Each of these pastoral gentlemen carried a crook in true Arcadian style, and two of them known as "the guardians" are distinguished by having their heads burdened with huge Hussar-like hats, evidently made of sheepskin, with the woolly fleece outside. One other notable member, the senior shepherd of the lodge, wore a similarly picturesque head-piece, besides leading at his side "the dog" with its fanciful apron and sash.[28] Altogether the procession was about three quarters of a mile in length. Under the guidance of Superintendent Fowler, of Prescot, and twenty policemen, it started from Widnes soon after twelve o'clock and reached Pex Hill in two hours. En route the procession received accessions at Appleton - that diminutive hamlet, and also at the village of Farnworth, which, by-the-by, from the number and merit of its washerwomen, has come, it seems, to be called the laundry of Liverpool.

The following is, as near as need be, the order of the procession: (1) Engineer Band of St. Helens; (2) The Local Board of Widnes; (3) the children, including Wesleyan scholars, Welsh Wesleyans, Roman Catholics, Welsh Presbyterians, Primitive Methodists, Appleton schools, Farnworth Church schools; next came the Oddfellows, and then the Shepherds, with instrumental bands bringing up the rear.

At old Stockswell, about half a mile from Pex Hill, are two beam engines, which have been furnished and fitted into the well by Messrs. Clayton & Goodfellow, of Blackburn. Each is of 40 horse power and can make 20 strokes a minute, with the capacity of pumping up about

---

[28] In addition to these local societies, in the early 1870s a Masonic Lodge was founded in Widnes. The inaugural meeting was thought to have been held on 10th November 1871 at the Simms Cross Hotel. Following this, the Widnes Lodge of Equity (1384) held their early meetings at Walker's Commercial Hotel in the town. Among the first members were: R.D. Simpson; J.W. Fowler; H.S. Oppenheim; W. Jamieson; J.W. Wareing; W.I. Thompson; James White; A Borthwick; A. Tippett; R.D. Simpson; J. Raven; W. Newsome; R. Neill; J.W. Carlisle and George Brown.

30 gallons at a stroke. About two o'clock the ceremony of christening and starting the engines was performed in the presence of a large number of ladies, various officials, and other friends, by Mr. John McLellan, chairman of the Local Board, assisted by Mr. Cross. As soon as the machinery had been fairly set a-going, guns were fired, and then followed a few congratulatory speeches. From this the party drove to Pex Hill, arriving in ample time for the fete there.

Soon after three o'clock, a select committee of specially invited guests assembled on the high ground above the reservoir, for the purpose of assisting at the central and important part of the day's proceedings. Mr. McLellan moved that the chair be taken by their friend Mr. Henry Deacon, who was the originator of the works, and had taken a most active interest in them, especially in arranging the preliminary steps (applause). He considered that these works would confer lasting benefits upon the township of Widnes; they would be productive of physical, social, and moral advantages alike (hear, hear, and applause). Being a strong believer in the old adage that "cleanliness is next to godliness", he did not think there could be much godliness without cleanliness, for without a clean body there was much less likelihood of having a pure and upright mind. It was pleasing to be now favoured with the presence of so many friends, especially of so many ladies, but he could not help regretting the absence of one lady, Mrs. Hutchinson, the widow[29] of the gentleman by whom, in the first instance, the manufacture and trade of the district has been extensively developed (hear, hear).

Mr. Deacon then took the chair, and after some humorous remarks, requested in the name of the Local Board that the respected wife of Mr. Knight, chairman of the gas and water committee, should inaugurate the works by turning the water on to the town for the first time. Mrs. Knight accordingly advanced and turned the handle which had been attached to the tap or turncock. The effect of this operation was almost immediately shown by the spray beginning to jet prettily from two ornamental water fountains that had been erected at the foot of the road. When the auspicious ceremony was completed a gun was fired, and an instrumental band struck up "God Save the Queen", all of which naturally tended to excite enthusiasm among the spectators.

---

[29] John Hutchinson died in March 1865

Mr. Gossage then moved a vote of thanks to Mrs. Knight, on whose behalf her husband briefly responded. A similar compliment to Mr. Deacon concluded that portion of the proceedings. In the late evening, about a hundred ladies and gentlemen sat down together at a banquet, in a spacious marquee which had been erected on the Reservoir ground".

As we have seen, before the formation of the Widnes Local Board of Health, and a partial planning overhaul, some districts had already been developed by private landowners and building speculators. Obviously, the influx of workers into the town had necessitated the rapid building of housing to accommodate them. The speed with which this population surge happened meant that the homes were built hastily and with little thought being given to the design of the homes or layout of the streets. In fact, the only real considerations were the speed with which they could be erected and the cost. When one looks at local plans it is clear that the greatest period of urban development in Widnes was in the mid-1870s as this era saw the large-scale development of West Bank. However, local records indicate that residential building first started around 1852 following industrial development in the Canal Region[30].

From maps of the area in 1861 and 1871 it is possible to see that Widnes was divided into three distinct residential areas separated by alkali works, railway lines and open spaces. Although there was a tide of residential construction by numerous builders in all these areas, we can notice that there were also large gaps in these building developments. It is assumed that the reason for this may have been that some landowners were asking too high a price for their land or put too many clauses or restrictions on the use of the land. Of course another reason was that some of this land had already been set aside for future industrial use. However, when looking at the mosaic of residential building in the three areas, local historical knowledge reveals that each of these districts subsequently acquired its own special character. These characteristics were usually associated with ethnicity or religion. Unfortunately, a regrettable result of this fragmented urban geography was that it sometimes served to underline social divisions and contributed to the isolation of groups from each other.

Newtown had one of the earliest concentrations of housing in the south of the town, but by the late 1860s and early 1870s some of the original parts of Newtown had already been knocked down to make

---

30 Industrially, the Canal Region had almost reached full capacity by 1865 and after that date only 2 more factories were opened there.

way for the railways. However, in the early 1860s construction began again on a larger scale in the Newtown and Simms Cross districts. This new spate of building resulted in sizeable residential developments in both these areas. In 1860 John Hutchinson leased land to the west of Waterloo Road from the trustees of the Wright family for housing development. Hutchinson subsequently sub-leased plots of this land to several builders including W.H. Kershaw, William Middleton, Richard Farrant, James Lea[31] and George Fleetwood. Unlike Newtown, the Waterloo area was not over developed at that time as space was purposely left for a possible extension to the canal. However, after 1865 there was an additional surge in residential building in the West Bank area. This was connected to the extensive industrial development which had occurred in the Marsh Region. Building development also progressed in Moss Bank immediately following the erection of the Sullivan and Pilkington factories[32] in the late 1860s. Mary Street and other nearby streets came into being around that time, the early houses in that locality being constructed by builders Hugh Williams, William Lightfoot and John Davies, who also built the Moss Bank Wesleyan Chapel and Schoolroom.

The development of our early residential districts and their positions was inexorably linked to the growth of industry. The location of factories usually had a bearing on the site of residential housing as at that time public transport was almost non-existent so placing homes near to factories seemed like a good idea. Unfortunately this meant that mass local housing developed cheek by jowl with places of work. Obviously, the close proximity of industry and housing created an unhealthy living environment as the polluting atmosphere of smoke and noxious odours saturated almost all residential districts in the south of the town. In addition to the unpleasant and unwholesome atmosphere, there was also the problem of the waste products of the alkali trade. This foul waste, which gave off toxic fumes, was disposed of by dumping in huge piles near to factories and homes.

It is possible to see, from building applications submitted to the Local Board from 1865 onwards, the names of the main builders of our

31 Mr. Lea, who was a native of Cronton, had previously been involved in a court case in May 1864, when he claimed to have been assaulted by a workman for using non-union labour.

32 Wm Pilkington & Son, who were involved in glass manufacture in St. Helens, opened the Mersey Chemical Works here in March 1865. Edward Robert Sullivan established The British Alkali Works in September 1867.

developing town. Some of their surnames were immortalised in what were once familiar street names such as Wood Street, Kershaw Street, Carlisle Street, Travis Street and Midwood Street to name but a few. It would appear that Edwin Wood was the most prolific of these builders having constructed in the region of 850 houses in the town. Behind him were William H. Kershaw and James W. Carlisle who built around 300 houses each. Incidentally, William Kershaw was one of the first tenants to obtain a lease on Hutchinson's West Bank Dock Estate. His lease was taken out in January 1865 at a rent of £50 per annum. At that time he was described as a Timber Merchant. His lease was extended in October 1874 and the company continued at this site until its closure in 1897 following the death of Mr. Kershaw.

We can see from early plans that there had been no thought or guidance given to the layout of streets or density of building development, nor had there been any attempt by the Highways Committee to control these issues. Although the Local Board did introduce new building regulations, this did not amount to a full planning overhaul nor did it necessarily mean that these rules would be implemented. Despite the Local Board claiming that all new building work would be subjected to regulations and strict scrutiny, the policies were not always put into practice. Even in terms of minimum supervision of individual building standards these controls seem to have been rather patchily applied. In fact, one case in 1867 shows how difficult it was to enforce some of these regulations. The case in question related to a number of houses in Waterloo Road which had been erected by local builder, James Lea. On completion of these houses, the Local Board's surveyor had inspected them but refused to issue an approval certificate as they did not comply with the by-laws which required adequate drainage to be installed. In the surveyor's opinion the dwellings were not, in the full sense of the law, fit for human habitation. Mr. Lea took his case to Court. He claimed that as building work had been started before the new by-laws came into operation the regulations should not be imposed retrospectively. Surprisingly, Mr. Lea won his case and was allowed to put tenants into the properties despite the fact that the dwellings did not meet the required standard and were considered to be unfit for human habitation.

Although Mr. Lea had claimed a legal victory over the Local Board it did not do him much good because shortly afterwards he was declared bankrupt. Sometime later he was convicted of obtaining money from a building society under false pretences. This resulted in him serving a two year prison term in Kirkdale Gaol for fraud. Unfortunately, James Lea was not an exception as business rackets and swindles were widespread at that time. Business morality in Victorian Britain was highly questionable and, as this was a period of speculative mania, fraud of all types, particularly insurance fraud and speculative investment fraud, were by no means unusual. In fact this type of crime was so common that several Victorian novelists, including Charles Dickens, based some of their most famous works on swindles and cases of investment fraud. Similarly, cases of bankruptcy were extremely common in all types of businesses. What is interesting is the fact that in many cases commercial fraud and financial scandal had little negative impact on the reputation of the businessmen who were involved in it.

Of course, high levels of borrowing to fund their ventures inevitably meant that bankruptcy was fairly common amongst our local industrialists and property speculators. Apart from Mr. Lea, another well-known local builder, J.W. Carlisle[33], who owned a total of 404 houses in Widnes, also went bust. Although Carlisle had undertaken a number of lucrative contracts, including building the Gresham buildings in Liverpool, in February 1885 he was summoned for non-payment of £292.14s.8d for Poor Rates. He was ordered to make an immediate payment of £258.5s.6d but was unable to comply with this order. As a consequence he was declared bankrupt in July that year. His liabilities amounted to £49,990 and his assets were less than £10,000.

Obviously, the new Local Board had huge tasks ahead of it and the members knew that their problems would grow as the population expanded. The vital work of making roads and paving streets, installing drainage and sewers, and providing gas and lighting would be an expensive burden on the pockets of the ratepayers. Consequently some local residents were extremely unhappy with the new arrangement. One of the new Board's first projects was to inspect existing property and report on the improvements which would be necessary. A surveyor was appointed to carry out this task. During the course of his investigation the new surveyor, Mr. Shufflebottom, discovered that many of the houses were in a deplorable state and lacked drainage and sewers and some streets were just a mass of mud and water and required paving. As a result, it was decided that landlords would be compelled to install drains in these houses and that all subsequent building projects were to be controlled and monitored.

---

33 J.W. Carlisle built many of the houses in the Simms Cross area, including Carlisle Street.

However, despite these new building regulations, as we have seen, it was not always possible to implement the rules.

The new Surveyor was given a dual role as he was also appointed Inspector of Nuisances. One of his responsibilities in that capacity was to control the operation of slaughter houses by compelling their owners to register and agree to regular inspections. Unregistered slaughter houses could be fined and shut down and those that were not kept in good condition could have their registration revoked. The Local Board also attempted to place some form of control over the numerous lodging houses in the town by introducing similar registration requirements. Public health was also a serious cause for concern. The lack of adequate sewage systems, or any previous laws to compel landlords to provide reasonable sanitary arrangements, had created a situation which had become a hazard to the health of the population. As stated earlier, smallpox,[34] cholera, typhoid[35], diphtheria and scarlet fever outbreaks were not uncommon and the infant mortality rate was extremely high. However, it was not until several years after the formation of our Local Board that *The Public Health Act* of 1872 was introduced. This Act divided the country into sanitary districts, each to have its own single Public Health Authority. In towns this was to be the Municipal Authority. Each authority was required to appoint a Medical Officer of Health and a separate Nuisance Inspector for the purpose of combating preventable disease.

At this point I should draw attention to the fact that across the river, in Runcorn, urbanisation had developed ahead of Widnes, and arrangements had been in place to oversee the development of that district long before the formation of the Widnes Local Board. Of course industrialisation and related population increases had occurred there much earlier and this prompted the forming of the Runcorn Improvement Commission in 1852. Prior to the Commission, the previous body which had been set up for administering the development and improvement of the town was the Board of Surveyors

---

[34] There was a smallpox outbreak in Widnes in 1883 – hospital tents were erected in Moor Lane to accommodate and isolate patients. A number of cases were reported in Milton Road, Gladstone Street, Market Street and Gerrard Street, Simms Cross.

[35] Henry Deacon fell victim to this disease and died in 1872 aged just 52.

and Highways, a similar organisation to that which existed in Widnes and most other small towns at that time. The last Runcorn Board of Surveyors and Highways was elected on 16th October 1851 and the following gentlemen were selected as members; James Cawley, J.L. Wright, James Rigby, Thomas Rigby, John Rigby, George Forrester, William Dutton, W.B. Gibson, William Howarth, William Forster, Thomas Hazlehurst, Thomas Johnson and Robert C. Whiteway. However, at that time, steps had already been taken to disband this body and replace it with an Improvement Commission. An application had previously been made to Parliament to pass an Improvement Bill for Runcorn. This request received a favourable response and after its third reading the Bill was duly passed by Parliament in the spring of 1852. *The Runcorn Improvement Act* officially came into force on 2nd October 1852 and the first commissioners, eighteen in total, were elected on 1st November. It had previously been agreed that the Trustees of the late Duke of Bridgewater and the proprietors of the Mersey and Irwell Navigation would each be allowed to assign a commissioner as their representative. Apart from these two nominated appointments, the qualifications required to be a commissioner were quite simple; they needed to be resident in the area covered by the limits of the Improvement Bill, be rated to the relief of the poor in an amount of £25, have a freehold estate of £50 per annum, or be in possession of a personal estate to the value of £1,000.

The bounds of *The Runcorn Improvement Act* comprised the whole township of Runcorn and certain parts of the township of Halton that were situated within the town of Runcorn. The new commissioners were empowered to provide for the paving, lighting, watching, draining and cleansing of the town of Runcorn and part of the township of Halton. They were also authorised to purchase gas works, to erect market places, slaughterhouses, weighing and measuring houses and to levy tolls. Permission was also given to borrow money on mortgage to provide for essential services. The specified amounts they were allowed to borrow were given as follows; on the general improvement rate, £40,000; on the highway rate, £3,000; on the sewer rate, £5,000; on the lighting and watch rate, £3,000. The new commissioners wasted no time in getting organised and committees were quickly formed to deal with the various sections of urban management. In December 1852, at the first meeting after the inaugural gathering to elect committee members, it was agreed by the Watching and Lighting Committee that Mr. G.T. Dawson would be appointed to the office of Assistant Constable for the town. The Highways Committee appointed Mr. John Buckley as Clerk to the Highways and Mr. William Pritchard was given the wide ranging and demanding role of Inspector of Nuisances, Surveyor under the Improvement Commissioners, and Superintendent of Highways. Mr. John H. Chorlton, solicitor, was appointed as Law Clerk and Secretary to the Board and Mr. Stenhouse of the firm of Messrs. Parr, Lyon and Company, who were Warrington bankers, was appointed Treasurer.

So, whilst Widnes was still striving to provide the most basic facilities and services, Runcorn was already up and running. More than a decade before its neighbour had decided to form a Local Board of Health, Runcorn was in the process of expanding its urban amenities. By the late 1830s, even before the forming of the Improvement Commission, the town already possessed a Town Hall[36] and a company had been formed to supply part of the town with gas. In the mid-1850s the Runcorn Commissioners were in the fortunate position of being able to enhance the town's facilities with the addition of a new Market Hall. It was claimed, when laying the foundation stone for this building that the market would be a great advantage to the working classes *"who would enjoy going in and being able to purchase agricultural produce cheaper than from small shops"*.

Although the new Market Hall provided a modern purpose built centre for sellers and buyers of agricultural foodstuffs, in fact, even before the existence of this Market the town residents had the means to purchase cheap farm provisions. Each week local farmers, gardeners and others had brought their produce into town and sold their wares from carts in the streets. Some forty years earlier, In April 1811, an announcement in a Cheshire newspaper informed local residents that a market would be established in the town to provide meat and other provisions each week. In addition, there would be two fairs held each year for the sale of livestock. Although this notice dates from 1811, in fact, unofficial fairs and markets had been part of local routine for a long time before this date. Markets everywhere were an essential feature of everyday life as they centred on the exchange and distribution of goods, particularly the agricultural produce of their hinterlands. They also provided a venue for the hire of labour. In addition, they played an important role in regular social interaction for both town and country dwellers.

---

[36] Runcorn Town Hall was built in 1831 on land provided by the Trustees of the Duke of Bridgewater.
Runcorn Gas Company founded in 1837

> ## FAIRS AND MARKETS
> ### At RUNCORN, in the County of Chester.
> *Notice is hereby Given,*
>
> THAT a MARKET will be established at Run-
> corn for the sale of Butcher's Meat, and Pro-
> visions of every kind, to commence on Friday the
> 3d of May next, at nine o'clock in the morning, and
> to be continued weekly throughout the year.
> And there will also be TWO FAIRS in the year,
> for the sale of horses, cattle, sheep, and all kind of
> goods, the one the last Friday in April, the other
> the last Friday in October.

By the early 1850s it is clear that Runcorn was an established and flourishing town, albeit with a population of mixed fortunes. The town had expanded considerably but despite the provision of a superb new Market Hall some people were dissatisfied with the overall management of the town. Residents and ratepayers were up in arms when it was discovered that there were serious failings in Runcorn's financial accounts. As a result of their discontent a public meeting was held in The Foresters' Hall in October 1857. At this meeting angry ratepayers and citizens voiced their concerns about the grave mismanagement of the town's affairs. Several of the town's commissioners and local shopkeepers were present at this meeting during which William Dutton, a local timber merchant, was unanimously voted to the Chair. Also present was Mr. White, a well-known Runcorn builder who had constructed several streets of houses in the West Bank area of Widnes. Mr. Dutton told the angry gathering that the town had been grossly mismanaged for a long time, and the rates had become so high that they had all started to ask questions. He said *"The new market had cost between £3000 and £4000, the poor rate was £1s.3d. in the pound and, in addition to this, they now had a serious defalcation in the town accounts to bear."*

Among the speakers at this extraordinary meeting was Mr. Samuel Shaw Brown, a well-known Runcorn businessman. Mr. Shaw Brown also had a business concern across the river at Widnes Dock and was from time to time actively involved in Widnes public affairs. This gentleman was known to residents on both sides of the river as a forthright but generally genial man with an acute social conscience. He had a reputation in both towns as a plain-speaking, vociferous and sometimes aggressive individual. Unfortunately his outspoken manner was not always appreciated, especially when on the receiving end of his attention. In spite of this, the fact that he had been elected onto various civic committees would suggest that he was fairly popular among his peer groups on both sides of the river. On this occasion, at the special meeting of ratepayers, Mr. Shaw Brown was given an enthusiastic reception. When he rose to address the meeting he was greeted with loud cheering and applause from the gathered crowd.

Mr. Shaw Brown started his statement by reminding the audience that the sanitary condition of the town was so bad that there had been 70 fatal cases of typhoid in Runcorn in the last three months. He then drew their attention to the fact that the Commissioners were not a democratically elected body but merely a group of influential people who had contrived by devious means to be nominated into office.

He also said that:

"...the main sewer in the town, where it ended, just reached the outside of the house of one of the Commissioners; but a few yards further along all the refuse and filth of the houses floated on the surface of the channel. He could have blamed the Commissioners less if they had been fairly elected by the town, but when that which they all knew to be the fact was borne in mind – when they considered that not only were the Commissioners not elected by the town, but had, by compelling all over whom they had influence to elect them in direct opposition to the expressed wish of the town, then the present state of things made it justifiable on his part to say their conduct had been even more disgraceful. It was agreed that Runcorn had been mismanaged, but not only had the Commissioners permitted, with their eyes wide open, the ratepayers` money to be taken but they had allowed the town money to be expended in a most scandalous manner; but a few weeks ago Mr. Howarth, a gentleman to whose honest exertions in the Commission the town owed much, raised his voice against the town expending £30 for the removal of the railings in front of Trinity Church. He was sure if the Primitive Methodists had desired the Commission so to do, all the eloquence and powers of reason they might have brought forth would not have got it done at the town's expense."

During Mr. Shaw Brown's lengthy and revealing speech, which was greeted from time to time with loud cheering, his complaints against the Commissioners took on a more personal tone. He referred to the fact that one of the Commissioners, Mr. Edwin Shaw, who I presume was unconnected, had recently reported him to the magistrates. He, (Mr. Shaw) had accused him (Samuel Shaw Brown) of being a persistent drunkard. Apparently, a complaint had been lodged but the magistrates had not acted upon it. Referring to this he said:

"I had received some little time ago a note from Mr. Shaw for having charged me before the magistrates with habitual drunkenness. One person, now a Commissioner, the moment it was issued, ran from one merchant's office to another to convey the glorious intelligence, and to assure them that now they should gag me. They have, however, since then discovered their mistake. The columns of The Liverpool Mercury afforded ample proof that it had not checked in the least my exposure of their public abuses. It had become a notorious fact that one or two of the Commissioners had rolled through the streets of Runcorn drunk, in companionship with the said Mr. Shaw. In addition, there have been several instances which prove that for a long time the Commissioners anticipated the results complained of, and knew that Mr. Shaw was outliving his income, and urged that after all the ratepayers had only themselves to blame.

The town's interest has been neglected, its healthiness impaired, and its rates increased until trade had sought a more congenial locality. It was an insult to our forefathers, who had fought and bled and died for the freedom and greatness we now boast as Englishmen, to neglect those municipal duties we talk about not being able to afford to do, and I hope we will act more wisely and honourably in the future".

At the end of what appeared to be a very lively meeting, the Chairman thought it would be prudent to appoint a committee of property owners to attend the meetings of the town's Commissioners in order to watch over the interests of ratepayers generally. It was hoped that their presence at these meetings would have the effect of improving the management of the town's affairs. A number of names were submitted to the meeting and were unanimously approved, after which a vote was taken. Subsequently, a committee known as *The Runcorn Ratepayers' Protection Association* was formed. The members elected were William Dutton (Chairman), John White, Samuel White, Samuel Shaw Brown, William Hopkins, John Williams, Mr. G. Hayes, Mr. G. Bowyer, Mr. W. Walker and Mr. J. Jannion.

The long-standing animosity between Samuel Shaw Brown and Edwin Shaw had come to a head earlier that year when Mr. Shaw

Brown applied to the Runcorn magistrates for a summons against Mr. Shaw for drunkenness. It was no secret that Edwin Shaw had an extreme fondness for drink. His self-indulgent and carousing lifestyle had come to the attention of the police in both Widnes and Runcorn and he had been cautioned by them on a number of occasions. As he was not a "quiet drunk", but a rather belligerent one, local people in Widnes had become increasingly fed-up with his antics. They could not understand why, despite continued warnings, he seems to have evaded prosecution while other lesser souls had been brought before the magistrates to be fined or imprisoned for drunkenness. Of course Mr. Shaw was personally known to most of the local magistrates in a social capacity. Naturally one would hesitate to suggest that these social relationships could in any way have allowed him to avoid prosecution. Perish the thought! However, if Mr. Shaw Brown's complaints are to be believed, then this was another example of the double standards which often existed in courts of law those days. I find a report of his original complaint to the magistrates to be rather disturbing:

"Mr. Samuel Shaw Brown stated that he had an application to make to the bench of a very unpleasant and painful nature. The bench had that day fined a man 8s.6d. for being drunk and disorderly, while there appeared in police reports of the same day on which that man's offence was committed, a similar charge against one of the town's servants. This town servant had even been previously charged with and admonished for the offence of drunkenness by one the magistrates on the bench. This man, whom he had frequently not seen sober, but concerning whom he never felt it his duty to take public notice until he found that his offences had been tampered with by one of the magistrates. Although a summons had been issued on the evidence of two policemen, and although the offender had so conducted himself as to disturb and cause to leave her bed the daughter of one of the most respectable tradesmen in the town, that magistrate had refused to sign a summons against him, he presumed on the grounds that the town's servant wore black cloth while the man fined 8s.6d. on that same day only wore fustian. There was a very strong and growing impression in the town, from such proceedings, that the bench was partial, which feeling must result in disrespect for the law. He therefore felt it had become the duty of any man who had, like himself, taken an interest in the public affairs of the town – especially as the matter had been given publicity through the columns of the "Liverpool Mercury" and was the cause of much feeling in the town for good or evil – he must, therefore, on public grounds, ask the magistrates to grant him a summons against Edwin Shaw, the Secretary to the Commissioners, for being drunk and disorderly in the public streets, near midnight, on the 1st May.

One of the magistrates – Mr. Whiteway said he should like to know what Mr. Shaw Brown meant when he said that Mr. Shaw had been admonished by one of the Bench? Mr. Shaw Brown replied, Mr. Whiteway himself was the gentleman who had reprimanded him. Mr. Whiteway said when he was a Commissioner he did have a charge of the kind against him, which the Commissioner overlooked on Mr. Shaw's expression of sorrow, but it did not come before him as a magistrate. Another magistrate, Mr. Johnson, said that as the matter had been brought to their notice now he would address the matter to the Chairman, Sir Richard Brooke – he would hold no further discussion with Mr. Shaw Brown but would use that discretionary power which he assumed his brother magistrates would also do. He must tell Mr. Shaw Brown that he would not do so from any Chartist, factious or vindictive feeling. The law was not vindictive. Mr. Shaw Brown said if the law was not vindictive it was assumed to be impartial; he could have no vindictive object; he asked no favour, but as an act of equal justice he asked the bench for the summons; if one man should be fined for such behaviour why not the other? Mr. Johnson (turning round to Sir Richard Brooke) said aloud - "He is that Shaw Brown that came into this town as a Chartist and upset the church rate and he did not know what else" – Mr. Shaw Brown said that the statement made by Mr. Johnson was absolutely false. He could not have come into the town as a Chartist, because he never was one; and with regard to the church rates, he (Mr. Shaw Brown) had never done more for them in public than Mr. Johnson had against them in private. He had come there, however, not to be insulted, but to do a public duty, and seek impartial justice; he therefore only had to ask the bench either to grant or refuse the summons. The magistrates refused the summons and Mr. Shaw Brown replied that he should at once lay the whole matter before Sir George Grey"[37].

From further accounts it is clear that Mr. Shaw Brown had the support of a large number of local residents who believed that the Magistrates were wrong in refusing to allow a summons against Edwin Shaw. Many believed that the magistrates were indeed partial. Subsequently, an outraged Mr. Shaw Brown wrote to the Home Secretary, Sir George Grey, to complain. The Home Secretary replied saying he believed that the Runcorn magistrates were quite wrong not to summon Mr. Shaw. However, nothing further was done. One might assume that Edwin Shaw decided to go on the wagon or moderate his behaviour in some way. The upshot was that, some months later, Mr.

---

[37] The Home Secretary

Shaw brought his own summons for drunkenness against Mr. Shaw Brown. The Magistrates refused this – to allow it would, no doubt, have opened another can of worms.

It is interesting to note that prior to that Runcorn ratepayers meeting of October 1857, Mr. Samuel Shaw Brown had previously been elected onto the *Widnes Highways Committee.* His eligibility for this post was due to him having ratepayer status because of his business concern at Widnes Dock. Therefore, Mr. Shaw Brown had a working involvement with the administration of Widnes and, being a member of *The Runcorn Ratepayers` Protection Association,* he also had a foot under the table at Runcorn. As a result he held positions of influence in both towns. Whilst it is quite clear that Mr. Shaw Brown had numerous enemies amongst the Runcorn Commissioners and the Runcorn magistrates, his popularity in other circles in both towns was clearly evident.

There are numerous examples of Mr. Shaw Brown`s rebellious and confrontational manner. At a *Widnes Highways Committee* meeting the previous year[38] he had raised objections to the serving overseers being re-elected. Never one to mince words, he opposed them on the grounds of their incompetence. He claimed that they were all unfit for office. His complaint arose from expenses the township had incurred in the heavy legal costs from their attempts to make the manufacturing part of the township pay an undue share of the rates. It was believed that this was a devious device to lessen the rates upon those who owned land. As a result of Mr. Shaw Brown's criticism some of the serving overseers offered to resign.   Mr. Barrow and Mr. Doward were subsequently appointed in their place and Mr. Shaw Brown was unanimously elected as Surveyor. At that meeting John Hutchinson, as a major manufacturer, agreed with Mr. Shaw Brown that it was a shameful fact that *"though Runcorn Gap district paid one-third of the whole rates their roads were utterly neglected while in parts of the town where little rates were paid the roads were well attended to".* He believed this unfairness would now be redressed by appointing an honourable gentleman such as Mr. Shaw *Brown "who would do his best to have low rates and yet maintain good roads".*

---

[38] March 1856

HALTON GRANGE
THE HOME OF THOMAS JOHNSON

Whilst Mr. Shaw Brown may have had some complaints regarding the Runcorn Commissioners and their mismanagement of the town finances most people were delighted with the new services the Commissioners had managed to provide. In addition to the impressive new facilities enjoyed by all the citizens of the town, several local manufacturers, shipyard owners, and businessmen were also benefiting from the fruits and prosperity of their own ventures. Some were building magnificent residences in the town and nearby. Of course, these dwellings not only served as their family homes they were also an important outward show of their success, wealth and status. In 1856 Thomas Johnson took possession of his beautiful and impressive new home which he called Halton Grange.

It is clear that Runcorn was a well-developed town providing excellent facilities for its residents long before industrialisation and rapid urbanisation made it absolutely necessary for Widnes to get its act together. Needless to say, although Runcorn had been faced with similar problems of urbanisation their problems were significantly less than those experienced in Widnes. The rapidity with which Widnes developed, and its population swelled, meant that the Widnes Local Board had been presented with immediate and overwhelming problems. However, once the Local Board had been formed it quickly attempted to put things in order. In fact, all things considered, The Board made remarkable progress in a fairly short space of time.

We can see from the earlier report on the opening of Pex Hill Waterworks that there were a large number of children in the town attending various local religious and non-denominational schools. It is evident from early newspaper references and archival documents that both towns had several private schools and church schools from an early date. A parish school, later to be known as a national school, was in existence in Runcorn from around 1811. An advertisement, reproduced here, which appeared in *The Chester Courant* in January 1828, shows that there was a *Free Grammar School* at Runcorn. At that time *The Grammar School* was inviting applications from suitably qualified gentlemen to teach at this establishment. It is interesting to note that a man with the required teaching ability could expect to receive a generous salary of £150 per annum.

TO SCHOOLMASTERS.

WANTED, for the Free Grammar School at Halton, near Runcorn, Cheshire, a MASTER well versed in the *Latin* and *Greek* languages, who must also be competent to teach *Arithmetic, Mensuration, Geometry, &c. &c.*

The school is endowed with Land, &c. of the annual value of upwards of £50 for teaching *English Reading* and the *Classics*; the other branches of education are charged *ad libitum*, by which a master of abilities might calculate upon the receipts averaging £150 per annum.

Letters of application (*postage paid*) accompanied by testimonials of qualification and character, addressed to Mr. WILSON, Norton Hill, Warrington, will meet with immediate attention.

THE COURANT, CHESTER, JAN 22 1828

In December 1841 the headmaster of *The Runcorn National School* was about to leave his post after serving the school for over thirteen years. At a meeting of the school subscribers, tributes were paid to the retiring master, Mr. Tinkler, who was presented with a bible as a mark of gratitude for his services. His wife, who had also been a teacher at the school, had left a short while earlier because of ill health. It was implied that Mr. Tinkler had resigned his post in order to act as her carer. The couple had both commenced teaching at the school in 1828 and it was said that over the following years they had stamped their personal ethos on this establishment. This glowing testimony of Mr. and Mrs. Tinkler's dedicated service was shared with readers of *The Liverpool Mercury*.

"Perhaps no parochial school in the kingdom has been more highly favoured in its master and mistress than the Runcorn National School under the superintendence of Mr. and Mrs. Tinkler. Under their care, children grew up in sound knowledge and true piety. Upon the retirement of Mrs. Tinkler from her important charge, the following resolution was unanimously passed at a general meeting of the school subscribers: "That this meeting desires to convey to Mrs. Tinkler its gratitude and best thanks, for the efficient manner in which she has discharged the duties of her situation, and for her fidelity and unremitting attention to the interests of the children committed to her care". The withdrawal of Mrs. Tinkler's services was occasioned by the very delicate state of her health, and, from the same cause, her excellent husband has lately found it necessary to relinquish his appointment also. His retirement is thus noticed in the last annual report of the institution: "Your committee, in closing their prefatory remarks, cannot take leave of the subscribers, without expressing their sincere regret at the loss which the school will sustain by the resignation of its much esteemed and valuable master, occasioned by his pressing domestic duties. A more kind and attentive master cannot be obtained, or one more truly possessing that highest of all qualifications in a teacher of youth, unaffected piety – and they trust that Mr. Tinkler, on relinquishing his charge, will feel assured that the subscribers and scholars will entertain sentiments of grateful respect for him, mingled with feelings of great sadness at his departure."

Another school, known as *Runcorn Hill School* situated, as the name suggests, on Runcorn Hill, offered a refined education for young ladies. The private school was owned and run by two sisters known as the Misses Marston. In January 1845 the school re-opened after the Christmas holiday with the owners commencing the new term by presenting their services in an eloquently worded newspaper advert. It was said that young lady pupils would be:

"Genteelly boarded and carefully instructed in the usual branches of an English education, with geography, the use of globes, etc. They will also be offered tuition in music, singing and dancing and will be instructed by masters of well-known ability from Liverpool; French will be taught by a lady from Paris who resides with the family. The house is pleasantly situated on an eminence half a mile from Runcorn, surrounded with spacious pleasure grounds, commanding extensive and delightful views. The locality of the neighbourhood has been long considered the most salubrious part of the county. Packets sail daily between Manchester and Runcorn."

Despite the presence of a number of established church funded and private schools in both towns, a Government Act of 1870 empowered local committees to establish and regulate educational services in their areas by setting up local Schools Boards. The Act allowed School Boards to build schools in instances where voluntary school places were insufficient. Also written into the Act was a duty placed on parents to ensure that their children received elementary instruction in reading, writing and arithmetic. The School Boards could charge a few pennies a week[39] for the education of children in Board schools and could also compel attendance. Surprisingly, there had been some opposition from members of the Widnes Local Board who believed that nothing should be done to establish a school committee until they were compelled to do so by the Government. For this reason Widnes was comparatively late in setting up a School Board. Although Liverpool had appointed a School Board by November 1870, and even small places like Prescot had agreed to form its own Board in March 1871, it was not until 1874 that Widnes decided to followed suit. In fact, Runcorn was also quite late in forming a Board and only did so in the same year as Widnes.

Although the Widnes Local Board prided itself on its advances and achievements, some members of the Board were not as forward thinking as their colleagues. The dilatory attitude of some members was partly the reason for the relatively late formation of the School Board. Some years earlier, in October 1871, it was reported in *The Liverpool Mercury* that steps were being taken to form a School Board in Widnes. This report concerned a meeting which had been held in the Public Hall in Hutchinson Street to discuss the possibility of forming such a Board in the town. A census had shown that more than one third of the children in the township of Widnes were not receiving education of any

---

[39] Poorer parents received exemptions

type. Despite this fact, and regardless of the insistence of the good Doctor O' Keefe that something should be done to promote education, some leading citizens and Board members still believed that Widnes should not form a School Board until they were forced to do so by the Education Authorities. Doctor O'Keefe's response to this was to say: *"There are always a number of stupid, selfish people in the world who have no public spirit!"* Therefore, as a direct result of the intransigence of both public figures and some Board members, it was a further three years before the first meeting of the Widnes School Board took place.

Over the period of its existence several of our local manufacturers were active members of the Widnes School Board and some also became managers of local schools. It is assumed that they felt it their duty to become involved in the provision of education for the children of their employees. However, this also ensured that they had a better educated workforce for the future. The first meeting of the Widnes School Board was held on 17th November 1874 in the Local Board room in Victoria Road. The first elected members of the new Board were Henry Deacon; Major James Cross; C. Sutton Timmis; Richard Bradshaw; Martin Taylor; Robert Shaw and the Rev. Father James Clarke. Mr. George H. Danby was appointed clerk and he was to retain that position for almost thirty years. In fact Mr. Danby was connected with the educational life of Widnes for over 38 years, first as clerk to the School Board and then as Director of Education. After his retirement he and his wife relocated to Chiswick in London. Shortly afterwards he was invited back to Widnes to receive a silver rose bowl in recognition of his services to the town. Sadly, Mr and Mrs Danby did not manage to attend this ceremony as he collapsed and died at Central Station in Liverpool en route to Widnes. The unhappy circumstances of his death came as a shock to the townspeople as he was a well-known and respected figure in the town. As a mark of appreciation of his lengthy commitment to Widnes and the education of its children, it was decided by the Education Committee of that time that a scholarship should be founded in his name. Incidentally, Mr. Danby's son, also George, later became the Director of Education for the town of Batley in Yorkshire.

At the inauguration of the Widnes School Board the town already had a number of schools. These included two National schools and three Roman Catholic schools, as well as the Grammar School. In April 1875 the School Board opened its first temporary school in the Wesleyan School in Oakland Street, offering accommodation for 200 infants. A month later a second temporary school was opened in Bank

Street. This was a mixed school offering accommodation for 200 children. Of course, one of the priorities for the School Board was finding suitable sites on which to build new schools. In 1875 they bought the land on which Warrington Road School and West Bank School were to be built. These schools were ready for occupation in 1877. They also purchased a large plot of land at Simms Cross for the purpose of providing a school. The Wesleyan School in Sutton's Lane was rented from the owners, The Sheffield and Midland Railway Company, until Simms Cross School was completed. The School Board appointed Mr. J.S. Snoddy as the Head Teacher of the newly opened West Bank School, while Mr. G. Faulkner and Mr. T. Showan filled the corresponding posts at Warrington Road and Simms Cross Schools.

Widnes School Board 1903

Back l to r: D. Lewis; S. Quinn; Mr. Dandy; Mr. Thomas; Mr. Dodd; Rev. Wright Williams
Front l to r: J.J. Williams; F. Neill; H. Wade Deacon; Dean Clarke; Dean Finnegan

Apart from erecting the schools, the problem of finding suitable teaching staff also proved to be a contentious issue. At a meeting of the School Board in June 1877 Board member Mr. Martin Taylor came in for criticism for a remark he had made at a previous meeting. His opinions had caused outrage among the teaching staff at some of the Board Schools. His comments, which included the phrase *"we will not be able to get first-class teachers in Widnes, no matter what salaries we pay"* was seen as a bad reflection on those who were currently employed as teachers in the town. Several local teachers wrote to the Board asking for him to retract his statement as it was *"detrimental to the interests of education in Widnes."* Mr. Taylor feigned personal indignation, claiming that his comments had been deliberately misinterpreted and asked the Board not to waste time in reading such letters again. However, the Chairman, Mr. Sutton Timmis, said it was not a waste of time to address the concerns of their teachers. Mr. Timmis also *said "It is a matter of opinion and while you are welcome to yours, I will maintain mine. I maintain that we have got excellent teachers in the town, and if we have not we ought to."* Father Clarke agreed with Mr. Timmis and the matter was then dropped. Unfortunately, the complaints rumbled on for several weeks and Mr. Taylor was compelled to give further explanations for his comments. He said:

"He did not wish to throw any reflection on the teachers, but he only meant to say that when masters could get £300 a year in London, with privileges that could not possibly be obtained in Widnes, he did not think such men would come to Widnes, where there were no such inducements. At the same time, he thought the Chairman of the School Board should not take notice of letters of complaint reflecting on a member's speech. Members were there to express their opinions for the good of the schools, and not for the benefit of individuals."

In 1876 the following list of Widnes schools appeared in Worrall's Directory:

PRIVATE SCHOOLS

Richard Bradshaw	*Appleton Academy*
Margaret Haddock	*Lune Hey, Farnworth*
Jane Hulme	*Bell House Farm*
Annie Kidd	*Farnworth*
Paulina & Caroline King	*Mersey Road*
Sarah Anne Moore	*(Boarding) Hale*
St. John O'Meara	*Irwell Street*
Annie Syred	*Bradley Cottage, Appleton*

Bank Street	*Sarah Ferguson, mistress*
Oakland Street Infants	*Mary Upton, mistress*
Grammar School Farnworth	*James Raven, master*
Farnworth	*Enoch Brown, master;*
Ditton	*Thomas Holbrook, master*
Hale	*Martha Lomas, mistress*
St. Mary's, Waterloo Road,	*John C. Crawford, master.*
St. Patrick's, Hutchinson St.	*William Atherton, master*
St. Bede's, Appleton	*Ann McKenzie, mistress*
St. Mary's, Newtown	*Amy Prout, mistress;*
St .Mary's, Hale Lane, Ditton.	*Ellen McGinty, mistress*
Suttons Lane Wesleyan School	*Edward Gleave, master*

At first it proved difficult to persuade parents to take advantage of the new educational facilities provided for their children. As education at this time was not free it is clear that cost was a disincentive for many parents who had large families. However, under a bye-law of the 1870 *Elementary Education Act,* the School Board was compelled to help in cases of difficulty. The Board had a legal obligation to disburse the whole or part of the fees if a parent was unable to pay. The proviso was that the child should attend a Board School and that the payment would not exceed six months or 4d per week for any one child. The fees charged at the Board schools between 1876 and 1878 were: senior boys and girls 4d per week; senior boys and girls (advanced classes) 6d per week; junior boys and girls 4d per week; infant boys and girls 4d per week. Obviously, after a six month period the parent became liable for the fees but this money was often difficult to collect. Not surprisingly, there are numerous incidents of parents being taken to court over non-payment of school fees

The Widnes School Board was only directly concerned with the three School Board establishments in the town. Voluntary and Church schools collected their own fees but they were unable to claim a share of the rates and the parents of these children were also exempt from claiming assistance with the fees. However, there were far more children on roll in the voluntary and church schools than there were in the Board schools. The non-Board schools were controlled by the school managers. These establishments were completely separate and totally independent from the School Board. As they did not receive any support from the ratepayers they did not send any attendance returns to the School Board. This made it difficult for the School Board to collate accurate information on the numbers of Widnes children attending school. In order to make an assessment, every year School Board attendance officers made house-to-house visits taking a census. In 1879, of the 5858 children of school age in the town there were 1276 that did not attend any school.[40]Interestingly, evidence suggests that in the early days it was the indigenous population of craft workers in the northern areas of the town who were unlikely to send their children to school. Families with skills or crafts usually apprenticed their children to the family trade. Therefore, they viewed education as a waste of time as their children's` employment future was already pre-determined and assured.

In January 1884 an extra-special and pleasing event occurred in Farnworth. The town's oldest educational establishment, Farnworth Grammar School, was re-opened after a long period of closure. The re-established Grammar School was to be housed in a new building, constructed at a cost of £2000 from a design by Messrs. F. & G. Holme of Liverpool. The opening ceremony was performed by Lord Winmarleigh, who had long associations with Farnworth through his personal connection to the Bold family. Mr. Walter A. Watts was appointed headmaster of the new school and his salary was to be £350 per annum. Mr. Watts had previously been employed as assistant Head Teacher at Chorlton High School in Manchester. On opening the new school, Lord Winmarleigh congratulated the Governors of Farnworth Grammar School on the fact that French, German and natural sciences were to form part of the curriculum of the school. He said that this would thus fulfil the object for which the school was originally created. After referring to Bishop Smythe, who founded the school in 1507, he expressed the hope that the building they had opened that day would prove the means of introducing many distinguished young men to public life.

Around this time there was also a growing consensus among the members of the Widnes Local Board who felt that the town needed to create a municipal environment in keeping with its rising importance and population. In August 1873 the Local Board had provisional plans in place for the development of Victoria Square as a civic area. Around 4000 yards of land adjoining Alforde Street and Brook House Lane were purchased from Mr. John Shaw Leigh for the site of a Town Hall and Market. Later, additional land was purchased from the Leigh

---

[40]*Into the Crucible* – Jean M. Morris (2005)

Estate for the improvement of Victoria Square. In November 1877 the Local Board purchased two semi-detached houses in Terrace Road from Mr. Midwood, for hospital services, at a cost of £1,250. The houses were modified to make them suitable and the Widnes Accident Hospital was established there in 1878.

It is obvious that the Local Board were keen to press ahead with their projects despite the fact that there was little or no money in the public kitty to fund their schemes. They had already borrowed £40,000 to build the new waterworks but, in order to proceed with their ambitious plans for the town; they urgently needed to borrow more money. The following request appeared in several editions of *The Times* during the months of May and June 1878.

"LOANS REQUIRED by Widnes Local Board, at 4% interest, to extend the Gasworks and Waterworks and pay off existing loans. Apply THOMAS BEASLEY, Solicitor, St. Helens."

In August 1886 a special meeting of the Widnes Local Board was held under the chairmanship of Mr. F.H. Gossage for the purpose of considering whether the construction of the proposed Town Hall should be carried out in conjunction with the erection of the public offices, which were then partially completed. The plans had been drawn by Messrs. F. & G. Holmes, of Liverpool, and the estimated cost of the entire building project was £15,000. In what appeared to be a rather tetchy meeting, Dr. O` Keefe said that work on the Town Hall should proceed at once as there *"was an urgent need for such a building in a town with the growing importance of Widnes"*. Mr. D. Wright seconded Dr. O` Keefe's motion, on the grounds that it would be more economical to erect the buildings at the same time. The proposals were opposed by Mr. Gaskell who believed that it would be unwise to proceed. He reasoned that because the alkali trade in the town was in a bad condition it would be unfair to burden the ratepayers with additional expense. After a vote, the motions were lost and it was agreed that only the public offices would be built at that time.

One can well imagine the amount of anger and frustration generated during that meeting, as Dr. O` Keefe was certainly not a man to take defeat lightly. Earlier that year, after a great deal of opposition and argument, he had persuaded the Board to provide a free public library for the town. His ambition to make Widnes *"a town to be proud of"* included a civic centre with a magnificent Town Hall as its centrepiece. A *Widnes Weekly News* report of a meeting held in January that year made the following comment:

"With regard to the question of a Town Hall for Widnes, a spirit of utter niggardliness seemed to pervade the meeting, and for once I could enter into the spirit of Dr. O'Keefe's righteous indignation. His love of Widnes is equal to his patriotism for Ireland, and it did one's heart good to see him as he hurled his metaphorical missiles right and left. If certain persons did not feel a little uneasy during the worthy Doctor's oration I am very much mistaken".

Although there had been great improvements since the Widnes Local Board was brought into existence, and there had been a genuine effort by the Board to upgrade facilities in the town, unfortunately some services still fell short of the standards required by the county authorities. In 1886, in response to Government directives, the Local Government Board was compelled to order an inspection of the urban sanitary district of Widnes. This was part of a general survey of all the sanitary districts within its jurisdiction. The Government had commissioned this countrywide survey because of the number of cholera incidents around the country. The purpose of the survey was to enable the Local Government Board and the local sanitary authorities to assess the sanitary requirements of each district. The result of the survey was presented to the Widnes Local Board at the beginning of September by Dr. Page, who was the inspector for the Local Government Board. Dr. Page told the Board that he was well aware of the difficulties under which the Widnes Board was placed as regard to their work. They had an exceptionally large population to deal with and because of the nature of local industry there were additional problems of pollution. He praised the Board for the efficient manner in which they had tackled the provision of a water supply and the installation of main sewerage. He also commended them for the provisions they had made for the isolation of cases of infectious diseases. However, he was less than impressed with other aspects of the sanitary condition of the town. He drew attention to the nuisances arising from middens and water closets which he claimed were generally of a substandard construction. He also told the Board that:

".....because of their defective construction there were other problems and there was an excessive accumulation of excrement through an inefficient method of removal. Many back-yards were in a very dirty and neglected state and temporary structures for the housing of pigs took up the necessary air space. Private streets and back passages in nearly every instance and every district throughout the town showed general neglect and want of scavenging. Sewers were badly ventilated, especially in private streets, and it was desirable there should be a

system of flushing. The bye-laws in connection with the registration of lodging-houses and slaughter-houses should be more stringently carried out. On the question of smoke, the Sanitary Authority he did not think had taken any action, and that consumption of smoke had not been adopted on any large and efficient scale in Widnes. He knew from his own experience that manufacturers tried to consume as much smoke as they could. He hoped the manufacturers of Widnes would do so. He recommended the Local Board to adopt the pail system of closets, and that the bye-laws with regard to air space should be stringently carried out".

In Runcorn, our neighbouring town across the river, things also progressed at a similar pace and authorities there had continued to add to and improve local services and infrastructures. However, the subject of sub-standard housing did not apply to Widnes alone. Runcorn too had many dwellings which were in an appalling and unhealthy state. At the beginning of 1894 *The Runcorn Improvement Commissioners* were compelled to issue an order to close down 18 houses at Zion Place, Mill Brow, belonging to a grocer named John Stringer, on the grounds that they were unfit for human habitation. New government regulations had come into force in 1890 when *The Housing of the Working Classes Act 1890* had been passed. The case against Mr. Stringer was the first time the Act had been enforced in Runcorn. The Commissioners made an order compelling Mr. Stringer and his wife Hannah, who was co-owner of the properties, to close the houses within fourteen days. Mr. James Percival, the Sanitary Inspector to the Runcorn Commissioners, said that the houses were in a deplorable condition. The Medical Officer of Health, Doctor McDougall, told the Commissioners that during the previous twelve months there had been 13 cases of fever among the residents of these houses, two of which resulted in death. Mr. Percival gave the Commissioners an account of his inspection and described the properties. His report was quite shocking. The houses, he said:

"....were built in a Delph hole and in several instances the rock formed the back wall of the houses. The properties were built 15 feet below the level of the soil of the ordinary gravel. The drainage had been conducted for many years by percolation into the quarry debris upon which they were built, and for a time this was capable of taking off the drainage. The properties were very dilapidated and the soil was saturated with sewage matter, and gave off gases of an offensive and dangerous character. The ventilation was very bad and the sub-soil was saturated to a depth of 7 feet, and it was as black as a soot-bag."

Although there were numerous urban problems in Runcorn, as there were in Widnes, nevertheless, improvements to the town's infrastructure continued. In 1892 a major new road was nearing completion which would offer great benefits to both pedestrians and vehicles alike. A report, under the heading *Public Improvement at Runcorn,* gave details of the funding and costs of the new road.

"There is now rapidly approaching completion one of the finest public improvements that have been carried out in Runcorn for many years past. This is the making of a new road from the thickly populated district of Halton Road and Hall-Brow to the rapidly growing neighbourhood of Newtown and the Railway Station; and the new thoroughfare is one of the finest in the town, and will be the most extensively used both by pedestrians and vehicles. The land for the road was given by Major Orred, who also contributes £1000 towards the cost of sewering and making of the road, and the share of the ratepayers will probably reach £1200. The most difficult part of the undertaking was to construct a bridge over a sheet of water connected with the Bridgewater Canal and known as the Big Pool. The Manchester Ship Canal Company, whose works are at that place, have constructed at their own cost the required bridge, which consists of six arches, and is well and substantially built of bricks, the foundation going down to the hard bottom of the Pool. The roadway is 30 feet wide, exclusive of the footpath, which is formed of granolithic pavement by Stewart and Co., of Liverpool. The contract for the sewering and roadmaking, which is being brought to a successful conclusion, has been entrusted to Mr. Valentine of Bootle."

Looking back on the 27 years that the Widnes Local Board had been in existence it is worth noting that members of the Board had always included some of our leading chemical industrialists and local manufacturers. In addition, these men always held prominent positions on the School Board and the local Magistrates Bench. In fact, it is correct to say that some of them had a say in almost every aspect of daily life in the town. The same could be said of Runcorn and other industrial towns of that era.

When we consider how much the town of Widnes had developed during the 27year tenure of the Widnes Local Board we can appreciate the great improvements and benefits that had been brought about by their endeavours. The lives of ordinary townspeople had been greatly improved by the installation of a waterworks and other important amenities. Nevertheless, to the outsider Widnes was still considered to be a blot on the landscape. In 1891, the writer Leo H. Grindon in his *"Historical and Descriptive Notes on Lancashire"*[41] described the town thus:

"The Chemical works are located principally in the extreme south-west of the county, especially near Widnes, a place which at once betrays itself to the passing traveller in the almost suffocating atmosphere, and the total extinction of the beauty of trees and hedges, spectres and gaunt skeletons alone remaining where once was verdure. Here we find in its utmost vigour the manufacture of "soda ash" (an impure carbonate), and of chlorine of lime, both for the use of bleachers; also prepared from the first named, "caustic soda" for the soap-boilers of Liverpool and Warrington. This discharge of stifling vapours was much worse before the passing of the Alkali Act than at present; and, curiously enough, though by no means without parallel, involved positive loss to the manufacturer, who now manages to detain a considerable amount of the good residuum previously wasted. The Act permits a limited quantity of noxious matter to go up the chimney; the stream is tested every day to see that the right is not abused: how terrible is the action even of that little the surrounding fields are themselves not slow to testify: everything, even in summer, looks dirty, lean, and dejected."

Over the years, usually at the instigation of the inimitable Doctor John O` Keefe[42], there had been several discussions among members of the Local Board and local ratepayers as to the question of whether Widnes should become a Municipal Borough. After officials from the Local Board canvassed the townspeople it was claimed that seventy percent of those consulted were in favour of petitioning Her Majesty the Queen to grant a Charter of Incorporation. Following some initial enquiries the Board was asked to submit a draft Charter, which was duly approved in June 1891. The following year, in June 1892, the Local Board received the Letters Patent under the Great Seal of the United Kingdom granting a Charter of Incorporation to the Borough of Widnes. The Widnes Local Board was dissolved later that year and held its final meeting on 8th November 1892.

In November 1894 the youthful Borough held its third local election. The Borough was divided into six wards and there were contests in two of them – the Victoria and Waterloo Wards. The

---

[41] *"Lancashire - Historical and Descriptive Notes"* – Leo H. Grindon (London 1891)
[42] See: *"Into the Crucible"* - Jean M. Morris (Countyvise 2005) 2nd edition (Arima Publishing 2009)

gentlemen representing the Farnworth, Simms Cross, and West Bank Wards were elected unopposed. The candidate for the Halton Ward lodged a complaint against his opponent, Mr. Andrew Quinn, which was successful, meaning that Mr. Quinn was eliminated and the other candidate was returned without further challenge. It would seem that the contests in the remaining wards, Victoria and Waterloo, were keenly fought. Reports suggest that there was a strong religious mood in both wards, particularly the Victoria Ward. The contest in the Victoria Ward was between Benjamin Brown, the iron-founder who lived at Brookfield in Ditton, and Samuel Quinn a grocer from Ann Street. Mr. Quinn received 391 votes to Mr. Brown's 292. In the Waterloo Ward, Charles Hemingway, a builder from Church Street, was the victor. He received 356 votes and his opponent, Charles Flynn, a grocer from Irwell Street, received 218. All four candidates stood as Independents.

Incorporation bestowed certain tangible legal and constitutional rights. It meant that the Corporation could sue or be sued in a court of law and could make and enforce its own bye-laws (within the framework of statute and common law). In practice, a Municipal Corporation constituted an independent unit of local government with its own administration and jurisdiction. Towns that had been granted Incorporation greatly valued their status. The dignity of their leading citizen, the Mayor, was upheld and enshrined in local protocol. He wore rich robes and a chain of office. The honour of being our first Mayor was bestowed upon local manufacturer Mr. F.H. Gossage. During his tenure as Mayor, Mr. Gossage made a most generous gift to the people of the town. He submitted and presented to the Council, for the use of the Mayor of Widnes, a magnificent gold chain of office and pendant. He expressed the hope that this mayoral chain might always be honourably borne by the gentleman selected as Chief Officer of the Corporation. The members of the Council placed on record their gratitude to Mr. Gossage by saying:[43]

"We wish to acknowledge this generosity and recognise the great care which he has exercised in selecting the appropriate devices, symbolising the staple industry to which the Borough owes its present position, which having been approved and embodied by the authorities of the Herald's College the grant of Arms recently made to the Borough"

---

[43] Ibid.

Part of the design for the Borough Coat of Arms, as prepared by the officers of the College of Arms, was a shield divided into four quarters, two of these contained a hive with bees and the remaining two quarters contained the red rose of Lancaster, taken from the arms of Henry VII. Beneath the shield was a motto bearing the words *Industria Ditat*. The hive and bees represented work and the red rose being the emblem of the county of Lancashire in which Widnes was then situated. The literal translation of the motto was *Industry Enriches*. Incidentally, in 1894 Runcorn achieved Urban District status and that town also had its own coat of arms which included a full-rigged sailing ship, as a tribute to its long history as a canal port.

THE WIDNES COAT OF ARMS

As the end of an eventful century approached, the population of Widnes had grown considerably and some aspects of the town had improved almost beyond recognition. Although the dire problems of pollution and unhealthy working conditions remained, the physical character of the town had been enhanced by the construction of several impressive public buildings and the provision of facilities that benefited the lives of the population. When the members of Widnes Corporation made an assessment of their domain in the final year of the nineteenth century they must have been well pleased with the fruits of their endeavours. Many of these improvements were based on the visions and aspirations of their predecessors, but were only brought to fruition by the determination and hard work of those who followed.

In July 1899, as the members of Widnes Corporation emerged from the Town Hall to assemble in the newly created Town Square, they must have been enormously satisfied with the sight before them. The Square was home to a cluster of elegant and imposing buildings, the Town Hall, with its neo-classical French Renaissance architecture; the new Library and Technical College; the beautiful church dedicated to St. Paul and the fine new Market Hall which was located close by. Of course, magnificent though they were, these buildings did not represent the full extent of the town's civic progress. From the Square the councillors were taken to West Bank to visit the Accident Hospital, which was found to be in excellent order. Whilst in that district, the members inspected the new promenade which was in the course of construction. The new promenade would cost £5000 and was being built in commemoration of the Diamond Jubilee of Queen Victoria. On leaving West Bank the councillors travelled onward to Ditton to inspect the huge gas holders and visit the nearby Highway Depot. From Ditton the group proceeded to the gas-works at Newtown. The next place visited was the Infectious Diseases Hospital at Crow Wood where large extensions, estimated to cost over £9000, were nearing completion. Visits were also made to the new cemetery at Farnworth, which had recently been completed at a cost of £12,500 and the pumping stations at Stockswell and Netherley from where the Borough obtained its water supply. At that time there were three pumping engines, with a total pumping capacity of five and a half million gallons per day. As the average daily consumption at that time was only about two and a half million gallons it was estimated that the town would be well provided with water for years to come. The tour of inspection was concluded at Pex Hill, where the Corporation possessed two covered reservoirs, one of which was said to be the largest of its kind in Britain. The water was sent from the pumping stations to this elevated point in the town so that

105

ample pressure could be obtained. When the long tour of inspection was over the members of the Corporation enjoyed a dinner in the pavilion on Pex Hill, the meal being provided Mr. J. Houghton of the Unicorn Hotel, Cronton.

And so, from its small beginnings and a population of 2209 in 1841, in a little over fifty years this pleasant rural corner of England was converted with almost magic rapidity into a teeming hive of industry. The resultant urban growth also happened with equal swiftness and the organisation of services to provide for the essential needs of a new urban population came about in a similar manner. In a relatively short space of time the district had become a flourishing Municipal Borough with a population of more than 30,000. The physical and social changes had been drastic and the fifty years had transformed the area and the composition of its society beyond recognition. Of course this was not the end of the story as, at the time of its Incorporation, the town was continuing to expand and the population was still increasing. Migration into the town from other places on this island, as well as from Ireland and other lands, was still an important ongoing social, economic and cultural process that linked or, in some cases, divided local communities.

INDUSTRY AND WORKERS

P rior to the development of the chemical industry in Widnes the majority of our inhabitants were employed on land owned by someone else. Although agriculture provided the main employment, mixed occupations were also common as families partly employed in agriculture could sometimes be engaged in carrying out work at home. This type of cottage industry typically involved workers manufacturing goods in their own homes. They usually worked for a businessman or larger producer who sold the goods on at a profit. In addition to these mixed occupation workers there was also a section of society who worked full time in home based industry. Some of these home-workers were highly competent craftsmen who specialised in specific trades such as precision tool making or watch making. Other *"cottage occupations"*, such as weaving, was routine semi-skilled work in which whole families, including women and children, became involved. From the early days, in addition to agricultural occupations and cottage industry, several other types of work opportunities were available to the indigenous populations in both towns. These were generally associated with the natural resources of the locality, which included the river and the presence of stone in great quantities. These two valuable assets were subsequently exploited by the more enterprising as a means of commerce and labour. In the beginning these ventures were usually quite minor affairs, offering employment to small workforces but in later times both became important sources of occupation.

Although Widnes was to make its name as a major centre for the manufacture of alkali, and its development as a significant town was inexorably linked with alkali production, it is worth noting that industrially Runcorn was a successful going concern decades earlier. In fact, Runcorn had been involved in the manufacture of alkali long before it became an established industry in Widnes. In the same way that Widnes had later benefited from its geographical location and improved transportation facilities, Runcorn's early development as a place of industry was aided by the presence of excellent transport communications.

The river Weaver was an important factor in Runcorn's industrial growth as salt, which was a vital commodity in numerous manufacturing processes, was shipped up the Weaver into the Mersey and onwards to numerous markets and destinations from the Port of Liverpool. Even though Runcorn already benefited from this important river link, the Duke of Bridgewater created further advantages when he chose Runcorn as the terminus for his canal. The Bridgewater Canal was initially intended to be a means of connecting the Duke's Worsley coal mines to Manchester and onwards to Liverpool via Runcorn. The additional benefit locally was that the new canal enabled Runcorn to become an important point of communication for several other industrial enterprises.

It is worth noting however, that in spite of the extra employment opportunities which the canals and docks produced, it was not until the early years of the nineteenth century that other significant industry began to develop in the town. Prior to that time agricultural work, fishing, and stone quarrying were the main occupations. In addition to these there were a number of other traditional forms of ubiquitous trade such as that of the shoemaker and the miller. Most small areas possessed at least one shoemaker and one or two corn mills. We can see from an auction notice (reproduced overleaf), from *The Chester Chronicle* of July 1804, that there was at that time a working wind-powered corn mill situated in Higher Runcorn. We can also see that this must have been a considerable and imposing structure as, in addition to its sails, it was eight storeys high and built of brick and stone.

One important natural asset which was known to be present in great quantities in the area was stone. In Runcorn, as in most places in Britain, the early quarrying of stone was primarily for local needs. The stone was usually quarried and shaped close to where it was needed and transported only a short journey away by horse-drawn carts or by barge. In the early days most of the local quarries were just small affairs but by the late 18th century the quarrying of stone had become a key activity in the Runcorn area. This change in fortune had come about in the wake of the Industrial Revolution. That dramatic event prompted the rapid development of industry and urbanisation, thus creating a constant demand for stone. As a result, the quarrying and supplying of stone became an extremely lucrative business. Because of the marked increase in demand local owners were encouraged to develop larger quarries which subsequently led to the expansion of the quarrying trade in Runcorn.

To Millers and Corn-dealers.

TO BE SOLD BY AUCTION,

At the house of Samuel Wylde, known by the name of the Bowling Green Inn, in Runcorn, in the county of Chester, on Monday the 30th day of July, 1804, at Four o'clock in the afternoon, subject to such conditions as will be then and there produced, and in the following or such other Lots as may be then agreed upon;

Lot 1. THE INHERITANCE in FEE SIMPLE of and in all that valuable substantial-built and well-accustomed WIND CORN-MILL, Warehouse, and drying Kiln adjoining, with the Stone Quay and Land thereunto belonging, situate in Runcorn aforesaid.

The Mill is 8 stories high, built of brick and stone, in an elevated situation in Runcorn, and the machinery is in excellent repair; consisting of two pair of French and one pair of grey stones, 5 feet diameter on the upper hurst, and 3 Wire Flour-machines beneath; and on the lower hurst 2 pair of Meal and one pair of Shelling stones. The Warehouse is commodious, and capable of holding 10,000 bushells of grain; and the whole of the premises convenient, and are well calculated for carrying on the corn trade on an extensive scale.

Lot 2. The Inheritance in Fee Simple of and in two excellent modern-built Dwelling-houses, situate in Runcorn aforesaid, adjoining to the last lot, with suitable Offices, Garden, and Yard thereunto belonging.

Immediate possession may be had of the above premises. Mr. FARRALL, on the premises, will shew the same; and further particulars may be had by applying at the Office of GEORGE ORRED, Attorney, No. 4, Exchange Alley, Liverpool.

By the end of the 18th century there were numerous thriving quarries in and around Runcorn. These quarries provided copious amounts of stone for industrial, urban and other purposes whilst at the same time creating employment for substantial numbers of men. I found several advertisements for quarry workers, such as the one below, which appeared in *The Chester Chronicle* in February 1791.

WANTED – A NUMBER OF HANDS

to be employed in getting STONE

Good workmen will meet with good encouragement

and constant employ

From Kerfoot Jannion of Runcorn, near Frodsham."

During this era the Runcorn and Weston stone quarries prospered and developed significantly. Not only had these businesses benefited from increased industrial growth and investment in public and private construction, they had also profited from the building of new canals which were criss-crossing the country at that time. The enhancement of Runcorn's own canals and waterway communications also assisted in this growth as local sandstone was used extensively for the construction of both the canal walls and the docks. *The Runcorn Hill Quarry,*[44] which was owned by John Linaker Wright, expanded considerably during this period. As an indication of its success the company built its own stone wharf at Weston Point Docks. The stone from this quarry was brought down to the dock by means of tramways which conveyed the stone down the hillside. At the same time several other quarries in the area, such as the *Stenhill Quarry* and Grindrod's *Mill Brow Quarry,*[45] both of which were located on the banks of the Bridgewater Canal, were also flourishing. The constant demand for stone prompted John Tomkinson, the owner of another Runcorn quarry, to open a further quarry at Weston[46] near to that of John Wright. Tomkinson regularly employed in the region of 150 men at his Weston quarry but it is believed that from time to time, to cope with periodic increases in trade, this number sometimes rose to around 500.

---

[44] Runcorn Hill Quarry Closed in 1900
[45] Mill Brow Quarry ceased production in 1894
[46] Weston Quarry was finally vacated in 1942

It is obvious, from the presence of so many profitable quarrying businesses, and the rate of their expansion, that the market in local stone was extremely buoyant. The superb quality of Weston and Runcorn stone was evident by the fact that it was the preferred choice of material for several well-known churches and important public buildings around the country. It was widely used throughout the north-west of England as well as at various locations in Wales, the Isle of Man and other places in Britain. Locally, it was used in the construction of numerous churches and municipal buildings, it was also the choice of material for some Liverpool docks, the Liverpool Anglican Cathedral and the city's magnificent Wellington Column. In Chester, Runcorn stone was used to build the Cathedral and County Gaol.

In addition to providing building material for British domestic requirements, Runcorn stone was in great demand abroad and was exported all over the world from Weston Point Docks. Interestingly, it has been said that Runcorn stone was used to build part of the docks in New York and San Francisco. Nearer to home, several harbours in Ireland including Dun Laoghaire, Howth, Belfast and Dungarvan were constructed with stone quarried in Runcorn. In fact, Ireland seems to have been a major importer of Runcorn stone as it was used for the construction of bridges and buildings in quite a few towns in the south-east of the country. Apart from the stone, there were also additional opportunities for quarry owners to make money from the by-products of stone quarrying. As well as the trade generated by supplying stone for building purposes, the waste from the quarries also provided a lucrative secondary business as this surplus material was widely used for road making and also utilised as ballast material for Liverpool's ocean going vessels.

The Runcorn quarries gave work to a relatively large number of local men and due to a high demand for stone this was generally fairly secure employment. Unfortunately, whilst a large amount of employment was virtually assured, some of this work was reliant upon favourable weather conditions. This meant that in inclement weather some parts of the quarrying process were unable to be carried out. This resulted in a situation whereby it was quite usual for large numbers of men to be laid off in bad weather. Of course, in those days there was no such thing as unemployment benefit or any other form of social support. This meant that workers could be without an income for long spells during the winter months. Throughout December 1819 and January 1820 a bout of severe bad weather meant that the quarrymen of Runcorn were unable to pursue their normal occupations. Naturally, this caused great hardship for the men and their families. In an effort to raise money and draw attention to their troubles some men hit upon a novel idea. The fact that they were willing to go to such extreme and arduous lengths to highlight their plight is indicative of their acute economic distress. In January 1820, *The Liverpool Mercury* gave the following information:

> A number of workmen, probably above 100, employed in the quarries at Runcorn, but now thrown out of employment by the present severe weather, yoked themselves, on Wednesday morning, to a large stone, which they dragged all the way from Runcorn to this town, collecting donations and Christmas-boxes on the road and in the streets. This novel method of exciting attention and commisseration, had a striking effect, and was very successful.

21ST JANUARY 1820

Despite the inconveniences associated with unpredictable weather, evidence suggests that during most of the early and mid-nineteenth century owners of our local stone quarries were enjoying a boom in demand and profits. Some quarry owners also enjoyed commercial success in other enterprises which were not connected to the stone industry. It was quite usual at that time for a resourceful individual to be associated with several ventures, some completely unrelated to their prime business concerns. Several local quarry owners and businessmen had interests in other separate and completely dissimilar commercial enterprises, either as owners or shareholders. Dennis Brundrit, who was primarily known as a shipbuilder, also owned a quarry in Runcorn. Furthermore, Brundrit had significant quarrying interests elsewhere as he held the mineral rights to the granite producing *Penmaenmawr Quarry* in North Wales. In partnership with Philip Whiteway, the firm of Messrs. Brundrit &Whiteway built their own ships to transport the Welsh granite to Runcorn, from where it was shipped on to the Port of Liverpool and other distant places. As an additional matter of interest, it is worth mentioning that Runcorn was also a distributing port for Welsh roofing slate which was shipped from the famous *Penrhyn Quarries* to Runcorn and onward to Liverpool for export. A resourceful Runcorn firm, Dutton & Company who were located in High Street, made use of the Penrhyn material which passed through the town by manufacturing school writing slates from this product.

John Tomkinson was one of those enterprising individuals who had interests in numerous ventures. Apart from his quarries, he was also the owner of a lime-works in the town as well as being the builder of several streets of residential housing. Tomkinson, who was originally from Liverpool, also had significant business concerns in that city. As a building contractor he became involved in the construction of some of Liverpool's most important public buildings. In 1840 he was given the contract to construct the Liverpool Collegiate Institution in Shaw Street. It was said at that time that:

"the contract for the entire work has been given to Mr. John Tomkinson, whose extensive means and liberal spirit will enable him to complete the building in the shortest possible period, and it is confidently anticipated that the Institution will be opened to the public in the spring of 1842"

The contract for the Liverpool Collegiate building was worth in excess of £21,000. In May 1843 Tomkinson successfully tendered for the erection of the new Liverpool Assize Court at a cost of £78,000. The *Liverpool Mercury* reported that *"It is a gratifying reflection that we have a townsman with sufficient capital and enterprise to undertake the erection of such a splendid building.* Although John Tomkinson was to carry out several other large contracts in the city and its environs, one of the most noteworthy was the prestigious St. George's Hall which was completed in 1854. Tomkinson's company was responsible for building the carcase of this magnificent building before handing over to Messrs. Furness & Kipling who executed the brickwork and joinery, after which the specialised masonry work was completed by Messrs. Nuttall & Hargreaves.

Interestingly, although there is no question of his ambitious and enterprising spirit, despite outwards appearances and claims to the contrary, it is doubtful that Tomkinson had sufficient personal capital to undertake some of these ventures. Like many men of his ilk, Tomkinson invested heavily and borrowed money in equal measures to expand his businesses. In July 1847 he made a substantial investment in machinery for his *Mill Brow Quarry* at Runcorn. This equipment was installed in order to make the work less arduous for his employees. However, it should be said that the installation of new machinery was not done for humane or altruistic reasons, it was a necessity. During the previous year the work in his quarry was deemed to be so hard that he couldn't get anyone to do it. No doubt it was also his hope that, apart from attracting labour, the new equipment would improve productivity and increase profits. This article tells us more:

"A new steam engine is now erecting at the Mill Brow Quarry, for the purpose of drawing out the rocks from the bottoms. It is calculated to draw the rock from any depth that may be required, and will release the stone-getters from that heavy task, which is considered such an annoyance that a gang of men left their employment last winter rather than undertake the job of getting up the bottoms. It has hitherto been a very laborious and unprofitable task, as the men can hardly make a common wage at this employment. At this quarry they are also filling up the land as the rock is taken out, and levelling the ground for building upon. A whole street of houses will be built by Mr. Tomkinson, a row on either side from the quarry to the main road".

In May the following year, after this major investment in machinery, John Tomkinson was experiencing serious financial difficulties. Like most entrepreneurs of that era he had borrowed money to finance and extend his businesses. As we will see, Mr. Tomkinson was not alone in his excessive borrowing as there are several other examples of that practice in this book. It was common for early industrialists to take out large loans or mortgages to fund their enterprises and then borrow further amounts to enlarge their premises and manufacturing potential. This was how most business was conducted in those days, mainly due to the fact that the Industrial Revolution had created a new complex economy which was dependent upon investment and finance. The new financial system was built on a base of credit, deals and insurance, all of which encouraged excessive borrowing. Unfortunately, many found they could not pay back the loans and defaulted on their payments. As a consequence there was an extremely high level of bankruptcy among Victorian entrepreneurs. In John Tomkinson's case, rumours quickly spread around the town that his connection with The Herculaneum Dock Estate in Liverpool had caused the collapse of his business. However, a newspaper article giving a report of his failure repudiates this. The article cites a number of other causes, including an unfortunate railway contract in Yorkshire and losses connected to a contract with the Birkenhead Dock Company as well as a considerable loss with the Assize Courts. It was also observed that he had made overly large investments in his Runcorn Quarries. It was said that:

"He has had great difficulty in obtaining money to meet such large commitments and this is amongst the causes which have led to the embarrassment of one of our leading tradesmen, whose industry and

benevolence have been for so many years the subject of admiration, and whose misfortune everyone deplores".

The unfortunate financial events of 1848 had been the culmination of several difficult years for John Tomkinson. Two years earlier, in March 1846, a horrific and most distressing accident occurred at his Runcorn lime-works. This site was just a minor enterprise with only a small workforce being employed on the premises. Details of the terrible catastrophe which happened at the works were reported in all local and national newspapers. Below is an edited extract from one report:

"On Tuesday the 17th March, a dreadful accident occurred at the lime works of Mr. John Tomkinson, the eminent contractor, which are situated near the Pool, Runcorn. From the best evidence obtained on the spot, the misfortune happened under the following circumstances: - William Edwards had the entire management of the kilns, which are five in number, they are each covered by a large brick chimney, commonly called "the funnel", which rises above the head about 45 feet, and is constructed for the purpose of carrying off the smoke and sulphurs, to prevent annoyance to the inhabitants in the immediate neighbourhood. At the bottom of the funnel every kiln has a doorway through which it is supplied with stone and coke, and a stage or platform connects all together. The manager, Mr. Edwards, lived at a cottage in the yard, and was assisted in the works by his sons and two youths. About four in the afternoon he went into his house to tea, the centre kiln being on a red glow with heat. He and the others had previously been "firing up", and they left a barrowful of broken stones on the stage at the doorway, ready to be added to the burning mass as soon as the fire had got through its present covering. One of the youths, named John Carruthers, was left on the stage, and Edwards desired him not to do anything at the kiln until he had finished his tea. Whilst he was sitting at his meal with his wife and family, his son, who as previously stated, worked on the premises, ran in to say that, missing Carruthers from the stage, he called, and received no answer, he went up and found him burning in the kiln; Edwards ran with a short ladder to the deceased to snatch him from the burning flames, the workpeople assisting. In this humane act poor Edwards was unsuccessful, for, grasping Carruthers with one hand, he tried to ascend the ladder; but, himself being dreadfully burnt, the sulphur and fumes overpowered him, and he fell with his dying burden into the awful abyss. Assistance being now collected, principally by the appalling screams of the awful stricken spectators, a man who worked at the soapery of Messrs.

Johnson, named Levi Knowles, generously volunteered to go down, by having a rope fastened to his middle, it was his intention to tie the one or other of the sufferers to him, and so by that means to have them dragged out. He boldly sprang in and a few seconds of breathless anxiety elapsed before the signal was given to haul up, but the flames had consumed the rope and it snapped, the greatest difficulty being experienced to get Knowles out alive. Richard Linaker, with a chain, attempted then, but the sulphurous smoke and stench soon caused him to become insensible. David Carruthers, father of the youth John Carruthers, and foreman at Mr. Tomkinson's Quarries called "The Duke's" at Runcorn, arrived, and the scene, which before was dreadful, now became more so from the force required to prevent Carruthers from jumping in headlong to rescue the young man. All hope of getting either of the sufferers out alive now being at an end, drags were thrown in, and the remains of poor Edwards and the youth Carruthers were pulled out, two scorched, blackened, lifeless cinders. Knowles and Linaker still continued in a very precarious state, but through the medical assistance of Mr. Wilson, surgeon, who was early on the spot and the kindness of neighbours, they partially recovered so as to be able to get home with help. It is not known how Carruthers fell in, but it is generally supposed, that whilst eating a little meat while the others were at tea, he must have sat on the barrow and either fallen asleep or the barrow capsized. Edwards was a steady man, and had been in the employ of Mr. Tomkinson for 22 years. He has left a widow and a numerous family".

An Inquiry was held before Mr. J. Caldwell, the Coroner of Halton Fee, a few days after this terrible tragedy. The Inquiry was short and the jury quickly brought in a verdict in both cases of *"Accidental death from burning"*. Mr. Tomkinson attended the hearing and it was said that in order to mark his appreciation of Mr. Edwards' long and faithful service he offered *"his sincere condolences and several comforting words to the widow to soothe her sorrows"*. The Rev. James Cox, incumbent of Holy Trinity Church, was reported to be unremitting in his attention and kindness to the bereaved families. It is not known if either family were offered any monetary compensation from Mr. Tomkinson or if his words of sympathy were all they received.

Seven months later, in October 1846, another of John Tomkinson's establishments became the scene of a dreadful accident. This time one man was killed and another five were badly injured. The accident happened at Tomkinson's quarry at Weston. An extract from a newspaper report of the incident tells us:

"A number of men were engaged in cutting under a portion of rock which suddenly fell bringing with it the seam or, as it is technically termed, the "back" that is the stratum intervening between two strata of solid rock, and a portion of the adjacent upper surface, burying six individuals. The last brought out, Peter Stubbs, had died from suffocation; no injury was observed except a fracture of the cheek bone.

The sides of the quarry are quite perpendicular to the depth of about 25 yards. The side of the quarry which fell in is skirted by a tram-road for the conveyance of loose soil, which is hoisted out by moveable windlasses of great power, suspended above by railway scaffolding. A few days since, the point of a "fault" or "back" was observed about three or four yards from the bottom, and the super-incumbent weight was secured immediately by beams which were considered to be of sufficient strength. On Wednesday, in consequence of the heavy rain, which penetrated from the surface downwards and insinuated itself into the "back", as this fissure is termed, the whole mass, to the weight of upwards of fifty tons, gave way. Happily, from thirty to forty men who had been working in the quarry were two or three minutes previously called off to assist in an adjoining quarry, or the loss of life must have been more fearful.

An inquest was held on Thursday before Mr. Caldwell, Deputy Coroner for the Honour and Fee of Halton, on view of the body of the ill-fated Peter Stubbs. There was no further evidence brought forward than is above stated, except that a hole had been cut for the purpose of introducing an additional beam two days previous to the accident, but it had not been supplied. A portion of the jury dwelt upon this, as an act of negligence on the part of the foreman of the quarry, Mr .J. Shaw; a portion of the jury we say, for it is an extraordinary fact, that the same Mr. J. Shaw was the foreman of the jury, and another three Weston jurymen were connected with the quarry and the Constable, Joseph Dean, was also in the employ of Mr. Tomkinson. The country will not be satisfied with such an inquisition, and we feel well assured that Mr. Tomkinson will not be satisfied with it. The verdict was "accidentally killed". It was recommended that Mr. Tomkinson should be requested to adopt all practicable securities for the preservation of human life hereafter. The worthy Deputy Coroner observed that he knew Mr. Tomkinson had given such directions. How far those directions have been carried out, the public will judge."

I am sure we all find it incredible that the foreman of the jury in this case was actually the man responsible for overseeing the operation of the quarry. In addition, there were four other men concerned in the inquest examinations who were in some way connected to John Tomkinson or his establishment. In these circumstances it seems highly unlikely that an entirely impartial judgement could have been reached. Apart from the obvious verdict of *"accidental death"*, and a few vague recommendations, there was no official censure of the owner or managers of the quarry. In fact, the recommendations of the Deputy Coroner regarding the practical measures which should be undertaken to safeguard human life were obviously not imposed. In June the following year another man, William Clarke, was killed at Tomkinson's Stenhill Quarry.

Of course I should point out that there were, from time to time, accidents in almost all the quarries. However it would seem that John Tomkinson's establishments had a significantly higher number of reported accidents and fatalities. An interesting point was raised by the District Coroner some years earlier, when presiding over the inquest of Thomas Blain who died in December 1840 when his barrow overbalanced and he fell over forty feet at Tomkinson's quarry in Weston. The Coroner remarked that over the previous four weeks he had had to record several fatal accidents from this district. It seemed to him rather strange that each accident occurred on successive Thursdays and that there was generally a high accident rate occurring on Thursdays. He did not offer any theory as to why Thursday was a particularly dangerous day for quarry workers.

Despite all the negative information included here about Tomkinson and the appalling accident record in his establishments, as an individual he was held in extremely high regard in Runcorn. He made several generous gestures for the benefit of the townspeople. Not least of these was his patronage of the church at Weston Point. When plans were being put forward for the erection of this church it was doubtful whether enough money could be raised to fund the project and proceed with its construction. When John Tomkinson was approached to supply some of the building materials, and requested to provide an estimate of cost, he wrote to the Clerk of the Trustees of the River Weaver offering a more practical solution. Included here is a transcript of that short letter.

Liverpool, November 7th 1840.

Dear Sir,

Your favour of the 2nd instant would have been replied to much sooner but I only arrived home last night. I beg to say, that feeling as I do the moral and spiritual wants of the inhabitants of the neighbourhood of Weston, I shall feel happy to supply the stone required for their church at Weston Point, put on board your barges under my crane – free of any expense whatsoever.

With every wish for its prosperity,

I am, Sir, yours truly, John Tomkinson.”

As news of Mr. Tomkinson`s generous offer became public *The Chester Courant* was moved to make the following comment:

“If there be in the minds of any persons a doubt as to the absolute necessity for the erection of a church at Weston Point, they have here a proof of it in the actions of a gentleman intimately connected with the place, and employing in his stone quarry there a large number of work-people. We have been led to understand, that the value of Mr. Tomkinson's generous offer to the Church Building Committee will not be less than £200. We do not pretend by any word of praise on our part to add to the gratification which Mr. Tomkinson must feel in the consciousness, that at a large cost to himself, he is helping to relieve the moral and spiritual wants of the poor inhabitants of Weston and the neighbourhood; but we beg to hold him up as a brilliant example worthy of imitation. The liberality of Mr. Tomkinson's conduct in this manner will be more appreciated when we state our belief that the gentleman is not even a member of the Established Church”

After a long and eventful business career in both Liverpool and Runcorn, John Tomkinson passed away at his residence in Church Place in Runcorn on 15th January 1865. He was 77 years of age. He had played an important role in both locations for numerous years and

119

had at one time been one of the largest employers in Runcorn. Less than a month after his death his Runcorn property was put up for sale, marking the end of an era.

Of course Tomkinson was not the only quarry owner in the district, nor was his quarry the only one enjoying a boom in business. By the 1850s the increasing trade in Runcorn stone created a situation where demand often exceeded production capacity. Sometime around 1853 the Runcorn firm of Brundrit & Whiteway[47] received an order to supply paving stone for the Clyde River Trust, to be used at their Springfield Quay and the Custom House Quay in Glasgow. After completion of the work the River Trust were so pleased with the quality and appearance of their paving that they subsequently paved several large areas in the city of Glasgow in a similar manner, the stone again being supplied by the Runcorn firm. The following year officials from Manchester visited Glasgow to inspect their paving with a view to covering the streets of their own city with the same type of stone. The Manchester officials were clearly impressed by the quality of the paving as they also placed a substantial order with Messrs. Brundit & Whiteway. Unfortunately, the order was so large that the Runcorn firm simply could not undertake it and it had to be offered elsewhere.[48]

Apart from the valuable trade derived from the presence of good quality stone, the geographical location of both Widnes and Runcorn, on the banks of the Mersey, provided opportunities for marine related enterprise on both sides of the river. Although little documentary or archaeological evidence remains, it is obvious that small boats had probably been built on the shores of the Mersey from the earliest time of settlement. In later times there was development of water communications in the area and by 1804 there were two canals with outlets onto the River Mersey at Runcorn and Runcorn Gap. Naturally, this prime waterside position, coupled with the canal communications, created a demand for small crafts. This resulted in several small boat building concerns being established on either side of the river where small crafts were built and repaired in fairly basic sheds and slipways. In later years, particularly in Runcorn, this trade amplified and became more advanced as a result of a substantial increase in river traffic and industry. In fact, much of the local shipbuilding business was created to provide vessels for local manufacturers who were expanding their trade connections. As a result of this, Runcorn gained a reputation as a key shipbuilding and ship repairing location. However, Runcorn's progress

---

[47] Primarily known as boat builders
[48] *The Glasgow Herald* – December 1856.

in this sphere was to the detriment of Frodsham which had, in earlier times, been the local leader in the shipbuilding industry[49].

From the latter years of the eighteenth century there had been some small scale commercial boat-building in the Runcorn area, but the increased canal trade and the subsequent rise of industry in the town created a need for bigger vessels. Because of this increased demand a number of new private shipbuilding concerns were set up in the area. Between the years 1792 and 1800 the Duke of Bridgewater commissioned a number of ships to be built in Runcorn. At the time of his death in 1803 it is believed that the Duke owned 3 large vessels and around 60 flat bottomed barges, all of which were built in Runcorn. In the 1850s there were several small enterprises operating in the town but the three main shipyards appeared to be the Castlerock Yard of John Anderton, the Belvedere Yard of Samuel Mason and the Mersey Street slips of Brundrit and Whiteway. The Johnson brothers also had a shipbuilding concern which occupied a small yard in Mill Street. Over the coming years, with the increase of trade, additional names were added to the list of shipbuilding yards in the town. As well as Messrs. Brundrit &Whiteway and John Anderton, the yards of Blundell & Mason, John Sothern and the Old Quay Company played a major role in the local shipbuilding industry. Also featuring significantly as registered builders of Runcorn vessels were William Rigby, William Wright, Charles Hickson, John Rawlinson, John Stubbs, John Weedall and Mr. Speakman.

Although most of the Runcorn shipbuilding businesses were independently run, many of the more prominent local manufacturers also opened shipyards where they built their own ships and had their own fleet to transport their products. With the increased trade and commerce in Runcorn and its hinterlands, shipbuilding became a lucrative business which offered substantial rewards, especially in the case of coastal and seagoing vessels. It is clear that private investment was an essential feature of the early Runcorn shipbuilding industry. Many of the ships launched from the Runcorn slipways were financed by local merchants and tradesmen who had no primary interest in the shipbuilding industry but saw it merely as an opportunity for financial speculation. The shipbuilders themselves were not immune to this type

---

[49] Shipbuilding also occurred at Sankey Bridges, Warrington, Northwich and Winsford. Between the years 1786 and 1805 there was also shipbuilding at St. Helens, on the Sankey Canal.

of financial speculation either. Apart from building for other people they sometimes owned vessels in partnership with other individuals and in some cases owned the vessels outright. Dennis Brundrit and Philip Whiteway, of the Brundrit & Whiteway shipyard, owned a number of ships both jointly and individually, as did Samuel Mason and John Anderton.

It is generally believed that the first significant commercial shipyard to be established in the Runcorn area was probably *The Castlerock Shipyard* which is thought to have opened around 1800. By 1840 this business was in the ownership of John Anderton. There is also evidence of an early boat building firm owned by *Messrs. Wylde, Mather and Co.* which was already operating prior to 1800. This company was in the process of being wound up at the beginning of 1799 and it was formally dissolved in April that year. The official notice of dissolution, which is reproduced here, provides no specific details of the location of the Wylde and Mather business or indeed the date it was originally established.

Runcorn, *April* 23, 1799.
WYLDE, MATHER & CO.
BOAT-BUILDERS, RUNCORN, CHESHIRE.

THE PARTNERSHIP lately fubfifting be-twixt Samuel Wylde, Thomas Mather, and James Riding, of Runcorn, and William Wright, of Wefton, in the county of Chefter, under the above firm, is this day diffolved by mutual confent. All perfons having any claims on the faid concern, are requefted to fend particulars of the fame forthwith to the faid Samuel Wylde : to whom alfo all perfons owing any thing to the faid concern, are defired to make immediate payment.—Witnefs our hands this twenty third day of April, one thoufand feven hundred and ninety-nine.

Signed by   Samuel Wylde.

In the prefence of   Thomas Mather.
B. Sothern.   James Riding.
J. Adam.   William Wright.

It is quite interesting to see the names of the other shareholders or partners. These were identified as James Riding of Runcorn and William Wright of Weston, who were presumably the anonymous "& Co". It is also worth noting that despite severing his ties with the Wylde and Mather business, William Wright continued his association with the local shipbuilding industry. He opened his own successful shipyard in Runcorn where he built numerous ships. As an additional point of interest, William Wright is often credited with being responsible for building the first ever steamship launched on the River Mersey.

I am sure that we are all familiar with the terrible statistics connected to the high death rate and numerous accidents and hazards relating to the Victorian chemical trade. Nevertheless, in spite of its notorious reputation, the chemical industry was not the sole culprit in this respect. The lack of collective health and safety awareness in most working environments meant that all types of employment included a high degree of personal risk. From inquest reports it becomes apparent that most of the occupations associated with our local industries were extremely dangerous. Boat-building, sailing and other river related employment could at times be just as hazardous as chemical work. There were countless accidents involving local crafts and crews. These incidents happened not only in the Mersey but also around our coastlines and much further afield. However, the fatalities which occurred on our local stretch of the Mersey, and in its nearby docks and quays, were plentiful and alarmingly frequent. In February 1834 three accidents occurred within days of each other. Two of these were associated with the lack of proper lighting near the basins at Runcorn. One man, a fireman on the *"Eleanor"* was drowned crossing one of the lock-gates. A few days earlier another man had drowned in similar circumstances at the same place. A local correspondent wrote:

"This is the second loss of life within three days, through the want of lights! Surely, if the proprietors of such extensive concerns as the Runcorn, Bridgewater and Old Quay Companies were aware of the great number of valuable lives which have been sacrificed, and the misery entailed upon the helpless families of many, thus left destitute, they would immediately strive to prevent the future occurrences of such calamities by appropriating a trifle out of the princely revenues they derive from the exertions of the mariner to preserve that mariner's life from being lost, owing to the want of light to point out the dangers which they themselves have made".

That same week another young man named Jonathan Porter, master of a flat, was killed at the Old Quay Dock. As he was getting his vessel into the dock on the night tide he was struck by the tiller and knocked overboard. As it was dark there was some difficulty rescuing him and he was drowned. The young man's body was found in the morning some distance up the canal near Halton. At the inquest into his death a verdict of accidental death was recorded. Despite numerous letters to the local press pleading for some lighting around the docks, all appeals fell on deaf ears. One correspondent described the management of the canals, locks and basins which surrounded the town of Runcorn as *"appalling! — on nights which might rival Egyptian darkness."* These fatalities were just a few of the numerous in which the lack of adequate lighting was cited as a contributing factor. It does seem incredible that no action was taken to fine or reprimand the owners of the canals and docks for their negligence.

In May 1839 an incident opposite the Boathouse Pier in Runcorn resulted in another loss of life. A boat belonging to the Bridgewater Trust had just had a new suit of sails fitted. The boat was known to be what is technically termed *"crank"* and the sail-maker, John Withington, believed he had cut the new sails in such a way as to remedy this defect. After fitting the new sails, Mr. Withington and several carpenters and others (seven in number) went for a sail up the river. At the time there was a stiff breeze and their intention was to go as far as the Old Quay and return. As they came to The Gap a sudden gust of wind caused the boat to capsize plunging all the occupants into the river. At the time there were a number of flats moored at the Pier waiting for the tide to turn, and two steamers had disembarked their passengers just a few minutes before. Despite the fact that there were plenty of people nearby, the poor sail-maker, John Withington, was drowned. Another sail-maker, by the name of Cooper, had his son, a child of about eleven years old, with him in the boat. Mr. Cooper managed to rescue his child by swimming with him on his back to the shore. Fortunately, six of the seven occupants of the boat were saved but what was expected to be a routine procedure resulted in the tragic death of the unfortunate Mr. Withington.

In its shipbuilding heyday the quality of vessels built at Runcorn was legendary. Some people believed they were far superior to those built in Liverpool and other shipbuilding locations. A fair degree of publicity was given to each new ship that was launched. This positive exposure meant that the shipbuilding industry in the town was well promoted. The favourable publicity also served to ensure that trade remained strong and lucrative whilst at the same time safeguarding local employment. In January 1842, the launch of a schooner called *"The Ellen"* was reported in *The Liverpool Mercury:*

"On Saturday last a beautiful vessel was launched from the building yard of Messrs. John Sothern & Co., Runcorn. From the buildings and vessels around flags were displayed and a large concourse of people assembled to witness the interesting sight of this fine schooner, "The Ellen", gliding from her stocks and dashing into the tidal water amidst the hearty cheering of the surrounding crowd. We are glad to find that shipbuilding in Runcorn is increasing, and from our own observation of the vessels, from time to time, sent forth to sea from this rising port, we do not hesitate to say that the workmanship of the Runcorn carpenters cannot be excelled in Liverpool or any other port in the Kingdom. After the launch of "The Ellen", the builders and their friends met at the Boat-House – (Mr. John Rigby's) – to drink success to their fine merchantman and coaster"

Although the boat-building fraternity in Runcorn was well accustomed to the sight of ships being launched into our stretch of the river, the completion of every new ship was a cause for local celebration. In September 1856 a great deal of excitement surrounded the launch of the largest vessel ever built in the town up until that time. This was an important event, not only in boat-building circles, but for all the residents of Runcorn and its hinterlands. The streets of the town were hung with banners and most of the boats on the river were decorated with bunting for the occasion. Runcorn was thronged to capacity. Thousands crowded the shore on both sides of the river adding to the lively and festive atmosphere. Mrs. Robert Whiteway was given the honour of performing the naming ceremony and, as the craft glided gracefully into the river, several cannons boomed out in salute. This noise was almost matched by the animated cheering from the crowds on the shore. The vessel, which was named *The Dennis Brundrit*, had been designed in-house by James Boot who was the manager of builders at the Brundrit & Whiteway shipyard. *The Dennis Brundrit* remained in service for almost forty years until it was wrecked near the Falkland Islands in 1892.[50]

Regardless of the general delight and excitement associated with the completion and launching of new ships, the downside was that

---

[50] The figurehead from this ship, which is a replica of a Victorian gentleman bearing the name *"Dennis Brundrit, J.P."*, was recovered from the waters around the Falkland Islands in 1942. It was at one time housed in a small maritime museum in Port Stanley.

tragedies involving river related work continued to occur. Unfortunately, at that time, when one worked on or lived near to a river this was a sad fact of life. The occurrences of boating and drowning accidents were numerous and residents on both sides of the river were no strangers to this type of calamity. The masters and crews of local *"Flats"* [51] from both towns were often involved in accidents and, regrettably, fatalities in this line of work were frequent. The flats owned by Coopers of Widnes seem to have had a particularly high rate of accidents and, alas, a great many of these incidents resulted in loss of life.

In July 1857 the inhabitants of Widnes were shocked and distressed by a drowning tragedy which involved some of their townspeople. A Northwich registered flat named *"The Sampson"* was being taken from the Canning Basin to the Nelson Dock in Liverpool when it sank in the river opposite the Clarence Pier. On board at the time was the barge's captain, Henry Hill, and his wife Elizabeth as well as two young children, an eight year old boy named Henry Woodcock and his four year old sister Ann Woodcock. Also on board was the captain's mate, a young man called Abel Goss from Widnes. When the captain realised the vessel was sinking he seized the lifeboat and got into it. His wife went to the cabin to get the children but before she was able to reach them the vessel sank with all on board. Despite the fact that there were several other vessels in the vicinity the boat sank too quickly for help to be summoned. However, shortly after *"The Sampson"* went down a successful attempt was made to attach a haul line to it. Subsequently a steamer towed the boat to the Potteries where it was allowed to remain until the tide subsided. The bodies of Elizabeth Hill and the little boy were found in the cabin. It was assumed that the bodies of Abel Goss and the little girl were swept away during the passage of the vessel along the river and they were not recovered. The flat was laden with salt when it sprung a leak. The captain and his wife, along with the young man, Abel Goss, were natives of Widnes. The children were being brought up by Mr. and Mrs. Hill who were their legal guardians.

During the early years of the nineteenth century Runcorn became increasingly more industrialised. By the mid years of that century, in addition to thriving shipyards and soap and chemical manufacture, there were several quarries, a brewery, a tannery and an acid works operating in the locality. The town's industrial development had primarily been aided by the area's excellent water communications and,

---

[51] Flat bottomed barges used for transporting raw materials and products to and from local industries.

of course, a railway facility had reached Preston Brook in 1839. However, although Runcorn had numerous and varied trade concerns and had become an important centre for commerce and shipping, we now know that, industrially, Widnes was destined to become the more important town. This supremacy was mainly due to the manufacture of alkali which became the town's core product.

Despite the fact that alkali manufacture was the prime reason for the development of Widnes as an important industrial centre, it should be pointed out that alkali production had commenced many years earlier in Runcorn. Although John Hutchinson was mainly responsible for bringing the industry to Widnes in the late 1840s, in fact, alkali manufacture was an established concern in Runcorn long before that date. Our neighbouring town across the river had already gained a reputation as an important centre of soap manufacture and alkali was being produced there profitably. So, despite Widnes being the recognised leader in the manufacture of alkali, we should be aware that the origins of the local alkali trade lay in Runcorn not Widnes.

The main driving force behind the development of Britain as an industrial nation is attributed to the enterprising efforts of a new entrepreneurial class of self-made men who emerged in the wake of the Industrial Revolution. These men were very resourceful and had the ability to anticipate and identify previously unexploited opportunities. They were extremely imaginative and prepared to take a risk, but this risk was often with money borrowed from others. One such man, the main engineer of Runcorn's industrial growth, was a farmer from Weston called John Johnson who developed several parcels of land on the south side of the Bridgewater Canal. This land had been inherited by his wife, Elizabeth Burton, from her uncle the Rev. Thomas Alcock, the Vicar of Runcorn. The Rev. Alcock had himself become the owner of this land through his marriage to Maria Harwood; this matrimonial union bringing with it the additional benefit of extensive land holdings in Runcorn. After the death of his wife, Maria, the Rev. Mr. Alcock remarried in November 1785. His new wife was Mary Breck the daughter of the Rev. T. Breck who had, before his death, also served as a minister in Runcorn. It is assumed that there were no surviving offspring from either of these marriages as, when the Rev. Alcock died in August 1798 at the age of 85 years, the Harwood land was handed down to his niece, Elizabeth Burton.

Three years after receiving the bequest of land from her uncle Elizabeth Burton married John Johnson. The astute Johnson was keen to make the most of his wife's inheritance and probably wished to increase its value. In an effort to do so he built a soap factory on the south side of the Bridgewater Canal in 1803. It is believed that Johnson raised the money to build his soapery by mortgaging the land to Thomas Pickering of Halton for a sum of £800. A few years later he obtained two more mortgages of £500 each which he invested in further industrial and residential development on his wife's land. Of course this investment was not a magic wand that would create economic growth unaided; it also required a huge degree of ambition and motivation on behalf of John Johnson. Fortunately he was endowed with both these abilities in great quantities.

Although John Johnson had borrowed substantial amounts of money to build his new factory in 1803, evidence suggests that by 1808 this business was not operating as a *"one man band"*. At that time Thomas Hazlehurst and his brother-in law, William Greenwood, were also involved in this venture and appeared to be part owners. Reports indicate that the company was recorded in 1808 as *"The Soapery of Messrs. Johnson, Hazlehurst & Greenwood."* At a later date Hazlehurst and Greenwood opened their own soap factory in the town; however, it would seem that their first endeavours in this line of work were in association with Johnson. This early combined venture was not without its problems. At the beginning of February 1809 a substantial fire at the factory caused a degree of damage to the ash-works on the site. Although the damage was not as serious as had at first been feared, in fact the cost of repair was just a little over £30; nevertheless, this represented a substantial financial and manufacturing set-back for the partnership.

Obviously, at some point after this date Johnson severed his business connection with Hazlehurst and Greenwood and he became the sole proprietor of the soap-works which eventually operated under his name. The powerful ambition to increase the returns from his land meant that by the time of his death in 1816, in addition to his soap factory, Johnson had also built a rope-works, a slate shop and some residential housing on the land. Furthermore, and most importantly, he had built the foundation on which a substantial business empire would be created by his sons. By 1841, several years before the alkali industry was established in Widnes, the Johnson Company in Runcorn, then under the control of John Johnson's two sons, was already producing alkali by the Leblanc process.

The first businesses to be created alongside the Bridgewater Canal were Masterman's Brewery and Walkers Skin-yard which were located on Heath Road and Halton Road respectively. The soapery which Johnson had built on the Greenway Road side of the canal prospered and after a few successful years of soap manufacture the business diversified into turpentine and rosin production. The Johnson business continued to thrive until the untimely death of John Johnson in 1816 at the age of 37 years. After his death two Liverpool based soap-makers, Mr. Hayes and Mr. Ollier, were appointed trustees of Johnson's affairs. These two men ran the business until 1821 when Mr. Johnson's son, John Junior, having reached the age of 21, took over the management of his father's company.

Of course, John Johnson Senior was no different to most other industrialists of those days who passed the commercial baton on to their sons. In that era most sons *did* follow in their fathers' footsteps and a system of nepotism rather than meritocracy was the accepted practice. However, in the Johnson case, John Junior would prove to be a more than worthy successor. After he had taken over the reins of the Johnson business young John kept a steady but progressive hand on the company. When his brother, Thomas, reached his majority he entered the firm as assistant to his brother. There is no doubt that the two brothers were certainly *"chips off the old block"* as they proved to be just as ambitious and determined as their father. It is quite evident that their business acumen was exceptional and together the brothers formed a truly formidable team. Through their hard work and commercial ability, coupled with a fair degree of ruthlessness, the Johnson brothers went on to build up a hugely successful business empire.

Sometime near the mid-1820s John Johnson Junior formed a business partnership with John and Henry Briddon of Weston Point who were soap boilers and ropemakers. It is believed that the Briddons also had extensive business interests in Manchester as well as Runcorn. However, by the summer of 1828 there had been a decision to dissolve the partnership and in August that year the formal dissolution of the firm of Johnson & Briddon occurred. After this, the Johnson brothers continued to develop their own commercial interests and during the 1830s the business underwent a period of rapid expansion. In fact, all the soap manufacturers in the district were flourishing during this era.

In 1835 Runcorn was the fifth largest soap producing town in England. The Johnsons took full advantage of this booming market and in 1836 the company acquired another soap works in Weston where they also produced rope, turpentine and alkali. The Weston factory had only been opened a few years previous by two Irishmen, Dennis

Kennedy and Thomas Maguire, who had come to the area from Liverpool where they had been operating as soap manufacturers. To fund their venture Kennedy and Maguire had taken out a mortgage of £1000 from the Bankes family, who owned large expanses of land in the area. The two men invested heavily and constructed buildings on the site and installed boilers, vats and other essential equipment. Unfortunately, due to this heavy investment and the large repayments on their loan, they soon found themselves in serious financial trouble. As a consequence they defaulted on their mortgage and, in order to pay off their debts, they were forced to sell the works to the Johnson brothers at a considerable loss.

Over the coming years, as the Johnson business increased substantially, the brothers also expanded their field of operation. During the 1840s they acquired interests in salt and coal mining. These acquisitions were intended to provide fuel and material for their own manufacturing business but they planned to sell the surplus for profit. Their interest in the coal trade in St. Helens proved to be extremely profitable as their mine managed to secure a contract to supply naval vessels at the Port of Liverpool with coal. It seemed that almost everything they turned their hand to at that time was successful and profitable. Apart from their business achievements, they also wielded enormous social and economic influence in the town. In fact, they were so dominant in the town that on several occasions they unashamedly used their patronage and power to influence commercial and civic decisions in Runcorn.

Like many other local manufacturers of that era the Johnsons also began looking at ways in which they could transport their products in a more cost effective manner. As a result they, like others, opened their own shipyard in Runcorn and acquired a large fleet of ships to transport their goods and materials. In October 1847 they took over the premises of Messrs. Stringer and Mather which was located near the river. The previous company had used the premises for cooperage work but the Johnsons set about converting the site into a ship building yard. They engaged as their foreman a Mr. Ronaldson, who had previously worked at the Old Quay. With their many acquisitions and assets the Johnson business went from strength to strength and seemed to be at the height of its achievements at the beginning of the 1860s. At that time the continued success of this long established business seemed to be assured. But, in spite of this confident outlook, a bad trade decision was to have a catastrophic effect on their business empire and regrettably it all came crashing down.

Even though the start of that decade had proved to be successful for most local industries it was not too long before trouble loomed on the horizon. In the spring of 1861 North America was plunged into a brutal civil war and as a result there was an imposed blockade on shipping. From then, until almost the end of the 1860s, the detrimental effects of the American Civil War upon British industry and commerce were felt in many areas of the country. These effects were most pronounced in parts of Lancashire where much of the population was reliant upon the textile trade. The blockade meant that Lancashire textile towns were completely cut off from their main source of supply, namely the cotton plantations in the Southern States of America. As a result of this imposed cotton famine, great economic deprivation spread throughout Lancashire as mills were forced to close. Although the effect was most keenly felt in the textile areas, it was not only that trade which was badly hit; there was a knock-on effect throughout the whole country. The shipping blockade meant that all types of British trade with America suffered disastrous consequences. The local alkali industry, whose major export market was in North America, experienced a drastic reduction in business which, in turn, impacted significantly on local employment.

As America was their largest customer, nearly all of our local alkali manufacturers were feeling the pinch as the lucrative American export market remained closed to them. This dramatic fall in trade meant that many manufacturers faced bankruptcy and hundreds of workers were threatened with the prospect of unemployment. The short-term measure was to reduce wages but this met with mass protest from workers. Early in 1861 hundreds of Widnes men and boys, who were employed in the Hutchinson & Earle works and Henry Deacon's factory, staged a three day strike in protest of a reduction of one shilling per day in their wages. Happily the manufacturers were able to agree a compromise but were still obliged to impose a significant wage reduction. The unfortunate workers were forced to concede in order to keep their jobs.

Most manufacturers were frustrated and powerless in the face of the American blockade on shipping. However, the Johnson brothers, who were always resourceful, decided to turn the damaging situation that had been created by the war to their own advantage. In order to maintain their American trade and outdo their competitors they decided to send their own ships to run the blockade. Whilst other manufacturers were helpless in the face of this obstacle, the Johnsons felt they had a lead over some of their competitors because they had their own fleet of ships. Of course this was a very risky and dangerous decision but one

131

they thought worthwhile in order to retain their trade links. Unfortunately, their plan backfired massively when most of their vessels were lost during a naval battle. This resulted in loss of life, loss of ships and a huge financial setback. The end result of this ill-fated endeavour led to the eventual bankruptcy and failure of the company.

One presumes that the Johnsons thought running the blockade was worth the risk as a considerable number of ships did manage to make it through safely. However, most of the successful blockade runners were small crafts with small cargoes; which meant they were usually fast enough to elude the larger ships of the Union Navy. One wonders how wise or profitable this was, even though it was a way of maintaining trade links. In some cases this could not have been of great economic benefit to the trader as the amount of cargo capable of being transported in these small ships was limited. On the other hand, sometimes the motivation was simply seen as a sympathetic attempt to help the Confederate States by bringing in supplies. However, in the Johnson case, they appear to have used their regular vessels for this purpose and their motives were neither sympathetic nor altruistic.

A rather bizarre co-incidence occurred at the beginning of November 1864 when a blockade running ship owned by Messrs. J. & T. Johnson of Runcorn was destroyed by a ship of the Union Navy. It appears that this vessel was owned by a company of the same name, from a town of the same name in America. The incident, which one would presume caused considerable local confusion, was reported in *The Manchester Courier* on 16th November. Unfortunately for the Johnsons this peculiar twist of fate was a forecast of things to come. Their own ships were sunk the following year at Charleston in South Carolina.

THE SHIPS BURNT BY THE TALLAHASSEE. — It will be seen by the telegrams from New York, brought by the steamer Belgian, that the Tallahassee has burnt two more ships, the Shooting Star and the Theresa. The Shooting Star was a vessel of 1,160 tons, and was on a voyage from New York to Panama with a general cargo, the principal items of which are hides, horns, and copper ore. She was built in Quebec in 1853, and is registered as the property of Messrs. J. and T. Johnson, of Runcorn, United States. [There is a similar firm at Runcorn-on-the-Mersey.] The Empress Theresa was bound from Rio Janeiro for Baltimore in ballast. She was a Virginian-built vessel, 316 tons, but five years old, and was the property of Mr. J. M. Bandell, of Baltimore.

The economic failure of the Johnson Company was certainly a sad and disastrous end to a firm which had been in operation in the town for around sixty years. The business had been built up from the original bequest by the Vicar of Runcorn to his niece, Elizabeth Burton, and through the assiduous efforts of her husband and their sons it had become a mainstay of Runcorn industry. It was indeed a dismal conclusion to a story of successful early entrepreneurial enterprise. After the disastrous failure of the Johnson Company most of the land and buildings belonging to the business were purchased by The Runcorn Soap and Alkali Company which was formed shortly afterwards. The sale was a rather unusual arrangement as it was not an outright purchase. It was agreed that the new company would pay Johnson's by instalments as and when the money came in. This rather flexible transaction which was, for the Johnsons, unusually accommodating, may have had something to do with the fact that both Johnson brothers retained a large interest in this new enterprise and acted as directors.

An offer of shares in the newly formed company was published in *The Times* and other national newspapers in November 1865. The prospectus of the new *Runcorn Soap and Alkali Company* informed would-be shareholders that the company had capital of £300,000 in 12,000 shares of £25 each, of which it was proposed to call up £20 a share. £2 per share was to be paid on application and £3 on allotment. Future calls of £3 per share to be made at intervals of not less than 3 months. The information contained in the notice gives a clear picture of the structure of the new firm and also provides details of the Directors as well as some useful background information. The Directors were named as Francis Shand of Liverpool; John Johnson of Runcorn; Thomas Johnson of Runcorn; William Keates of Liverpool; William Hayes of Runcorn and Thomas Fielden Campbell of Liverpool. It was stated that the Directors would have the power to add to their number at any time. The registered office was at Walmer Buildings, Water Street, Liverpool. The advert informed prospective investors that:

"This Company has been formed for the purpose of purchasing and carrying on the Alkali, Soap, Rosin, Turpentine and Salt Works, situated at Runcorn, Weston, Widnes and Winsford, belonging to the well-known firm of Messrs. John and Thomas Johnson, which have assumed dimensions almost beyond the limits of private enterprise. The Alkali and Soap Works have been in existence during a great part of the present century, and Messrs. Johnsons` manufacture of these

133

productions has acquired a very high reputation both in this country and in America.

The works are in perfect working condition, and capable of turning out about 150 tons soap, 150 tons soda ash, 100 tons saltcake, 100 tons bleaching powder, 100 tons sulphuric acid, 30 tons soda crystals and 80 tons refined rosin per week. After a careful valuation, and after a strict examination by Messrs. Banner and Son of the books and profit and loss accounts of Messrs. Johnson, the purchase-money for the above works, including the Freehold and Leasehold Property, Plant, Machinery, several valuable patents and the goodwill (taken at one and a half year's purchase), has been agreed at the sum of £153,724.

The stock-in-trade will be taken at valuation, Messrs. Johnson retain for themselves, in part payment of the purchase-money, one third of the capital, and they guarantee that the net profits of the concern for three years, from 1st November instant (from which date the works will be taken over), shall average not less than 10% per annum on the capital for the time being paid up. The Directors, however, believe that, considering the terms of the purchase, and the great impulse given to the trade by the cessation of the war in America, larger profits may be reasonably expected.

A copy of the agreement with Messrs. Johnson of the Articles of Association may be inspected at the Office of the Solicitors of the Company. Applications for shares must be accompanied by a payment of the deposit of £2 per share. In the event of no allotment being made, the deposit will be returned in full. Should a less number of shares be allotted than are applied for, the deposit will, as far as required, be applied towards the payment due on allotment. Applications for shares will be received at the Bankers, Brokers, Solicitors and Offices of the Company."

Of course, the Johnsons were not the only soap-makers in town, nor were their contributions any more important to the history of the Runcorn soap industry than the Hazlehurst one. In 1816, the year of John Johnson's death, Thomas Hazlehurst who had previously had a business alliance with Johnson, resurfaces on the Runcorn manufacturing scene. In that year Hazlehurst opened a turpentine and rosin factory on the opposite side of the canal to Johnson's Soapery. This factory was built on the site of an old farm called *Camden Croft* which was located between the canal and High Street. Happily, Hazlehurst retained a sentimental echo of this old farm by naming his new factory the *Camden Works*. In the beginning Thomas Hazlehurst was in partnership with his brother-in-law, his sister's husband,

William Greenwood, but this partnership was later dissolved and Hazlehurst continued the operation alone. As we know, sometime later Hazlehurst turned his attention to the manufacture of soap at this works and by 1850 this soap company had grown into a large concern.

There were several marked similarities in the operation of the Johnson and Hazlehurst ventures. Like the Johnson business, the drive and determination of its owner meant that the Hazlehurst soap-works soon developed into a very successful and prosperous company. When Thomas Hazlehurst retired in the early 1820s the company was taken over by his sons, William, John, Thomas and Charles. In later years, after the retirement of his brothers, the company was in sole control of Charles Hazlehurst who steered it to great commercial success. Like the Johnson Company, they developed huge markets for their products in America and several other countries. In the 1870s, after the deaths of Thomas Hazlehurst Junior and his brother Charles, the business was run by a board of directors and in 1891 it was absorbed into the United Alkali Company[52].

The enormous success of the Johnson and Hazlehursts companies was derived from the growth of the textile industry. The rapid growth in textile manufacture after the Industrial Revolution meant that there was an increased demand for acids, alkalis, soaps and chemicals of all kinds. In addition, the escalating use of soap all over the world created an increased demand for the alkalis used in its manufacture. This meant that there was a strong connection between the chemical and soap making industries. In recognition of this, around the mid-1830s the firms of both Johnson and Hazlehurst diversified into chemical production. At the Rocksavage works, which the Johnson's had taken over from Kennedy and Maguire, the Johnson's built a large vitriol plant to produce sulphuric acid while at their Runcorn works they began producing alkali by the Leblanc process. A short while later, the firm of Hazlehurst followed suit and diversified into alkali manufacture. Both companies built huge chimneys at their works in order to disperse the waste gases from the alkali process into the atmosphere. At the time, the erection of such large chimneys caused something of a stir. The newspapers made much of the height of each chimney and gave detailed accounts of their construction, even down to

---

[52] In 1911 the business was sold to Lever Brothers and subsequently soap production ceased and the site became a tannery.

the number of bricks used in each one. The Johnsons' were the first to construct. *The Manchester Courier* of December 1834 reported thus:

"There has recently been erected at the extensive soap and chemical works of Messrs. J. and T. Johnson, of Runcorn, a circular brick chimney of immense magnitude, surmounted by a capital of hewn stonework, the whole forming a column of surpassing height and beauty, probably exceeding in height any structure in the world upon the same base. Its dimensions are as follows: Diameter at the base, 30 feet, height 272 feet. It contains upwards of 500,000 bricks, and is estimated to weigh about 2000 tons. This beautiful column, erected under the superintendence of Mr. Livingstone of Newcastle, is 9 feet higher than the celebrated chimney of Mr. Clapham, of that town: 43 feet higher than the chimney of Mr. Muspratt at Liverpool; and 70 feet higher than the Monument in London."

Two years later the Hazlehurst Company built their own magnificent chimney which eclipsed the Johnson structure both in height and weight although it would appear that a similar number of bricks were used in its construction. This time *The Liverpool Mercury* supplies us with an account:

"The spirited proprietors of the Camden soap, turpentine and chemical works at Runcorn, have set their brother chemists an example which is worthy of their imitation, by erecting a chimney to carry off anything which may be deleterious to the health, or injurious to the comfort of the inhabitants. It was commenced on May 8th of this year (1836), and was finished on Saturday November 28th, at the works of Messrs. Hazlehurst and Sons. It combines elegance and strength in a superior manner; it is circular, and appears a beautiful object either viewed near or at a distance. In height, it is unrivalled in the Kingdom, exceeding one hundred and two yards. It contains more than half a million of bricks, and may be reckoned to weigh 2,803 tons. There is a neat ornamental stone cornice at the top, the whole forming one of the most stupendous specimens of the kind in modern art."

Apart from these significant industries Runcorn had several other types of business and manufacturing enterprises at that time. Rooke Hunter & Co. (this works became Earp & Co. later) had an acid works in Halton Road; Wright had sold his quarry and opened a tannery in Bridge Street and two other tanneries were also operating in the town. In addition to these establishments there were also seven shipyards as well as several ships' chandlers and sail-makers in the locality. All these ventures contributed greatly to the buoyant economy of the town, offering numerous work opportunities as well as healthy profits for the employers.

We are all probably familiar with the numerous complaints about the noxious odours, gases, and smoke which were associated with Widnes in later times. Earlier, Runcorn had also received a fair share of grumbles from its inhabitants concerning the environmental nuisances created by the chemical trade in their own town. Apart from the obvious nuisances produced by smoke and other pollution, there was clearly some real concern about safety issues in the chemical industry. A letter published in *The Liverpool Mercury* in the spring of 1838 (reproduced on another page) gives an insight into the feelings of local residents. At this time there was a great deal of publicity surrounding a court case which had been brought against James Muspratt.[53] This related to the adverse effects of the chemical fumes which emanated from his Vauxhall plant in Liverpool[54]. The numerous complaints about this factory, which were widely reported in the national press, had been going on for some considerable time. As early as 1827 Muspratt's Vauxhall Works in Everton had been considered a public nuisance because of the smoke and fumes being discharged from the premises. Ten years later Muspratt was indicted before the Liverpool Spring Assizes for *"creating and maintaining a nuisance within the borough of Everton to the annoyance and injury of the inhabitants thereof"*. During this period posters were pasted on walls around Liverpool attacking James Muspratt and his operation at Vauxhall Road. The publicity surrounding this case highlighted the unpleasant and damaging effects of the chemical industry on neighbouring areas. This helped to heighten the fear of local residents as there was a genuine worry that Muspratt might decide to relocate to Runcorn.

Of course it should be said that Muspratt was not the only producer of chemicals in Liverpool at that time, nor was his works the only culprit when it came to pollution. There were a number of objections raised against other manufacturers in the city. In March 1838 a Captain Burgoyne, who lived in Anne Street near to Mount Pleasant, made a

---

[53] Muspratt arrived in Liverpool in 1822. Although Thomas Lutwyche and William Hill had been producing alkali by the Leblanc process in Liverpool from 1814, it is widely accepted that the Muspratt factory was the first *significant* alkali factory in Britain.

[54] *Gore's Liverpool Directory* of 1823 – The named the owners of the works are listed as Muspratt & Abbott. *Gore's Liverpool Directory* of 1825 - Listed under Muspratt's name alone.

CHEMICAL WORKS AT RUNCORN.

To the EDITOR of the LIVERPOOL MERCURY.

SIR,—Observing a paragraph in your paper of last week, intimating the probable intention of some spirited individuals erecting chemical nuisances in Runcorn, because of no complaint being made against those already existing there, I take the liberty of informing the parties and the public, that the chemical works and soap manufactories are severely felt and much complained of by the inhabitants of Runcorn, not only as nuisances, but also as erections likely to endanger the lives of those living near them; and the very elements, as if aiding the complainants or condemning these nuisances, have attacked them; for on Monday last, during the storm, the two tall chimneys were struck and severely injured by the electric fluid or thunder, the one being cracked or rent, and the other having bricks knocked out or torn from it.

For the benefit of those who may contemplate carrying on chemical works at Runcorn, I can tell them that, although we have not a wealthy corporation to protect us from injury, we have our Brookes, our Cholmondeleys, our Astons, and many other spirited owners of property and men of mettle, who only want the spark lighted to rouse them into action for their mutual defence; consequently we warn them to keep off from our healthy little village, for it will be only going out of the frying-pan of Liverpool into the fire of Runcorn, in which they may come off worse and experience a more signal defeat than they have lately done at Liverpool.

A CONSTANT READER.

Runcorn, April 18, 1838.

complaint about the noxious odour and vapours caused by a chemical works in Canning Street. Although he lived a short distance from Canning Street, he said that when the wind blew from that direction he was aware of a nauseous smell that came into his house, making it necessary to close all the windows. He also talked of fire-brasses, door furniture and silverware being tarnished. In addition to the offending establishment in Canning Street, local directories [55] name several manufacturers of borax and other chemicals in the vicinity of Parliament Street and Duke Street[56]. Obviously James Muspratt's Everton works were on a much larger scale to any of these establishments and therefore caused significantly more pollution and received more publicity.

When reading newspaper reports about chemical operations and their consequences we can well understand why members of the indigenous communities of Runcorn were concerned about the effect further industrial development would have on their own town. Issues of safety and pollution appear to have been a major concern and the much publicised Muspratt court case served as a vehicle for more public alarm. The challenging tone of the letter which is reproduced on another page implies that Muspratt had seriously considered opening a factory in Runcorn because he thought there would be less likelihood of complaint in that area. However, this was clearly scaremongering as there is no significant documentary evidence to suggest that this was ever the case. Obviously the circumstances and publicity surrounding the Muspratt prosecution prompted a great deal of speculation as to what he was likely to do if he was forced to relocate. This probably gave rise to a good deal of conjecture which resulted in a case of people adding two and two together and coming up with five.

Obviously, it was not only the residents of the town who were against the expansion of industry; many of the major landowners in the district were also strongly opposed to it. Some eminent historians, when writing about the effects of the Industrial Revolution on the country in general, have alluded to the fact that most landowners had a hypocritical nimby-like approach to this subject. Although landowners profited greatly from the sale of land to developers they did not want industry on their own doorstep. Indeed, some of the landowners mentioned in the correspondence relating to Runcorn, who were viewed

---

[55] *Gores Liverpool Directory*
   Slater's Directory of Lancashire
[56] Areas of Liverpool 8 – near to the present day Anglican Cathedral

as protective champions of the area, had previously sold land to industrial developers. It would appear that whilst they were quite happy to benefit from the proceeds of land sales, they did not want the unwholesome environment created by chemical manufacture to encroach upon their own estates. Unfortunately it seems they could not have one without the other. It is obvious, from this letter, that Runcorn residents felt that the existing works were already generating an unacceptable level of pollution and that further development in the area would be intolerable.

This correspondent was clearly alarmed by the possibility of any additional chemical manufacture in the area. One has to admire the defiant stance of the writer and the threats of further action if Muspratt or others should dare to come to Runcorn. However, in spite of alleged complaints about the adverse effects of existing local soap and chemical factories, it is interesting to note that this *"Constant Reader"* describes the town of Runcorn in April 1838 as being a *"healthy little village"*.

Regardless of the fact that the writer and others opposed further industrial development in the town, over the following years various portions of land were offered for sale or lease for that specific purpose. Interestingly, whilst some people genuinely believed that the Trustees of the Bridgewater Estate were ultimately responsible for hindering Runcorn's industrial progress, the Trustees did from time to time offer land for industrial development. An advertisement also reproduced here, appeared in *The Liverpool Mercury* and several other northern newspapers in August 1853. On the face of it, it would seem that the Trustees were promoting development rather than obstructing it.

Nevertheless it is worth mentioning that, despite the tone of the advert, there were numerous unsuccessful attempts by various companies to set up chemical factories in Runcorn. Although the Bridgewater Trustees had advertised land to lease for industrial use there was a general feeling that the requisites of these leases were not fair. Several efforts to acquire land for factories were thwarted by the Trustees who declined to release land on reasonable terms.

It has been implied over the years that there may have been other underlying reasons for not making land more easily available and that the unfavourable terms of the leases were indicative of this. In 1854, just a year after this advertisement, an application from Messrs. Haddock & Parnell for land, for the purpose of building a chemical factory, was refused by the Trustees. The main objector to that application was the Trustee, Lord Ellesmere, who was a personal friend of Sir Richard Brooke the owner and custodian of Norton Priory.

Land for Works, to be Let or Sold.

THE TRUSTEES of the late Duke of Bridgewater and the Old Quay Company are desirous to encourage the erection of Works of various kinds at and in the neighbourhood of Runcorn, and are prepared to treat on the most favourable terms with parties requiring sites contiguous to their navigation.

Runcorn offers peculiar advantages for either sea or inland traffic, which constitute it a most eligible situation for works requiring cheap and ready transit of their manufactures.

Villa and other House BUILDING LAND on SALE.

Apply to Mr. W. Howarth, Bridgewater Canal or Old Quay Navigation Office, Runcorn; or to Mr. J. S. Paterson, Bridgewater Offices, Manchester.

THE LIVERPOOL MERCURY - AUGUST 1853

Sir Richard Brooke was a major landowner in the area and a man of considerable influence in Runcorn and the surrounding districts. He was also a prolific complainer regarding the effects of industrial pollution on the environment. His complaints particularly concerned the adverse effects of the toxic fumes and smoke created by the local chemical industry. These polluting emissions had resulted in the contamination of his lands at Norton and Cuerdley and, he claimed, this had greatly reduced the monetary value of his land holdings and caused distress to his tenants. It is believed that Lord Ellesmere's objections to the Haddock & Parnell application mainly arose from a feeling of loyalty to Sir Richard. It is thought that he did not want to cause further annoyance to his friend nor any additional nuisance to the Norton Priory estate. This type of interference from the Trustees, coupled with their continual refusal to release land for factories on equitable terms, has caused many local historians to believe that the Trustees were indeed responsible for hampering further industrial development in Runcorn.

141

Despite the concerns of local residents regarding pollution, there *was* an increase in local manufacturing and trade. With this growth of industry Runcorn's population during the period 1801 to 1841 increased significantly, rising from 1,474 to 6,951.[57] It would certainly seem that towards the middle of the nineteenth century Runcorn looked destined to become a major industrial area. It possessed all the necessary transport requirements and its existing industries were thriving and profitable. The Runcorn businesses of Johnson and Hazlehurst were two of the largest soap and alkali concerns in the north of England and were employing hundreds of men. Johnson's Runcorn works alone employed 760 men. As we have seen, by the late 1860s Johnson's had been absorbed into *The Runcorn Soap & Alkali Co. Ltd* and the company had replaced their concentration on soap manufacture with the manufacture of heavy chemicals. In addition to several successful manufacturing industries, Runcorn stone was still in great demand and as a result over 1000 men were employed in quarry work. Furthermore, the foundations for the extensive tanning trade that matured in the area in the later years of the nineteenth century had also been set down. In fact, by the late 1840s the area was flourishing.

In addition to all this industrial expansion, and to add to its commercial advantages, on 5th April 1847 Runcorn became a Bonded Port. This meant that it was free from the excessive dues put on goods by Liverpool. Maritime trade was booming at that time and ships docking at Runcorn brought in commodities from various parts of the world, particularly timber from the Baltic regions. In February 1848 two large vessels arrived in Runcorn with cargoes of railway sleepers from Russia. The first vessel, which berthed at The Old Quay Dock, was *The Hope* carrying 2700 sleepers. The other ship, *The Hebe*, at that time the largest vessel ever to arrive in Runcorn, had been carrying 4000 sleepers but had been obliged to lighten her load at Garston before sailing up the river to Runcorn. After unloading the sleepers at Runcorn both ships returned to Russia with cargoes of fine salt. All in all, it would be fair to say that in the 1840s the economic future of Runcorn certainly looked set to remain rosy. Its canals and docks were thriving and several successful manufacturing industries were offering plentiful employment.

However, despite the optimistic outlook and the advantage of being a Bonded Port, by 1850 Runcorn's fortunes began to show signs of a slowdown. The transportation of products and raw materials was of

---

[57] By 1901 the population figure had risen to 16,941

prime importance for all manufacturers and the availability and convenience of transport links played an important role in the development of the town. However as railways and improved road networks developed in the area the canals became less important. These artificial waterways, which had been responsible for Runcorn's growth and prosperity, ceased to offer a dominant advantage and the profits on the canals fell drastically. Of course water transport was notoriously slow, especially in the winter months when ice was often a problem for traffic on the canals. Therefore the new railway infrastructures were considered a more efficient and speedier way to transport materials. With the subsequent growth of rail communication as a means of industrial haulage Runcorn's role as an important transport hub was greatly diminished.

Apart from the loss of business due to rail expansion, in 1850 Runcorn's status as a Bonded Port was annulled. From the 5th April that year it was reduced from being an independent port to being *"a creek"* within the port of Liverpool. Later it was listed as a sub-port of the Port of Manchester. From that time it remained essentially a canal port but, whilst there was a general decline of trade on the old waterways, there was still a reasonable degree of coastal trade and barge traffic. Interestingly, when its status as a Bonded Port was annulled in 1850 some special concessions were granted. These privileges, which were not ordinarily granted to common *"creeks"* which could normally only receive *"reports inwards of coasters"*, now included the reports of shipmasters *"inwards from foreign parts"*. Runcorn also retained its Bonding privileges as regards bonded timber as well as being able to receive duties on imports. In the 1880s there were around seventeen countries trading through Runcorn with exports to the Baltic generating a substantial amount of business.

In much the same way as the canals had been responsible for the early increase in commercial activity and employment in the town, shipbuilding and sailing had also been an important element of daily life in Runcorn for most of the nineteenth century. Up until the early 1880s the local trade in shipbuilding had been pretty buoyant and numerous ships were launched into the Mersey from local yards. In spite of the fact that Runcorn had ceased to play a major role in water transport communication, local shipbuilding continued to be a going concern till the latter years of the 1880s when trade eventually started to fall off. There were numerous reasons for this decline, not least was the unfavourable state of the river due to silting. Besides that, the sea wall which was being constructed between the new Manchester Ship

143

Canal and the river was an added hindrance. Unfortunately, after 1890 shipbuilding as a significant trade and source of local employment became almost non-existent. All that remained of the industry which had once been a central part of the local economy were a few small concerns which concentrated mainly upon building and repairing barges.

In matters of industry and commerce there are often winners and losers. Whilst Runcorn's star was beginning to fade in the mid nineteenth century, Widnes, on the opposite side of the river, was on the rise. The unique geographical position enjoyed by Widnes, where railway, canal and river met, contributed significantly to the development of industry in the area. The manufacture of alkali, which remained the town's core product for an extraordinary length of time, became directly responsible for an unprecedented growth both in industry and population. Nevertheless, it should be pointed out that regardless of the fact that the alkali trade in Widnes expanded at a vast rate; there was still a considerable amount of alkali being produced in Runcorn. However, by the early 1860s the volume of chemical trade in Widnes had completely overtaken that of its neighbour. It is also worth noting that Runcorn, although not matching Widnes in manufacturing stakes, still had a degree of industrial growth due to the Wigg works and increased output from the local soapworks after 1860. Towards the end of the 1880s there were still three Runcorn firms[58] producing alkali by the Leblanc process.

Obviously, it was not only the favourable geographical location that was responsible for the growth of Widnes. Numerous other important factors came into play. Not least of these were the availability of cheap land and a high level of the private enterprise and speculation which was widespread during the Victorian era. Like the pioneering industrialists and innovators of Runcorn, Widnes also had its own group of enterprising men. John Hutchinson and men of his ilk led the way in creating an atmosphere of commercial endeavour and advancement. This was truly an era of great commerce and creativity. There is absolutely no doubt that without the highly entrepreneurial flavour of the times, which offered tremendous scope for enterprising men of limited resources, industry would probably not have developed in Widnes on such a major scale.

---

[58] These three firms were subsequently absorbed into the United Alkali Company when this was formed in 1890.

Workers on The Manchester Ship Canal

We have read here about the transformation of Runcorn from a renowned place of scenic beauty and tourism into a busy industrial canal port. We have also seen how industrial and other development changed the landscape and ethos of the area. Whilst these changes were dramatic and damaging to both the environment and the population, they were to be eclipsed by the scale of changes which occurred in the neighbouring town across the river. The rapid and spectacular alteration which took place in Widnes drastically affected both the physical and social environment of the immediate area and its hinterlands. The unprecedented rise in industry and population was to give the town an unenviable reputation throughout the length and breadth of the land. This once unremarkable rural area became notorious as a place of noxious odours, smoke, gas, devastating pollution and violent behaviour. The transformation which occurred in Widnes was extreme in every sense. Apart from destruction of the landscape and contamination of the environment, the coming of industry into the area also brought about a complete shift in the social and employment habits of a whole new section of society.

Prior to the inception of the chemical industry in Widnes the main employment had been of an agricultural nature. In addition to the normal rural occupations there were a small number of cottage industries in the northern regions of the town. These were mainly concerned with the production of canvas for the sails of ships or the

145

manufacture of pinion wire, watch parts and precision tools. These activities were, in the main, domestic based industries which were carried out in the homes of the workers, who were usually employed as *"outworkers"* for larger manufacturers. In the southern area the traditional occupations associated with the river, such as fishing and boatbuilding, were also evident. In fact, archaeological discoveries of a number of small log boats on the upper Mersey would suggest that boats were being built on the shores of the Mersey from the earliest times. Even though Runcorn eventually became more noteworthy in the realm of boat building, this time honoured occupation did take place on both banks of the river. Fishing was also a particularly sound source of income as the river Mersey was unpolluted and filled with salmon and other fish. Also available in this stretch of the Mersey were an abundance of eels, a popular epicurean delicacy known locally as snigs. So, apart from bringing in an income, fishing also had the additional benefit of providing food for the family table.

Although most of the small industries in the area in the early days were domestic based, the manufacture of pinion wire was more of a commercial enterprise by 1800. An early ledger belonging to the Warrington firm of Peter Stubs (1756-1806), [59] refers to the purchase of pinion wire from Appleton in the late 1790s. This was most probably purchased from the firm of Copple and Heyes who operated a small wire-drawing factory in Appleton village around that time. This factory, which employed a small local workforce, was located in the centre of the village near to the spot which was occupied in later times by a company called *Park Insulated Materials*. It is now the site of a residential apartment building. By 1815 the Copple and Heyes business had passed into the sole ownership of Thomas Heyes whose family subsequently owned and operated this company for several generations. In the early 1860s Thomas Heyes was employing 79 men as well as a number of young boys.

In addition to the wireworks, Appleton village was also home to a number of toolmakers and watch-movement makers as well as a blacksmith and wheelwright. Some of these tradesmen lived and worked in a collection of cottages known as Tithebarn Row which was located near the site of the old Tithe Barn. This group of dwellings was reached through an archway situated almost opposite the Heyes wireworks. Other village residents followed traditional agricultural occupations on the surrounding lands and there was also a small

---

[59] An 18th century industrialist – Peter Stubs of Warrington – T. S. Ashton (1939)

workforce employed in the local quarry. As one can imagine, this mixture of occupations, both skilled and unskilled, meant that Appleton village was a hive of industry. In almost all cases the native inhabitants of the village had adopted an established pattern of living and working which had been practised by their families for generations.

The local watchmakers and precision toolmakers, who were mainly based in Cronton, Ditton, Upton and Appleton, were skilled craftsmen who usually worked in small workshops in their own homes. They owned their own tools, worked at their own pace, and sold the products of their labour. However, instead of working for themselves and earning a fair price for their skill, they were employed as outworkers by master watchmakers from Prescot. The master watchmaker paid his outworkers an amount which was determined not by the intrinsic value of their labour but by what the market would allow. In most cases the men were paid in provisions or with watches rather than in money. This practice was known as the *"truck system"* and was an extremely dubious and unfair arrangement. Workers were usually given a ticket to obtain provisions from a named shopkeeper, who was often the master watchmaker himself or his wife. The men who received watches in payment usually sold them at a considerable loss. This system of payment was widespread throughout the country but, in an attempt to curb this practice, various Government Acts were introduced in 1842, 1853 and 1867. However, despite legislation being brought in to prevent payment in goods and to protect workers from unscrupulous and tyrannical employers, these Acts did little to curtail this unfair system.

I would imagine that almost all of our local precision craftsmen were subjected to the unscrupulous practices of the truck arrangement. It is believed that most of the outworkers employed in the watchmaking industry throughout the country were victims of this deplorable custom. This was the *"sweated trade"* of the time. Renewed attention was placed on the *"truck system"* in 1871 when a Government Commission was formed to investigate its procedures. The purpose of the Commission was to inquire into any arrangement whereby an employer gave goods in lieu of wages, or vouchers for goods sold at any shop in which the employer had an interest. Many outworkers who worked for Prescot based watchmakers gave evidence at this Inquiry. One outworker told the panel that he had worked for a Prescot watchmaker, Mr. Beesley, for over eight years and during that time had never once had his wages in money. Mr. Beesley had given him tickets to get provisions at his shop. The witness's wife often complained that if she had the money in hand she could buy provisions much cheaper at other shops. Other witnesses claimed that they received payment in the form of watches but, in all cases, they would have preferred to have received their wages in cash. During the proceedings it was stated that there were around 500 men employed in the watchmaking trade in Prescot, but when one included outworkers from St. Helens, Rainhill, Cronton, Upton, Widnes and other neighbouring places the number employed was in excess of 1200. The witnesses included several from Rainhill but I found no record of any worker from the Widnes area being called to give evidence. After the 1871 Inquiry, the Act was enforced more stringently, nevertheless, the practice was not entirely eradicated; it still existed to some degree for a considerable time afterwards.

Although there is no denying that watchmaking was a highly exploitative industry this, and toolmaking, provided employment for many of the inhabitants of the villages and hamlets around Widnes. Dozens of small workshops were set up in cottages in these areas, many of them having existed for generations. Usually several members of a family were involved in the work, even young children who were often employed from an early age and were given simple tasks to perform. There were a number of marked divisions of labour in the process of watchmaking and some families concentrated on the manufacture of just one or two particular components. Because of this distribution of work it was estimated that it took about 25 men to complete one watch. Each complex stage of production was undertaken by a different specialised craftsman and then passed on to the master watchmaker who assembled the parts and put his own name on the plate which identified him as *"the maker"*.

It has generally been supposed that the watchmaking and toolmaking trade sprang up from an earlier period when local men made armour, weapons and various types of fine metalwork for the Barons and retainers of Halton Castle. Several nineteenth century historians have made claim to the suggestion that when the blacksmiths, who had previously been employed forging these types of items, were no longer required to do so they channelled their skills into the manufacture of metal tools such as shears, pliers, pincers etc. *"The Hammer and Pincers"* pub in Hough Green is said to have been so named to reflect this association. This assumption is based on the fact that the *"Hammer and Pincers"* symbol was the original insignia of The Armourers Company which was founded in London around 1423. It is certainly a compelling hypothesis when one considers that the armour was largely chain mail and that wire was produced locally at Appleton. Wire and fine chain work was also produced nearby at

Sankey and Warrington. The more delicate metalwork, which was later evident in the watch and toolmaking trade, was produced in several areas around Widnes.

In addition to these skilled craftsmen there was also a colony of handloom weavers in the northern regions of the town who worked in the canvas industry, making cloth for the sails of ships. Like watchmaking, this was also a common domestic occupation in all parts of south Lancashire. This home-based industry was comparable to watch and tool making in that it was conducted in a similar *"piece-work"* manner, which meant that domestic weavers and spinners were exploited as ruthlessly as operatives in other domestic trades. Early census records identify numerous weavers in the Farnworth area. Like other cottage crafts, whole families were involved in this work. Even when this occupation transferred to factories children were still being put to work as bobbin winders, although in later times it was illegal to employ children.

By the beginning of the 19th century a series of inventions gradually began to take weaving out of the homes and into factories. Subsequently, the introduction of power looms brought about a long drawn-out destruction of hand loom weaving. This meant that the repetitive clack of the loom became a thing of the past in the little cottages of Farnworth and Lunts Heath. We can see from various records that, locally, this process had moved from cottage into factory as early as 1815. An advert from *The Lancaster Gazette* on 1st July that year gives an indication of the size of one Farnworth operation.

WANTED,

A STEADY, SOBER MAN, to SUPER-INTEND a FLAX SPINNING-MILL, containing from three to four hundred Spindles, with Preparing Machinery, worked by a Steam-engine.— Testimonials of character will be required; and suitable wages given.

⁂ For particulars apply to Messrs. THOS. and W KIDD, sail-cloth-manufacturers, Widnes, near Warrington

PINNOCK'.

By 1825 there were at least five commercial weaving sheds located around Farnworth and Lunts Heath. The most notable of these were owned by William Norland, Thomas Shaw, Thomas Smythe, Longton & Leather and the brothers Thomas and William Kidd, who also owned a sailcloth factory in St. Helens. The Kidd family had a particularly long association with the canvas industry. In the early 1860s we find that another member of the family, Robert Kidd, was in business as a canvas merchant in Farnworth. He was working in partnership with a man called John Woodhouse and their company, trading under the name of Kidd and Woodhouse, was listed as canvas manufacturers and brewers at Farnworth. Unfortunately, the company went bankrupt in October 1865 and the partnership was dissolved shortly afterwards.

Although this occupation was no longer entirely based on cottage industry, where the weaver used a small hand loom, nevertheless, the weavers were traditional artisans who worked in a time honoured occupation which required a degree of skill and experience. By the mid-1870s the chemical industry had become the main employer in the area. Although there was initially a degree of reluctance on the part of local artisans to enter into that trade, nevertheless, there was a gradual decline in the number of skilled weavers. The shortage of experienced workers in the canvas trade prompted local factory owners to advertise for workers outside this area. These adverts were placed in localities where there was likely to be an abundance of suitable labour. The following advert appeared in *The Belfast Newsletter* of 13th May 1876.

CANVAS POWER-LOOM WEAVERS. — Wanted, at once, Men and Women with families, accustomed to Millwork preferred. Apply at NEW MILLS, Farnworth, near Widnes, Lancashire. 6118

In addition the toolmaking, wire-drawing and weaving, there were also several stone quarries located around the area which offered employment to small numbers of men. Besides these traditional occupations there were a few mills in the vicinity, although these would generally have operated as one-man-bands. Mill Brow was the site of two mills which were owned by the Smyth family of Peel House. One mill was driven by wind and the other by water. There was also a mill near to the Horns[60] but unfortunately this structure was completely destroyed in December 1823 when a hurricane hit the area. It was

---

[60] It is believed that this mill was sited near to the site of the present day *Rivendell Nurseries* in Mill Lane.

reported that the mill went on fire because of the violent friction caused by the speed of the sails rotation. Both the mill and the miller's house were totally wrecked in the storm. We can also see from an advert placed in *The Manchester Courant* in October 1819 that there was an established mill at Pex Hill, Cronton.

As we saw earlier, in the mid-1840s whilst Widnes had remained relatively untouched by industry, its near neighbours Runcorn and St. Helens already had a number of thriving industrial activities. Alkali, which became the core manufacturing product in Widnes, was already being produced profitably in both these towns. However it should be said that although Runcorn and St. Helens were by that time established places of chemical manufacture, the production of chemicals was still a relatively new activity. Indeed, at the close of the eighteenth century, apart from the manufacture of gunpowder and a few drugs and acids in small quantities, there was scarcely a chemical factory anywhere in this country. Probably one of the first chemicals produced in quantity was sulphuric acid. Then, when the value of chlorine as a bleaching agent was discovered, this opened up a whole new field of industrial activity. When Charles Tennant opened a bleaching-powder works in Glasgow in 1797 he launched what was to become a significant manufacturing outlet. Within a few years the manufacture of bleaching powder was an important industry in many parts of the country.

The production of alkali in Widnes and other places in Britain was enabled by a process devised by a Frenchman named Nicholas Leblanc. He developed a method of producing soda using common salt with sulphuric acid. As I am not a chemist, nor do I possess a great deal of knowledge on the subject, I am therefore ill equipped to go into specific detail relating to the techniques of producing alkali. So let it suffice to say that the process involved using common salt with sulphuric acid, thus making sodium sulphate and liberating hydrochloric acid gas, then roasting the sodium sulphate with limestone and charcoal to obtain sodium carbonate and calcium sulphide. At the time this innovative process was formulated it was viewed as a major breakthrough. Nicholas Leblanc was subsequently awarded a prestigious prize by the French Government for his valuable discovery. The ground-breaking process invented by Leblanc was afterwards adopted by several manufacturers in this country, including the alkali manufacturers of Widnes, Runcorn and St. Helens. Unfortunately, whilst countless firms in England and other countries made their fortunes from this process, Leblanc himself was never to profit financially from his discovery. During a period of acute poverty and depression he committed suicide

151

TO BE SOLD BY AUCTION,

On Thursday the 18th of November next, at two o'clock in the afternoon, at Sharples's, the Golden Lion, in Dale-street, Liverpool, subject to conditions to be produced, and together or in lots as may be agreed on,

A MOST desirable FREEHOLD ESTATE, the greater part in Cronton, the rest in Rainhill, in the county of Lancaster, consisting of a capital Mansion, called Cronton-hall, or Brook Stones, and several Closes of Land held therewith, containing about 176 acres, statute measure, including the reversion, after the death of an old life, in a detached Estate in Cronton, containing about 9 acres, like measure.

And a Wind Mill, called Pex-hill Mill.

Cronton hall is in the possession of Bryan Riding The Outbuildings are new, extensive, and well-arranged, and it may be truly said, that there are few, if any, such Estates to be purchased in this part of the country.

The situation on its southern aspect embraces all the prospects which that much admired place called Pex-hill so peculiarly affords, as well of the River Mersey as of the Cheshire shore, near Runcorn, and its eminence commands the views on the Lancashire side.

The Land is remarkably good, in a highly cultivated state, and there are some thousand Forest-trees growing thereon, which have been planted about ten years, and are making great progress in their growth.

It is situate about a mile and a half from Farnworth Church, in which there is a large as well as a smaller Pew belonging to the Estate: 10 miles from Liverpool, 7 from Warrington, 3 from Prescot, and 3 from Runcorn.

For further particulars, in the mean time, apply to Mr. Ashworth, of Turton, near Bolton; Joshua Goring, Esq. of Everton; or to Messrs. LEIGH and SON, Solicitors, Basnett street, Liverpool.

in the study of his home in France, by shooting himself. This was a sad and tragic end to the life of such a talented man. It is especially poignant when one considers that Leblanc had been responsible for creating the chemical process which had such a profound influence on the business and working lives of so many people around the world. The riches which his discovery created were vast by any standards, so it is quite shocking to learn that he died in abject poverty while others made fortunes from the technique he devised.

When researching Nicholas Leblanc's process I found an interesting report of a speech made by Mr R. G. Perry to mark the centenary of the founding of the alkali industry. Mr. Perry was at that time the President of the *Association of British Chemical Industries.* He described the alkali trade as having been:

"...conceived in revolution, fathered by war, and nourished by strife." Indeed, this was very true, as the product was first heard of towards the end of the French Revolution, when the French Government, in need of alkali, offered a prize to the inventor who could come up with a process for producing soda ash from salt. In 1794 the prize was won by Nicholas LeBlanc whose process then, and for the next ninety years or so, became the established method of producing alkali."

I should point out that even after Nicholas Leblanc had invented his process it was some time before the production of alkali took off to any degree in this country. Much earlier, during the Napoleonic Wars, England had introduced a devastating tax on salt which meant that the production of alkali in this country was economically prohibitive. However, as soon as this tax was repealed James Muspratt brought the first significant production of alkali to the Merseyside area[61]. Alkali manufacture soon became one of the country's principal and most profitable industries and, in keeping with the pioneering and entrepreneurial flavour of the times, scores of enterprising young men like John Hutchinson were tempted to set up their own alkali factories.

The use of salt in the Leblanc process prompted many alkali manufacturers to establish their factories near to where salt was readily available or easily obtained. Therefore, an efficient transport infrastructure was essential. The alkali industries in Runcorn and St. Helens relied heavily on the canal waterways to bring in their raw

---

[61]Thomas Lutwyche and William Hill had been producing small amounts of alkali in Liverpool as early as 1814; however, Muspratt's Vauxhall works at Everton was the first factory in Britain to produce alkali on a large scale.

materials, which included salt from Northwich, limestone from North Wales and oils and pyrites from Ireland and Spain. The convenience of these water highways had facilitated the expansion of industry and employment in both those towns, as well as an increase in their populations. Despite Widnes having no major industry or employment prospects before the birth of the alkali trade, the completion of several schemes including the extension of the Sankey Navigational Canal from Fidler's Ferry to Widnes and the opening of the Runcorn Gap Railway[62], did provide new opportunities. Although significant heavy industry had not yet reached the area and the population was still moderately small, the opening of the railway and canal heralded the beginning of change. These additional services brought a minor stream of new workers into the area which enabled a small residential district, consisting mainly of railway and canal workers, to develop in the region of Widnes Dock. This was the first community of incoming migrants to be established in the area. By 1841, although the population had grown slightly, the overall figure was still relatively low with the census of that year listing just 2209 inhabitants

The St. Helens and Runcorn Gap Railway gave Widnes an important rail link. Although the official opening was not until 1833, the service actually started operating in 1831 for the transit of coal from the collieries at St. Helens to the Dock at Widnes. In 1833 it was estimated that around 600 tons of coal were being transported along that route each day. It has generally been assumed that prior to John Hutchinson's arrival in Widnes in 1847 there was no real industrial development in the area. In fact, this is incorrect as there were already three industrial facilities operating close to the Runcorn Gap Railway as early as 1833. These were described in one report as *"three large establishments for the manufacture of copper, glass and chemicals"*. The report also informed us that these concerns had been built by the side of the railway and that *"other important works were in contemplation"*. Unfortunately, apart from a few vague references, there is no noteworthy documentation to give further information about these establishments. Nevertheless, despite the acknowledged existence of these manufacturing concerns, it was most certainly John Hutchinson and the alkali trade which put Widnes on the industrial map.

Although the canals were an established and reasonably reliable form of transport, the arrival of the railways provided a welcome and

---

[62] Located near Widnes Dock

effective alternative for alkali and other manufacturers. The new St. Helen to Runcorn Gap Railway offered many benefits to local manufacturers as it was a speedier form of transport, especially in bad weather when transport on the canals could be slowed down. When it opened in 1833 its costs also compared favourably with the old canal system so, overall, it was a practical and reasonable option. However, despite running profitably for around 10 years and offering local manufacturers an alternative transport facility at an acceptable cost, by the beginning of 1844 there were plans afoot to change the structure of the company. In March 1844 a special meeting of the proprietors of The Sankey Brook Navigation was held. At that meeting, which was chaired by Mr. Case, it was agreed that the navigation company should be sold to the proprietors of the St. Helens and Runcorn Gap Railway. Following this, a formal merger in 1845 of The Sankey Brook Navigation Company and the Runcorn Gap Railway Company resulted in the St. Helens Canal and Railway Company being formed.

From a commercial point of view the merger of the Canal and Railway Companies was an economically sound amalgamation of two profitable businesses. Alas, for their customers it was not such a welcome development. The merger meant that the new company virtually dominated transport facilities in the area and eliminated competition. Almost immediately, the new company set about planning extensions to their system. In order to raise revenue for this expansion they announced an increase in freight charges on almost everything except coal. The reason for not increasing costs on coal lay in the fact that, originally, the railway company had been financed by St. Helens mine owners who remained major shareholders in the new combined venture. The proposed increase in freight charges was a terrific blow to the St. Helens alkali manufacturers as around ten to twelve tons of raw materials were needed to produce just one ton of alkali by the Leblanc process. The price rise meant that the alkali makers were faced with hugely increased transportation costs which obviously impacted negatively upon their profits.

The story of John Hutchinson's arrival in Widnes in the late 1840s, and the circumstances leading up to it, are well-known and have been documented many times in books by myself and others. However, for the benefit of readers who may not be familiar with the details and reasons which prompted this event, I give an account again here. There is no doubt that the increased freight costs imposed by the newly merged canal and railway company played a significant part in Hutchinson's decision to set up his factory in Widnes. Hutchinson, then a very young man, was employed in the alkali trade in St. Helens and was aware of the detrimental effect additional costs would have on the local industries. He came to the conclusion that Widnes would be a more profitable location for producing alkali. He reasoned that setting up a factory in this area would be more cost effective and convenient for a number of reasons. The railway and extended Sankey Navigational Canal had created an effective route of communication between the Lancashire coal-fields and the Cheshire salt-fields at their convergence at Widnes. This meant that the raw materials required for the alkali process already came together at Widnes. Coal was brought from St. Helens, the salt from Cheshire came via the river Weaver by barge to Runcorn Gap, pyrites imported from Anglesey and Ireland came via the Mersey to Runcorn Gap and the limestone from the North Wales coast came by the same route. So, whilst St. Helens manufacturers were disadvantaged by their location, it was obvious that a works in Widnes, located at the southerly end of the canal, would be more cost-effective as it was geographically better placed to bring in raw materials at a greatly reduced cost.

John Hutchinson did his homework and realised that he could derive several advantages from this location. In addition to the more favourable transportation costs, the fact that Widnes was more sparsely populated meant that there was less likelihood of complaints about atmospheric pollution and the dumping of offensive waste, which were unavoidable by-products of the alkali industry. In St. Helens, manufacturers had been involved in numerous expensive legal actions as a result of complaints from local landowners about the noxious effects of the alkali trade. One prolific and influential complainer was Sir John Gerrard, Lord of the Manor of Windle, who declared that the alkali industry was responsible for killing off trees and hedgerows on his estate. However it was not only the landed gentry who were complaining about the noxious effects of the chemical industry in St. Helens. There were numerous letters to local newspapers from residents who were becoming increasingly alarmed. One correspondent who wrote to the editor of the *Northern Daily Times* regarding the health of the St. Helens population said:

There are nuisances, worse than many suppose, and which the Improvement Commissioners have very unwisely permitted, encouraged, and may I say courted to be allowed I mean the nauseous and poisonous "burning blue waste", the refuse from all the chemical and alkali works of this town. Hundreds of new houses, cottages etc., have been erected upon it, streets raised, railways made, and canal banks raised, and who could have predicted anything else but a fearful scourge, and great desolation to be the consequence. Look at the once crystal brooks, formerly swarming with fish, now one stream of poison, the fogs and vapours rising from which are indeed shameful. Surely, when it has, and continues to turn the copper, silver and gold in the peoples' pockets as they walk the streets, is it not sure to hurt both vegetable and animal life, when we know that it is impregnated with arsenic, muriatic and other strong acids? Some days the appearance of the brooks are orange, others blue, next green, perhaps the following a foamy milky colour. Fertile fields are forever ruined, once grand and majestic trees are now leafless and branchless stumps. Our once good hedges are also laid low, and if these smokes and vapours do these things, can it be wondered that the inhabitants of this town should be so sorrowfully infected, and how may I ask must the more tender crops of the vegetable kingdom be? Nay, there are abundant proofs to show these deadening effects, pages might be filled with horrifying accounts of the dangerous state of this town."

At the time of writing this letter St. Helens was experiencing above average cases of infectious fevers including cholera, typhus and inflammatory fevers. It was estimated that well over 1,200 inhabitants had been infected and were dangerously ill at that time. Of course, most of these diseases were due to bad housing, water borne infections and lack of adequate sanitary provisions. However there is no doubt that some serious pulmonary illnesses were down to the effects of working and living in close proximity to the noxious vapours which were created by the alkali process.

The complaints and fears expressed by residents of St. Helens were numerous and constant. As a consequence of the undeniable pollutions caused by the alkali trade the St. Helens manufacturers were frequently faced with huge claims for compensation. John Hutchinson, as well as considering transport costs, had taken this into account when contemplating setting up his own factory. In Widnes there was cheap land available and any claims for compensation, due to damage caused to crops or trees from the unavoidable escape of hydrochloric acid gas, would be lower because of the nature of the nearby agriculture. He also reasoned that, as it was a sparsely populated rural area, the fumes and effluvia from the alkali process could be distributed without too much complaint. The availability of land meant that there was also plentiful space for the disposal of solid waste (galligu) and the liquid waste could easily be run off into the river. Of course at that time there was little initial understanding of either the medical or environmental implications of pollution on a large scale. Indeed, it took some time for

157

the cumulative effect of pollution to become apparent. Generally, it was considered to be an unpleasant nuisance but not actually harmful.

Before coming to Widnes John Hutchinson had worked as a manager and chemist at the alkali factory owned by Andreas Kurtz[63] in Sutton, St. Helens. His association and employment with Kurtz had come about through his friendship with Andreas' son, Andrew, who had been a fellow student at the Paris Polytechnic School where Hutchinson had studied chemistry. The fact that both families lived in the same area of Liverpool may also have reinforced this friendship. Hutchinson's employment at the Sutton Alkali Works was probably his first experience of industry. It is almost certain that his practical knowledge of alkali manufacture was acquired during the short time he worked there, which was probably for little more than a year. As we have seen, having gained some experience in the trade, by 1847 he was already thinking of striking out on his own. It is quite amazing to think that he was just 22 years of age at that time and yet he was already formulating plans which would have such a lasting effect upon our area and its population[64].

Clearly, he was not slow to recognise the fact that the increased freight charges being imposed by the Canal and Railway Company would have a negative effect on St. Helens industry, therefore, it would be unwise to open his factory in that area. As stated earlier, he did his homework and identified the many convenient advantages which our area presented. Hutchinson was aware that land at Widnes, which was adjacent to both rail and water communications, was available for development and that ample acreage could be secured cheaply. The superb location of this land would ensure that transportation from Widnes would be cost effective and complaints regarding environmental pollution would be negligible.

Obviously we have no way of knowing just how long Hutchinson had been contemplating opening his own factory. However we do know that within a few weeks of the first increase in transport costs he applied for a lease on land at Widnes. As what might be viewed as a twist of fate, this land was the property of the newly merged St. Helens Canal and Railway Company. It was generally believed that this land had originally been set aside for improving their dock facilities and for

---

[63] Andreas Kurtz, the owner of the Sutton Alkali Works, was originally from Reutlingen in southern Germany.

[64] Hutchinson was 22 years old when he set up his works in Widnes around 1847. By 1851 he was employing about 100 men.

providing storage accommodation. It has sometimes been suggested that the newly merged Company only started to release land for other purposes because they began to place more importance upon the railway, to the detriment of the canal. This is not strictly true as, in fact, the Railway Company had been offering surplus land for industrial development since shortly after the opening of the railway and long before the two companies merged. Evidence shows that the Railway Company was offering parcels of land for lease at Widnes as early as 1835. Furthermore, emphasis was given at that time to the suitability of this land for the erection of chemical works. On the 28th January 1836, at an auction held at the Fleece Inn in St. Helens, the Railway Company offered leases on several plots of land at Widnes. These lots were described as an eligible investment for manufacturing chemists, smelters etc. It was claimed that the lots would benefit from:

"The facility of their communication, by Railway with the coal-field of St. Helens, the River Mersey and the Liverpool and Manchester Railway. They could be suitably adapted for the erection of chemical works and smelting houses, or any other places of manufacture in which the cost of fuel is considerable".

From the description of the lots on offer in 1836 we can easily recognise some of the Widnes locations where industry and housing was subsequently developed.

"Lot 1: A field adjoining a house called The Vineyard situated on the west side of the St. Helens and Runcorn Gap Railway, bounded on the north and west by land called Brickhouse Lane, leading to Runcorn Ferry, and on the south by land belonging to Mr. Knowles.

Lot 2: A field called Great Hay, separated from Lot 1 by the Railway, bounded on the north by Brickhouse Lane, and on the south by land belonging to Mr. Knowles, on the east by land belonging to the Trustees of the late Henry Rawson, Esq. and on the west by the Railway.

Lot 3: A field called Little Burdley, situated on the east side of the Railway, bounded on the north by land belonging to Mr. Johnson and on the east and south by Brickhouse Lane.

Lot 4: A field, formerly two fields, situated on west side of the Railway, bounded on the north by land belonging to the Trustees of the late Matthew Gregson, Esq., on the north-west by land belonging to Sir

159

Henry Hoghton, on the south by land belonging to the Trustees of the late Mr. William Ashton and on the west by a land leading to Runcorn Ferry, called Lugsdale's Lane.

Lot 5: A field situated on the east side of the Railway, bounded on the north-east side by land called Page Lane, which separates the said field from the estate of David Bellhouse, Esq., and on the south by land belonging to Mr. Johnson.

Lot 6: A field or piece of land, situated on the east side of the Railway, at the Widnes Incline Plane, bounded on the north and east by land belonging to J.S. Leigh, Esq., and on the south by other land belonging to the Railway Company."

Apart from the Railway Company's holdings, in 1840 there were in the region of 90 landowners in Widnes. Each owner's land was divided into several plots which were occupied by the owner or lessees. In the 1840 Applotment books, or Apportionment records, the number of occupiers of plots was given as 175. Although this number included several persons who owned small acreage, there were also a number of owners who held significant amounts of land throughout the town.

Sir Henry Bold Hoghton, the owner of Bold Hall, owned over 30 plots of land in Widnes which were mainly situated in and around Farnworth village and Lunts Heath. These plots were sublet to persons named Daniel Whitfield; James Abbott; Peter Alcock; Peter Antrobus; Edward Moss; Thomas Howard; John Moss; Alice Punlet; James Rigby and the Rev. William Jeff, the Vicar of Farnworth. William Hurst, another major landowner, was the proprietor of a large area of land in West Bank. Although occupying 80 acres of land in West Bank the entire Hurst landholding extended to over 180 acres and included land situated near Norland's Lane and the junction of Cronton Lane and land at the junction of Norland's Lane and Lowes Lane. The lessee of this land was Ann Rimmer. Joseph Gerrard also owned land in West Bank and his holding was around 37 acres. In other areas of the town David Bellhouse owned over 80 acres, divided into three main plots, which were chiefly occupied by Mr. Bellhouse himself. His principal holdings included land to the east of Tanhouse Lane and Beech Grove; a plot to the north and south of Simms Cross and a further plot facing onto the St. Helens Canal. He also owned several smaller plots, one of which was sited in Farnworth Street which he leased to Peter Bradshaw and another on the northern side of Puzzle Pate (Derby Road), leased to Thomas Shaw who also leased three smaller plots to the west of Chester Lane (Birchfield Road). Among other landowners in the town was Matthew Gregson, who owned around 57 acres north of Tanhouse Lane which was mainly occupied by John Edwardson. A lady named Dorothy Grimson owned and occupied 68 acres to the west of Chester Lane.

Around a decade after the Railway Company had offered parcels of land for auction at The Fleece Hotel in St. Helens, they still had plentiful land available for industrial development in Widnes. So, within a few months of the merged Railway and Canal Company implementing their increased freight costs, John Hutchinson had left The Sutton Alkali Works and successfully acquired a strip of land at Spike Island, between the canal and dock. On 20th November 1848 a draft lease was drawn up by the directors of the St. Helens Canal and Railway Company, giving John Hutchinson a 42 year lease *"with the option of the Company to take it at any time within 21 years on allowing the lessee to remove all buildings, giving in either case 12 months' notice."* An official lease was dated 11th March 1850. On 20th May a further notification indicated that the lease was extended from 42 years and was now to run for a period of 75 years from 31st March 1849 on payment of 2d instead of 1½d per sq. yd. On 13th August 1853 an adjoining plot of land was leased on the same terms. On 11th July 1856 it was agreed to accept 20 years purchase.[65]

Despite the date of the original lease being March 1949 it is supposed that Hutchinson began manufacturing on the site well before that time. Records suggest that he came to Widnes around 1847 and started off in a small way, probably having been allowed a rent free period before formally signing the lease. The most reliable indication of his having come to Widnes in 1847 is taken from the evidence he gave to *The House of Lords Select Committee on Noxious Vapours* on 18th June 1862. During questioning he told the Committee that he had started manufacturing at Widnes in 1847. From those modest beginnings in 1847 he gradually increased his production and by the end of 1853 he was looking to further enlarge his manufacturing capabilities. This resulted in an additional plot of adjacent land being leased on 1st May 1854.

It is generally believed that John McClellan arrived in Widnes around the same time as Hutchinson, or possibly a short time before.

---

[65] Albert Constable notes.

He had previously been in partnership with a man called Holden, operating as Borax manufacturers from premises at 6 Temple Court in Liverpool. However, the partnership with Holden was officially dissolved in July 1846 and it is believed that he came to Widnes shortly after this. After the arrival of Hutchinson and McClellan, other manufacturers began appearing on the scene in fairly quick succession. In 1850 William Gossage opened his works on the opposite side of the canal to Hutchinson. William Gossage was probably one of the greatest inventors of his era and was the architect of several ground-breaking innovations relating to the manufacture of chemicals. He appeared to have a real aptitude for invention and lodged his first patent in 1823 which was for a portable alarum for clocks and watches. After this he began a long series of patents which some people have described as *"a summary of the alkali trade."* Long before he came to Widnes he was already looking at methods of reducing the nuisances caused by the manufacture of alkali. In 1836 he patented his condensing tower, which was designed to dispose of effluvia by absorption in coke therefore producing a by-product of muriatic acid. In 1856 he perfected his process for producing caustic soda. This process was to revolutionise soap-making.

In May 1839 a public notice appeared in a number of national newspapers. The advert was placed by William Gossage who was at that time working at Stoke Prior in Worcestershire where he had started a salt and alkali works in partnership with Jonathan Fardon. The notice was accompanied by a letter from Messrs. Clough of St. Helens, who were alkali manufacturers. Messrs. Clough claimed that the Gossage condensing apparatus, which had lately been installed in their works, had reduced the escape of muriatic gases and enabled them to produce significant amounts of sulphur from residual alkali waste. To support Clough's claim the results were tested by an independent panel who issued a certificate to verify their findings. The certificate was published alongside the Gossage advertisement.

CHEMICAL NUISANCES.

MR. GOSSAGE requests the attention of Alkali Manufacturers to the annexed Documents, which prove that the condensation of Muriatic Acid Gas is perfectly and readily effected by the use of his Apparatus, therefore, that the continuance of any nuisance arising from the discharge of Muriatic Vapour from Alkali Works may be completely prevented.

Mr. GOSSAGE is prepared to grant Licenses, under his Patents, for condensing and using Muriatic Acid, on such terms as will yield great advantages to the Licensees; and he thus offers to the Manufacturers of Alkali an opportunity to make the total suppression of nuisance a source of immediate and continued profit.

Communications to be addressed to Mr. GOSSAGE, Stoke Prior, Bromsgrove.

GOSSAGE ADVERT - MAY 1839

In December 1849 Jonathan Fardon and William Gossage parted company and sold their interests in their British Alkali Works at Stoke Prior. It is believed that the parting was entirely amicable and that Gossage was eager pursue other ventures. Fardon and Gossage had obviously been good employers as, at the time of their departure, both men were presented with silver inkstands by their appreciative workforce. The inkstands were said to be valued at six guineas, the money having been raised by voluntary contributions from the workforce. Each inkstand was inscribed with words which included the following phrase:

> *"In testimony of the sense of the kind and considerate treatment which they evinced on all occasions towards those employed under them."*

At the time of his arrival in Widnes William Gossage was engaged in copper smelting, which he did with only limited success. It was not until 1855 that he turned his attention to the manufacture of the product with which we most readily associate him – soap. In time, the Gossage Soap Works was trading internationally and was to become one of the most important works of its kind in Britain. By the end of the century Gossage was employing in the region of 800 people.

Following on from Gossage, in 1852, Frederic Muspratt arrived in the area and opened his Woodend Works. The following year, after a brief period working for John Hutchinson, Henry Deacon also opened his own works in the town. As these new businesses swiftly developed Widnes soon became a magnet for other would-be alkali manufacturers who recognised the geographical and economic benefits of the area. In what appears to have been a comparatively short space of time the district had become a thriving hub of dense industrial activity, with alkali manufacture at its core.

WILLIAM GOSSAGE

Although there is not a vast amount of reliable historical data available about the early period of alkali manufacture in Widnes, we do know that the industry developed with extraordinary speed due to the achievements of a few exceptional men. As we saw in Runcorn, where the likes of John Johnson and Thomas Hazlehurst played a key role in the town's industrial development, in Widnes also a few remarkable men played their part. As we have observed, John Hutchinson was ostensibly the first to see the potential advantage of establishing a factory in the area and other similar minded men were quick to follow his lead. Their arrival and their subsequent activities were to determine the whole course of our local industrial and commercial advancement.

What is particularly interesting about the mid-Victorian period in Widnes is that the chemical industry offered enormous opportunities for ambitious men of limited resources. Furthermore, it is obvious that the size of their business ventures increased rapidly and dauntingly even though open and unrestrained competition prevailed. Ludwig Mond, when writing to his parents in 1872, gave us some idea of how quickly industry developed in the area even though some manufacturers had little start-up finance.

"Here, where we have some 50 factories in a few square miles, are many factories, some of which have started in a very small way and which deal with only part of the soda manufacturing. There is nowhere in the world where a factory could be set up with such ease and small capital, and where such working power can be found".66

Even though information about many of the early Widnes alkali factories is extremely limited, we are fortunate, with the help of archival material and letters,[67] to be able to piece together a reasonable picture of the development of John Hutchinson's company. From this information we get a brief understanding of Hutchinson's business methods. We can see how quickly he expanded his factory and land holdings. When reading these documents it is obvious that, despite possessing extraordinary business acumen, this talent was coupled with a ruthlessness which did not particularly endear him to others. Nevertheless, the speed with which he developed his company, and the vision which he applied to this, suggests that had he lived longer he would have gone on to achieve even more success. However, perhaps Hutchinson's greatest legacy is to be acknowledged as the founder of the chemical industry in Widnes and subsequently having the title *"The Father of Widnes"* bestowed upon him.

Despite the fact that there is scant information relating to Hutchinson's industrial activities before he came to Widnes, an inventory of his holdings in 1865 states that he owned a one-sixth share in the Cowley Hill Estate in St. Helens, which was valued at £1,500. Unfortunately this document did not reveal the name of the other five shareholders or the date the share was originally acquired. Perhaps this preceded Hutchinson coming to Widnes and may suggest that he had previously planned to produce alkali in St. Helens. Maybe it was simply the increased transportation costs which prevented him from doing so. Of

---

[66]The History of the Chemical Industry in Widnes: (D.W.F. Hardie)
[67] Archival material held by The Catalyst Museum.

course this is only a hypothesis; there is no corroborating evidence so we have no way of actually knowing if this was the case. Hutchinson's share in the Cowley Hill Estate was subsequently sold to the St. Helens industrialist J.C. Gamble in 1867 for £1,670. Mr. Gamble's works at Gerrard's Bridge shared a boundary with the Cowley Hill Estate and one would have supposed that his intention was to extend his works onto this site. However, contrary to expectations, the Cowley Hill land was not developed for industrial use but, instead, it was utilised for residential development, most probably housing Gamble's own workers.

Among the interesting documents relating to Hutchinson's business dealings in Widnes are details of several early land leases with the St. Helens Railway and Canal Company. A lease dated 11th March 1850 cites the two previously mentioned leases dated February and March 1849. These leases refer to land situated between the canal and the dock on the site now known as Spike Island. The lease issued in March 1850 was revised in May that year extending the period of lease from 42 years to 75 years.[68] It is interesting to read the negotiated clauses in these leases, which gave John Hutchinson extensive rights. These included the right to take water from the canal for production purposes; to lay a waste pipe through the St. Helens Railway and Canal Company's land to the river Mersey; to load and unload barges berthed in the Widnes Dock adjacent to the works site; preferential use of a berth in Widnes Dock and permission to construct a branch railway across the Railway and Canal Company's land to connect with the St. Helens and Runcorn Gap Railway.

It is quite clear that John Hutchinson had only limited capital with which to set up his Widnes enterprise and so he started off quite modestly. Circumstantial evidence suggests that he probably began operations in 1847 and it is possible that, initially, his factory was only involved in part of the manufacturing process. At the same time, in order to deal with the commercial side of his business, he set up an office in Liverpool where he leased rooms at 9 Lancaster Building, Tithebarn Street. By a strange coincidence, another John Hutchinson, a cotton broker, was also listed as a tenant in the same building. I do not know if the two men of the same name were connected in any way. By 1850, with his Widnes landholding having gradually increased, the site would then have become large enough to accommodate a full scale

---

[68] Information from the Albert Constable notes, in possession of Catalyst Museum.

alkali plant. At this point one would assume that he would have been able to undertake the complete alkali manufacturing process.

The swift growth and success of Hutchinson's business meant that by 1851 he was able to take on a works manager. The first person to hold that position was a young man called Henry Deacon. It is likely that Hutchinson first became acquainted with Henry Deacon when they both worked in St. Helens. Deacon had previously been employed at the St. Helens glassworks of William Pilkington where he gained distinction by having invented apparatus for grinding and smoothing plate glass. A declaration concerning this invention was dated 17th December 1844. It is evident that Henry Deacon was highly valued at the Pilkington works and quickly rose to the position of chief chemist and engineer. At the time of his leaving he was the highest paid member of staff. One might assume that, in order to lure him away from this well-paid job, John Hutchinson was able to make him a better offer.

Henry Deacon did not reign long at the Hutchinson Works, which is surprising in view of the fact that he had left a lucrative position with Pilkington's to come to Widnes. Some accounts have claimed that there was an *"incompatibility of temperaments"* between Deacon and Hutchinson. However this may not be the only reason for Deacon leaving, as he was very ambitious and probably had not intended to remain *"managing"* someone else's works for too long. We should also remember that many years later Ludwig Mond had said that nowhere else was it possible to set up business with such ease and small capital. This climate of enterprise obviously motivated ambitious young men to try their luck in the alkali trade. Therefore, rather than leaving Hutchinson's employment for reasons of incompatibility, it is quite possible that Deacon only took the position with Hutchinson to gain some practical experience in the alkali trade so that he could go into business for himself. He left Hutchinson after only two years and then, in partnership with his former boss, William Pilkington, opened his own alkali factory in Widnes. Deacon and Pilkington each agreed to advance £3000 to build the Widnes factory. Two years later this partnership was terminated and it would appear that the parting was somewhat acrimonious. When writing to Major James Cross, William Pilkington had said he was *"pleased and relieved...to get rid of such an unsociable, selfish and arrogant fellow as Deacon"*.

HENRY DEACON

We will never know what prompted Mr. Pilkington to have such a negative opinion of Henry Deacon but it could simply be that there was a conflict of personalities or attitude. Deacon was known to have exceptional mechanical and scientific ability, having been a student of the renowned Michael Faraday who was a family friend. Deacon was also deeply spiritual and belonged to a religious group called *The Sandemanians*[69] who practised a simple and literal form of Christianity based on the scriptures. It is possible that, because of his brilliant brain and unusual religious preference, Deacon, through no fault of his own, may have come across as overconfident or antisocial. Nevertheless, for all his faults, real or imagined, he appears to have been a decent man. Indeed, our local history shows that he and his descendants were outstanding in their compassion and benevolence to the poor of this town (a quality few of our early industrialists shared).

---

[69] This sect, also known as *Glassites*, ceased to exist around 1890.

Naturally there has been much speculation about the disagreement between Henry Deacon and William Pilkington, though the real reasons behind this are obscure. There is no doubt that the two men were vastly different in temperament and outlook. Deacon was known to be a perfectionist and an innovator, whilst Pilkington was more business orientated. Some observers suggested that, apart from a possible conflict of personalities, protracted experiments and deferred profits did not suit Pilkington. Whatever the reason, there is no doubt that Pilkington left Deacon in the lurch. He was forced to carry on as best he could until he could raise further capital to continue his work. Fortunately, shortly after his acrimonious parting from William Pilkington, Henry Deacon found a new partner called Holbrook Gaskell. Deacon and Gaskell set up business together in 1855 and the association between them proved to be far more durable and amicable. In fact, they formed what was to become one of the town's leading and long-lasting alkali firms, subsequently known as Gaskell, Deacon and Company. Within six years of forming their partnership Gaskell and Deacon were employing over 180 men at their works, with this number growing considerably in the following years.

Sometime between 1853 and 1854, after the departure of Henry Deacon, John Hutchinson took on a business partner called Oswald Earle. Shortly afterwards the trading name was changed to *"Messrs. Hutchinson & Earle"*. Oswald Earle was the son of Thomas Earle of Hull. The Earle family were known to have considerable interests in shipping and limestone industries in Hull and other parts of the north-east.[70] The timing of this partnership is interesting as John Hutchinson and Oswald Earle had recently become related through marriage. They were brothers-in-law, being married to sisters Elizabeth and Georgina Kynsey, the daughters of an Anglo-Irish doctor from Athy in County Kildare. The marriage of Oswald Earle and Georgina Kynsey had taken place at St. Mary's Church in Dublin in August 1853, not too long before the partnership with Hutchinson occurred. There is no documentary evidence to indicate if Hutchinson and Earle had been friends or business associates before the marriage of Oswald Earle to Hutchinson's sister-in-law. However, as the business partnership was commenced around the time of this marriage, the timing might suggest that Hutchinson may have taken advantage of this connection to persuade Earle to invest in his venture.

---

70 The Earle family were in partnership with the Wilsons (Lord Nunburnholme).

There is no reliable information available as to the exact details of Hutchinson's partnership agreement with Oswald Earle or what capital investment was involved. One would surmise that Earle put a significant amount of money into the Company because Hutchinson, who was extremely shrewd, was unlikely to have taken him on without some major financial contribution. When the partnership was dissolved some years later, apparently with a degree of acrimony, Earle was said to have been *"bought out"* although the money due to him appears to have been paid in several instalments.

During his time with the Hutchinson Company, Oswald Earle had a clearly defined role in the business, his work being confined to sales and shipping activities. There is also evidence to suggest that in addition to the Hutchinson & Earle business he had operated his own commercial agency for a number of other manufacturing enterprises. He was based at the Liverpool office at Lancaster Building in Tithebarn Street, opposite Exchange Street East, where he employed an office manager called Thomas Snape[71]. In later years, when writing of this time, Snape described this building as *"a rabbit warren of small offices owned by Mr. Nathaniel Reyner"*. Although Thomas Snape's career in the alkali trade started in the office of Hutchinson & Earle, many years later he was to enter the Widnes chemical industry on his own account. In 1876 Snape acquired The Phoenix Chemical Works which was located near to West Bank Dock. Thomas Fleetwood had previously owned this factory from around 1866. It is believed that Snape had some business association with Fleetwood prior to his taking over the works in 1876. Regrettably, three years after Snape bought The Phoenix Works it became the scene of a brutal murder. On the 10th March 1879 a 38year old Irishman called Michael Delaney was killed on the premises by two unknown assassins[72].

As trade developed, John Hutchinson acquired an adjacent plot of land in May 1854. The now extended site offered ample room for extra burners, additional acid tanks and for regulus production[73]. The land leases of 1850 and 1854 had provided Hutchinson with sufficient

---

[71] In later years, after selling his business to The United Alkali Company, Thomas Snape became Liberal M.P. for Heywood in Lancashire from 1892-95. He was also an Alderman and Justice of the Peace for the county of Lancashire. He died at his home in Liverpool in August 1919 aged 77 years.

[72] *"Yesterday's People"* (Jean M. Morris – Springfield Farrihy Publishing - 2012)

[73] Regulus is the first stage in copper refining and is produced by a second burning of copper pyrites.

space to construct and expand his No.1 Works.   Thomas Robinson[74], an enterprising iron-founder who owned the Atlas Works in St. Helens, was commissioned to build and equip the new works.   It is thought that Robinson had become acquainted with Hutchinson during his time managing Kurtz's Sutton works.   History shows that Robinson's subsequent involvement with Hutchinson was to have a far-reaching effect on his own business. Recognising the growing needs of our local industries, Robinson decided to set up an iron foundry in Widnes which he ran in addition to his St. Helens Works. This proved to be a smart move and an extremely sound business decision.   Afterwards he became the chief artificer to the Widnes chemical industry.

Thomas Robinson built his first foundry in Widnes at Lugsdale near to the railway line. This foundry was the first of its kind to specialise in making plant for the chemical industry.   However, when Robinson observed the rapidity with which the alkali industry in Widnes was developing he decided to build another, larger, foundry. This was located on a site near an old farmhouse called Brook House, close by Bowers Brook on the east side of the L & N.W. Railway. The new larger foundry was well designed and extremely modern.   It had the added advantage of having the first steam-driven overhead travelling crane for handling the heavy ladles of molten metal. Robinson's new foundry also claimed the distinction of manufacturing the first private locomotive used in Widnes, which was commissioned by John Hutchinson. Over the following years, with the continued expansion of industry in the town, the Robinson business became enormously successful.   In later years, although continuing his primary business as an iron founder, Thomas Robinson also had substantial financial interests and involvement in several local chemical firms.

Hutchinson's No.1 Works was erected quite quickly as in those days factory buildings were mainly constructed in wood, being little more than large sheds.   Although Robinson had constructed and equipped the No.1 Works with great speed it was obviously fit for purpose as over the following years there appeared to be little change or improvements made to the original building or layout. The works were built of wood with pitch pine being used for the saltcake house as this wood was known to be particularly resistant to the effects of muriatic acid. The curved roofs were formed and supported by a lattice of cross members (known as a basket roof) then felted and tarred.   The

---

[74] The works of the Widnes Limestone Company were also equipped by Thomas Robinson.

structures were ventilated by means of a long louvered section which ran along the entire length of the roof. The exception to this form of roofing was in the sheds where chlorate was manufactured. These buildings usually had slate roofs because of a possible fire hazard. In the day, lighting was provided in the buildings by means of side windows positioned high in the walls. At night the factories were illuminated by means of small lamps which burned colza oil, or duck-oil as this was commonly known. This type of lighting was notoriously smelly and smokey, which meant that that the light and atmosphere at night was both inadequate and unpleasant.

The 1854 lease of additional land enabled Hutchinson to sub-lease a plot at the northern end of his site. The sub-lease was granted to the Widnes Limestone Company who agreed, as part of the deal, to supply guaranteed quantities of crushed limestone to Hutchinson at a favourable rate. The leasing of land to the Widnes Limestone Company was a shrewd business move by Hutchinson because another suitable site would have been difficult for them to find and, of course, he was able to get his limestone from them at a reduced price. At the same time, William Gossage was also expanding his soap making activities on the western side of the canal which included the site of an earlier limestone processing works. It has been suggested that Hutchinson and Gossage may have struck a deal whereby Gossage transferred two leases to Hutchinson, which related to land between Gossage's Works and Snig Lane (Waterloo Road). The owners of this land were the trustees of the Wright Estate.

There is an allegation that Hutchinson used a devious and rather unpleasant blackmail tactic to persuade William Gossage to assign the leases to over to him. This was in connection with Gossage's failure to use Hutchinson's alkali waste in soap manufacture as he had previously contracted to do. There are a number of theories regarding the deal between Hutchinson and Gossage and any one of them is a possibility. D.W.F. Hardie, in his *History of the Widnes Chemical Industry,* tells us that Gossage was convinced that he had found a viable way to recover sulphur from alkali waste. As a result, he entered into agreements with several local alkali manufacturers to take their waste in order to recover sulphur from it. Unfortunately, after further experiments, Gossage realised that he had been a tad over optimistic and asked to be released from these agreements. All the manufacturers, with the exception of John Hutchinson, were happy to free the bitterly disappointed Gossage from his contract.

It is said that Hutchinson was uncooperative and adamantly refused to release Gossage from his contract, subsequently using the strip of land as a bargaining tool. However, despite this being the accepted theory it is pointed out by Albert Constable, in his notes about the Hutchinson Company,[75] that there is no evidence to support this statement. He says that, in any event, Gossage would not have needed the land if he was not going to go ahead with the sulphur recovery process. We can also see from area maps that Bower's Brook split Gossage's site from the land he let Hutchinson have. As Hutchinson was unable to expand on his existing site the switch involving the Widnes Limestone Company was probably a satisfactory outcome for all parties. The fact that Hutchinson subsequently culverted Bower's Brook and Bower's Pool may suggest that this was also part of the deal.[76]

As with many historical hypotheses we will never know what is actually true, so one can only make an assumption based on the information that is currently available. Nevertheless, despite numerous modern conjectures, it was generally believed at the time that Hutchinson had been quite ruthless and very unfair in his dealings with William Gossage. This opinion is borne out by a statement, included here, which was published in *The Leamington Spa Courier* on 5th May 1877. The extract is taken from a report of William Gossage's death and although not naming John Hutchinson specifically, it does tell us that the manufacturer in question was responsible for inflicting severe financial damage upon Gossage and his business. In fact, it clearly states that the anonymous manufacturer almost wiped Gossage out. So, despite any attempt or wish to believe otherwise, it would appear that the widely held opinion of those times was that John Hutchinson had behaved in both a shameful and unreasonable manner towards William Gossage. Fortunately Gossage did recover from this serious financial setback and he was able to continue and expand his business considerably over the following years.

The fact that Hutchinson was prepared to let Gossage go to the wall in order to gain some commercial advantage, and to get his own way, was just one example of John Hutchinson's hard-nosed business dealings. There are several other incidents which display a ruthless attitude towards his competitors.   However, in spite of this difficult aspect of his personality, there is no denying that he had a brilliant

---

[75]*Catalyst Archives* – (Albert Constable notes)
[76] Ibid.

talent for being able to recognise potential business opportunities, not only in alkali production but in all manner of other areas. In these cases he grasped the initiative before others could do so.

> In a patent, dated 1837, he proposes to decompose this residue by means of hydrochloric or carbonic acid, and to burn the resulting sulphuretted hydrogen for the production of sulphuric acid, while the carbonate of lime formed was to be employed for purposes connected with the manufacture of alkali in place of ordinary limestone. So certain did the patentee feel of the practical applicability of this principle that, in 1854, after taking out a further patent, he contracted with various alkali manufacturers at Widnes to take from them the whole of their waste for a given number of years to be so treated. This method was not, however, found commercially remunerative, and the contract became a source of great anxiety and loss; for, although, with one exception, all the manufacturers relieved him of his contract to take their waste, one firm refused to do so, and stripped him of nearly all he then possessed as an equivalent for non-fulfilment of his undertaking.

THE LEAMINGTON SPA COURIER – 5TH MAY 1866.

In 1861 Hutchinson and Earle decided to dissolve their partnership and evidence suggests that the parting was somewhat acrimonious. There is no documented reason available to indicate what prompted this split. Maybe it was simply a consequence of a precarious financial situation and rising debts. Despite the fact that some historians have recorded 1861 as being the date of the end of the partnership, records show that it was not officially terminated till January 1863. Although it was not until 31st December 1864 that the financial matters of the partnership were brought to a satisfactory conclusion. A week earlier, on Christmas Eve, Hutchinson had written to Earle to inform him that he would be able to pay him the last instalment of the partnership money on 31st December. The sum involved was £1800. The parting appears to have caused some bitterness which was unfortunate in view of their family connections. Hutchinson had said in his letter to Earle that *"he hoped that any unpleasant recollections connected with the partnership would be buried in the past"*. Subsequently, Oswald Earle, who was then living in Seaforth, opened his own shipping office at 11 Old Hall Street in Liverpool and for a short while afterwards the Hutchinson Company used him as their agent[77].

Oswald Earle was to experience mixed fortunes in the years following his split from Hutchinson. In August 1861 he was granted a patent for an improved lubricating compound. At the time the patent was issued he was described as a chemical manufacturer and his business address was given as Old Hall Street. In the autumn of 1865 he became involved in a new chemical venture at St. Helens. In partnership with three others, Henry P. Grayson, J. W. Williams and L. B. Armstrong, he took over an existing alkali factory at Pocket Nook which had previously been owned by William Henry Balmain. Mr. Balmain had operated this factory successfully since 1852 but, like many other manufacturers of that era, he had increased his capacity enormously and in doing so had overstretched his financial resources. As a consequence he was heavily in debt and his factory was mortgaged to the hilt. Unsurprisingly, Balmain was declared bankrupt in 1865 and his factory was taken over at the beginning of 1866 by Oswald Earle and his associates, who were to trade under the name of The St. Helens Chemical Company. In their prospectus they stated that they would have a working capital of £50,000 and were offering 5000 shares in the Company at £10 each. Their offices were to be based at Victoria Chambers in St. Helens and at 11, Harrington Street, Liverpool.

Shortly before becoming involved with the St. Helens Chemical Company, Earle and his wife Georgina suffered a dreadful personal tragedy. In the autumn of 1865 they were dealt a serious blow when their twin daughters died within weeks of each other. Blanche died on September 10th and her twin sister, Ann Edith, passed away at their home in Seaforth a short time later on 20th October. One cannot imagine the grief this double loss created. However, Earle continued to devote as much time as possible to his commercial activities. Records show that, apart from the St. Helens venture, Earle continued with his own independent business in Liverpool. In 1869 he was sued for breach of contract by a Mr. George Curzon Dobell. Earle was the sole named defendant in this case and is described as a Liverpool chemical manufacturer, which indicates that he was operating this particular

---

[77] He later traded as a general merchant in Liverpool. He died in June 1873.

business on his own account. The case involved the sale of "Redenda Guano", (artificial manure), to Mr. Dobell. The product had been advertised as containing a high level of phosphate of lime but on analysis this was found to be well below the level expected. Mr. Dobell was awarded damages of £400.

Unfortunately Oswald Earle was to follow a route which many of the early manufacturers found themselves upon, the road to the Bankruptcy Court. On 15th November 1871 a report in *The Liverpool Mercury* contained the following information:

"Yesterday, before Mr. Registrar Watson, a meeting of creditors was held under the failure of Mr. Oswald Earle of Old Hall Street, merchant. The unsecured debts are £2645 those fully secured are £6323. The assets are - debts, £100; furniture, £306; and surplus of securities in the hands of creditors, £242. Debts amounting to £900 were proved, and Mr. Bolland chosen Trustee, with Mr. G.C. Dobell and Mr. Ernest Dronks as a committee of inspection."

In view of their earlier court case it would seem a trifle unfortunate for Oswald Earle that Mr. George C. Dobell was part of the inspection committee. Some months later Earle was able to pick up the pieces and, having settled many of his debts, the bankruptcy order was annulled in August the following year. Sadly, just nineteen months after first being declared bankrupt, Oswald Earle passed away on 13th June 1873. As we have seen, his career in the chemical trade had been one of mixed alliances and fortunes which resulted in varying degrees of success and failure. Nevertheless, his brief association with Widnes was during an important time in the development of industry in our town. It is fitting that his connection to that episode is remembered by a street that still bears his name.

By 1861 John Hutchinson was the largest employer in the district with around 600 workmen on his payroll. Although 1861 had seen the departure of Oswald Earle from the Hutchinson Company, that year witnessed the arrival of John Brunner. Brunner, who was only nineteen years old at that time, had previously been employed as a clerk with a Liverpool shipping agency. It has been claimed that he had been made redundant from this post because of a fall in business due to the civil war in America. However, as this was at the very start of the American Civil War one wonders if this statement is accurate.

When John Brunner commenced employment at the Hutchinson works his brother, Henry, who had trained in chemistry in Zurich, was already employed by Hutchinson as chief chemist and process manager. In fact, young John Brunner would have felt immediately at ease in his new workplace as Richard Powell, who was employed in a senior role by Hutchinson, was also known to him.   Powell had been a former pupil at the school run by the Brunners' father[78] in Everton. Evidently John Brunner settled into his new role quite well and by 1862 he was being described as the chief clerk of the Hutchinson Company. Prior to that time most of the official company work was undertaken by Hutchinson's private clerk from an office he had set up at his home in Appleton Lodge. After this date all company business was carried out by Brunner and conducted from the works premises, although Hutchinson still maintained an office and clerk at Appleton Lodge to deal with his personal affairs.

As we have seen, John Hutchinson was always one step ahead of the game and his flair for spotting business opportunities was almost without equal. One example of this was related to the construction industry and illustrates his resourceful and clever attitude towards profit and enterprise. Obviously, with rapid development in local building, both of houses and factories, there was a constant need for bricks. By 1858 there were also outline plans to construct a railway bridge across the River Mersey and this, with its associated viaducts, would also require large quantities of bricks.   In response to this, Hutchinson sent several boatloads of local clay to a London brickmaking machine manufacturer for analysis. The clay required processing to remove the stones found in it, which was a feature common to all the local clay. After the clay had been tested for suitability, Hutchinson set up his own brickworks.   On 8th February 1863 the Hutchinson accounts show entries relating to the purchase of three *"process brickmaking machines and associated equipment"*.   However, entries elsewhere in the accounts show that the machines were in use well before that date. Hutchinson eventually sold his brickworks to Mr. Thomas Brassey who, in partnership with a Mr. Ogilvie, was involved in the construction of the railway bridge over the Mersey and the associated viaducts. A royalty was paid to Hutchinson for the clay used. The brickworks, which had continued to trade as John Hutchinson Ltd.,

---

[78] The Brunner family had come to this country from Switzerland in 1832 and their father, John Brunner Senior ran a school in Everton.

closed down after the viaducts were completed. It was estimated that they had supplied some 18 million bricks for this project.

In addition to providing bricks from local clay, Hutchinson also utilised his alkali waste for building purposes. Some of the waste was found to be useful in the construction of local railway embankments or for levelling the ground on which houses were to be erected. In fact much of the very early alkali waste, both in Widnes and St. Helens, did not get dumped onto tips but was used for ground preparation prior to building. There is no way of knowing exactly how much of this waste was used or where it was used. It is generally acknowledged that many local dwellings, particularly properties in the West Bank area, were built on levelled waste tips. It is also known that several local churches, including the old St. Mary's Church in Waterloo Road and St. Ambrose Church in Halton View, were among those built on a ground base of alkali waste. Both these buildings were to experience problems with their foundations at a later date.

Almost all of our local manufacturers borrowed heavily to finance their new factories and then borrowed further amounts to expand their premises and manufacturing capacities. Of course they were not alone as most business dealings in those days relied heavily on borrowing excessive amounts of money to fund and expand commercial ventures. This was an age of enterprise and the fact was that capital was, and had always been, the parent of all progress. Britain was still in the process of radical change as manufacturing industry developed and grew while agriculture declined drastically. Because of this alteration, the financial institutions had started to restructure themselves to cater for the needs of an industrial based economy instead of an agricultural one. This new industrial economy was established on a network of credit, finance and business deals. However, it would seem that the more complex the framework of business the greater the possibility and scope for sharp dealings. Unfortunately, during this period of expanding enterprise, many a small thrifty investor was ruined by financial speculation and businesses often went to the wall because of heavy borrowing and debt.

John Hutchinson was extremely proficient in borrowing money and was a self-confessed master of persuasion when it came to finances. It is claimed that he often advised his fellow manufacturers in the art of obtaining money. When Brunner and Mond needed to raise the then enormous sum of £26,000 for the purchase of Winnington Hall in Cheshire, Brunner is said to have remarked to Mond that *"We could easily borrow upon it, after Hutchinson's fashion, who as we know was an expert borrower* "[79]. It is quite clear that most of John Hutchinson's business activities stretched his own resources to the limit. It is also interesting to note, when writing about other local industrialists of that era, that whilst some of them did become spectacularly wealthy others died leaving relatively little capital and their estates were burdened by huge debts. In the case of Brunner and Mond, they used up all their personal savings to buy Winnington Hall but were also able to persuade Mr. Charles Holland to supply the bulk of the remaining investment capital for their venture. As we now know, their business enterprise was to be hugely successful and Mr. Holland was handsomely rewarded for the confidence he showed in them and their project.

John Hutchinson is generally credited with bringing the first significant manufacture of alkali to Widnes. Therefore we have to acknowledge the important role he played in the industrial development of the town. However, whilst there is no doubt that Hutchinson was endowed with vision, skill and business acumen, he was by no means a technological innovator like his fellow industrialists William Gossage and Henry Deacon. In fact, it is widely acknowledged that William Gossage was probably the greatest inventor in chemicals of his generation. On the other hand, Hutchinson had many other attributes which enabled him to build up a significant company in the town; not least of these was his shrewd and sometimes ruthless business ability. Of course, in those days, ruthlessness in matters of business was by no means unusual and was often looked upon as an admirable quality rather than a shortcoming. So, like the Johnsons in Runcorn, Hutchinson displayed a rather hard-nosed attitude both to his business dealings and towards his workforce.

When we examine the roles of our early manufacturers, in both towns, we should acknowledge not only their commercial abilities and their part in developing our areas but also the difficult tasks they were required to perform. We should remember that in the early days the new industrial entrepreneur needed to be able to turn his hand to every aspect of business. He had to design and set up his plant, engage and train his workforce, organise all the various stages of production and handle the day to day finances as well as act as salesman and market analyst. The manufacturer was essentially the practical force which initiated the economic cycle. He conceived the ends, found the means,

---

[79] Ibid.

bore the burden of risk and paid out the other factors of production. Of course things did not always go to plan, and it is probable that some of our early local industrialists were disheartened when the return of a profit from their endeavours did not meet their expectations. As the profit was generally fixed by a competitive market, this meant that profit had a natural tendency to fall with fluctuating manufacturing costs or over production. Obviously, in the case of the local alkali trade, as more and more factories opened there was more competition for business. Nevertheless the manufacturers were the lynchpin of local society and, although labour was the source of all wealth, we should remember that it was capital and entrepreneurship which moved it forward and set it in operation.

All of our new industrialists were extremely hardworking and ambitious men who, quickened by the spirit of the times, took advantage of every opportunity available to them. History shows that some of our early manufacturers had brilliant creative talents while others were simply men of vision with good commercial skills. We have seen that not all manufacturers were evenly endowed with talent, skill, application, honesty or success. As I have previously stated, some were technical inventors like Gossage and Deacon, whilst others were just highly competent businessmen like John Hutchinson. Nevertheless, whatever their manner of participation or the level or nature of their abilities, the foundations of the Widnes chemical trade were laid down by men of this ilk, both the businessmen and the innovators. It was a very potent mix, and because of this powerful combination of talent and vision the town rapidly developed into a scene of vigorous industrial activity and fertile invention. Of course, the unfortunate downside was that the area also expanded into an ugly agglomeration of factories and densely packed housing.

Not surprisingly, the development of our alkali industry attracted workers from the length and breadth of the land. Most of these had come from rural backgrounds; therefore the new factory system which brought these men and their families into our town was a sharp contrast to their previous work and their established way of life. Because of the acute change, this novice and expanding workforce was faced with almost insurmountable problems associated with the process of industrialisation and urbanisation. The rhythms of the seasons were replaced by the rhythm of furnaces and shovels and fresh air was exchanged for smoke and fumes. These country dwellers now found themselves gathered together and organised in an unfamiliar systematic fashion which was ruled by work patterns and timetables. The age old division between the master and the worker had become more recognisable and heightened and, in addition, industrial relations were formalised by legally enforceable rules and laws.

The changes for the new inhabitants of our town were extreme on every level. Not only were their working patterns changed from a system where their occupations had relied on seasonal demands and the tempo of the countryside, they were also residing in an unfamiliar environment of concentrated housing and overcrowding. They had been thrust into the midst of great acreages of new bricks and mortar which had been thrown up rapidly by speculators for instant profit. To add to this scene, the town was full of mixed and teeming life which consisted of a multitude of people from different cultures, ethnicities and creeds. All these elements presented the potential to create great divisions and frictions in society. To make matters worse, in the early days there was no formal infrastructure to generate the rudiments necessary to provide a healthy environment or civilised social life for the bulk of the population.

I have previously stressed that the experiences of our towns were not unique as most of the nation's workers and the country's landscape were undergoing similar patterns of adjustment at that time. Change, in a variety of ways, also affected the indigenous populations in the areas where industry had developed. In fact environmental changes, as well as drastic changes in the structure of society, touched all areas of life. One cannot imagine how people, both incomers and native communities, coped with the extreme changes that had been forced upon them. An interesting view regarding the composition of early industrial workforces in Victorian England is expressed by A. Redford in his book about *Labour Migration in England*. He says that factory work in the early period might be described as casual employment for itinerant labour. He also says:

"..all the scanty evidence confirms the migratory and disreputable character of the early factory population and the reluctance of the settled population to enter factory life".[80]

We are able to accept the accuracy of this final statement as census data confirms that in the early days of our industrialisation very few of the native working population were employed in the new chemical

---

[80]*Labour Migration in England* – A. Redford (Manchester 1964)

factories. It would seem that the indigenous workforce was immune to the attraction of factory work and unwilling to abandon their time-honoured way of life. Even the promise of regular work was not sufficient to prise men loose from their traditional occupational anchorage. Even later, as industry became more established, relatively few of the young men from the northern parts of the town left their ancestral trades to undertake factory work. Those that did so usually had a certain degree of competence in manufacturing, even though the end product was entirely different. They had been trained in their fathers' workshops in the old craft centres of Cronton, Appleton, Upton and Farnworth and were therefore disciplined in the principles of routine work patterns. Because of this experience, and the practical expertise acquired in their previous occupations, these young men were able to enter the chemical factories as semi-skilled workers. Of course, after 1871 there *was* a general movement of Widnes born men into the chemical trade. This subsequent departure from their old occupations was the result of a general decline in the old traditional crafts which were once prevalent in the area, especially canvas weaving. The deterioration of this trade was a natural consequence of the change from sailing ships to steamships.

In reality, by the late 1850s some sailcloth manufacturers were already selling off their workshops. Although some of these factories continued to operate under new owners it is clear that this trade was declining. Thomas Shaw's factory in Farnworth was put up for auction in 1857. The text of the advert is reproduced here. It gives us an idea of the extent of Mr. Shaw's property holdings in the village of Farnworth. However we have no way of knowing if this sale was prompted by a general deterioration of the sailcloth business or if it was due to the retirement or death of the owner.

"Important and valuable property, in the village of Farnworth for Auction on Monday 21ˢᵗ instant, at five o'clock in the evening, at The Ring-of-Bells, Farnworth in the County of Lancaster.
ALL that capital MESSUAGE or DWELLING HOUSE, situate in Farnworth aforesaid, on the north side of the public highway from Hale and Cronton to the town of Warrington, with the garden, coach-house and other outbuildings thereto belonging, now in the possession of Mr. Thomas Shaw. Also the FOUR DWELLING HOUSES adjoining, in the occupation of Mrs Mills, Charles Goolden, Michael Cooke and Edmund Wilde. Likewise, THREE FACTORIES in the rear of the said messuage or dwelling houses, and wherein an extensive sailcloth business has for many years been carried on by the late proprietor.

The house is replete with every convenience and well adapted for the residence of a respectable family. The factories may, at little expense, be rendered applicable to any other trade or manufacturing business. The property is freehold of inheritance, in good repair, and well worthy of attention of sailcloth makers and manufacturers, being within a short distance of the St. Helens and Garston railway, and only five miles of the respective towns of Warrington, Prescot and St. Helens. Early possession may be had."

The arrival of the chemical industry and other influences meant that there was an inevitable decline in the old traditional crafts that had once been prevalent in the area. However, some old occupations such as boat-building were given a new lease of life. Rather than dwindling, this trade received a boost as a result of expanding industry. Although Widnes never achieved the volume or reputation of the Runcorn shipyards, nevertheless, there were several profitable boat-building concerns in Widnes between 1860 and 1890. Samuel Stock, William Cooper, Edward Gandy and William Jamieson were the primary Widnes builders during that period. The revitalisation of boat-building was due in no small way to the new chemical trade in the area; this had created a strong demand for flat bottom barges to transport raw materials and products. Most of these barges were built locally and were specifically designed to navigate the local canals and the shallows of the River Mersey.

Despite the fact that the flats were primarily intended for canal and river passages, many of them did travel much further afield and were involved in coastal trade around Britain, including the Isle of Man and Ireland. In fact, some flats even made longer sea voyages. In order to do this they were converted into schooners but were dangerously unstable in bad weather due to having so much extra canvas. Unfortunately the loss of flats seemed to be a fairly regular occurrence. There are countless reports of flats being sunk both in local waters and much further away. Although the flats owned and built by Coopers at Widnes were extremely high on the list of casualties, other companies also had significant levels of loss. One local vessel, reputedly the largest boat ever to be built at Widnes, was wrecked off the coast of Rio Grande do Sol in Brazil on 26th September 1884. This was a 172 ton vessel named *"Janie"* which was constructed at the Widnes shipyard of Samuel Stock in 1875.

When we study employment statistics it is interesting to note that from the 1870s onward there was a significant change in the occupational structure in several areas of the town. Prior to that date there was still a mixture of old and new industries. Initially, the canvas factories and the small workshops which produced tools and watch parts carried on their work alongside the new alkali factories. Nevertheless, things were changing and all these occupations eventually became victims of technological progress. By the mid-1880s canvas weaving was declining and the outworking system of watch manufacture became redundant as more modern methods of manufacture were introduced. In 1889 some local watch-part makers closed their own workshops and joined in a co-operative venture by opening a small factory to produce complete watches. This business enterprise did manage to run successfully for a number of years but due to diminishing trade it was forced to close within twenty years of opening. The toolmakers coped much better, some having successfully made the transition to making miscellaneous types of small tools for the chemical trade and other emerging industries. In fact, toolmakers were still in evidence in the Cronton area as late as the 1940s. Trade directories show that up until that period Frederick, Thomas, and James Glover were still working from premises in and around Hall Lane; John France, John Sparks and Thomas Manifold were working in Chapel Lane; Joseph Anders in Smithy Lane and John Brimelow at Pex Hill. One toolmaker, Joseph Anders, was still in business as late as 1945.

Although there were a few notable exceptions, many of our local employers were quite harsh in their dealings with their workforces. Most workers were bound by contractual obligations, making it impossible for a worker to leave his employment without the agreement of his employer. *The British Master and Servant Law of 1823* was just one of a number of draconian labour disciplines which had been introduced in the wake of the Industrial Revolution. It would appear that the purpose of this unfair law was to impose a new industrial work ethic. Interestingly, there were no real restrictions applied to the employer who could sack a man as and when he pleased, even without good reasons for doing so. In fact, in most cases employers were free to break their contract without any penalties, sometimes they received a small fine but this was the exception rather than the rule. Amazingly, the law which imposed such dreadful penalties upon workers for petty violations was considered by some employers to be too lenient.

In 1844 there was an attempt to insert a clause into *The Master and Servant Act* which would involve use of the treadmill as part of the punishment. The clause also sought permission which would mean that an employer, or his foreman, could bring an action against any workman or female employee without the need for substantiating evidence. Fortunately, there was a huge outcry amongst the more liberal members of parliament and the Bill to insert this clause was defeated. A description of the clause was given thus:

"By this clause all persons engaged to do any work – joiners, shoemakers, milliners, domestic servants, manual labourers, &c., may be made liable to imprisonment and the treadmill, on the single and unsupported oath of an employer, or his foreman or agent."

The Master and Servant code which punished the workforce for petty infringements was just the tip of the iceberg. When one explores living and working conditions in the Victorian era it is plain to see that a common strand of hypocrisy and double standards ran through many areas of daily life. The rules and laws which were imposed upon workers were draconian to say the least, whilst, at the same time, the employers` behaviour was completely unregulated.

To be fair, the harsh attitude displayed towards the workforce by some manufacturers should perhaps be viewed in the context of the times. Obviously there were great difficulties of adjustments for workers and manufacturers alike. The workers, who were new to factory regulation, and the factory owner needing to impose a work ethic on an inexperienced workforce, were both struggling to cope with the new system. This resulted in a regime being established in which factories were ruled by strict regulations. Of course, in practical terms, factory owners needed to enforce firm factory discipline on a workforce that was often unwilling to conform to the new routines. On the other hand, despite manufacturers imposing rules and procedures in the workplace to enhance productivity, the welfare and physical safety of their workers came very low down on employers` lists of priorities. Although chemical work was an inherently hazardous business some manufacturers were seemingly indifferent to issues of safety or welfare. This meant that accidents were a regular occurrence and countless workers paid the ultimate price. For the employer, who had a capital investment in the venture, profit was of paramount importance with the worker generally viewed as a hireable and expendable commodity. A grave lack of concern, or interest in safety or working conditions, was the inevitable result of that perspective.

Apart from ruthless conduct and indifference towards their employees, some local manufacturers were also extremely hard-nosed in their business transactions. There is absolutely no doubt that some of their dubious business dealings and the attitudes displayed towards their employees would be totally abhorrent to us today. On the other hand, we should remember that the mind-set in Victorian times was vastly different. Many years ago I attended an interesting lecture about nineteenth century business ethics and the problems relating to historical interpretation. I came to the conclusion that it is impossible to apply modern standards to the type of behaviour that in Victorian times was acceptable; though today that behaviour would be viewed as unreasonable, unethical or downright illegal. Although difficult, one has to try to judge the actions of Victorian industrialists and entrepreneurs in terms of the values which were current at that time. There is no doubt that some of our Victorian manufacturers were gentlemen whose word was their bond and who exhibited truly noble and Christian characteristics. However some could be viewed as archetypical hypocrites. These were the men who went to Church each Sunday yet spent the next six days exploiting their employees and trying to outdo their business rivals, or boost profits, by whatever means were necessary – no matter how underhand or cruel. Whilst John Hutchinson could almost fall into the second category, the only difference was that he rarely went to Church!

In that era of enterprise and industrial development sharp practice in business dealings was widespread. Over the past years I have written several books about Victorian Widnes. While researching for these works I have been particularly shocked by the scale of fraudulent crime which was present both locally and nationally at that time. In fact we have only to look at the tremendous increase in the representation of fraudulent behaviour in the literature of that period to see that this type of crime was commonplace. As stated earlier, Charles Dickens based several of his works around cases of fraud and stories of this nature also appeared in newspaper reports and parliamentary debates of that time. This would indicate that fraud was present in a variety of situations. Some local crime of this type was committed by people in positions of responsibility who were highly respected in the town. Many of these fraudsters held public purse-strings and abused the great trust that had been placed in them by the leaders of our community. Other crime included insurance fraud, and as this was a period of speculative mania, speculative investment fraud by businessmen was fairly common. Of course there are countless incidents where technically the law was not actually broken but, nevertheless, a degree of dishonesty and corruption was obviously present. A town like Widnes, with new factories and businesses starting up, was clearly ripe for unscrupulous dealings. However, I am not suggesting that this went on to any significant degree but merely pointing out the huge opportunities that were present for this type of activity.

Obviously the concepts of business morality and ethics are loaded with complications. It is only to be expected that, in a highly competitive environment, business is about coming out on top in a struggle for existence. Distinguishing between shrewd, sharp and unethical business practice is not easy. However, it is interesting to see how far some businessmen thought it acceptable to go in pursuit of profit. While successful men like Deacon and Muspratt were generally judged to be reasonably considerate employers, John Hutchinson was, without doubt, a sharp-witted and tough operator. Although there is much to admire in his entrepreneurial skills, there was a strain of ruthlessness present in much of his business and personal dealings which, to me, seem rather distasteful. His treatment of workers could be regarded as particularly callous at times. In one instance, following an attack on one of his foremen, supposedly carried out by three Irishmen, he sacked every Irishman in his employment. Of course, as a great percentage of the working population of the town were Irish most of these men, who were totally innocent of any wrongdoing, were reinstated a few weeks later. However, their blameless families had suffered great economic hardship in the intervening period. Despite this, I did find several reports of works outings and excursions and indications that many workers held him in high regard. A report in the 30th July 1859 edition of *The Warrington Guardian* gives an account of the annual works outing organised for the employees of the Hutchinson & Earle Company.

"ANNUAL HOLIDAY AND EXCURSION"

On Saturday last the employees of the extensive alkali works of Hutchinson & Earle, through the liberality of their employers, enjoyed their annual holiday and excursion. The passenger steamer "MANCHESTER" was chartered for the day and placed at the disposal of the excursionists. At an early hour in the morning the excursionists to a number of 450 employees boarded the steamer and it proceeded to Eastham. A field had been hired and the men sat on a grassy bank to partake of their plentiful breakfast. It was a source of hearty enjoyment, reminding one of the primitive and substantial nature of a baronial breakfast of medieval times. After this activities took place on the field, including: Wrestling; Daring Leaps; Racing; Rounders; Dancing. Some wandered amongst the trees.

At noon the men had another substantial replete and when "The Health and Prosperity of the Firm" had been toasted with vociferous cheering, the men re-embarked for a trip down the river. John Hutchinson and Oswald Earle embarked at the great landing stage. They received a most enthusiastic welcome from the men and the loudest strains from the band. John Hutchinson before leaving addressed the men with congratulations, assuring them of his cordial sympathy with their interests and a desire to promote their welfare in every way.

The steamer then went downstream around the man-o-war ships stationed in the river, the men saluting each other with good old English Cheer. As it continued homeward the amusements continued so far as the limits of the ship permitted in a most splendid manner. The health of "the clerks and foremen of the works, coupled with the names of Kellett and Powell" were reciprocated by the toast of "the clerks and staff of the Liverpool office, coupled with the name of Mr. Snape". Toasts were interrupted by songs. Many in vocal power of artistic character. The steamer arrived back at 5.00 p.m. The men who could not go because of the exigencies of the works received an extra days pay."

From this account it would seem that many of his workers had a high opinion of him. There was also a significant presence of workers at his funeral which means that some of his workforce genuinely mourned his passing. I found several other examples of local firms organising annual outings for their workers. On these occasions it seemed to be traditional for employees to cheer the management at the end of an enjoyable day. Nevertheless, I am sure that many would agree that one day of pleasure does not adequately compensate for 364 days of indifference, coupled with low wages and gruelling working conditions. However, as I pointed out earlier, there is a danger in applying modern interpretation to past conduct. It is quite impossible to employ the values of our modern age to that of the past; so it may be grossly unfair of me to judge the actions and attitudes of John Hutchinson and other employers by the standards of today. However, I suspect that all historical accounts contain either implicit or explicit moral judgements and this work is probably no exception.

As we have seen, there was an extremely high level of borrowing among industrialists at that time which often resulted in financial problems or complete ruin. Unfortunately, it was not only the manufacturers who suffered financially when a company faced difficulties. Usually, the key action to avoid going to the wall was to cut production costs. This often meant that the wage bill was the first expenditure to be trimmed down, either by laying men off or drastically cutting their wages. This created a climate of uncertainty and insecurity among a concentrated mass of wage-earners who had no natural protection to turn to in times of economic distress or instability in employment. Therefore, in trade slumps, it was inevitable that financial distress was more concentrated and more visible in newly developed towns where there had been a large influx of workers. Furthermore, unemployment and the inescapable poverty associated with it, created additional social problems. There is evidence to show that crime swelled to a peak in every economic slump. It is certainly no secret that Widnes, from the middle of the nineteenth century, was plagued by poverty and violent crime. Despite unemployment or inadequate wages being the obvious causes of poverty, the common belief amongst the middle-classes was that poverty was a moral and individual problem rather than a social and economic one.

When contemplating the negative social effects of the alkali trade, which were appalling, we should also consider the effect of the chemical trade on the environment. The degradation of large areas under fumes, effluents and tips shocked observers both locally and nationally. However, the chemical trade was enormously successful and after 1850 vast amounts of alkali was being exported abroad. Because of this, and an increasing sense of importance of chemicals to modern industry, official criticism was usually fairly subdued. Even so, when the environmental damage caused by the alkali trade became so obvious in Widnes and St. Helens, as well as in Glasgow and Tyneside, the Government was obliged to take steps to manage the problem. In 1864 an Alkali Act was introduced. This was the first of several Acts which would be established to make provision for the

189

control of chemical nuisances, with the aid of an inspectorate.	It should be noted that all these Acts were designed to lessen the effects of the trade on the environment. In fact none of the early Acts examined the effects of alkali production upon the workforce or local communities.

Despite the introduction of Alkali Acts and the endeavours of an Alkali Inspector, the complaints regarding atmospheric pollution increased rather than abated as industry expanded.	The effect of industry on the health of the population, as well as bad working conditions and the high number of workplace accidents, had all become serious causes of concern.	In some manufacturing towns local authorities brought in their own by-laws which sought to lessen the damaging effect upon the environment.	However, these by-laws were a weak weapon in the face of the might of industrial development, especially when local authorities themselves were generally composed of industrialists, as was the case in Widnes.	Therefore, because of the lack of firm action to penalise the offending companies, the impact of insidious industrial blight and pollution was accepted almost as a force of nature and areas continued to be plagued by acrid smoke and poisonous gases.

During 1878 a further report was presented to both Houses of Parliament by members of a *Royal Commission Inquiry on Noxious Vapours*. This Inquiry followed a deputation by Lancashire landowners who had solicited the aid of Lord Derby to speak in Parliament on their behalf. It was hoped and expected that stronger legislation would be brought in to compel manufacturers to clean up their act.	Among the local manufacturers called before the Commission were Major James Cross, representing Widnes manufacturers; Mr. Gamble from St Helens; Mr. Wigg from Runcorn and Mr. Muspratt who was then operating in Flint.	The published findings of the Inquiry included the following summary:

"That alkali manufacture is injurious to health; that it is demoralising to those engaged in it; and that it destroys the picturesque and agricultural value of property in its neighbourhood"

In July that same year Sir Richard Brooke had brought a legal action for damages against Charles Wigg. The case was heard in the High Court of Chancery in London.	Sir Richard claimed that land and vegetation on his estate at Norton Priory had been damaged as a result of the effluvia and gases from Mr. Wigg's works.	The extensive demesne consisted of an area of around 5500 acres which, apart from the magnificent structure known as Norton Priory, included the home farm, parks, plantation gardens and pleasure grounds. It was alleged that the timber and fruit trees on the estate had been completely destroyed and, in addition, cattle could not be kept on farms because of the state of the grass in the fields, which had been poisoned by chemical pollution. Sir Richard told the court that the rents of the farms on the parts of the estate near to Wigg's works had steadily diminished. Charles Wigg contested these claims, saying that the Widnes chemical works were mainly responsible. Both parties produced a large number of eminent scientific witnesses to reinforce their cases. However, the court found in favour of Sir Richard Brooke and Charles Wigg was ordered to pay compensation for the damaged trees and loss of farm rents.

Cases such as this strengthened the resolve of members of *The Royal Commission Inquiry* to introduce additional legislation to force manufacturers to reduce pollution. Naturally manufacturers were apprehensive about any new legislation being brought in, as any modifications to plant or processes were likely to be expensive or detrimental to production schedules. At the end of the year, in December 1878, there were many conflicting letters to *The Times* from landowners and manufacturers alike. Amongst these was one from Edward Sullivan, the owner of a Widnes alkali factory based at Moss Bank. Although many of the points he raises are predictable and biased in favour of manufacturers, nevertheless, some of his arguments, particularly those regarding the hypocrisy of landowners, are quite valid. This edited extract from Mr. Sullivan's letter gives an indication of his position:

"The indictment of the deputation of Lancashire landowners against the alkali manufacturers, as recently stated by Lord Derby, would be damning indeed and would more than justify your most powerful advocacy if there was nothing to be said on the other side; but I think that those who take the trouble to read the "Report of the Royal Commission on Noxious Vapours" will allow that there is something to be said on the other side, and that it is possible to paint the devil even blacker than he really is.

As regards the work being injurious to health and demoralising to those employed in it, the report states at page 7 "The manufacturers speak uniformly as to the good health of their workmen". Dr. Richardson, who has paid especial attention to this subject, was unable to discover any evidence which showed to him proof of special deterioration of health. It may be added that the work as a rule is free from all danger;

191

accidents of any kind are very rare, and these only of a trivial kind. Alkali workers are as respectable as their neighbours; their wages are good, their work is regular, they are employed by the piece, no women or children are employed, no unions, no strikes.

As regards the injury done to the picturesque value of land by alkali manufacturers, I am afraid there is no doubt they must plead guilty. In some cases, especially in that of Sir Richard Brooke, the damage is most distressing; but there is a concurrence of evidence from Widnes, Weston, St. Helens and Flint, that during the last four years, since the passing of the Alkali Act of 1874, the damage has very much diminished, and that in districts where the number of works has not increased the present damage is inappreciable.

The alkali industry is a necessity in a manufacturing country. If it is an evil it is a necessary one. Sulphuric acid, the base of all alkali products, may be called the heart of all manufacturing industries. The consumption of it is the surest gauge of their condition. There is scarcely a manufactured article in daily use that is not more or less dependent upon it. To enhance the cost of its production by hasty or ill-judged legislation would enhance the cost of half the industrial products of the country. It is not the greed of the manufacturers that has increased the number of alkali works, but it is the increased trade of the country that has demanded an increased supply of an indispensable element of production.

If new works had not sprung up at Widnes and St. Helens they would certainly have sprung up elsewhere. It is to be regretted that so many works have congregated at Widnes and St. Helens. The consumption of coal alone, a million tons at the former and a million and a half at the latter annually, would of itself cause great nuisance to the neighbouring districts; but who, pray, is to blame for this evil? Not, certainly, the manufacturers who bought and leased the land offered to them by the landowners; but the landowners who offered it.

Complaints of injury done to trees and to the picturesque value of ornamental property does not come with very good grace from the proprietors who have sold and leased contagious land at very high prices for the expressed and avowed object of erecting and extending the very works they now wish to destroy.

Sir Richard Brooke, whose name most frequently occurs in the report, and who is undoubtedly the greatest sufferer in the picturesque value of his estate, has within the last few years leased land immediately opposite his house, at a very high rental, for the erection of alkali *works and the deposit of alkali waste and, I understand, has hundreds of acres more to be let for the same purpose; nor is he by any means the only landowner who has lately let and sold land expressly for the erection of alkali works.*

There is a general desire among alkali manufacturers to minimise the nuisance and injury caused by their works. Recent legislation has undeniably tended to that result, and any further legislation in the same direction that is reasonable and practicable will, I know, receive their hearty support; but it will be a fatal mistake if a somewhat one-sided statement of local grievances should cause any hasty legislation that would destroy an industry that is absolutely indispensable to the manufacturing prosperity of the country.

Signed: Edward Sullivan, Widnes (December 2nd 1878)

Despite Mr. Sullivan's honest acceptance of the environmental damage caused by the alkali processes, his claims regarding the health of workmen were certainly not borne out by the reports of many medics and independent observers who visited the area. Not too long after Mr. Sullivan's wordy submission to *The Times* a Manchester journalist visited the town to report on the matter. This was the same journalist who had written the famous lines *"there are few people who have not heard of stinking Widnes and its melancholy surroundings, where trees and hedges, and grass alike have the look of being scorched up as if by fire"*. He now wrote of working conditions in our chemical factories:

"The conditions under which the workman in the chemical works carries on his daily labour are most injurious, although the death rate is not nearly as high as might be expected. The main harm is done by the vapours which, when inhaled, set up certain and characteristic diseases. For instance, the vapour of sulphuretted hydrogen produces severe diarrhoea, rapid pulse, and symptoms of low or typhoid fever; chlorine produces suffocation, cough, and laboured breathing; vapour of nitric acid produces throat affections; the vapour of muriatic acid will produce disease of the membranes lining the mouth, nose and throat. The work is so detrimental to clothing that many of the men wear suits of paper – some of them having a new one every day.

History also shows Mr. Sullivan's claim that *"accidents of any kind are very rare, and these only of a trivial kind"* is patently untrue. Our local newspaper is liberally sprinkled with reports of horrific accidents and deaths in our chemical factories. A vast amount of documentary evidence totally disproves Mr. Sullivan's assertions. In actual fact

193

serious accidents in Widnes workplaces were a regular occurrence rather than a rarity. It is therefore astonishing to read Mr. Sullivan's phrase relating to conditions in the workplace and his belief that the work was free from all danger. Just a few months earlier a workman called Frederick Jones, of West Street, was killed at the Gossage Soapworks while working in the black-ash shed and shortly before that another man had a fatal accident at the Goulding & Davies chemical works. In the period between these deaths there were innumerable other accidents of a serious nature.

It is quite obvious that in the early days most industrial accidents and deaths occurred because there were no significant safety precautions in place. There was also an extremely casual attitude to the handling of materials and equipment and, in addition, inadequate fencing, flooring or lighting meant that many deaths were caused by men tripping and falling into vats of dangerous chemicals. One such incident happened at the Muspratt Works in July 1882 when a young man called Peter Kinsey met his death by falling into a tank of caustic liquor. Kinsey was required as part of his duties to keep the caustic tank filtered. On the day of the accident the syphon on the tank did not work and while pushing it with a stick he fell headlong into the corrosive liquid. No help was at hand so he was unable to scramble over the top. By the time he was discovered he was still alive but frightfully burned. He died a few hours later at Widnes Accident Hospital. At the Inquest into his death the jury expressed the opinion that some proper appliance ought to be provided for pushing the syphon. Mr. Lewis, the manager of the works, submitted a method he intended to adopt in the future. There is no record to show if this modification was ever implemented.

In reality, because industrial accidents were so numerous, casualties seem to have been accepted as a matter of fact and there was almost a fatalistic approach by both employers and workers. As well as these serious safety issues, the intensity of their work, the excessive hours, and the continuous contact with heat and noxious gases left men ill and worn out before their time. Many workers suffered from serious respiratory problems although Mr. Sullivan appeared unwilling to accept that the work was detrimental to health. Instead, he tells us that *"Dr. Richardson, who has paid especial attention to this subject, was unable to discover any evidence which showed to him proof of special deterioration of health"*. Interestingly, several other doctors, both in Widnes and St. Helens, were of a different opinion. The outspoken Widnes medical practitioner, Doctor John O'Keefe, is on record as having said:

"It is a very unhealthy trade and if published statistics show but a small death-rate in the chemical trade, it is because the chemical yard only kills a man three parts out of four, leaving the workhouse to do the rest. The men are dismissed before they are actually dying. As a general rule, the men go from forty-five to fifty-five years of age. The tubes become blocked up and asthmatical; the gases destroy all elasticity of the tubes. The lime-men get soft stone. All get more or less anaemic. Asthma, kidney disease, chronic cystitis are the prerequisites of all. It would not be wise to pass a Widnes chemical yard man at the ordinary rate for life insurance. The work certainly shortens life. For one thing the men cannot do their work unless they are half drunk. They drink and drink. I have one patient who drinks a half cask (eighteen gallons) of beer a week. They drink because they cannot eat. I know men who have brought their breakfasts, dinners, and teas back home because they could not touch them. A man cannot be healthy under these conditions".

Despite Mr. Sullivan's claims to the contrary, the alkali industry was most certainly harmful to health. Industrial accidents which caused loss of limb or loss of life were neither uncommon nor trivial. It is quite shocking to discover that one of our leading industrialists did not consider the number of incidents to be significant or of a serious nature. One might assume that his stance probably reflected the general attitude of manufacturers. It would seem that many were insensitive to the dangers or oblivious of their responsibilities in ensuring that factories were safe for their employees. What is also alarming is that in many instances it was the workmen themselves, rather than the employers, who were blamed for negligence. In a number of cases fellow workmen were accused of murder or manslaughter when one of their colleagues died. Some men were arrested and put through the ordeal of a trial before being acquitted. In all these cases the manufacturers were let off scot-free and were not censured in any way for failing to make their workplaces safe.

In 1868 a 35year old workman was killed at the factory of Wells, Taylor & Edwardson which was located in Earle Street. The dead man, who was working on the night-shift, had fallen into an uncovered vat of caustic liquid in the dark. After a cursory investigation by the police, three fellow workers were taken into custody and held at the local police station on suspicion of murder. The three were subsequently cleared of all charges when it became apparent that this had simply been a tragic accident. The owners of the factory were not criticised or reprimanded for their laxity but the three accused men were subjected to the most dreadful treatment. Another example was the case, in 1873, of a workman called James Burns who was accused of the manslaughter of his colleague Edward Callaghan. Both men were employed at the Hutchinson Works and had been operating a steam hoist when the incident occurred. Callaghan's clothing had accidentally caught onto the hoist and he was carried upwards, striking his head on an iron bar and afterwards dying from his injuries. Burns was immediately accused of negligence and charged with manslaughter. The unfortunate James Burns was arrested and imprisoned but when the trial came to court the Judge ruled that there was no case to answer, as it was clear that Callaghan's death was entirely accidental. The case was dismissed. However, the dismissal was not before Burns had suffered the trauma of being accused of involvement in the death of his workmate and the disgrace and stigma of being taken to court.

Mr. Sullivan rightly pointed out in his interesting letter to *The Times* that the chemical trade was an absolute necessity to a successful manufacturing country. The demand for alkali was increasing in Britain and abroad. By this time it had become the town's core industry employing large numbers of men, all producing alkali under the most arduous circumstances. Working conditions in the alkali trade were extremely unpleasant and dangerous. Although Mr. Sullivan had said that *"the manufacturers speak uniformly as to the good health of their workmen"* it is obvious that some manufacturers were more sensitive than Mr. Sullivan to the appalling state of affairs in local workplaces. Speaking in the late 1880s, about ten years after Mr. Sullivan wrote his letter, local industrialist Holbrook Gaskell described conditions in the early factories and acknowledged the difficulties which workers had to endure. His description of the environment and working conditions some forty years earlier lead us to believe that things had improved considerably by the 1880s. However we know that despite the later introduction of various health and safety regulations some processes hardly changed over the years. We also know that work in local chemical factories remained gruelling and hazardous. Holbrook Gaskell said of earlier days:

"At night one had to go around with duck-lamps which generally smelled, always smoked, and almost invariably burned the legs of one's trousers when carried about......The generation now reaching old age – at least those who have survived the ordeal of the old working conditions – could unfold a picture, almost incredible, of the long hours under suffocating conditions, with the mouth gags and improvised wooden screens for the face as men laboured almost bare to the skin at the black ash furnaces and the old fashioned bleach and soda plants.

Those were the days when process men worked 12 hour shifts with an appalling 24 hour change at weekends. If a man was struck down by illness or accident he had to depend on the charity of his ill-paid fellow workers who contributed to collections at the works gates on payday."

It should be said that Mr. Gaskell, although displaying several examples of altruism to the people of Widnes, was not an entirely perfect employer either. He showed a more callous side to his character In February 1882 when a young worker sued his company under the *Employer's Liability Act.* A young man called John Mannion had suffered a serious accident in the Gaskell Deacon Works which had left him permanently disabled. During the operation of his duty Mannion had been required to convey chemical materials in wagons along an elevated tramway to the revolving furnaces. While riding in a wagon one of the temporary wooden pillars which supported the tramway collapsed. This wooden pillar had only recently been substituted for an iron one which had been removed to repair the foundations. It was clear that the replacement pillar had not been put up safely and that it was probably not strong enough to hold the weight of the tramway. Mannion, a young man in his twenties, fell from a height of over twenty feet and received severe head, neck and back injuries which left him badly and permanently disabled. He was given compensation which amounted to £260 or the equivalent of three years basic wages. As the young man would be unable to work for the rest of his life this amount was obviously inadequate and he was advised to bring an action against Messrs. Gaskell, Deacon and Company for an improved offer.

The Gaskell Deacon Company proved to be a formidable opponent. Although clearly at fault, the Company produced a long line of eminent witnesses in its defence. The people appearing for the Company included Major James Cross; Robert Carlisle, a Manchester builder; Edward Reed, a surveyor and architect based at Westminster Chambers Liverpool; Mr. J.M. Wilson, a mining and land surveyor; Mr. A.G. Kyle the engineer from Messrs. Hutchinson & Co.; and Mr. Pritchard the Manager of the Tharsis Sulphur & Copper Co. Mr. Deacon himself also gave evidence. All these witnesses gave unanimous testimony that the wooden pillar had been constructed carefully, correctly, and safely. Mr. Deacon however, was unable to account for the accident or deny the fact that the pillar had collapsed, causing Mannion's injuries.

When the case came to court, the foreman of the jury was of the opinion that there was no gross negligence on the part of the Company but the jury thought the plaintiff should have sufficient compensation for the injuries he sustained. However, the foreman said that one of the jury wanted to know whether negligence affected compensation. The Judge said they could not consider compensation until they found negligence. After further consultation, the foreman said the jury were now agreed that there had been *"a little bit of negligence"* and assessed the damages at £50. It was later reported that *"four out of the five jurymen wished to make the damages £100 instead of £50 but they were "instructed" to do otherwise".*[81] If one were cynical it could be pointed out that several local manufacturers were also prominent members of the Magistrates bench.

Despite the countless problems and dangers present in our chemical works, we sometimes overlook the fact that the population at large were being subjected to the inhalation of dangerous fumes from nearby factories. In October 1884 two young Runcorn children died after inhaling fumes from the works of the Runcorn Soap and Alkali Company. The children, Thomas and Grace Spencer, aged four and three respectively, were sleeping on a boat which was moored in the canal opposite the works. The father of the children, Charles Spencer, was the captain of the boat which was owned by a Mr. Speakman. Although the family lived in Welsh Row, Gilbert Street, they were sometimes in the habit of sleeping on the boat. During the night of the accident Mr. Spencer had been woken by a feeling of nausea and was struck by the extremely strong smell of gas in the cabin. On realising the danger and feeling dizzy, he and his wife carried the children out of the cabin and headed towards another boat which was moored about a hundred yards away. However, before reaching it they both collapsed and, unknown to them at the time, the children were already dead. The occupant of the other boat, Joseph Brown, also of Welsh Row, went to their assistance. He had also been woken by a feeling of nausea. After offering some aid to Mr. Spencer and his family, the Browns were also forced to flee from the scene because of the overpowering fumes. In giving evidence at the inquest into the children's deaths, Mr. Brown told the jury that *"often when passing the works with his flat, there was a very strong smell of gas and his horse would stagger so that he had to go and seize its head in order to get it past"* The inquest lasted four hours and a verdict of *"accidental death due to suffocation by a gaseous poison"* was returned. The end of the report gave the following information *"We may state that Mr. Wigg, the managing director of the works, has visited Spencer's home, and promised to bear*

---

[81] *"Into the Crucible"* – Jean. M. Morris (Countyvise 2005) 2nd imprint (Arima Press 2009)

the expenses of the interment of the children and of Mrs. Spencer's convalescence"

It should be said that things *did* improve after the publishing of 1878 *Royal Commission Report.* A new Factory Act was introduced in that year and in the following years several other new Acts, including the Alkali Act of 1881, were introduced. The result of these Acts included recommended changes to the layout of chemical works. Soda vats were to be covered, gangways and gangplanks were to be fenced and dangerous places illuminated. Where Weldon chlorine was used, tests had to be made on the chlorine content of the atmosphere and the figures recorded in a book. Respirators had to be provided for rescue purposes and places were to be set aside for washing down those splashed with caustic.[82]

Although all these improvements were welcome there was still a long way to go. The chemical industry continued to be an unpleasant and highly risky occupation for its workforce. Fifteen years after the recommendations cited in the 1881 Alkali Act, the investigative journalist, Robert H. Sherard, wrote his famous *"White Slaves of England"* articles for *Pearson's Magazine.* Sherard's controversial 1896 articles highlighted the working conditions in a number of trades around the country. They included harrowing descriptions of the alkali trade in Widnes. Just a few months before these articles appeared three men died at the Muspratt Works after being gassed while working in a drain. The men, Luke Farrell, Patrick Fahey and Thomas Atherton were some 300 yards down the drain doing a routine cleaning job when they were overcome by gas and unable to get out. A man called Handley, with the aid of an air tube, tried to rescue them by going down the drain and attaching ropes to their bodies but unfortunately they were all dead when they were eventually brought up. At the inquest into their deaths Dr. O` Keefe said the cause of death was suffocation from sulphuretted hydrogen gas. He said that if the necessary appliances, such as ropes etc., had been used Mr. Fahey's life would have been saved. The Doctor recommended that rules regarding the use of ropes and respirators should be more stringently enforced. Of course the provisions of the Alkali Act of 1881 had already imposed these regulations but, as we can see, companies did not always comply.

"The White Slaves of England" articles caused quite a stir in several areas around the country, especially in those districts where attention

---

[82] *"Dangerous Trades"* – T. Oliver (London 1902)

had been drawn to their industries. The alkali trade in Widnes and St. Helens featured largely and created an outraged reaction from manufacturers in both towns. In his article about the chemical industry Sherard gave an account of the shocking working environment and arduous practices in Widnes factories. He also gave an alarming description of the unwholesome living conditions in the town. As might be expected, there were a number of letters written to *The Times* in which Widnes alkali manufacturers condemned his article as complete exaggeration. However, Sherard's disturbing description of life in an alkali town shocked the nation. Several newspapers carried reviews of his contentious work. One reviewer, when referring to the section about the alkali workers of Widnes, quoted directly from the article saying:

"One of the salt-cake men, who had been working on the process for eighteen years, told the journalist that: "I am standing eight hours on end in front of a fiery furnace, melting with heat, drawing, shoving, and turning the salt with an iron bar, which weighs fifty-six pounds. The heat is so intense that I am perspiring all the time. I have two towels to wipe myself on. One is drying whilst I am using the other. I'm not often hungry, and the gas makes me sick". He continued by telling Sherard that he had lived for weeks on milk and eggs "my stomach won't stand anything solid". He added "Not a man of my time but what is gone off or in the workhouse".

He also told us that:

"Many of the alkali workers lead intemperate lives. Alcohol has become a necessity for these wretched people as alkali workers drink because they cannot eat, and they often bring home all their meals untested for want of appetite. A note in Mr. Sherard's appendix shows that the chemical workers of Messrs. Brunner, Mond & Co., and of Messrs. Lever Brothers, who manufacture all their own chemicals, are perfectly well cared for. "Port Sunlight" says Mr. Sherard, "is spoken of in the slums of Widnes as the El Dorado of the chemical worker's ambition, where men in health can come to possess their own cottages, and make provision for their old age, and in sickness receive careful attention and humane treatment."[83]

The welfare facilities offered to the workers employed by the Brunner Mond Company at Winnington and the Lever factory in Ellesmere Port show that not all manufacturers were impervious to the needs of their workforce. Throughout this period there were a small

---

[83] Port Sunlight was the model village created by Lord Lever for his workforce.

number of prominent industrialists who were also kindly paternalistic employers, these included John Brunner and William Lever as well as the philanthropic Quaker families of Fry and Rowntree. John Brunner was known to be a particularly good local employer. He provided some outstanding benefits for his workers and had an extremely enlightened attitude to Trade Unionism. He once told his employees *"that nothing would please me better than that you should band together for your common good"* [84]. William Lever also had a progressive outlook towards the wellbeing of his employees at Ellesmere Port. He provided modern well-built housing and numerous other benefits which contributed to the creation of his *"model community"* at Port Sunlight. It is little wonder that Widnes workers who resided in jerry-built, overcrowded, insanitary houses had an overwhelming aspiration to live and work in the more beneficial environs of William Lever's new village.

During this chapter we have seen how the inception of the Industrial Revolution and the subsequent arrival of industry into our areas changed both the landscape and character of society forever. Historical hindsight allows us to see that the march of progress was particularly swift and relentless in Widnes as the area took on a new industrial role with a novice form of social order. The population increased at a rapid pace, which meant that the indigenous society was swallowed up by a mass of migrant workers who misguidedly believed they would better themselves. It is also worth mentioning that relationships between employers and their workforces also underwent a radical change. In previous times, before the advent of concentrated industry and the influx of a new diverse society, small local employers shared similar customs and allegiances with their workers. These mutual communal values meant that interaction between employer and employee was often close and personal. Of course the sheer scale of new industry and the diversity of its workforce meant that this type of relationship no longer existed.

Obviously when considering the impact of industry on Widnes we should not view this influence solely in human terms. For apart from the social context, the process of industrialisation meant that the local landscape was also changed forever. A forest of smoking chimneys replaced the tree lined shoreline of West Bank and clean fresh air and

---

[84] Stephen E. Koss - *"Sir John Brunner: Radical Plutocrat 1842-1919.* (Cambridge University Press) 1970

crystal clear streams gave way to noxious vapours and toxic watercourses. We should also remember that Runcorn had undergone significant changes in landscape and population too. Regardless of the fact that it was later overshadowed by its neighbour, Runcorn did continue to enjoy a significant commercial presence. This success was sustained by several profitable industries which included the manufacture of soap and alkali as well as shipbuilding and tanning concerns.

When reflecting on the interesting process of evolution in our two towns, we can see that progress was not without serious problems associated with work, society and environment. However, despite these difficulties both towns continued to expand and develop their own manufacturing bases. Needless to say these developments had been made possible by the determination and ability of the early founders of industry in both Widnes and Runcorn. These outstanding men were responsible for creating industries which at one time enjoyed enviable reputations in many parts of the country and, in the case of Widnes, in the world.

Although many of the accomplishments of our early manufacturers and the achievements of their workers may seem fairly commonplace today, we should remember that these achievements were far more impressive more than a century ago. At that time the tasks they were expected perform in order to produce alkali, soap, or any other manufactured product, were carried out with wholly inadequate facilities and under horrendous operating conditions. Therefore, we modern townspeople owe a huge debt of gratitude to both the workers and the far-sighted entrepreneurs who made it all possible.

THE RIVER, CANALS AND CROSSINGS

From early times the passage across the Mersey from Widnes on one side of the Gap to Runcorn on the other had been performed in ferry boats. Although there are no records to provide a precise date for the establishment of the ferry, it is widely believed that it dated back to Norman times and the period when the area was governed by William Fitz Nigel the 2nd Baron of Halton, who inherited the title and lands from his father-in-law, Yorfrid. Charles Poole, in his fine and informative book *"Old Widnes and its Neighbourhood"*, tells us that a formal charter was granted in 1190 when the baronies of Halton and Widnes were united during the time of the 6th Baron, John Fitz Richard. However this was the second deed to have been granted and, unfortunately, there is no known date for the first one. Mr. Poole also refers to an action taken out by a Henry Ackers in 1529 with regard to the operation of the ferry. Despite these records and many other interesting references it is impossible to establish an exact date for the setting up of a formal service. Suffice to say that a recognised ferry service had been in operation across this short stretch of the Mersey for many centuries.

Even though it had obviously been in existence and in continual use since early times, there is not enough documentary evidence to provide a detailed history of the ferry service much before the 18th century. However, from that date we can find numerous references to the ferry and its operation. In 1728 the ferry, along with the Baronies of Halton and Widnes, were transferred by the Crown to the Marquis of Cholmondeley. The following year the Marquis leased the ferry, for three lives, to John Chadwick of Runcorn. At one point in time William Hurst, the owner of West Bank House in Widnes, lodged an unsuccessful claim to the ferry and the neighbouring marshland. Although his claim failed, he was allowed a number of concessions which included being permitted to cut rock for his own use from the strand at West Bank. He was also given free passage on the ferry for himself and his tenants and permitted to impose a toll on pedestrians and vehicles passing over his land en route to the ferry. He set up a toll bar for this purpose in Snig Lane (Mersey Road) about half a mile from the river.

The ferry which operated from Runcorn Gap in Widnes to the other side of the river in Runcorn was notoriously challenging for passengers and boatmen alike. Problems associated with unreliability and danger persisted for generations and various owners and operators did little or nothing to improve the service. The journey across this short stretch of river was perilous, unpleasant and erratic. It became the cause of constant complaint by passengers who said that it was certainly not a trip to be undertaken by the faint hearted. Over the years there had been persistent public demands that the owners of the ferry should make vital improvements to the facilities to ensure the safety and comfort of its users. Local and national newspapers printed letters from innumerable disgruntled passengers who raised several areas of concern regarding the ferry, each one serious in its own right. It was alleged that the boats were rotten and unsafe; the walkways to the ferry were slippery and actually getting on board the boats was daunting and treacherous, especially at night. In spite of continual criticism all appeals to the owners of the ferry fell on deaf ears. They were seemingly immune to complaints and reluctant to make any financial investment or improvement. Of course, as this was the only means of crossing the river at this point, they knew that no matter what condition the ferry was in, or how appalling the service was, custom was virtually assured.

From time to time over the years there had been several impressive plans by enterprising individuals and groups to build a bridge to span the Mersey at Runcorn. Most of these plans had been abandoned due to impracticalities or lack of adequate funds to see the projects through. Despite the enthusiastic desires of local travellers, and the aspirations of numerous speculators and engineers, it was some considerable time before this ambition would finally come to fruition. Nevertheless, over the preceding years there had certainly been no lack of support for a venture of this type. Several well-known engineers competed for an opportunity to build a bridge at this spot. In November 1813 James Dumbell of Mersey Mills, Warrington, and William Nicholson of London both put forward plans. In later years Charles Blacker Vignoles, who was involved in the construction of the St. Helens and Runcorn Gap Railway, also expressed an ambition to build a bridge across the river at Runcorn.

By 1814 a group of prominent gentlemen had already formed a committee for the purpose of promoting a bridge at Runcorn. The committee was made up of businessmen, clergymen, landowners and members of the gentry including Sir Richard Brooke, Viscount Kilmorey, The Earl of Derby, The Earl of Sefton and Sir John Chetwode. Although this was primarily a local scheme the Runcorn Bridge Committee attracted a substantial number of sponsors from other locations in Cheshire as well as from Liverpool and Staffordshire. This meant that not all the committee meetings were held in Runcorn. Some meetings took place at a venue in Sandbach, some at the King's Arms Inn in Liverpool and locally at the White Hart Inn[85] in Runcorn. Judging by the number of attendees at these meetings it is clear that there was a huge amount of public support for the project. Although a surprisingly large number of people had become members of the *"Bridge Group"* it is not clear if all of them had pledged financial investment or if some had simply expressed an interest in the scheme. At one meeting, held at The Royal Hotel in Runcorn in October 1816, there were upwards of two hundred persons present.

Over the period of its existence a considerable number of bridge designs and estimates had been submitted to The Runcorn Bridge Committee for their consideration. At one early meeting plans had been tendered by Captain Brown of the Navy; Mr. Rowland of Ruabon; Mr. Turner of Whitchurch; Mr. Moneypenny of London; Mr. Mitan of London and Captain Bye of the Royal Engineers. In addition, letters of interest were received from Thomas Telford at Edinburgh; Mr. Jesse Hartley of Pontefract and Mr. Ralph Dodd of London, who all sought permission to submit plans. At the Runcorn meeting in October 1816 a further six plans were offered to the Committee for their contemplation. The plans put forward to the meeting included one for a stone bridge with seven arches; an iron bridge with five arches; a timber framed construction with five arches; a timber framed bridge with two arches; a suspended chain bridge of 1000ft span and a similar one but with lengths of iron riveted together, instead of links. After due consultation the Committee decided that from all the plans submitted on that occasion only two plans were to be short-listed.

The final decision as to which plan would be adopted was reached in April 1817. Although there had been a large number of plans of varying design and construction to choose from, the Runcorn Bridge Committee finally narrowed the choice down to the two suspension type bridges. At a general meeting of the promoters, the Committee, which was chaired on that occasion by Sir Richard Brooke, advised its

---

[85]This was later renamed *The Royal*.

members that they had decided to adopt the plan submitted by the renowned engineer Thomas Telford. This plan was for a 1000 ft. span suspension bridge with two side spans of the same construction, each 500 ft. wide, forming in the whole a range of iron 2000 ft. long. It was estimated that, with the road, it would cost in the region of £100,000. The announcement was met with unanimous approval and support. It was reported that *"before the end of the meeting a subscription was commenced with great spirit, which promises speedy success."*

The scheme to build a bridge at Runcorn was received with great enthusiasm not only by local residents and long suffering ferry passengers, but also by the many holidaymakers and invalids who came to the town for leisure or recuperation. The proposed bridge became a recurring topic of reportage in the national press as well as in the newspapers and journals of our neighbouring towns and counties. The *Manchester Chronicle* took a special interest in the subject as many residents from Manchester and its hinterlands were regular visitors to Runcorn. In 1817 the following article appeared under the title *"Runcorn"*.

"We know of no place that has more to recommend it, in point of scenery and situation, than this flourishing little town and the advantages it offers to sea bathers are not surpassed in this part of the kingdom. New houses are everywhere erecting, and should the projected Bridge over Runcorn Gap be carried into effect, the welfare of the town will vie with that of its (at present) more prosperous neighbours. That delightful spot, Halton Castle, still possesses all its well-known attractions. The picturesque and romantic beauties of this once proud seat of baronial magnificence are more than ever visited by the curious, and those who delight in the contemplation of the deeds of the days of other years. The views from this "Castle-crested" hill extend over an immense tract of country."

By September 1818 the Committee, now styled the Runcorn Bridge Company, had preliminary preparations in place to put their bold project into operation. It seemed almost certain at that time that the scheme was about to go ahead as tenders were invited for construction and other ancillary work. The following advertisements, which appeared in *The Liverpool Mercury,* give us an idea of the scale of the proposed undertaking. In addition to the massive amount of building work involved, the project would also require a great deal of financial backing. The expectation was that the main bulk of this money could be raised fairly quickly by private subscription. It was anticipated that investment costs would be recouped by imposing a system of tolls for passengers crossing the bridge or using the approach roads. Although it would be a long term investment, it was believed that there would eventually be a handsome profit for all subscribers to the scheme.

ROAD AND APPROACH TO THE INTENDED BRIDGE AT RUNCORN.
TO BE LET BY PRIVATE CONTRACT.

THE MAKING of a ROAD for Carriages, Horses, and Foot Passengers, with requisite Embankments, Drains, large Culvert Flood-gates, &c. to lead from Ditton Mill, in the county of Lancaster, upon and over Ditton March, to the present Ferry over the River Mersey, called Runcorn Ferry, according to a plan and specification thereof, which will be lodged on behalf of the Runcorn Bridge Company at their Office in Runcorn, on or before Saturday the 8th day of August, 1818, at which place all requisite particulars may be learnt.

The Work will be Let in several Contracts of moderate extent, so as to secure its completion during the present Season. Sealed Tenders, with the names of two Sureties for the due performance of the work, are to be left at the said Office, on or before the evening of the 17th August inst. and on the following day, at eleven o'clock in the forenoon, the Runcorn Bridge Committee will attend at the White Hart Inn, in Runcorn aforesaid, for the purpose of taking such Tenders into consideration, selecting the most eligible, and agreeing to such of the proposals as the Committee may think proper.

By order,
JOHN FITCHETT, Secretary.

RUNCORN BRIDGE.

NOTICE is hereby Given, that application is intended to be made to Parliament, in the next Session, for leave to bring in a Bill, in order to obtain an Act for erecting a Bridge over the River Mersey, at a place called Runcorn Gap, from a certain place in the Township and Parish of Runcorn, in the County Palatine of Chester, at or near the Castle Rock there, to the opposite shore in the Township of Widnes, and Parish of Prescot, in the County Palatine of Lancaster, near a certain Dwelling-house, in the Township of Widnes aforesaid, called the Ferry-house; and for opening and making proper and convenient Ways, Roads, Avenues, and Approaches to the said Bridge, or to the Ferry across the said River Mersey, at Runcorn aforesaid, through Lands in the several Townships of Widnes and Ditton, in the said Parish of Prescot, and in the Township of Halewood, in the Parish of Childwall, in the said County of Lancaster, and through Lands in the several Townships of Runcorn, Halton, Clifton, Sutton, Aston, and Preston-on-the-hill, in the said Parish of Runcorn, and in the several Townships of Dutton, Bartington, and Little Leigh, in the Parish of Great Budworth, in the said County of Chester, and for creating and establishing a Toll or Tolls, to be paid on passing over the said Bridge and Roads.

By Order,
JOHN FITCHETT, Secretary.

THE LIVERPOOL MERCURY –SEPTEMBER 1818

Although the Runcorn Bridge Company had formally approved Mr. Telford's plan there was still a great deal of dispute as to whether the overall scheme was practical. Concerns were voiced by merchants with shipping interests who feared that arches of a bridge would narrow the passage for sailing ships and cause serious damage to their masts. They also believed that their sailing vessels would not be able to manoeuvre with ease if there were piers in the river. In addition to the concerns and general misgivings of merchants, plus a growing national interest in the subject of its viability, there was also mounting criticism of the scheme from Liverpool Corporation. The Runcorn Bridge Company had initially asked the city Corporation to offer their support for the undertaking but they had refused to comply. At that time the City Council feared that the erection of a bridge in that location would have a detrimental effect on the ebb and flow of the river.

Obviously Thomas Telford was extremely keen to build his bridge. In an effort to counteract the amount of negative or sceptical misinformation being circulated, he started to involve himself in the debate by issuing statements on the subject to the national press. In September 1817 the *Manchester Chronicle* included the following observation:

"We have noticed a paragraph which appeared in the "Globe" London newspaper, making silly remarks on the impracticability of erecting a bridge across the Mersey at Runcorn. The contradiction we gave to it was founded upon the best authority this, or perhaps any other country in the world, could produce. We are glad to see that the paragraph in question has not escaped the notice of our contemporaries; and we copy, with much satisfaction, the following from the last "Manchester Chronicle":- "We are informed from reliable authority, that so far from the projected bridge at Runcorn Gap being impracticable, as asserted in a late paragraph, that it is the recorded opinion of Mr. Telford, who must be allowed to be one of the ablest and most experienced engineers in the Kingdom, that it is not only practicable, but would not be in the least detrimental to the navigation of the river Mersey."

Despite their earlier opposition to the scheme, in December 1818 Liverpool Corporation presented a Parliamentary Bill relating to the erection of a suspension bridge at Runcorn. The plan for this undertaking was again prepared by Thomas Telford. However this proposal was eventually abandoned due to the high costs involved. The first estimate given to the Corporation was for £84,890 but this was later reduced to £62,500. Nevertheless, even the lower costing was considered to be far too expensive. Although the expenditure was said to be the main reason for rejecting the scheme there were other contributing factors. At the time there was still a considerable amount of dispute in Liverpool as to whether or not a bridge would have a negative effect on the flow of the river. There was also the ongoing fear that arches in the river might impede navigation. These persistent doubts were thought to be additional reasons to dispense with the idea of bridging the river at that time.

The debate about the feasibility of erecting a bridge at Runcorn was to rumble on for many years and during all that time there was no significant progress in the matter. However, after a prolonged period of limbo, the question of the Runcorn Bridge resurfaced in August 1825. This was in connection with proposals made by the Post Office to establish a Mail Packet service between the ports of Liverpool and Dublin. Up until then all mail to Ireland had been directed through Chester and Shrewsbury to Holyhead. The provision of a mail service between Liverpool and Dublin would be of great benefit for both public and commercial purposes. In order for this to be viable the mail coming from London and the south would need to be at Liverpool by 5 o'clock each evening. To accomplish this it would be necessary to make the journey to Liverpool shorter and quicker. If a bridge was erected at Runcorn the route could be shortened by fifteen miles. The Post Office subsequently invited Thomas Telford to investigate this course of action again, with a view to suggesting a way of improving and shortening the mail service route to Ireland.

Notwithstanding the fact that the Telford plan for a suspension bridge was still officially under consideration, a Post Office spokesperson made the following comments which indicate that they had already decided that this was not the preferred option. A much earlier bridge/canal design devised by James Brindley, the canal builder, was regarded as a better solution for the reasons stated:

"Although a suspension bridge of 1,000 feet span, at Runcorn, is thought to be necessary for this purpose, we now conceive that the idea originally suggested by Mr. Brindley and revived by Mr. Giles, of constructing a bridge there, for the double purpose of a carriage road and canal, would be infinitely preferable; the former would answer not only the end proposed, but contribute greatly to the convenience and interest of the country. By extending the canal from Runcorn to Liverpool, and a branch to Sankey, the immense concerns of the Duke of Bridgewater's Canal, of the Old Quay Company, the River Weaver,

and the Sankey Canal, would all be united into one commodious, safe, and certain line of commercial intercourse. The execution of the scheme does not appear to be attended with any extraordinary difficulties or expense: the aqueduct is the principal; but stone, the chief material, is abundant and cheap in the vicinity, so that the work may be executed at a small expense, compared with the immense advantages that will arise from the undertaking. It may suffice to point out (independent of the road) a few details that immediately present themselves to our view: 1) The immense danger and loss attendant on the river navigation, will be avoided. 2) Vessels of lighter construction, of considerably less expense, and capable of carrying greater burdens than the present, will be sufficient for every purpose. 3) The communication betwixt the port of Liverpool, as well as Northwich, with the Lancashire Collieries, will not be interrupted by neaps, as is frequently the case at present. 4) The great expense, delay, and damage incident to loading and unloading goods to and from flats to the boats navigating the Trent and Mersey will be completely annihilated. These hints, it is conceived, are of sufficient importance to excite the attention of the public to the investigation of a subject that presents so many valuable consequences to the country."

In fact there was a great deal of support for James Brindley's original plan which he had submitted to a group of Liverpool businessmen as early as 1768. Most people were of the opinion that it was only his untimely death which had prevented this project from being executed. However historical retrospection and acquired knowledge provide us with other reasons for the plan being abandoned. It would seem that the primary reasons for Brindley's plan being rejected were the same as those which had hindered Telford – namely the high costs involved and opposition to the scheme by Liverpool shipping merchants. Of course we modern readers have the benefit of hindsight but in 1825 it was said that:

"Had that self-taught genius, Brindley, the engineer for the late Duke of Bridgewater, lived a few years longer it was his intention to have carried the Bridgewater Canal and a turnpike road over the River Mersey at Runcorn Gap. A bridge at that place for a turnpike road would be of infinite advantage to Liverpool, it would shorten the distance from London through the Wiches by nine miles; the London mail would then arrive by five o'clock in the evening, in time to be forwarded by the steam-packets, and the facilities to Cheshire and Lancashire would be invaluable."

Two years later, in May 1827, Thomas Telford's ambition to build his bridge at Runcorn was dealt a further blow. At a meeting of the Liverpool City Corporation, whose views had been flipping between negative and positive from the outset, a decision was made to formally oppose the Runcorn Bridge Scheme. The Corporation had previously employed engineers to survey the embankments of the Mersey in order to assess the effect such a bridge would have on the river. According to their findings, if a bridge was built at Runcorn there would be serious and harmful effects on the flow of the river. A statement issued by the members of the Corporation gave the following information:

"The members unanimously concurred that a bridge across the Mersey at Runcorn would have an injurious tendency on the ebb and flow of the tide, and the Corporation are, therefore, opposed to the plan, as conservators of the port and harbour of Liverpool."

Regardless of this damning decision, there were those who still hoped that it would be possible to bridge the river at Runcorn. Obviously we now know that Thomas Telford's ambitious project was never accomplished. His superb plan was destined to join all the other unsuccessful schemes to bridge the gap across the Mersey at this point. In spite of the disappointing failure to implement his Runcorn plan, happily, Telford was able to make use of the work and the time he had put into preparing his design. A modified version of his Runcorn Bridge proposal was chosen for the bridge across the Menai Straits to Anglesey[86]. When Parliament was asked to approve the building of a bridge across the Menai Straits, Telford provided them with the following written information to support his suggestions. This offers us a valuable *"straight from the horse's mouth"* account of how his design for the Runcorn Bridge evolved:

"In 1814, when being applied to for a design for a bridge across the Mersey at Runcorn, where it was necessary to preserve a water-way of one thousand feet in breadth, a bridge upon the principle of suspension occurred to me as the only practical means and, with that view, I instituted a regular set of experiments upon rods of malleable iron, viz. from thirty to nine hundred feet in length, and from one twentieth of an inch to two inches in diameter; and these both in regard to elementary parts, and also when combined, partly by welding and partly by joining in a model. The nature and results of these experiments are detailed

---

[86] The Menai Bridge needed to be strengthened in the 1930s.

and commented upon in an excellent Treatise on the Strength of Materials, lately published by Mr. Barlow of the Royal Military Academy at Woolwich. From these I had reason to conclude, that by means of malleable iron properly combined, a substantial bridge of one thousand feet might be constructed; and accordingly gave a design for that purpose."

As we have seen, Telford's plan to span the river at Runcorn had gone the way of several previous schemes and was subsequently abandoned. It was a bitter disappointment to everyone concerned and it was to be some considerable time before the dream of a bridge across the Mersey at Runcorn would be realised. To add to this disappointment, our loss of Thomas Telford's brilliant design and talent was Wales' gain. There can be few who catch a glimpse of his bridge on their way to Anglesey who fail to be impressed by this magnificent feat of engineering. At the time the Menai Bridge was built this type of suspended construction was viewed as a pioneering form of bridge design in Britain. However, although the concept of suspension bridges was fairly new here, a man called Joseph Finlay had already built an iron chain suspension bridge in Pennsylvania as early as 1800 and in 1825 a Frenchman called Marc Seguin also constructed an innovative wire suspension bridge. But unfortunately, for the people of Runcorn and Widnes, a bridge of *any type* failed to materialise at that time and Telford's wonderful and innovative Runcorn plan was subsequently consigned to local history.

In the meantime, deficiencies in the old ferry service continued to frustrate all those wishing to cross the river for business or pleasure. However as this was the only public conveyance between the two shores it was a case of needs must. The service had become notorious throughout the whole country because of numerous letters in the press regarding the deplorable state of its boats and the hazardous embarking and landing conditions. Although most complaints emphasised these particular problems, in earlier times the attitude and inefficiency of its boatmen, rather than the condition of the vessels, were regular topics of dissatisfaction and criticism. The Runcorn boatmen were notoriously truculent and unhelpful. It would seem that their fractious conduct often added to the discontent and overall frustration of the passengers. One traveller, in May 1823, had a very low opinion of our local ferrymen and felt compelled to write an open letter to Lord Cholmondeley, via *The Liverpool Mercury*. I can say with some degree of certainty that this letter, like countless others, failed to bring about any action or change in the behaviour of boatmen or the general operation of the service.

RUNCORN FERRY

TO THE RIGHT HON. LORD CHOLMONDELEY.

MY LORD,—I understand that you are the proprietor of a ferry on the river Mersey, at Runcorn Gap. Your Lordship will, I feel convinced, do your utmost to prevent imposition, and to correct those abuses which materially affect the comfort and convenience of travellers. Permit me to inform your Lordship, that the ferry to which I allude, is, without exception, one of the worst, if not the very worst, I have ever seen in the kingdom. The boats are good and the passage very short; but those who manage the boats are to the last degree careless and insolent.—Trusting your Lordship will order men of decency and ability to be employed on this important station, I remain your Lordship's obedient servant,

VIATOR.

MAY 1823 - LETTER TO LORD CHOLMONDELEY

Complaints about all aspects of the ferry journey were numerous and unremitting and most passengers were left feeling exasperated, dissatisfied and irate. Unfortunately, as I pointed out earlier, because it was the only frequent form of transport across the river travellers had to put up with it. Whilst being far from perfect the ferry provided an essential service for the residents of the two towns. It was an indispensable local facility which allowed thousands[87] of people to travel across the river each week. The daily packet service from Runcorn to Liverpool was another important transport link. This public river communication between the city and several northern towns helped to ease the isolation of Runcorn and its residents. In fact it appeared to be safer and far more convenient and comfortable to get to Liverpool from Runcorn than it was to cross the short stretch of river to Widnes.

By the 1780s there was a regular packet service to and from Manchester operated by the Bridgewater Company along their canal. These boats were fairly comfortable and the 100 or so passengers they could accommodate were able to get drinks and light refreshments on board. As well as being able to embark at Runcorn, passengers on this service could also board or disembark at Preston Brook, Stockton

---

[87] It was estimated in the mid-1860s that the numbers of passengers was around 3000 per week.

Heath, Lymm and Altrincham. The downside was that the entire journey took around 8 hours to complete. By the beginning of the nineteenth century the Mersey and Irwell Company had also introduced packets from Runcorn to Manchester, sailing from the Old Quay Docks to Knott Mill Wharf. This service was in direct competition with the Bridgewater Company. Although not good news for either concern, the rivalry[88] between the two companies was obviously a godsend to Runcorn residents. The competition in ferry trade gave local residents a choice of services on this route. However it would appear that the fares on both routes were identical, three shillings first class and two shillings for second class.

Whilst it is obvious that water transport was vital to industrial growth in the area, it is sometimes easy to overlook how important canal travel was for the general population at that time. The Bridgwater and The Mersey and Irwell packet services were of great benefit to all inhabitants in the towns and villages situated along the canals between Runcorn, Liverpool and Manchester. The arrival of these services meant that travellers from Manchester could journey on to Liverpool via the Runcorn packets and vice versa. These ferries provided an effective transport link between these two important cities as road travel between the two places was still quite difficult and took a considerable time. In addition, passenger trade was a welcome and valuable supplement to the local economy as Runcorn was a stopping off point for passengers who had travelled from places along the canal en route for Manchester or Liverpool. It is probable that some people halted in the town for refreshment or shopping before continuing their journey in either direction. Of course the ferries also made travel to Runcorn more accessible for those visiting the town for holiday or recuperation, and this type of visitor provided a significant contribution to the local finances.

The importance of the river and canals in relation to local history goes without saying. The water highways in our region enabled the growth of industry in both towns and offered employment to many hundreds of men, as well as essential travel facilities for our populations. Unfortunately the story of transportation on our river is liberally peppered with accidents and drownings. Although the majority of these marine accidents involved Mersey flats, some were associated with the ferries that plied the Runcorn route. In September

---

[88] The two companies were merged in 1844 when the Bridgewater Trustees purchased the Mersey & Irwell Company.

1811 the Runcorn to Liverpool Packet, which was carrying about thirty passengers at the time, struck a sandbank near Dungeon Point. Fortunately, a Mersey flat was sailing close by at the time and its crew managed, with a large degree of difficulty and danger, to pick up some of the passengers who had been put into the ferry's lifeboat. The lifeboat then returned to the stricken ferry to collect the rest of the passengers, who at that time numbered around fourteen. When the boat containing the second lot of passengers came alongside the flat it began to sink rapidly. In spite of gallant rescue attempts by the flat's crew and other passengers three people were drowned. One was the young daughter of the captain of the Runcorn Packet, another a gentleman from Manchester and the third unfortunate victim was a young lady called Collier who was from Runcorn.

Despite this sad incident, and numerous other accidents on the Liverpool Packets, the condition of the boats which ferried passengers from Runcorn to Liverpool and Manchester were still far superior to the Runcorn Gap Ferry. Apart from being considerably larger, the packet vessels were more up to date than the local ferryboats. The ferryboats were still being operated by human manpower whilst the packets were driven by modern steam powered engines. The introduction of steamships had prompted a flurry of activity on several rivers around the country. This was especially noticeable in shipbuilding localities like the Clyde where the first steamship to appear on the Mersey was actually built. This ship, which arrived in the Mersey in July 1815, was called *The Elizabeth* and was built on the Clyde in 1812 by John Wood. *The Elizabeth* was subsequently bought for £1,200 by Lieutenant Colin Watson, a young officer in the East Yorkshire Militia who was stationed at that time in Liverpool. Watson had previously witnessed the success of the steam vessels operating on the Clyde and came to the conclusion that they would be equally successful on the Mersey. After purchasing the boat, Lieutenant Watson formed a small company with the intention of operating the vessel between Runcorn and Liverpool with the expectancy that in the future this service might also be extended to Warrington.

The story of Colin Watson's venture into the ferry trade is a short but interesting one. Having purchased the vessel from John Wood he travelled to Glasgow to collect it and bring it down to the Mersey. I don't know if he had previous sailing experience, but one would assume that he hadn't as the journey was beset with the type of problems a skilled mariner might have avoided. He was accompanied in his mission by his cousin, a young naval officer called Hargrave, and

215

another young man. They left the Clyde early on the morning of June 2nd 1815 and set sail for Liverpool. That night they hit a dreadful storm and were sent off course. Their journey took them to Ramsey Bay in the Isle of Man where they lost one of the paddles. They anchored at Port Patrick to buy some supplies but because they had run out of cash they had to stay on the island until some money could be sent to them. Setting sail again, they next made a mistake with their compass and eventually found themselves off the coast of North Wales. After this, the vessel apparently drifted westward near to Dublin on the Irish coast. They finally arrived at George's Dock Pier in Liverpool at midnight on the 28th June. The journey from Glasgow to Liverpool seems to have taken them over three weeks to complete!

It might be interesting to point out that at this time neither Watson nor his cousin, Hargrave, had yet reached their twenties. In fact, the unfortunate Hargrave died of alcohol addiction before he was twenty. Regrettably, despite their epic journey from Glasgow and his great ambition to operate a ferry service on the Mersey, Watson's business venture did not last long. It is thought that *The Elizabeth*, under the ownership of Watson, only plied this route for a few months. He sold the vessel in the spring of 1816 to Robert Welburn, a Liverpool blockmaker, after which the Watson Steamship Company was subsequently dissolved. Although Colin Watson was unable to make a success of his ferry business, *The Elizabeth,* which could carry 100 passengers, continued on the Mersey for another few years. Afterwards she was converted by her new Liverpool owner into a horse-drawn vessel and in that capacity she continued the Runcorn to Liverpool service until she was put up for sale in 1818 After the demise of *The Elizabeth* another steamer, *The Greenock*, ran between Runcorn and George's Dock at Liverpool Pier Head. However this service was also very short-lived and appears to have been in operation for less than a month. It seems rather sad that young Watson's ambitious venture did not succeed; nevertheless, he should be remembered as the person who brought the first steamship onto our river. On 1st March 1816, after selling his steamship, he entered the service of the Customs at Liverpool and he can be found listed in Liverpool directories up until the late 1820s. Sadly, Colin Watson died in Liverpool on 4th June 1830 aged just 33 years.[89]

Of course Runcorn was already known as a boat-building town and the arrival of steamers on our rivers meant that local shipbuilders were

---

[89] Colin Watson is buried in Walton Cemetery, Liverpool.

keen to be part of this new trade. Furthermore, there was no shortage of financial backing from local businessmen for this type of venture. In 1816 the Runcorn shipbuilder William Wright built *The Duke of Wellington*, which is thought to be the first steamship built on the Mersey. She was registered at Liverpool in the names of John Davies of Runcorn, victualler; John Askey of Halton, victualler; William Wright of Runcorn, shipbuilder; James Radley of Liverpool and Richard Edwards. Also built in Runcorn around the same time was *The Prince Regent.* This vessel was built by William Rigby and jointly owned by Job Wilson, a local innkeeper; Thomas Parr, a local mariner; John Bott, a local waiter; John Prescott, a local butcher; Thomas Barker Smith, a Chester schoolmaster and John Heyes who was described as a gentleman. Both *The Duke of Wellington* and *The Prince Regent* sailed between Runcorn and Liverpool.

The agents for the new steamship ferries were keen to highlight the benefits of their individual services. One advert for *The Duke of Wellington* gave the following information:

"Packets on Sunday last. The Duke of Wellington departed from Runcorn at 5 o'clock in the morning and arrived at this port at seven. She sailed hence with passengers about eleven, and landed them at Runcorn. She departed from Runcorn to Warrington, where she arrived at two o'clock. She again left at half past two for Runcorn, where she landed her passengers and having taken in a fresh cargo sailed for Liverpool and arrived here at half-past seven in the evening. The whole distance which she sailed in the course of the day was upwards of eighty miles, a distance we imagine which no vessel ever performed in the same time on this river."

The agents for *The Prince Regent* were no less enthusiastic in promoting their ferry. They provided newspapers with the following information:

THE PRINCE REGENT RUNCORN STEAM PACKET

The New and commodious Steam Packet called the Prince Regent, built upon the most improved principle, fitted up in an elegant style, and conducted by a careful and experienced crew ; starts daily from the New Slip on the West Side of George's Dock, and after remaining there for two hours, which affords a sufficient time for viewing Runcorn, returns to Liverpool. The distance from Liverpool to Runcorn is 21 miles, which the Prince Regent Steam Packet performs with perfect safety and certainty in under two hours. The Passengers with all their Luggage, and for the carriage of which no additional charge is made, are safely and conveniently landed at a new and highly commodious landing place lately made at considerable expense exclusively for the use of the Prince Regent Steam Packet at the entrance to the Canal belonging to the Company of the Proprietors of the Mersey and Irwell Navigation ; from whence there is a short and excellent road to Wilson's Hotel in the higher and most beautiful part of the romantic village of Runcorn, by which road the Passengers will avoid all the personal inconvenience and expense which have been so long and generally experienced and complained of in landing at the Stone Wharf at the lower part of Runcorn. Such of the Passengers as are proceeding to Warrington or Manchester or any of the intermediate places are commodiously forwarded with their luggage in the Company's Packet Boat on the Canal, which sails every morning in the Summer Months at 10 o'clock, and the Winter Months at 8 o'clock, from a part of the Canal which lies opposite to and within about ten yards of the above new landing place.

The advantages which the Steam Packet has over the Sailing Packet are that the Prince Regent Steam Packet is always in an upright position ; as there is little motion, is unencumbered with sails, rigging, and oars which often alarm the Passengers and obstruct their view of the beautiful scenery of the River; at all times proceeds and arrives with the greatest punctuality, and is in many other respects preferable to any other public conveyance for the removal of families, aged and infirm persons, and invalids.

For particulars, apply at the Prince Regent Steam Packet at the Slip;

To T. Parr, No. 4 George's Dock Passage; or to J. Bolton, Mann's Island, in Liverpool; and at Wilson's Hotel, in Runcorn."

I am sorry to say that despite being built to the highest specification and having an experienced crew on board, neither of these things were a match for unpredictable and extreme weather conditions. *The Prince Regent* met a disastrous end in December 1822 when she was sunk in a violent storm near Ellesmere Port with the loss of nine lives. A survivor of the tragedy gave the following account of the disaster which, apart from atrocious weather, was caused by a collision with a sailing flat:

"The Packet left the George`s Pier-head, about three o`clock in the afternoon, having 23 persons on board, including the crew. At this period, the wind blew fresh, and was ahead of the Packet, though there

was no appearance of weather to justify suspicion of danger. About five o'clock the wind had greatly increased, and at six the packet had reached within a quarter of a mile of Ellesmere Port. The wind now blowing a complete hurricane, the Captain found it impossible to make the port. He then contemplated a return to Liverpool, and veered the vessel round for that purpose, but was soon convinced that the tide had so far receded as to render that object impracticable. For several hours the vessel beat about, and, from the darkness of the night, it was impossible to attempt steering to any particular point. At nine, the anchor was cast, but the Packet drifted considerably, and at about twelve it fell foul of a Flat, whose cable was also out, but dragging her anchor. The shock was tremendously alarming, every person on board believing they were going down. At this time, several of the passengers were in the cabin, and were violently flung down, from the heaving of the Packet, one side of which was actually under water. The confusion and alarm were now at their height. As the Flat remained for some short time at the side of the Packet, several of the crew and passengers caught hold of the side of the Flat and got on board her. Among these were all the hands belonging to the Packet (except the Captain) Mr. Burtt, and an artist from Chester and another man, in all six.

The circumstances of Mr. Burtt were peculiarly afflictive; he had run upon the deck, when the alarm created by the two vessels coming in contact was felt, and, standing on that side of the Packet which appeared to be sinking in the waves, caught hold of the edge of the Flat, or he must otherwise have been precipitated into the sea; and at this moment the flat and packet separated, he had no opportunity of returning to the latter, however anxious he might have been to do so. It is supposed that this gentleman hung by the side of the vessel in a perilous situation, for the space of ten minutes without being able to raise himself upon the deck, and no person on board being acquainted with the condition in which he was placed. Fortunately, however, after long struggling he succeeded in gaining the deck but not before he was exhausted with the effort. But, to return again to the state of the packet, there was now one foot of water in the cabin and it was decided to cut the cable, and let the vessel drift with the wind and the tide, the sea dashing over her in all directions. About one o'clock the tide began to flow and the packet was driven about two miles above Ellesmere Port, where she ran against a sandbank continuing for several times to recede from and approach to it. At length, she stuck first in the sand opposite Stanlow House and the feeble glimmering of the moon discovered the shore at about seventy yards distance, most of the intervening space being sand or mud. It was now four in the morning.

Captain Diamond here pressed as many of the passengers as he could prevail upon to make the shore; when Mr. H. Whittell, son of Dr. Whittell, and Mr. William Leatherbarrow, both of Chester, and Mr. Nixon from near Stanney, leaped into the water and succeeded in reaching the land. There were now fourteen individuals on board, five only of whom got safe to shore. The Captain, with his son in arms, was washed overboard, while in the act of endeavouring to disengage himself of his greatcoat. Mrs. Deakin, a stonemason's wife, with her infant in her arms, and her niece about ten years old; the blind fiddler who accompanied the son of Mr. Burtt, a promising youth of about five years of age; Mr. Davies, a millwright of Chester, and an elderly person, all perished in the attempt to gain land. The whole of the individuals who escaped were, we are happy to say, found ready and abundant accommodation suitable to their distressed situation at Mr. Smith's of Stanlow House and Mr. Hickson`s at Ellesmere Port."

Apart from the regular steamship services which had been introduced from Runcorn to Liverpool, an additional service was advertised in May 1819. This was to ply between Liverpool and Weston Point on a new steamboat called *The Ancient Briton*. Shares in the new steamboat were offered to the public at ten pounds each. The launch of *The Ancient Briton* service coincided with the opening of Mr. Cornelius Baynes' new *Weaver Hotel* at Weston Point. Mr. Baynes advertised his hotel as being *"ideal for families and company, being only one mile from Runcorn where a new road has recently been made just over the hill from Runcorn"*. Adverts for the new Weston Point Packet appeared in *"Gore's Advertiser"*. The adverts described the vessel as being:

"The swiftest packet on the River Mersey and her engine is so constructed that it cannot possibly be forced past its usual speed. The only communication with the safety valve is a chain instead of a rod of iron; therefore no weight can be placed upon it as to prevent the over-plus of steam escaping"[90]. The agent at Liverpool is James Wright, of Powell and Browne, merchants, 64 Sparling Street."

The Runcorn to Liverpool ferry service continued to grow and was well supported by both locals and travellers from further afield. The ferries provided a great means of transport to the city and beyond for travellers in both directions. For obvious reasons the summer months

---

[90] This reassurance was necessary owing to the frequent boiler explosions on the early steamships.

were particularly busy and the service proved to be a boon not only for families and the solo traveller but also for organised groups. A small insert from an edition of *The Liverpool Mercury* in 1843 gives an indication of the popularity of the ferry service.

> OLD QUAY BOATS.—These boats have been fully employed during the week. On Tuesday and Wednesday from eight hundred to a thousand passengers were conveyed by them to Runcorn, for Liverpool, the boats leaving here at one and two o'clock in the morning. On the three first race-days several thousand Sunday-school children were also conveyed to Eccles, Barton, Flixton, and other villages in the neighbourhood.

THE MANCHESTER TIMES – JUNE 1843

As an additional point of interest, up until the late 1840s it was possible to purchase alcoholic drinks on board the packet boats that plied the Bridgewater Canal. However in 1848 the Bridgewater Trust issued a notice informing the public that alcoholic refreshment would no longer be available on the Runcorn Packet. This move followed numerous complaints from passengers who claimed to have witnessed a lot of drunkenness and acts of immorality on board the boats.

Although the ferry services on the canals seem to have been reasonably efficient operations, with fairly reliable boats, the local ferry from Runcorn to Widnes continued to be a nightmare for passengers. Over the years the old Runcorn Gap Ferry had been in the hands of several lease holders and being the only public means of passage across the river it was probably a fairly lucrative undertaking. In addition to the passenger fares there were also the tolls and other privileges connected with ownership of the ferry. Over a ten year period from 1810 the lease had been held by Mr. Peter Brown at a yearly rent of £20, passing then to a Mr. Gilbert at the same rate. In 1826 The Mersey and Irwell Navigation Company took over the lease for £50 per annum. By the beginning of 1854 the ferry lease was again being offered for rent by auctioneers, Messrs. Churton, who invited bids for the lease in February that year. The auction took place at The Royal Hotel in Runcorn and the successful purchasers were the directors of *The St. Helens Railway and Canal Company* who agreed to pay the princely sum of £920 per annum for the ferry and its associated rights. The specific conditions of the lease required the lessee to offer three reliable boats and enough ferrymen to provide a regular service. The boats were to be kept in good repair and the embarking and disembarking places were to be well maintained. The lease, which was granted to Mr. Gilbert Greenall as the representative of the directors of the railway company, was for a period of twenty-one years. After seven years the rental would rise to £1000 per annum and after a further seven years this would increase to £1100.

Although the terms of the lease had included certain stipulations regarding the condition of the boats and the landing facilities, there was little done initially to comply with these requisites. In the years immediately after the Railway Company had secured the lease the Runcorn Improvement Commissioners made numerous unsuccessful efforts to persuade the company to act in accordance with their responsibilities. These requirements referred mainly to the maintenance of the ferry boats and their approaches. Despite continued appeals, all requests were routinely ignored. As a consequence the Commissioners, feeling they had no other option open to them, subsequently petitioned Lord Cholmondeley's officials to take action against the Railway Company for not observing the terms of the lease. However it was not until one of the ferries capsized in 1858[91] that action was eventually taken by Lord Cholmondeley's representatives. Shortly after this unfortunate incident there was a sudden flurry of activity which resulted in a new waiting room being built. A narrow stone causeway was also constructed which terminated in a flight of steps leading down to the moorings. However, this hasty activity had not yet taken place when the correspondent quoted below made his epic journey in November 1858.

"Gentlemen, Allow me to call the attention of the St. Helen's Railway Company to the filthy and disgraceful state of the Runcorn ferry. Last Monday week, wishing to come per first train to Liverpool, I proceeded to the ferry at an early hour. On arrival at Castle-rock there was a boat waiting, which I got in, and in a few minutes off we set. Being a stranger, and the morning being thick, and not knowing the nature of the ferry, I expected very soon again to land on terra firma; but behold my surprise when in about a minute and a half I found that we were alongside a sandbank, and told to get out. I inquired the cause of this and was told that it was in consequence of there not being sufficient water to go around the bank, and that they always had to put them on the bank when the tide was out. With this I got out, little expecting

---

[91] On this occasion there was no loss of life.

what I had next to encounter. In I went, ankle deep in puddle and water, getting, as one would say, a jolly good wetting to start with. I thought that I must have missed the plank and asked the boatmen where it was. To my surprise, they said there was none, and that I should have to walk in that manner over the bank. Well, there was no alternative; go I must, or stay where I was; so, turning up my trousers, on I went, flipperty-flopperty, and in a few minutes arrived at the opposite side of the bank, only to find about one hundred or more, evidently train passengers, apparently as badly off as myself, having been ankle deep in mud; some standing contented in the mud, and others growling like angry bears, and lifting up one foot after another to keep from sinking, waiting patiently for a boat to come to take them off. It is an old saying that patience is a virtue, and well it tried the patience of us all. We waited fully thirty minutes before a boat made its appearance; on it coming as close as possible, they put out a short plank, about one half of the length required, and all wishing to get on it must go half up to their knees in puddle, or if preferred, they might stay on the bank; of course it was optional with the passengers which of the two they chose. They seemed to prefer the former, for no sooner was the plank put out than they all rushed to it, regardless of the water, and in a few minutes the boat was full. Then came the most difficult task: they were in the boat, but she was on ground and all the exertions of the boatmen combined with the passengers could not move her. Some of them were then requested to get out, but would not, and after staying another 30 minutes some of those in the boat got out, and off she went with about 20 of the 100. In a short time she returned. At the same time we could perceive another boat making round the bank to render assistance. With great difficulty I managed to get in this, and after having been on the bank for an hour and a half, landed on the Lancashire side, the slip here being ankle deep in mud, and the train having left Runcorn Gap half an hour before we landed. On inquiry, I was informed that this was no unusual occurrence, and that frequently rail passengers are thrown late though having to go over the banks, there not being sufficient boats to take them off. Now, this is an abominable nuisance which I am surprised the Runcorn people do not abolish; and it is a disgrace, and an everlasting disgrace to the railway company that they do not provide more accommodation. If they cannot do without banking them, let them make the banks and slips fit for human beings to go over, and not, as they are at present, unfit for the traffic of pigs; and let them provide a sufficient number of boats to take any quantity of passengers, more especially railway passengers."

The provision of a waiting room and improved approaches to the moorings was completed by 1860 but there was still a great deal of dissatisfaction surrounding the state of the ferry and the journey across the river. The addition of a causeway across the rocks and a flight of steps did little to improve the overall experience. In fact, just a few years later there would be additional complaints concerning the slippery state of the steps. By the early 1860s the grumbles regarding the ferry had regained a pace. It was obviously a matter of grave concern to passengers that the boats which transported them across the river were not seaworthy, and that the public walkways to the ferry were still in a deplorable condition. In addition to this, the service was notoriously unreliable. This unreliability was a cause of great annoyance and frustration to travellers, especially those who were planning onward journeys. It should also be remembered that the advancement of industry in Widnes had increased the number of passengers who were travelling across the river to work in the neighbouring town. Because the ferry service was so unpredictable this created serious difficulties for both workers and employers alike.

Many aggravated passengers vented their anger by writing to the local and national newspapers. There are countless examples of angry letters about the Runcorn Gap Ferry which take in a wide span of years. A considerable number of these letters are scattered throughout this chapter and I make no apologies for including so many. I feel that each one contributes to the overall history of our *"old ferry"* and they each give the reader a sense of the times and conditions. The complainants usually cited as their main cause of grievance things such as hazardous embarking and disembarking conditions, badly maintained boats as well as the shocking incompetence and insolence of the boatmen. Unreliability was very high on the list and, even though climatic conditions dictated the regularity of the service, it was often claimed that delays were entirely due to inefficient work practices or the dilatory and sullen attitude of the boatmen.

The following letter appeared in *The Liverpool Mercury* on 3rd February 1863. It tells an alarming tale of a type of journey which would shock and horrify modern travellers, not to mention our present day health and safety Tsars. In addition to the obvious inconveniences and perils the ferry traveller had to contend with just to reach the boat; he also had to suffer the indignity of having to be carried on the back of the boatman. As the river crossing relied on the tides this meant that when the tide was low it was only possible for the boats to go halfway across. Because of this, boats coming from either side of the river usually swapped passengers when they reached a midway sandbank.

Naturally this was a great inconvenience for everyone, passengers and boatmen alike. The traveller also faced the added difficulty of having to transfer from one boat to another by balancing on very narrow planks. One can only imagine the hassle and difficulties this presented, especially for less mobile passengers. The whole process seemed to be an ordeal from start to finish. It was a fairly primitive arrangement but I am sure the owners of the ferry could have come up with something better, even if it was only longer and wider planks! If all this were not enough to daunt even the most determined traveller, at the end of his journey, when he eventually reached dry land, his shoes and feet were usually soaked through.

> Being a resident near Runcorn, and having business in Liverpool which required my presence, I left Runcorn 15 minutes before the advertised time for train boat, purposing to have plenty of time. The boat took us a portion of the way over, and left us on a sandbank, which the tide was just leaving. After walking to the other side of the bank another boat came to meet us from the Lancashire side, but could not get to the bank within 80 yards. The boatmen bring two trestles and planks, which are not half long enough to reach to the boat, and place them about midway; then we walk over the shoe tops in water to the planks; then along the same with much difficulty (on account of the strong wind) to the end, where one of the boatmen is waiting to take us on his back and carry us to the boat, which is a very tedious operation. We then sail for Lancashire, and run some half-mile to the station with our boots full of water. When we arrive there we are told we must wait an hour and a half, as our train is just gone. The picture is rather under than over drawn. I have only spoken of what would be derived from the ferry. But we must not forget that Runcorn is an increasing seaport town of upwards of 10,000 inhabitants, extending its docks and warehouses, surrounded with land to be let cheap for manufacturing purposes, which are springing up on all sides, and which only wants a railway through the town to cause their further development. Shareholders need not fear for dividends on the Aston and Runcorn line.—Yours, &c., HALTON CASTLE.

It is no wonder there were so many disgruntled passengers and irate letter-writers. Perhaps one can also understand why the boatmen were notorious for their grumpy and discourteous manner. I am sure there was little job satisfaction in dealing with exasperated passengers, or in having to hoist people of all shapes and sizes onto their backs to transport them from one boat to another. It was probably a hard, unpleasant and very low paid job which gave them little reason to be cheerful or accommodating.

The dangerous state of the walkways, especially for those crossing the river in the dark of night, was often singled out as one of the main causes for complaint. Previous owners had made no significant capital investment or improvements to the facilities and it would appear that *The St. Helens Railway and Canal Company* did only the minimum amount possible. The small improvements they did make were only carried out under coercion from the Runcorn Commissioners. Ten years after taking over the operation they sold their interest in the ferry to *The London and North-western Railway Company*. The regular passengers probably hoped that this sale would finally be the answer to their prayers. Alas, the new owners, like their predecessors, had no plans to improve either the boats or the embarking and disembarking routines. As usual, the only platform for open and public complaint was through the columns of local newspapers. In September 1864 one hopeful Runcorn resident wrote a letter to a northern newspaper in which he gives a sardonic response to some previous correspondence about the Runcorn Ferry.

"Gentlemen, - I am glad to see, from your paper of today, that you Liverpool people are taking pity upon us poor Runcornites, and do not want to see us go down to Davy Jones's locker by the score during the ensuing winter. In sober earnest, the state of the ferry and approaches between this and the Lancashire side has been a disgrace to a civilised country these many months past. Your correspondent has probably, when he crossed, been in luck's way, not having to scramble over slippery stones or ankle-deep in mud before he could get in or out of the old rotten tubs of ferry boats, as we have to do at low water, or else he would have spoken still stronger. He had probably not, as we now and then have, the pleasure of being accompanied in his transit by horses, oxen, sheep, or swine, alive or slaughtered, in the same boat.

Having for eighteen months back brought the matter over and over again under the notice of the St. Helens Railway and Canal Company, the then owners of the ferry, without any result, I despaired of any remedy till some fine day the Coroner had been sitting upon a dozen of us, and the ferry managers, etc. committed to Kirkdale or Chester Castle, as the case may be.

However, there is a better time coming. Ferry, railway and docks have now passed into the hands of the London and North-western Railway Company, and they sent down last week their surveyors to report on the state of their new acquisition – say, four rotten boats, and the exclusive privilege of ferrying across the Mersey some 3000 or more passengers per week. People now, at any rate, know when they break their limbs in getting into or out of the ferry boats, or running a good chance of being drowned in crossing, that they or their executors will have a good paymaster to fall back upon.

I trust however, for their own sake, that the company will remedy matters – not only get clean new boats efficiently manned, but also get the approaches to the ferry out of a state which beats Californian or Australian diggings – yours etc. "A Runcornite"

Nevertheless, for countless generations of travellers the old ferry had been the sole means of crossing the river and despite its continuous hazards and inconveniences they were forced to put up with it. Over the latter years of its existence most people became resigned to the fact that, in spite of the constant complaints which had gone on since the early 18th century, little would be done to improve it. Local people despaired of things ever changing and, to compound their despondency, the numerous proposals to build a bridge across the Mersey at Runcorn had been abandoned for one reason or another. Every scheme to bridge the river had been greeted with great interest and enthusiasm locally. But, regardless of this enthusiasm and the sterling reputation of some of the engineers who submitted plans, none of these projects materialised. As we have seen, two of the greatest engineers of their age, James Brindley and Thomas Telford[92], were among those who had hoped to span the Mersey at Runcorn. It is to be regretted that neither of these remarkable men was able to realise his ambition.

After so many years of discontent and frustration, during the late 1860s *The London and North-Western Railway Company* were finally to fulfil the hopes and dreams of all those early engineers and planners, not to mention the thousands of ferry passengers who had risked life and limb crossing our river. By the early years of that decade the rail company had ambitious plans in the pipeline to develop their communication system. A particularly important element of their

---

[92] Thomas Telford, whose pioneering work produced new methods of engineering, became the first President of *The Institution of Civil Engineers.*

scheme was a plan to link Liverpool with London. The first step towards the improvement of the line of communication between the two cities was the opening of the Liverpool to Garston line in 1864. The intention was that when all the other improvements, of which the Garston line was only a small part, were completed they would form a direct line of communication between the port of Liverpool and the Capital. By far the most ambitious plan in this improvement scheme was the building of a railway bridge to span the river at Runcorn.

THE OLD FERRY AND LANDING SLIPWAY

Naturally the plan to link Liverpool with London with a crossing over the Mersey would have a tremendous beneficial impact on local travellers. Not only would there be easy access to Runcorn and Widnes from either side of the river, there was also the added advantage of another local rail link. The coming of the railways and their growth as an alternative means of passenger transport had significantly improved travel throughout Britain. Rail transport offered greater mobility for everyone and gave people access to previously inaccessible regions. As it took considerably less time to travel the same distance than by road, it also made travel quicker and more comfortable.

Apart from making it possible for people to seek employment opportunities further afield, the railway also created other work prospects through building or other types of rail related employment. Despite the undisputed benefits the railways brought to remote regions, there were obviously downsides for residents in some of the areas they passed through. The construction of railways throughout the country was a major undertaking and one can only imagine the huge disruption this caused in places where cuttings, embankments, bridges and viaducts were needed. In addition to all the major construction work there was the additional paraphernalia of stations and signal boxes to be built and sited. Today, as we await the completion of a second modern road bridge across the Mersey, and see the amount of excavation work and disruption this entails, we can more easily appreciate the amount of hard manual labour that was required to construct our old railway bridge. We should also remember that this astonishing feat of Victorian engineering was carried out without the benefit of modern machinery.

Locally, the formation of railways commenced around 1826 when the first line from Liverpool, running almost directly from west to east, was formed for the purpose of connecting Liverpool with the city of Manchester. A second shorter line was then constructed which was intended to unite the town of Warrington with Liverpool and Manchester.

TO RUNCORN GAP.

FROM LIVERPOOL.		FROM MANCHESTER.	
7 0 Morning ....Second Class		7 30 Morning ....Second Class	
11 45 ,, ...	,,	11 45 ,, ...	,,
5 30 Afternoon ..	,,	5 30 Afternoon ..	,,
ON SUNDAYS.			
7 0 Morning ....Second Class		7 0 Morning ....Second Class	
5 30 Afternoon ..	,,	5 30 Afternoon ..	,,

RUNCORN GAP (WIDNES) RAILWAY TIMETABLE – SEPTEMBER 1840

In theory rail travel was supposed to be quicker and more convenient than the journeys undertaken by the turnpike roads. However, an account of a rail journey between St. Helens and Runcorn Gap in May 1840 might lead us to believe otherwise. The writer of this letter describes an overly long trip to cover a relatively short distance and correctly suggests that it might have been quicker to walk.

"There is a railway from St. Helens to Runcorn Gap, a distance of four miles. One Tuesday evening the journey was thus accomplished: the author of this paragraph booked himself by the quarter to six o'clock train from St. Helens to Runcorn Gap and received a ticket from the bookkeeper at the former place. At ten minutes to six the train, one coach, started, and in a few minutes arrived at the foot of the incline

which carries the railway across the Liverpool and Manchester line. Here Runcorn passengers alighted, and a walk to the stationary engine followed. There the Parr engine, with a train of coal wagons, was waiting. After some ten minutes delay the writer was told to mount the tender of the engine, no carriage being there to take him on to the end of the journey. Another short ride brought him on to the end of this part of the journey, after which another short ride brought him to the top of the second incline, on reaching which he was told to dismount from the coal box and walk on to Runcorn, some two miles distance. After a walk and a wait he was picked up by the Runcorn engine, and on that finally arrived at the station at Runcorn Gap at twenty five minutes past seven o'clock; having traversed the whole line of the Runcorn Gap and St. Helens railway, some seven miles, in the amazing short space of one hour and forty minutes, which is about five minutes longer than would take a tolerable pedestrian to walk over the same distance. Should this meet the eye of any directors, they ought to make at least an attempt to manage their matters differently, or at once cease to pretend to convey passengers along their line."

We are quite fortunate to have a number of records relating to early train journeys on the Runcorn Gap Railway. All of them offer contemporaneous descriptions and give an insight into the thoughts of travellers and their opinions of our area. They provide a sense of what it was like to travel on the railway in the early days. The following account is from a gentleman who made the trip along this route in April 1842. This description is particularly entertaining and enlightening, especially as one is given to assume that one of his travelling companions was either a Mr. Johnson or a Mr. Hazlehurst.

"I was one of a party of six, in a railway carriage, viz., a Liverpool merchant, going to Manchester; a blind woman, engaged to shampoo the Earl of Derby; a butcher, for the Old Swan cattle market; a Runcorn chimney rival, and a St. Helens coal factor. The Liverpool gentleman shaded his Conservative importance behind a Tory paper; the shampooing rib entertained the butcher; the Runcorn and St. Helens were talking about coals and soda; and I was looking on.

Our wheels being well fed with Henry Booth's patent soda and palm oil mixture, the departure bell having sounded, the "go on" command echoed through the tunnel, and in less than fifteen minutes we were roped out of the darkness. During our subterraneous slide, I was thinking about the nonsense of those railway managers who imposed on the travelling inspectors, the servitude of wearing a livery; I believe I saw two of those gentlemen in blue with gold laced collars; the superintendent seems alone to have escaped this servile distinction; no doubt they could not for shame oblige the old gentleman to be wrapped up in this police coat. I wish the authors of this tyranny to be compelled to appear in such like accoutrement every Sunday, at the church door.

At Broad Green Station we lost the butcher, and with him, the cow`s perfume; a good thing for consumptive subjects, says our milk woman. A female of an enormous obesity, quite an African Venus, made her appearance to fill the empty stall. The guards being occupied somewhere else, the Liverpool gentleman next to the door took hold of the hand that was stretched in for assistance; the task, however, was above the limits of his dragging power; the lady, with a good grasp and a heavy pull, tumbled back, taking her cavalier with her, on a heap of snow, where both were safely extended, no serious mischief being the consequence. Now, three men backing her centre of gravity, she was at last hoisted into the vehicle, and all was right save the loss of ten minutes. The newcomer was a good acquisition for the blind traveller; having lost the benefit of the show, she was all the time wetting her lips to make up with the tongue for what her eyes had left her short.

The board which tells you that you have reached the St. Helens and Runcorn Gap Station is a good plan; similar indication should exist at every stopping place, as is the case already on the Birmingham and London lines.

A litte further, up on the right, stands Muspratt`s monster chimney which has spoiled the Runcorn soapboiler`s pride. All the trees in the neighbourhood, as far as you can see, were sick from the soda-ash effluvia before this chimney was built. Nothing will restore them to health again; and the money spent in erecting this post-mortem monument would have been better applied in indemnifying the agriculturists. They say this chimney threatens to reduce itself by half. Let it come down to any height it pleases, and smoke away, the mischief is already all done.

At the Parkside station a marble tablet tells you Huskisson's sad tale; they forgot to add in an N.B. that the enlightened Corporation of Liverpool have shut up his statute in a Diogenes lantern. People should not remember that the town was formerly represented by a clever man, for comparisons are odious"

The traveller in this eventful journey of 1842 seems to have enjoyed the companionship of either of the soap manufacturers, Mr. Johnson or Mr. Hazlehurst, during his excursion. Sadly, the railway proved to be a curse rather than a blessing for one of these men. On another journey, in June 1869, a son of Mr. Hazlehurst met with a fatal accident. The young man, Thomas Alfred Hazlehurst, who was just a month short of his 21st birthday, was accompanying a group of workmen from his father's works on a special excursion train from Runcorn to Buxton. As the train approached Broadheath Station he leaned out of the carriage window to see whether a friend he had invited along was on the platform. Unfortunately, in doing so, his head hit a coping stone near a girder bridge and he was knocked unconscious. The young man's skull was fractured in two places and he died shortly afterwards at Cheadle Station. It was one of several similar accidents that had happened at this point. After this particular incident the Coroner requested the North-Western Railway Company to remove all coping stones from this girder bridge.

We can gather from these examples that early railways were not efficient, but things did improve as rail travel became more commonplace and advanced. As we have seen, some twenty years later, in the 1860s, when proposals were made to link Liverpool with London via a bridge across the Mersey the plan was greeted with widespread eagerness by the new railway enthusiasts as well as the residents of Runcorn and Widnes. The proposed new bridge would cut off the angle at Warrington and allow an almost direct line between Liverpool and London. It was remarked, at the time, that when this work was completed it would be the greatest rail improvement that had been achieved in modern times. There was also a plan to incorporate a footbridge alongside the railway which would allow pedestrians to cross the river at the point where there had previously been nothing but the dangerous and unreliable ferry. As one can imagine, the regular and long suffering ferry passengers were overjoyed at the prospect.

However things did not happen overnight and until the railway bridge was completed travellers were obliged to continue crossing the river by means of the old ferry. It must have been a cause of great frustration for passengers knowing that the end of their ferry days were in sight, yet having to persevere with the same old problems. Despite the early optimism of those travellers who had hoped that new owners, *The London & North-Western Railway Company,* would invest in new facilities, by the autumn of 1865 it was quite obvious that this was not likely to happen. There had been no improvement in the service and criticism increased rather than abated. In a letter to *The Liverpool*

Mercury in October 1865 we read what had become a familiar feature in that newspaper, another complaint about the Runcorn Gap Ferry. This correspondent gives a graphic account of what pitfalls a passenger may encounter on a night-time journey across the river. It was certainly not a trip for a timid traveller nor was it advisable for ladies to make the journey alone. This rather satirical letter, extolling the dubious merits of this form or transport, was titled "*A Model Ferry*".

"Gentlemen, I have ventured to intrude upon your valuable space to introduce to your readers, who have not had the (mis)fortune to see it, what I am happy to say is a great curiosity in this age of progress – I mean the Ferry at Runcorn Gap. It is so well managed, and the Company are so afraid of interfering with the liberty of the passengers, that you are positively allowed to find your way in the dark across the bank of the river alone, to the other deep end, but are told by the ferrymen "if you keep a bit to the right you will find the boat"; then if the night is not too dark, and you are fortunate, you will not find the boat but something else – namely about 30 feet of planks about 12 inches wide to walk without light or anything to guide you. If you accomplish this safely you arrive at the boat and flatter yourself that you have accomplished successfully a rather nice bit of navigation; but wait until you have gained the other end of the boat, and if your eyes are good you will see another plank and find what immense service the little practice you have had on the planks is to you, for you have now a rather different sort of plank, not quite so wide as the last or so long, but, if the boat is not on the ground, just sufficiently unsteady as to make the walk exciting. This sort of thing might not be so pleasant to gentlemen who are near-sighted, for they might not find either boat or plank, or they might find the planks, and when in the middle of them would most likely miss their footing and find the river; but this would be a refreshing bath after a long day's travel, so that they would not after all be much the losers as they would have it so cheap. Ladies also might not admire the passage, but they are not supposed to travel at night, and if one or two do happen to cross, perhaps they will find some gentleman who will endeavour to make the journey pleasant. If not, why, it could scarcely be expected that a light should be placed on the boat and a man on the bank to guide the few across; it would be such a waste of oil and entail no end of trouble to the collectors of tickets. The trustees of the Duke of Bridgewater, although having nothing to do with the ferry, have endeavoured to improve matters by making an opening in the pier to accommodate the ferry; but as the place requires washing as the tide recedes, and the ferrymen have quite enough work to do as they can get through, the sand and mud have

233

accumulated on the steps to such an extent and makes them so beautifully slippery, that you have to bring all your activity to your assistance to save a fall. This brings all your muscles in play on a cold night, and imparts that pleasant glow one feels after an hour's skating, and puts you in a nice position for getting to your house or hotel (as the case may be) as quickly as possible and immediately going to bed. If any of your readers who may be fond of pleasure and excitement would like to try this intricate piece of navigation, I would recommend them to start from the Widnes side of the river on a dark night, about an hour before floodtide, when I am sure they would come to the same conclusions as Yours & etc."

Although the ferry conditions were appalling, I suppose one should not feel too surprised that *The London & North-Western Railway Company* was reluctant to invest in improvements. The Company already had ambitious plans in place to build a bridge across the river which would cause the ferry to become obsolete. However, in the intervening time, the ferry was still in daily operation and the complaints continued to come thick and fast. It seems as though a week could hardly pass by without some reference being made in both local and national newspapers to the terrible dangers of the Runcorn Ferry. Even from the limited research period covered in this book, we can see that complaints about the ferry had been constant for well over forty years.

One cannot help but wonder what those early travellers would make of our modern preoccupation with health and safety. These days we often think that legislation has gone over the top. Nevertheless, it is gratifying to see how far we have come using the simple principle that it is better to be safe than sorry. Thank goodness we are now far more enlightened and safety conscious and, fortunately, there are strict legal procedures in place to penalise those who put lives in peril. When reading all these complaints it does seem incredible that, even in those distant days, the owners of the Runcorn Ferry were allowed to operate such a slip-shod and dangerous service without some form of legal penalty or reprimand. This lack of official action might lead us to assume that there were no provisions or rules in place at that time to safeguard the travelling public. However, as we can see from the following complaint, this was definitely not the case. The Board of Trade was responsible for implementing safety regulations but it would seem that in the case of the Runcorn Gap Ferry these rules were simply not put into practice. A passenger travelling in September 1864 wrote:

"I beg to direct attention to the dangerous condition of the communication by ferry to Runcorn. The boats are utterly rotten, patched with any driftwood which may be found floating in the river, and actually padded with spadefuls of clay to reduce the leakages. They are badly found with the needful means of working, the steering apparatus is not in order, and in this condition run the momentary risk of drifting and foundering among the bridge-work piles in a strong tide. As to cleanliness, that is not expected; but the lessees are morally if not legally bound to provide for the safety of their passengers, inasmuch as they have exclusive privilege of ferriage; and unless safe boats properly found and manned are not speedily provided, loss of life will probably occur during the stormy weather, dark nights, and fogs of winter.

It is usual for the public to be protected by public inspection of the various modes of conveyance, if a person leave, say Seacombe ferry for Runcorn, the Seacombe ferry boat carries and exhibits a certificate of efficiency from the Board of Trade, stating also the number of passengers allowed to be carried; the cab to Lime Street must obtain a license to ply, which would probably be withdrawn if it became dilapidated and unsafe. The railway can only carry passengers after obtaining sanction of the Board of Trade, yet the same railway company send the passengers across the river to Runcorn in leaky tubs totally unequal to the requirement; consequently all the former precautions may be frustrated."

Fortunately, the numerous hazards of passage on the Runcorn Gap Ferry were destined to become a thing of the past. We all know that history often paints a romantic picture of ancient activities and conduct. The early ferry which transported our ancestors from one side of the river to the other is no exception. I suppose its antiquity alone has been responsible for conjuring up quixotic visions of the ancient ferryman rowing his passengers across the Mersey in an open boat. However, as we have seen here, it was not romantic at all. In fact, in the Victorian era it was a rather unpleasant experience and most probably far worse in earlier times. Obviously this was a case of *"needs must"* and the old ferry, despite its numerous nasty pitfalls, offered an essential service for local residents and general travellers alike.

At the beginning of June 1867 the new railway bridge was well on the way and the second stretch of the structure was about to start with the installation of the fourth girder. The girder was to be set in place with an official launching ceremony. It was an exciting occasion for the citizens of both towns and, as was the custom in those days, the event was marked with some festivity. The whole of the structure was decorated with flags and banners and huge crowds gathered on both sides of the river to witness this historic event. Immediately prior to the launching ceremony the architect of the bridge and the resident engineer hosted a visit from members of the Mersey Docks and Harbour Board. No doubt these esteemed gentlemen would have voiced their admiration for the superb quality of the work.

The honour of "launching" the 700 ton girder, which had taken eleven weeks to construct, was given to Mr. Philip Whiteway of Runcorn. In order to reach the girder Mr. Whiteway, who was preceded in his journey to the new bridge by a fife and drum band, was drawn along the part-built bridge on a trolley. The huge girder, which was about to be dropped (or launched) into place, was supported in its temporary position by a framework of timber beams. At the appropriate time a group of workmen, armed with rams, knocked the frame away and the girder settled down into its designated spot. When this huge iron support moved into position Mr. Whiteway released a bottle of champagne which was attached to the girder by a ribbon. As the champagne smashed against the iron structure Mr. Whiteway declared it duly launched. This act was immediately followed by the firing of cannon and lusty cheers from the workmen and the crowds of spectators who had gathered to witness this historic scene.

It was a long time in coming but the eagerly awaited bridge across the river finally materialised towards the end of 1868. The hugely impressive structure, to be known as *The Ethelfleda Bridge*, was designed by Mr. Baker who was *The London and North-Western Railway's* chief engineer and constructed by several teams of hardworking labourers under the command of Mr. Wells, the resident engineer. The new railway bridge was by any standards an incredible feat of engineering. The approaches to the bridge footpath included flights of steps at either end, with turnstiles to record the number of pedestrians crossing the bridge each day. On opening, the toll for crossing the bridge was 2d (two pence) for a single ticket or 3d (three pence) return. A weekly contract ticket was one shilling. These fares were exactly the same amount as the ferry tickets and, although it might not have been ideal for those who were less mobile, it was certainly a safer and more pleasant way to cross from Runcorn to Widnes or vice versa. Although pedestrians were safely shielded from the trains by a barrier, initially, some people were apprehensive about walking alongside the railway as it was said that there was a possibility that the trains could whiz past at an *"alarming speed of up to fifty miles per hour"!*

The arrival of the railways in our area brought ease of travel to the masses and improved mobility for all sections of society. Although the local Liverpool to London railway link did not open till the end of the 1860s, the Runcorn Gap Railway had officially opened to traffic in Widnes in 1833 and the first railway in the Runcorn area reached Preston Brook in 1838. In September 1864 the old Runcorn Gap Station in Widnes was renamed, afterwards becoming known as Widnes Station. Travel to and from Widnes by rail was further improved when a new railway station was opened at Farnworth in 1873.

When the new bridge was finally opened to pedestrians it was thought that the ancient ferry would become immediately extinct. However the ferry continued to operate for some time afterwards as it was still the only means of transporting livestock across the river. In addition, a clause had been inserted into the Act stipulating that the Railway Company must continue the ferry in the manner that it had previously been maintained. Which I suppose meant that it carried on as usual with the same dangerous methods of operation. The Company also had to pay compensation to those who owned the rights of the ferry. As a result, the old ferry continued to cross the river for a considerable while afterwards, although few people took advantage of the service. The main custom in its latter years was related to the transport of farm animals and light freight. Surprisingly, the old ferry managed to survive till 1905 but by that time very few passengers were interested in using it. When it no longer became a viable proposition the ancient ferry service was finally terminated and consigned to *"romantic"* history.

Crossing the Mersey to our neighbouring town had long been an important element of local life for both Widnes and Runcorn residents. After the ferry, the pedestrian footpath across the railway bridge was the first improved step towards enabling a safe and easy journey across the river. However, despite the provision of this new pedestrian feature, there was still the problem of transporting light cargoes or vehicles across the river. In May 1891 the Runcorn Improvement Commissioners approached the Widnes Local Board asking them to consider the possibility of connecting Widnes and Runcorn by means of a vehicular bridge. They believed that the two towns should approach the county councils of Lancashire and Cheshire with a view to inducing them to build such a bridge over the river. The Widnes Local Board agreed to receive a deputation of the Runcorn Commissioners to discuss this matter. Fourteen years later the problem of a vehicular crossing was solved by the erection of an ingenious piece of engineering known as the Transporter Bridge, which was constructed at a cost of £137,663.

The much loved Transporter Bridge was brought into operation in 1905, almost corresponding with the termination of the old ferry service. The official opening ceremony was performed by Sir John Brunner on 29th May 1905. The *"Trannie"*, as it was affectionately known, made around 150 crossings a day and enabled the transportation of both vehicles and foot passengers. It was an imaginative piece of engineering with a span of over a 1000 ft. with girders suspended from four steel towers, two on each side of the river. The towers were 190ft above high water level and were fastened to cast iron cylinders bolted onto solid rock on the Widnes side, but were sunk 35ft below the level of the ship canal on the Runcorn side. A frame on rollers was attached to the girders and hanging from this was a cage-like structure suspended from overhead cables. This cage was the *"Transporter car"* in which passengers and vehicles were carried across the quarter of a mile from one town to the other. The car was 55ft long and 24ft wide and was operated by electric power to pull it along the rollers from one side of the river to the other.

The Transporter Bridge gave Widnes and Liverpool direct road access to Runcorn and other parts of Cheshire without the need to go via Warrington, meaning a travel saving of around 17 miles. The Transporter became a local landmark and operated successfully between the two towns for almost sixty years. Regular bus services from various areas in the two towns took passengers down to the Transporter terminal. The service gave access to railway routes from both towns and was a boon for those wishing to shop on either side of the river, especially as the early closing days in the two towns did not coincide. It was also the preferred method of travel for countless generations of young people going to dance-halls across the river in their neighbouring towns. Of course, those that missed the last late *"Car"* needed to put their dancing feet to more mundane use by walking home to their respective towns across the Old Bridge.

The short expanse of river between the shores of Runcorn and Widnes has witnessed innumerable accidents over the centuries.

Countless mariners and ordinary citizens of the two towns have perished in the unforgiving waters on our stretch of the Mersey. The vast majority of these deaths were the result of work related accidents involving men who earned their living on the river, in the docks, or in other marine related occupations. Deaths among mariners were often connected to weather conditions or the seaworthiness of the crafts they sailed in. Although the greatest numbers of deaths from drowning were connected to river occupations, particularly among the *"River Flats"*, there were countless shocking drowning tragedies involving ordinary men, women and children. Of course, in later years, as people became more aware of safety procedures and the occupational structure of the

THE TRANSPORTER BRIDGE

area changed, the instances of drownings lessened. By the beginning of the 20th century there was a noticeable reduction in river related tragedies. However despite this decrease there was still an unacceptable level of accidents. In 1901 a voluntary organisation called *The Runcorn District Life Saving Corps* was formed to help rescue those in danger of drowning in our river. During the first four years of its operation the organisation had been called upon numerous times to help and, despite a marked degree of success in saving people, it was estimated that during that time over fifty dead bodies had been recovered from the river, docks and canal.

239

Although every single loss of life is dreadful and sad, the cases of multiple drowning are even more distressing. As we have seen, there were a number of ferry accidents which involved several deaths. On one occasion, in November 1795, the ferry boat which sailed between Liverpool and Runcorn overturned in the river and seven people were consigned to a watery grave. Also particularly sad were those incidents where the victims met their fate whilst enjoying what had promised to be a pleasant day out. One case, in August 1825, occurred on a sunny Sunday afternoon when seven cheerful young men left their homes in the village of Farnworth to go and bathe at Widnes Wharf, opposite Runcorn. Only three of these young men were able to return home that day. The other four, whose surnames were Dwerryhouse, Parr, Rose, and Piercy drowned after being swept away in the river. It was said that their surviving companions were greatly traumatised by the tragedy and were inconsolable for a long time afterwards. It was some weeks before the bodies were recovered and when their distraught parents were called upon for identification purposes their bodies were unrecognizable.

Another tragedy also involved a group of young men who had gone out in pursuit of a good time. One Sunday afternoon in October 1843 six young men had spent the afternoon drinking at various public houses in Runcorn. After finally being ejected from their last place of refreshment they headed down to the small boat they had moored near the ferry pier. With them they had several bottles of ale which they had purchased for the journey home. As they were making their way to the opposite shore the weather became stormy and the boat overturned. Four of them were drowned and two were saved. A report of the incident said that the two saved men were so intoxicated they didn't know what had happened and the following day they had absolutely no recollection of the accident at all. This event prompted a great deal of comment about the effects of excessive drinking and of the growing and worrying trend of breaking the Sabbath. It was said that there were more accidents of this nature occurring on a Sunday than on any other day of the week. Of course the obvious reason for this was that most people worked a six day week and Sunday was usually their only day off. The young men who died were named as Abel Chadwick, Samuel Clarke, William Higginson and Adam Maddock. The two rescued men, George Chadwick and John Maddock were the brothers of two of those drowned.

Needless to say tragic events are especially heartbreaking when it includes more than one member of a family. A boating accident in February 1848 involved a man called Burrows who lived in Higher

Runcorn with his wife and six young children. One evening whilst he was having supper he was visited by his three brothers, who were boatmen. They asked him to accompany them over the river to Widnes to bring back a load of coal. They decided to mix business with a bit of pleasure and planned to stop off at the *Snig Pie House* in Widnes for refreshment. One of the brothers took his wife along for the ride. The brothers' sister and her husband also accompanied them, making a party of seven in total. On their way back to Runcorn with the coal, between seven and eight o'clock in the evening, the water was rather rough and the wind had increased considerably. When they were near the Duke's Dock a squall struck the sail and the boat was overturned. Two of the men could swim but all the rest were drowned. All seven were related to each other, four brothers and a sister, along with her husband and the wife of one of the brothers. The husband of the sister was one of those who could swim and he managed to escape; he had only been married six months and his wife was pregnant. He told the inquest that he had tried to save her but was unable to hold onto her as they were both sinking. The rest of the party, three brothers, a sister and sister-in-law, were all drowned, leaving three widows and numerous fatherless or orphaned children.

The number of townspeople from both towns who drowned in our river and canals is far too high to recount. There are countless incidents of single drownings including several people who fell from ferries. Obviously one feels an overwhelming sadness for every family who suffered a loss in this manner. When the tragedy involves children it is particularly distressing and when this also includes more than one child from the same family this is especially upsetting. An incident in July 1867 involved two young brothers called Charles and William Parkinson, the sons of a labourer named James Parkinson who lived in Ann Street, Widnes. The lads were aged 12 and 14 years respectively. One sunny afternoon they had gone down to bathe in the canal with several other children. It was said they were opposite Mr.Pilkington's chemical works in Moss Bank where they stripped and walked into the water hand in hand. They had only gone a short distance when they suddenly disappeared. Apparently they had stepped into a hole where the water was around 12 feet deep. They never rose to the surface again after going down. Help was sought from nearby houses and several people dived in and tried to find them but the bodies were not recovered until the following day. Therefore another dreadful and tragic accident was added to the long list of local families who had been left devastated by loss of life in our river and canals.

241

The sailing conditions in the Mersey could be unpredictable especially in times of bad weather or high tides. Sometimes the consequences of high tides had detrimental results not only on river crafts but also on the land around its shores. At the beginning of October 1873 the effects of unusually high tides meant that a number of properties near the river were destroyed. One night the midnight tide rose to a height of 10 feet 10 inches at Runcorn – which was more than two feet higher than stated in the tide tables for that year. The height of the river was at one point level with the Old Quay bank. Across the river Cuerdley Marsh, which was at that time used as a ley for cattle, was entirely under water and in some places it was more than five feet deep. About one hundred sheep were drowned. A large number of animals grazing on Frodsham Marsh, near the River Weaver, were also drowned and a considerable amount of damage was done to nearby properties. It was said that the tides on the night of the 5th of October 1873 were the highest they had been for almost twenty years.

I regret to say that not all incidents on our local stretch of the Mersey were accidental. In October 1876 it was alleged that there was a deliberate attempt to murder a local man called Thomas Ogden by drowning him. Fortunately, in this case the outcome was not fatal. This incident was the result of a dispute between Ogden and several members of a family called Ford. Joseph Ford, who, like Ogden, was a river pilot, was charged along with his son, William, with having attempted to murder Thomas Ogden by ramming his boat and beating him. What I found surprising, when researching various accidents and incidents relating to river occupations, was the high number of men who were employed in this type of work who could not swim. The victim in this case, Thomas Ogden, a mariner, was also unable to swim.

This particularly unpleasant episode happened at around eleven o'clock at night when Ogden was working on the river. His boat was suddenly and deliberately rammed by another boat being operated by Joseph Ford and his son, along with another member of the same family. After his boat had been rammed Ogden managed to get near to the shore and succeeded in mooring it at Widnes Marsh, near to where all the men resided. Once on shore, the three men continued their pursuit of Ogden and a fight broke out on the land. Ogden was badly beaten and then thrown into the river at a point where the water was extremely deep. It was common knowledge that Ogden could not swim but, despite this, the men left the scene making no attempt to rescue him. It was alleged that they believed he would drown. Fortunately for Ogden, after the men had left the scene he was able to grab onto a projecting rock and succeeded in getting back onto the bank. Although badly injured and greatly distressed he managed to make his way to his lodgings where someone alerted the police.   Shortly afterwards warrants were issued for the arrests of the three men but they had all absconded.   Joseph and William Ford, father and son, were subsequently found and sent for trial charged with attempted murder; the other man was never apprehended.   There is no information available to suggest the reason for the dispute, but at their trial the Fords stated that it was a trivial disagreement which had got out of hand. The prosecution claimed that it was a callous and cold-blooded act which, to all intents and purposes, was likely to have left a man for dead. As we are not privy to all the facts of the matter, or the evidence which was presented to the court, it would be unfair to make a judgement but, in any case, it was certainly an uneven fight, three against one.

The incidents of Sunday drownings were numerous and many involved young men who had been drinking to excess.   These sad episodes gave an opportunity for local temperance organisations to use the events as clear evidence of the evils of drink.   One of these tragic incidents commenced on a Sunday morning in July 1884 when seven young men arrived at Weston Point in a small boat with a fixed mast. After spending several hours in the pubs around the neighbourhood, they arrived back at Weston Point Pier at around five o'clock in the evening. It was quite obvious to those who saw them that they were the worse for wear.   On reaching their boat there appeared to be some disagreement which resulted in one of them deciding not to get into the boat. This young man said he had no money left so he asked his companions for 3d to pay for his fare over the Runcorn Bridge. He then set off alone to walk across the bridge while his six friends boarded the boat and set sail towards the Frodsham part of the river. They had only gone a short way when several people on the river bank saw the boat capsize and the occupants fall into the water. A mate and second engineer from a steamship which was moored nearby launched a small boat to go to their rescue and the captain of a small flat also set sail to offer assistance. Unfortunately, as the tide was two hours on the ebb, it took them almost an hour to get to the boat.   When they eventually reached the craft it had resumed an upright position and they found a young man in a state of semi-consciousness lying in it.   Later three bodies were discovered on the river bank near Frodsham and another was found the following day in the same vicinity. One young man had managed to swim ashore and the man who had been discovered in the boat made a full recovery. Three of the dead men were named as John Woodward, John Swiney, John Barber and the

243

other man was unnamed. Those who survived were James Wood and Bryan Lofter. It was rumoured that the accident occurred as the occupants of the boat tried to retrieve a companion's hat which had fallen overboard. It was also said that there had been some concern regarding the question of whether the occupants were fit to sail the boat. When the boat was setting sail from Weston Point a captain of a nearby boat observed that the boat was very low in the water and that the occupants seemed ignorant of how to manage the sails. He said he called out a few instructions, but the only response to his help was a curse.

Temperance became a constant theme during Victorian times and the regularity of drink related accidents on the river created many opportunities to highlight the iniquities of drink. In the case of Sunday drownings, it is true that many of these involved groups of young men who were in an advanced state of intoxication. Perhaps excessive alcohol consumption was part and parcel of Sunday afternoon socialising for young men who had spent a hard week in the confines of hot and noxious chemical factories. However, alcohol abuse was not a nuisance peculiar to young men; it was a widespread problem among all ages of the male populations of both towns. Regrettably, the damaging effects of excessive drinking were noticeable not only as a cause of drowning accidents, but in many areas of everyday life. A large amount of violent crime and domestic violence was directly fuelled by drink and in some cases an intolerable portion of a man's weekly wage was spent on alcohol. Of course this added to the existing deprivations of family life.

Apart from the abnormal rate of drownings which were attributed to drunkenness, there was no shortage of other alcohol related incidents to give ammunition to the temperance movement. In 1888 another event a little further down the river received a huge amount of sensational publicity in local and national newspapers. Middle-class Victorian readers were suitably shocked by reports of drunken behaviour by groups of men and boys on the banks of the Mersey. They viewed the incident as a prime example of the debauched state of the working classes, believing that this occurrence served to compound their opinion that the working classes lacked self-control and had no concept of decent behaviour. The episode sparked renewed calls to curb the widespread drunkenness which plagued Victorian society. One cannot help but feel that had this *"whiskey galore episode"* happened further up-stream, nearer our own towns, there would have been a similar state of affairs.

The incident, which drew large crowds to the banks of the Mersey near Otterspool, happened one Wednesday afternoon in March 1888. The Liverpool police received information that a large crowd had gathered on the banks of the river near to Otterspool where a substantial number of barrels containing methylated spirit had been washed ashore. Several constables were despatched to the area to investigate. On reaching the shore they encountered what could best be described as a scene of drunken bedlam. Dozens of people, mainly men and boys, were standing around a hogshead and several barrels of methylated spirit, while others were rolling barrels away and trying to conceal them with the intention of collecting them later and taking them home. Some of the barrels had been opened and there were numerous men and boys lying on the ground in a state of helpless intoxication. They had no proper drinking vessels so the only way of consuming the spirit was by one man holding the cask up for another man to drink from, and they appeared to be taking turns in doing this. However, a number of men were just lying on the ground and drinking straight from the casks. From the hopeless state of some of the men it was clear that they had been there some considerable time.

Several descriptions of the scene conjure up images of Hogarth's portrayals of wanton inebriations. However the arrival of the local police soon put a stop to these alcoholic activities. The barrels were immediately confiscated by the police and put under guard until the arrival of the Customs Officers. Those men who were physically able to do so made a quick getaway. However, some of the men were so drunk they had to be removed from the scene in wheelbarrows and taken to the nearest police station where they were put in the cells to await charges being brought against them. Unfortunately some had drunk so much of the liquor that they were in a bad state, almost unconscious, and the local doctor had to be called. The doctor found it necessary to use a stomach pump on several of the drinkers. He claimed later that, had he not done so, there is no doubt that they would have died from alcoholic poisoning. Despite the ill effects of drinking raw spirit, and the possibility of being arrested, the following day the beach was full of men and boys again, no doubt hopeful that some more barrels might be washed ashore at the same spot. It was also said, as news of this incident spread, that there were dozens of men and boys on the shorelines of the upper Mersey, near to Widnes and Runcorn, hoping that some barrels would be swept up to their stretch of the river.

In this chapter we have seen that the river Mersey played a vital role in the development of both Widnes and Runcorn. Over the centuries the river brought us benefits and joys as well as countless tragedies. We have also seen how difficult it was in earlier days to traverse the short distance between our two towns, a span of only a quarter of a mile. The numerous perils and shortcomings of the old ferry, which served as the only means of crossing at this point, make for uneasy reading. Furthermore, the subject of bridging this narrow stretch of water seems to have been a recurring theme for centuries as numerous unsuccessful efforts by engineers and enterprising individuals were subsequently abandoned and consigned to history.

Because of all those long standing difficulties and disappointments we can well imagine the euphoria which greeted the completion of the magnificent Ethelfleda Bridge in the late 1860s. We can see that, by any standards, this was a magnificent feat of engineering. Today, as we await the opening of another new crossing to add to the existing structures, we are keenly aware of the disruption and scale of work involved in such an enormous project. Therefore we can more easily appreciate what a hugely difficult enterprise those early engineers and builders embarked upon in order to build our *"Old Bridge"*. We have certainly come a long way from the days of the ancient and treacherous ferry but the story of this early service, and the ensuing difficulties involved in providing a link between the two towns, is an important and fascinating part of our local history.

EVERYDAY LIFE

When reflecting on the lives of local residents during the past few hundred years, we can see that changes in the daily habits and working routines of the indigenous populations of both towns were extreme. We are also keenly aware of the radical physical and environmental changes which occurred, especially in Widnes. However some parts of the local topography remained relatively unscathed and, happily, we still have some ancient buildings which link our past to the present. The Castle Pub in Halton is one example. An advertisement reproduced here, from May 1796, demonstrates a case in point. This notice also serves to remind us of the salubrious atmosphere and reputation that Runcorn and its districts enjoyed in the late eighteenth century.

HALTON-CASTLE, NEAR RUNCORN, CHESHIRE.
JOHN DARWELL,
(Succeſſor to Mr. WHITE)

RESPECTFULLY informs his Friends and the Public, that he has, at a conſiderable Expence, fitted up the above Inn, in the moſt commodious Manner, for the Reception of Travellers and Viſitants to this ſingularly ſalubrious and pleaſant Situation.—The Proſpect is extenſive beyond Compariſon, and beautifully diverſified with Towns, Seats, Woods, and Water, to a great Extent; the River Merſey running juſt beneath, renders it very Convenient for Sea-bathing, to which great Numbers reſort from Mancheſter and other Places.—The BOWLING GREEN, for Pleaſantneſs and Beauty of Situation, is not to be equalled in the Kingdom — The beſt Wines, Spirituous, and Malt Liquors, have been ſelected; and every Exertion and Endeavour will be made to give Satisfaction, and merit a Continuance of that flattering Encouragement which they have been pleaſed to confer.
☞ A WAITER wanted.

THE CHESTER CHRONICLE – 13TH MAY 1796

THE CASTLE AT HALTON – IN THE 20TH CENTURY

Of course at that time The Castle Inn was catering specifically to a well-heeled type of patron. The best wines, spirits and malt liquors on offer at this establishment would most certainly have been beyond the means of ordinary working people. Furthermore, I am sure that its proprietor, Mr. Darwell, would have been somewhat disconcerted if his clientele had been anything less than the refined class who were affluent enough to visit the area for leisure rather than work. At that time status boundaries were evident in all aspects of daily life, and the vast disparity in fortunes and lifestyle which existed between different sections of society created great divisions among all classes. But in spite of the huge inequalities which were a feature of everyday life, the populations of cities, towns and villages were conditioned to accept that wealth and power, or privileges of birth, brought with it certain rights. Working men had a strong sense of dependency and were accustomed to showing subservience to their masters and a fierce loyalty to the ruling sovereign and all members of the royal family. Although society was fundamentally unequal, it was totally embedded with an acute sense of hierarchy which existed in men's' minds and habits. Naturally, the Monarch was at the pinnacle of this hierarchy and he commanded allegiance and unwavering commitment from his subjects, whatever their social position.

When Prince William, the Duke of Gloucester, visited Runcorn in December 1804 as a guest of Sir Richard Brooke there was a great display of loyalty from the local inhabitants. A report of this event paints a picture of uncompromising patriotism:

"His Royal Highness Prince William of Gloucester has been spending a few days at Norton Priory, in this county, the beautiful seat of Sir Richard Brooke, Bart., and on Wednesday visited Runcorn, for the purpose of viewing the extensive works of the late Duke of Bridgewater there. We have the pleasing task of recording the prompt and loyal conduct of the patriotic Corps of Volunteers belonging to that place. It was not until a late hour the preceding night that the report of this amiable Prince's intended visit reached Runcorn, notwithstanding which, and the circumstance of many of the men, from the nature of their employment, being dispersed amongst the farmhouses in the neighbouring country, there was a very respectable muster, parading at an early hour to welcome the Royal visitor; on his entrance into the village, he was received with opened ranks and presented arms, the band playing and the colours saluting; on his arrival in front of the line he alighted, and after conversing for some time with the Commanding Officer, with his usual condescension, and asking a number of

249

questions relative to the Corps, he desired the men might march past in review order, which they did in a very soldier like manner; he expressed much pleasure in this unexpected mark of loyalty and attention, and pronounced a high panegyric on the appearance and discipline of the Corps. This must have been highly gratifying to the Prince, to find that every corner of this district is filled with men prompt and ready for the defence of their King and County."

During this period the country was ruled by George III a popular and hardworking King who had managed to exert some significant influence on Parliament. However a debilitating disease subsequently incapacitated him and the nature of this illness, which has been described as madness, required that authority was passed to his son. At the time he became Prince Regent, in 1811, the son was already known for his lax morality and lack of honour. By the time he succeeded to the throne as George IV there had already been a marked decline in royal political influence and authority. In fact, his reign was tainted by numerous scandalous activities. His wife, Princess Caroline of Brunswick Wolfenbuttel, was no less profligate in her behaviour. The marriage was not a happy one but the union resulted in the birth of a daughter, Charlotte, their only child.

Although the demeanour of the Regent and his wife left much to be desired, Princess Charlotte was extremely popular among the people. When she married Prince Leopold of Saxe-Coburg the whole country celebrated the happy event. Alas the story did not have a happy ending as the young Princess was to die within hours of giving birth to a stillborn baby boy. After Charlotte's death her mother, Caroline, went to live abroad where her shameful conduct, which included numerous adulterous affairs, became the subject of salacious gossip at home and abroad. Nevertheless, despite all the controversy which surrounded the Monarchy at that time the vast majority of the population, which was inherently dutiful in character, remained intensely loyal to the Crown. Although it is clear that this allegiance did not necessarily include respect for royal behaviour.

Despite that ingrained loyalty, and perhaps not surprisingly, there *were* many among the working population who were beginning to voice their dissatisfaction through public protest. The clamour for fairer parliamentary representation was becoming more insistent. By 1817 the voices of discontent were growing louder and, in January that year, the Prince Regent's coach was surrounded by an angry jeering mob who threatened the terrified Prince. The social injustices and inequalities which had always existed, and caused great discontent among working men, came to the fore during the nineteenth century. Previous generations had accepted their condition with resignation and had lacked the courage to protest simply because they felt it was not within their power to change things. They believed that their situation was inevitable. Nonetheless, the country was changing in many ways at this time and, as industry replaced agriculture, the lives of working people were irrevocably altered. As a result of the transformations which were happening all around, attitudes as well as working practices started to alter and the new urban masses began pressing for a fairer society. Consequently the country started to seethe with unrest and a series of revolutions in Europe stimulated thoughts of civil upheaval.

Some historians believe that this new growth of confidence was a direct result of the French Revolution and that this event, coupled with the process of industrialisation, was the agent of a rising movement of popular agitation. There was, indeed, a marked shift in the mood of the working classes after the success of the Revolution in France. Ordinary people started to develop the courage to remonstrate against intolerable economic exploitation and political oppression. It would seem that the incidents in France had cultivated the aspirations of ordinary men and women who began to call for reform and a fairer society. Of course the other element cited as a source of increased confidence was the Industrial Revolution. This was essentially a phase of transition between two ways of life, a chapter which became a driving force for change in the working and living habits of ordinary people. Both revolutions were important factors which contributed to a palpable alteration in the attitude of working people, as they developed a new sensation of self-respect and political consciousness.

During the nineteenth century, as a result of this new found confidence amongst working men, there were a series of unsuccessful attempts to reform the workings of Parliament. Some of these attempts resulted in violent clashes between the authorities and those who challenged parliamentary procedure. One of the worst incidents occurred not too far from our own area, in August 1819, when a peaceful meeting attended by thousands of suffrage and anti-poverty protesters ended in massacre and injury. That infamous meeting, held at St. Peter's Field in Manchester, would subsequently become known throughout the land as the Peterloo Massacre[93]. In fact, despite the

---

[93] The word *"Peterloo"* was a derisory term intended to mock the soldiers who attacked unarmed civilians, in contrast to the soldiers at "Waterloo" who were seen as genuine heroes.

terrible events of that day occurring some miles away, the incident did have a direct impact upon our area. It caused a huge degree of panic among local landowners and town worthies. The upper classes feared that the discontent which was becoming evident among the urban masses would lead to them becoming organised and radicalised into a new political force.

On that fateful day, 16th August 1819, the crowd had gone to St. Peter's Field to hear the famous orator, Henry Hunt, speak about reform and the repeal of the Corn Laws. Mr. Hunt, who was calling for universal suffrage, attracted crowds of people wherever he went. On this occasion Mr. Hunt's makeshift platform was a simple wooden cart which was located in an open area not far from what is now St. Peter's Square. The atmosphere was quite festive, with a band playing and many of the crowd carrying flags and banners bearing the words *"Reform, Universal Suffrage and Equal Representation"*. The presence of such a huge crowd caused the local authorities to panic. In the aftermath of the event it was claimed by local magistrates that, fearing trouble, one of them had arrived to read the Riot Act. It was also alleged that this magistrate gave an order for the crowd to disperse. Despite these claims many of the local journalists who were attending the meeting were adamant that no such order was given, nor was the Riot Act ever read. One of the journalists, when describing the event later, wrote:

"The meeting assembled in the most peaceable manner, the usual complement to our monarch was performed by the bands playing "God Save the King". The chairman of the day arrived at length, and was beginning to address his countrymen when the cavalry rushed upon the people, cutting right and left, taking forcible possession of the conductors of the meeting, and then proceeding by direct charges upon the multitude to force them to the ground. I saw numbers of men and women cut down on every side of me; and even a few who stood against the farthest wall of the area, as spectators, were sabred without distinction of sex or circumstance.

Was the language used by the speaker seditious? No, it was to urge silence and good order, politics had not even been introduced. Were any of the banners and inscriptions seditious? No, they might have been seized or their carriers prosecuted. Was the exhibition of caps of liberty and inscriptions a matter of bad taste, which I think it was, because it offended the prejudices of political opponents? Surely the people must not be cut down for bad taste. Was the attendance of women bad taste? Still, the sword is not the proper corrector of it.

Were warrants to be served on the speakers for some particular reason? Even if this was so, why was this not done on the ground, without wounding scores of unresisting innocent people after the prisoners were secured. Had the Riot Act been read, and the civil power found insufficient to quell the riot? No, certainly not, there was NO riot. Was it read, as stated, soon after twelve o'clock? No this was impossible, the hour would then have expired before the great procession arrived; and the crowd then present might have been dispersed with comparative ease. Was it read at all? I think not! Numbers of persons who stood in every different part of the meeting are ready to swear they never heard any mention of it. And if it was read, there having been no riot, was the meeting to be dispersed? And if it was so dispersed, was the killing and wounding of unresisting people necessary?"

Despite hundreds of claims to the contrary, and a genuine belief that it was not, to be entirely impartial one should say that it is possible that the Riot Act may have been read. There is no clear evidence to prove or disprove either claim, it could be that because the crowd was so large the Magistrate's words were inaudible because of the noise level. However the widely-held opinion is that there was certainly no riot or any legitimate reason for The Act to be read. In retrospect, one can believe that the overwhelming size of the crowd led to panic amongst the Magistrates and their initial reaction was to call in the troops. However to do this would have been an unlawful action unless the Riot Act had been read. In view of the dreadful outcome the Magistrates probably lied about the Riot Act being read to cover themselves. The subsequent arrival of groups of militia, which included a local volunteer cavalry and several hundred Hussars on horseback, had a devastating result. As the crowd who, according to numerous contemporary reports were conducting themselves in an orderly and peaceful manner, remained in place an order was given to the militia to charge. Within ten minutes the area was a mass of human carnage with an estimated twenty dead and over seven hundred men and women seriously injured from sabre wounds and trampling. The lively festive atmosphere had been replaced by a field of dead and injured bodies and blood soaked banners. The organisers were arrested and put on trial accused of high treason. In contrast, an official inquiry cleared the Hussars and Magistrates of any wrongdoing and they received messages of congratulations from the Prince Regent.

The general panic that followed that dreadful event at Manchester caused several hasty meetings to be called locally. Landowners and

253

people in power feared that there would be a civil uprising around the country. It is important to understand that the Manchester meeting occurred during a period of immense political tension and it was primarily an attempt on behalf of the organisers to stir the nation's conscience. To place these events in context we should remember that at that time fewer than 2% of the population were eligible to vote and the appalling Corn Laws were making food unaffordable for poor people. Unfortunately, whilst this form of protest awakened a social conscience in some, it only served to strengthen the opposition of those in entrenched positions of power.

Needless to say, this event raised a great deal of concern in our own area as Manchester was not too far away. However, just a week or so before this terrible and tragic event, emergency meetings had been called in Stockport, Knutsford, Middlewich, Warrington and Runcorn. The meetings were in anticipation of trouble arising from public gatherings relating to the repeal of the Corn Laws. In Runcorn the meeting was presided over by Sir Richard Brooke and a list of over 750 residents signed up to be sworn in as Special Constables should the need arise. A notice of intent was posted in several newspapers by Magistrates in various towns. Unfortunately the visual quality of the newspaper report of the Runcorn meeting is not good enough to reproduce here; therefore I include a full transcript of the text below:

MEETING AT RUNCORN.

At a GENERAL MEETING of the Community at large of Runcorn and the adjoining townships in the county palatine of Chester, convened by public notice, and held at the National School Room, in Runcorn on Thursday the 5th day of August 1819, for the purpose of adopting such precautionary measures as may be judged expedient in support of the Laws and Constitution of our Country, against the designs and practices of the disaffected, which were they to succeed, would entirely put a stop to trade, manufactures and labour.

SIR RICHARD BROOKE, BART, IN THE CHAIR;

RESOLVED FIRST: That this Meeting is unanimously of the opinion that every well affected subject should come forward at the present crisis, and declare his determination to support to the utmost of his power the civil authorities in the maintenance of the Laws and Constitution of our Country as at present established against the evil designs and practices of the seditious and traitorous conspirators, who though few in number, nevertheless whose objects by factious publications and inflammatory language artfully disseminated among the labouring class of society, tends to delude and lead them into the commission of violent and unlawful acts, by no means calculated to obtain a redress of grievances, or to remove temporary distresses of the country, but which, if not checked by the firm arm of the law may be productive of greater evils and worse times.

RESOLVED SECONDLY: That a Declaration to this effect be drawn up and signed by the Meeting, and that a copy of our proceedings be transmitted by the Chairman through the Acting Magistrates of the Hundreds of Bucklow to the Lord Lieutenant of this county; and that the same be inserted in the CHESTER CHRONICLE, MANCHESTER ADVERTISER, and in the COURIER LONDON Newspapers; and likewise that printed copies be posted up and circulated in this part of the country.

That the following Declaration be agreed to:

We, whose names are undersigned, being seriously impressed with a sense of the danger which threatens the community from the designs and practices of the disaffected, and which, were they to succeed, would entirely put a stop to trade, manufactures, and labour; deem it indispensably necessary to declare our determination to support the Laws and Constitution of our Country, and to co-operate with the legal authorities for the preservation of the public peace. For which purpose we do hereby further declare our readiness to be sworn in and to act as Special Constables or otherwise, and do call upon our neighbours and others, to join us in taking every necessary measure which the urgency of the case may require, to accomplish these most important objects.

RICHARD BROOKE, CHAIRMAN.

The Chairman having left the Chair, and General Heron being called to it. General Peter Heron, as Chairman, then resolved that the thanks of this Meeting be given to Sir Richard Brooke, Bart, for his cordial co-operation and able and judicious conduct in the Chair. [94]

I found no record of any similar meetings having taken place in the vicinity of Widnes, but as the area was only sparsely populated at that

---

[94] Extract from *The Chester Chronicle and North Wales Advertiser*: 20th August 1819

time this is not surprising. The after effects of *"Peterloo"* were felt most keenly in districts where there were significant populations of working men. In these places local magistrates called for leading citizens to be sworn in as Special Constables in case there was trouble. Liverpool of course had a substantial working population and special measures were taken by leading civic members in the city and its immediate environs.

There is no doubt that *The Peterloo Massacre* left a profound impression, not only on those who were present at St. Peter's Field on that day, but also on generations of labouring men in the north of England. In addition, many of the journalists who witnessed the event were arrested just for being at the scene. Some were so shocked by the unprovoked violence of that day that they became involved in the reform movement themselves. John Edwards Taylor, a Manchester businessman, also became an avid supporter of reform. As a result of his shock at the barbaric brutality of Peterloo, and especially by the mendacity of the authorities in denying many of their actions on that day, he became instrumental in setting up *The Manchester Guardian* newspaper. Many other reports of that dreadful event, along with original eye witness accounts, are now housed at Chetham's Library in Manchester and make for interesting but rather sad reading.

It is indicative of the attitude of the upper classes at that time that, after this horrific event, the Prince Regent praised the soldiers who cut down innocent men, women and children. Of course by this time respect for the Monarchy, though still strong among the upper classes, had begun to lessen considerably amongst ordinary working people. There were several notable incidents where the Prince Regent was heckled by angry crowds. His fulsome tributes to the soldiers who murdered innocent bystanders in Manchester caused particular outrage. Naturally the upper classes believed that the established social order should be maintained at any cost, and bringing in the troops was the most common form of restoring public order at that time. In fact in 1831 the Hussars were sent for to deal with striking miners during a coal strike in St. Helens and there were numerous civilian casualties.

During the early decades of the nineteenth century life in the small villages that comprised Widnes was fairly uneventful. Men laboured in the fields or in the time honoured occupations of their districts. Many village women worked as laundresses for the wealthy families of Liverpool, washing and pressing their linen which was collected and delivered by cart each week. Others worked in cottage crafts such as weaving or watchmaking. The inhabitants of these small places were part of long established rural communities and their lives followed a quiet, simple, traditional pattern of continuity. This steady tempo of life was occasionally disturbed by some minor local event or interesting occurrence which created a welcome diversion from the insular environment and slow pace of village life.

A pleasant distraction for the villagers of Farnworth and Bold took place in the summer of 1823, when news reached the district of the forthcoming marriage of Mary Bold, the daughter and heiress of the late Peter Patten Bold of Bold Hall. It was said that Miss Bold had inherited a fortune estimated to be in excess of twenty thousand pounds per year, which was a vast sum in those days. To add to the enthusiastic anticipation of this event, Miss Bold was marrying into royalty as her bridegroom was Prince de Sapieha, a distinguished Lithuanian Prince who also had connections to the Polish nobility.

Although the forthcoming nuptials created great excitement in the village, in actual fact the happy couple were already married. A civil marriage ceremony had been performed by the Rev. Dr. Trevor at the residence of the British Ambassador in Florence, Italy, on 21st December 1822. It had been a rather grand but relatively quiet affair with the Princess being attended by her mother and one of her sisters. As her father, Peter Patten Bold, had died in the autumn of 1819 the honour of giving the bride away was bestowed upon a family friend, his Excellency Lord Burghersh, who was married to the Duke of Wellington's niece, Priscilla Wellesley. The Prince de Sapieha was attended by Prince Potemkin, the Russian Charge d'Affaires at Florence, and by the Russian Ambassador to Naples. A small number of close friends, including Lord Dundas and Mr. Dixon of the Guards, gathered to witness and celebrate the event. Despite the fact that a civil ceremony had already been performed, the bride wished to have the union formally consecrated in the rites of the established church. Therefore, it was natural that Princess Sapieha[95] should wish to return to her local church for this religious ceremony as her family had a strong and lengthy connection with Farnworth Church.

Incidentally, Mary was not the only member of the Bold family to marry around this time. The 1820s saw all four daughters of the late Peter Patten Bold enter into a matrimonial state. In May 1820 Dorothea, the second daughter of Mr. Patten Bold, who was two years

---

[95] The full title was Princess Sapieha-Rozanski

younger than Mary, married Mr. Henry Hoghton[96] at St. George's Chapel in London. Mr. Hoghton was the heir to Sir Henry Phillip Hoghton of Walton Hall and Hoghton Towers. In 1827 another sister, Frances, married John Digby Murray who was later to become a Baronet. In April of 1828 Anna Maria Patten Bold[97] married her cousin, John Wilson Patten[98] of Bank Hall, also at St. George's Chapel in London.

Prior to their marriages all four daughters, along with their widowed mother, Mrs. Patten Bold, had regularly graced the elite social events known as the *"London Season"*. The family mixed in the highest of circles and all four daughters had been *"Presented At Court"*. The youngest of the girls, Anna Maria, being presented at Court on the occasion of the Prince Regent's official birthday on 24th April 1818. From all accounts it would seem that the sisters were very popular among their peer groups. Their status was such that their presence at fashionable balls and smart gatherings were worthy of note in the social columns of national newspapers. A newspaper report of one high-class event tells us that *"Mrs Patten Bold and her delightful daughters were in attendance"*. Apart from attending as a guest at prominent events, Mrs Patten Bold[99] also hosted her own balls and parties at Bold Hall as well as at the family's London residence in Hanover Square. Reports of these lavish affairs summon up images reminiscent of the novels of Jane Austen.

Even though there was a great deal of pleasure surrounding the forthcoming nuptials, Princess Sapieha had already made news of her civil marriage public. The tenants and workers on her estate were advised that the Princess had decided to spread a little of her happiness by making a benevolent gesture towards them. On their arrival at Bold Hall from the Continent at the beginning of August 1823, the Prince and Princess had summoned their land agent, Mr. Cookson, and instructed him to reduce the rents of all the tenants on the home estates of Bold, Burtonwood, Sutton, Rainhill and Widnes. The reduction for each tenant equated to around 12½% per annum. This decrease was in addition to a previous allowance of 20% which had been made in 1818 by her father, Peter Patten Bold[100] for the purchase of manure, which

---

[96] He later added the name "Bold" to his surname.

[97] Anna Maria, Lady Winmarleigh, died in 1846

[98] Later to become Lord Winmarleigh

[99] Mrs Mary Patten Bold died on 9th February 1835

[100] Peter Patten (later known as Peter Patten Bold) inherited the estates from his aunt Anna Maria Bold in 1813. She was the daughter of Peter Bold of Bold Hall. At the time of inheriting, Peter Patten was the MP for Malmsbury.

was to be bought under the supervision of the Estate Steward. It should be said that there are several other examples of Princess Sapieha's kindness, all of which give us a measure of her compassionate nature. Of course the substantial rent reduction served to endear the Princess even more to her tenants and labourers. This generous act was obviously appreciated, especially as most landowners of that time were completely immune to the need to improve the condition of their dependant tenants and employees.

In spite of the excited and happy anticipation of the forthcoming nuptials, it was general knowledge that the Princess Sapieha did not enjoy the best of health. Because of the delicate state of her wellbeing the couple planned to return to the more agreeable and kinder climate of Italy shortly after the wedding ceremony. Their Widnes marriage subsequently took place at St. Wilfrid's Church[101], in the village of Farnworth, on 19th August 1823. The service was conducted by the Rev. William Thompson and the witnesses to the marriage were named as Anna Maria Bold, Isaac Bold, Thomas Parker and Dorothy Parker. All the witnesses to this religious service were relatives of the bride. There is nothing to indicate if any members of the Prince's family were present at the ceremony.

As planned, the couple returned to their home in Italy at the beginning of October 1823. However in April the following year they arrived back in England for a short visit. They took an apartment in Chester for the duration of their stay and it is believed that the purpose of the visit was to seek medical advice relating to the failing health of the Princess. Sadly, despite consultations with some of the top physicians in England, on her return to Italy the health of Princess Sapieha continued to decline and she passed away in Rome on 13th December 1824. In accordance with her final wishes, her remains were brought back from Italy to Bold Hall and afterwards interred in the family vault at Farnworth Church. [102] A dramatic account of the journey of her body from Rome to Widnes and the terrible anguish of her bereaved spouse makes for extremely sad reading. The body of the Princess, accompanied by the Prince on her final journey home, arrived at Dover on 12th January 1825 on board the steamship *Monarch* which had set sail from Calais. It was said that the grieving and inconsolable Prince sat beside the coffin during the entire sea voyage to England.

---

[101] The church was re-dedicated to St. Luke in July 1859.
[102] The funeral took place at Farnworth in January 1825.

On Saturday 13th of January the remains of the young Princess passed through Warrington in a closed carriage drawn by four horses. The funeral coach was followed by the Prince in another carriage and four. On the final leg of this sad drive the funeral carriage halted for a short stop outside Bank Hall, the old family residence of the Princess' late father, Peter Patten Bold. It then proceeded in a slow journey to Bold Hall where the body of Princess Sapieha lay until her removal the following Monday to Farnworth Church. Unlike the large public funerals of most well-known landowners of those times, the funeral of Princess Sapieha was a small private affair and consisted only of the immediate family and a few close friends, including the Rev. Mr. J. Hornby, the Rector of Winwick, who preceded the hearse in his own coach. It would seem that, apart from the Rev. Hornby's coach, the hearse was followed by only two other carriages. The first of these was occupied by the Prince and his brother-in-law, Mr. Henry Hoghton, and the second carriage conveyed Colonel Parker the uncle of the late Princess.

The funeral service was simple and, as requested by the Princess some time before her death, it was conducted by her friend the Rev. Mr. Hornby. It was said that the clergyman found the task extremely difficult and such was his grief and distress that his words and a good deal of the service was almost inaudible to the gathered mourners. The coffin was covered with plain black silk velvet, without any ornate furniture; except a few brass nails on the lid on which was a plain black plate with white letters bearing the following inscription: *"Mary Sapieha, died 13th December, 1824, aged 28"*. The Prince was heartbroken. A quote from a report of this sad event gives us an impression of his grief.

"His Highness bore the trying scene much better than was expected, but his inward grief we are informed was very great. He has, we understand, scarcely left the corpse since its departure to its interment, and after it had been lowered into the vault and he had proceeded to his mourning coach, the horses being not quite ready, he again went to the vault, and, descending down two of the steps, he gave a small cry and left the vault much affected. His Highness set off immediately from the church with Colonel Parker, to Astley Hall, where he intended staying only one night, and then setting off for London, and from thence directly home to the Continent.

The carriage in which her Highness's corpse was brought to England was one purposely made for her to sleep in during her illness, and it was so complete, and had so little the appearance of a carriage capable of holding a coffin, that scarcely any person, during their route from Rome to Bold, had the least idea of such a thing; and it was equally kept a secret; the post-boys occasionally complaining that the carriage was a great weight for the horses. She arrived at Bold the very day month she died, so that they must have had a wearisome and busy journey – the coffin was nearly 1100 lbs in weight.[103]

Shortly after her death a memorial was erected inside Farnworth Church. The Prince commissioned an eminent Italian artist, Pietro Tenerani, who had sculpted the tomb of Pope Pius VIII, to carry out the work. Tenerani's beautiful bass-relief depicts the deathbed scene of the young Princess and bears a Latin inscription, which translates as *"Farewell, sweetest spouse; I do not give thee up, but I look for thee again."* In addition to the customary details of her birth, death and marital status, a long inscription commemorates the many virtues of the late Princess and ends with the words

"For 27 years she tasted whatever of delights could be enjoyed, by a heart expanding with social intercourse in friendly sympathies, in the devotion of filial piety and the reciprocation of affection in the bosom of a family of perfect love. For two short years of wedded union all that earth could minister of bliss was hers. Under circumstances of rare, but chequered felicity, happy beyond the common lot, she proved the insufficiency of this world, and died in the full faith of Christ, content to exchange time for eternity and life for death".

It was an extremely sad end to what appears to have been a fairytale romance. The Prince, who bore the official title of Eustachy Kajetan, Prince Sapieha-Rozanski, left England immediately after the funeral of his young wife. His marriage to Mary Bold had been a short but obviously a very happy one. At a time when many marriages were made, not in heaven, but by arrangement between parents or guardians, this union appears to have been a genuine love affair. The Prince remained single for the next eighteen years or so, but after this long period as a widower he remarried in Boulogne in May 1842. He died in Paris in 1860 and his second wife survived him by only four years.

---

[103] Interestingly, when her nephew Sir Henry de Hoghton died in 1876 he left instructions in his Will that he should be buried in three coffins, one a shell, one of lead of extra thickness, and one of polished oak an inch and a half thick. Had the Princess Sapieha's coffin been of similar construction then this would account for the heavy weight.

Following the death of Princess Sapieha her sister, Dorothea Hoghton, the second daughter of Peter Patten Bold, inherited the estate. The following month her husband, Henry Hoghton, applied for a royal licence to assume the surname *"Bold"* in addition to the name Hoghton. Permission was subsequently granted by the King, this consent also including the authority to add the *"Bold quarterly"* to that of the Hoghton coat of arms. From this date onwards the family were to be known as *"Bold Hoghton"*. Interestingly, Dorothea's father, Peter Patten Bold, had previously been simply Peter Patten. He had also added the *"Bold"* surname to his own in 1813 when he inherited the estate from his aunt, Anna Maria Bold, who died at the age of 82years on 25th November that year. She was the eldest daughter of Peter Bold of Bold Hall. It is worth mentioning that Anna Maria was the benefactor of a school which was built in Farnworth Village in 1810. The building later became a pub which is now known as *"The Griffin"*. A plaque, which bears the initials AMB in honour of Miss Bold's generous patronage, is still visible above the doorway.

The Bold estate remained intact and in the hands of the Bold Hoghton family for the following twenty odd years until it was offered for sale in the summer of 1848. On the 10th June 1848 a firm of London based auctioneers placed the following advertisement in *The Times*:

"Offered for sale in August unless sold earlier:

Valuable estate and lands, including the manors of Bold, Burtonwood and Sutton. Comprising a splendid mansion, gardens, park, noble woods, lake and plantations which include 4,300 acres superbly timbered and well stocked with game. The Burtonwood and Sutton estates consist of 1030 acres and numerous farms and other property skirting St. Helens and containing mines of superior coal and also beds of clay of great value for pottery purposes. These produce £12,000 per annum exclusive of royalties and rents receivable from coal mines, which must annually increase.

The Mansion of Bold stands upon a fine elevated part of the park, richly studded with noble timber and sheltered by oak woods of the finest growth. Within the park are the remains of the ancient hall, moated round, and which, from a period little later than the Conquest, has been the seat of the maternal ancestors of the present owner.

For further particulars apply to Daniel Smith & Son, Waterloo Place, Pall Mall, London."

Apart from the Bold estates, Sir Henry Bold Hoghton also owned substantial property in the form of the paternal Hoghton estates in Lancashire, namely at Walton Hall which was located on the banks of the Darwen near its confluence with the Ribble. The old family estate at Hoghton Towers, which had been abandoned for the newer Walton Hall, had a unique claim to fame as it was there that his ancestor, Sir Richard Hoghton, entertained King James I on his way from Scotland to London in August 1617. During his three day stay at Hoghton Towers the King amused himself by hunting deer in the parklands. He also enjoyed sumptuous banquets each evening and it was, allegedly, at one of these meals that the King knighted the loin of beef. Afterwards this cut of beef was given the name *"sirloin"* by which name it is commonly known today. However, whilst the Bold estate was entirely free of encumbrance, the Hoghton estates were mortgaged to the Bank of England and other parties to the tune of over £81,000. In spite of this hefty mortgage, the Hoghton properties produced an income of around £8,000 per year and the Bold estates brought in £13,000 per annum, which meant that there was combined revenue of over £20,000 a year for the Bold Hoghton family.

When Dorothea Bold, Lady Bold Hoghton, died in December 1840 (at the age of 43) Sir Henry suffered a marked reduction in his income due to clauses in the Will of her father, Peter Patten Bold. At that point the Bold Estates were passed down to their eldest son, also named Henry. Following this alteration in ownership, several sections of the Bold Estate were put up for sale. Stipulations connected to the inheritance of property also created changes in other aspects of Sir Henry Bold Hoghton`s landholdings. The paternal Hoghton properties also had several complex inheritance clauses relating to the estate. As with the Bold estate, this property passed to the eldest son on his coming of age. However, up until the time young Henry reached his majority the estate had been held in trust, with his father as principal trustee and manager. This situation proved to be rather contentious when Henry junior eventually came of age. In March 1852 a rather sensational court case occurred in which Sir Henry Bold Hoghton was sued by his son and heir, Henry Bold Hoghton junior. The son claimed that, prior to his coming of age, his father had coerced him into signing several agreements relating to deeds and mortgages on the Hoghton estates. He said he had not fully understood the implications of the documents he had been asked to sign and that he had not been offered legal representation or advice in the matter. Young Henry also said that he had trusted his father, but his father had forced him into signing documents he did not now agree with. In retrospect, he realised he had unwittingly signed away several rights relating to his properties.

However reasonable his argument may have been, it was a rather sad and undignified case brought by a son against his father. No doubt a great deal of mutual bitterness resulted from this action. In the end, the court found in favour of Sir Henry and his son was ordered to pay the court costs. I suspect these costs were the least of his worries as the relationship with his father had deteriorated almost beyond repair. The father, Sir Henry Bold Hoghton, the 8th baronet, died at his home in Hampshire in July 1862. He had remarried in 1847 and later served as Deputy Lieutenant of Lancashire. Interestingly, sometime after this date his son stopped using the "Bold" surname and was afterwards known only as Sir Henry Hoghton.

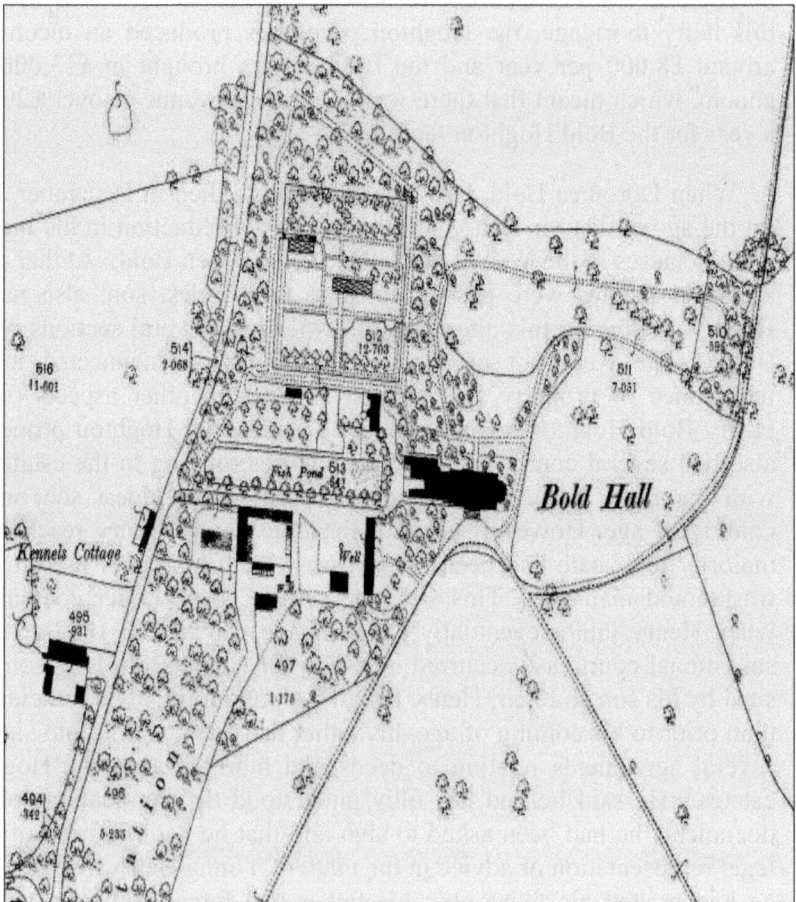

Although several portions of the Bold Estate had been sold off in the intervening years, the huge section which included the house was eventually sold in 1860 to Mr. William Whiteacre Tipping, a wealthy cotton manufacturer from Wigan who was the stepson of Henry Robinson, the owner of the Wigan Brewery. Mr. Tipping's purchase comprised of several thousand acres of land which included a number of small farms, 400 acres of park around the hall, 140 acres of plantation and nearly 17 acres of pleasure grounds and gardens as well as the magnificent house known as Bold Hall[104]. Sadly, this meant that the Bold family association with this ancient estate was finally at an end. The demise of the family's personal relationship with the area would no doubt have been a sad matter for tenants and retainers whose own generations of ancestors had served the family in one way or another.

The arrival of Mr. Tipping to Bold Hall brought drastic changes. For the old retainers, who had been used to the refined ways of the Bold family, the comparison between them and the new owner must have been shocking. Genteel behaviour amid the grandeur of Bold Hall was now a thing of the past, as the new owner was neither cultured nor inclined to preserve the magnificent interior or gracious routines of his new home. Mr. Tipping has been described as crude, unpleasant, uneducated with rough manners and dress. One might suppose that this description may have resulted from the fact that he was a self-made man and not a member of the gentry, for at that time the "nouveau riche" were treated with condescension by the upper classes. There are countless descriptions of Mr. Tipping and his eccentric behaviour. He has generally been portrayed as an unkempt braggart whose main passion lay in drinking, gambling and the cruel sport of cock fighting. We are also told that during his frequent visits to the nearby *Tipping Arms* (now *The Griffin)* he flashed money around in an attempt to impress the patrons, often boasting that he carried a thousand pounds in his pockets. Naturally we modern readers have to rely upon these previously written works to make a judgement. Unfortunately most of these reports do not favour him.

Despite these unflattering descriptions, one might wonder if perhaps Mr. Tipping may possibly, in some circumstances, have been unfairly represented and maligned. Among other things, he has been

---

[104] The original Bold Hall (a moated house) was built in 1616
The new Bold Hall was built by Peter Bold in 1730

accused of destroying the Bold woodland for profit by indiscriminately cutting down trees on the estate. However, it is a fact, that long before he took possession there were several advertisements by the agents of the previous owners offering vast quantities of wood for sale. This would indicate that significant parts of the woodlands were destroyed well before Mr. Tipping started to fell trees. It is also said that, during his occupancy, the interior of Bold Hall fell into serious disrepair. Of course this was quite true. He seems to have been unconcerned about his surroundings and, being a bachelor, only used four rooms. His interests lay in hunting and shooting rather than furnishings and draperies. Had there been a wife or daughter on the scene no doubt things would have been vastly different.

Although he could certainly be found guilty of neglecting to maintain the Hall to an acceptable standard, Mr. Tipping did show concern for his land and the tenants on his farms. In 1865 he took out an injunction against the St. Helens Smelting Company preventing them from further activity. He claimed their noxious vapours were destroying vegetation on his land and causing injury to his tenants' cattle. Another point worth mentioning is that he was considered to be a fit person to serve as a governor of Farnworth Free Grammar School. He served in this position for a period of ten years, from 1875 to 1885. One would assume that a person described as an uncouth drunkard would not have been viewed as a suitable person to hold such a position. Mr. Tipping died intestate in 1889 and the estate was passed to his next of kin, a Mrs. Wyatt who lived in Hampshire. After his death several of his friends wrote to local newspapers giving far more complimentary accounts of the man and his life. Many of them deplored the negative manner in which Mr. Tipping had previously been portrayed. His next of kin, Mrs. Wyatt, did not take up residence and the estate was immediately put up for sale.

In Farnworth, the close community and parishioners of Farnworth Church would have been particularly sad to witness the end of the Bold era. It has been suggested that the Bold family had been resident in the area which bore their name from the time of Edward the Confessor[105]. There is certainly evidence that the family were settled in the area during the reign of Henry IV. Over the following centuries their presence and patronage had offered reassuring continuity to the residents of Bold and Farnworth. It must have seemed almost inconceivable that their links with the area had finally been severed. As village life at that time was very insular and communities were tight

---

[105] Charles Poole – *"Old Widnes and its Neighbourhood"*

knit, families having lived alongside each other for generations, change in any form did not come easy. When a member of their community died the loss was felt by everyone. After an old man called John Pullen, who was in his 90th year, died at his home in Farnworth village in September 1828 his body was borne to the nearby churchyard on the shoulders of four of his neighbours whose combined ages amounted to 309 years. Mr. Pullen, who was described as a yeoman of the manor of Widnes, had lived his whole life in the village as had his father and grandfather before him. He would have been as familiar and important to his neighbours as the landscape around them, and his loss would have been keenly felt. I am sure the departure of the Bold family from the area was viewed in a similar manner.

Whilst events surrounding the marriage and sad death of Princess Sapieha had created both excitement and grief in Farnworth in the 1820s, at the other end of the town, in November 1825, the residents of the small district of Halebank were fascinated by a less important affair. Although certainly not a riveting occurrence, nor as exciting as a royal wedding, the fact that it caused so much interest gives us an idea of how uneventful daily life was at that time. The incident concerned the local wheelwright, Mr. Rutter, and the extraordinary exploits of a cat. It seems that Mr. Rutter was on friendly terms with a Mr. Clegg who was a publican at Winwick near Warrington. One evening while Mr. Rutter was visiting Mr. Clegg he was persuaded to take a cat home with him. For want of a better way of transporting the animal it was put into a sack and the sack was tied to Mr. Rutter's cart. It was said that Mr. Rutter set out from Winwick about half past four in the evening and took a route which entailed the crossing of two turnpike roads and the canal once or twice, travelling via Burtonwood, Bold Heath and across to Hale. He arrived back in Halebank quite late at night and brought the sack into the house. When the cat was let loose she ran about the house for a short while before finding a small hole in the door from which she made her escape to freedom. After a search outside there was no sign of the cat so Mr. Rutter gave her up for lost and thought no more of it. Several weeks later, having occasion to go to Winwick, he called in to see Mr. Clegg. On entering the house he was astonished to see the sleeping cat stretched out by the hearth. The poor animal had returned only two days before, emaciated and weak. It must have taken it at least two weeks to find its way back to Winwick. Needless to say, neither Mr. Rutter nor Mr. Clegg suggested removing the cat from its home again.

When contemplating the unavoidably long-winded journey Mr. Rutter had taken from Winwick to Halebank we can appreciate how isolated some communities were, and why such a relatively unremarkable occurrence caused so much excitement. The lack of public transport meant that some areas were cut-off. Villagers often had to rely on spasmodic visits from the mail cart or occasional visitors to bring in news from other parts of the town or county. It was a fairly insular existence and any event which was out of the ordinary became a welcome and exciting departure from routine. It is easy for modern readers to have a rose-tinted view of rural life in the early nineteenth century, but this can sometimes blind us to the harsher realities of those times. Apart from the lack of transport and decent roads, which contributed to a sense of remoteness, there were countless other forms of hardship. When viewed in human terms we see that this was a period of acute rural poverty, coupled with a general repression of the country's working population.

As I have previously stated, at that time there was a great imbalance in social and constitutional privileges which meant that ordinary working people had no real voice in civic and national affairs. They were denied political rights and in periods of trade depressions the first action of employers was to cut wages. However, inequality was not only present in matters of employment and political reform; civil law was also heavily weighted in favour of the landed and middle classes. Most sentences given to ordinary people were totally disproportionate to the crimes involved. It is quite astounding to discover that during this period men or women could be hanged for any one of 200 offences, and children could receive severe punishment or imprisonment even for quite minor misdemeanours. In some cases the death penalty was commuted to transportation, which was in itself a dreadful and much feared sentence.

Transportation of local offenders was fairly common at that time. During the period this type of punishment existed, a significant number of men and women from both towns received hefty sentences. In April 1822 three Runcorn boatmen were each transported for a period of seven years for breaking into a boat at Preston Brook and stealing a truss of raw silk. The men, Richard Howard, Joseph Owen and Robert Prince were all in their early twenties. This was a fairly lenient sentence compared to that of 24year old Samuel Robinson who, at the same court, was sentenced to death for stealing a horse. In October 1833 Edward Waterworth, aged 36, was transported to Botany Bay for seven years for stealing a dog collar, the property of John Bradshaw of Runcorn. At the same court, a young 22year old local woman, Amelia

Laurenson, also received a sentence of seven years transportation for stealing an item of wearing apparel from Frances Salkend at Runcorn. In March 1846 a young Widnes man, 18year old Richard Forster, who had been convicted of a felony once before, was transported for a period of ten years for stealing a silver watch from James Abbott, a watchmaker, at Widnes.

Whilst judgements such as the death penalty and transportation were obviously extreme and brutal sentences, especially in cases which might today be viewed as worthy of short prison terms, other forms of less strict punishment did exist. One of these was the *"stocks"* which was intended to publicly humiliate the offender rather than deprive him or her of their freedom. An example of this occurred in Runcorn in July 1854 and is described below:

> SITTING IN THE STOCKS.—On Wednesday, the centre of the town of Runcorn was all astir, owing to a person named Jacob Bradbury, of Pennington's-row, being placed in the town stocks, from half-past ten in the morning until half-past four in the afternoon, for neglecting to pay a fine for being drunk and disorderly on the 11th of March last. After his liberation he was called upon to pay the rent of the stocks, the cost of police attendance, warrant, &c., or go to prison for one month.

Apart from the seemingly unfair sentences given for minor misdemeanours, the ferocious Game Laws were also a huge source of indignation and social division. The game, which was preserved for the amusement of wealthy landowners, was protected by law from half-starved labourers who wanted it for food. The law provided regulations by which rich landowners were able to protect their living property and the penalties for poaching or trespassing were extremely severe. Any man found catching rabbits or birds for the dinner table could face a long term in prison with hard labour or, in some cases, transportation to Botany Bay. In fact capital punishment for crimes against property was also fairly common and after 1816 long sentences of transportation for poaching were not unusual.

It should be pointed out that the majority of magistrates who sat on the bench at our district Petty Sessions were landowners or local employers. Some of them were very people the law was designed to favour – namely the landowning classes who delighted in hunting and shooting. It was often the case that magistrates were passing sentence on men or women whom they judged to have encroached upon their own territory. Therefore it is not too surprising to discover that a poacher could expect no mercy if caught. The same situation arose in employment cases, as local employers were well represented on the magistrates' bench and were often passing sentence on their own employees. In cases where a man had left his employment without permission the sentences were unreasonably harsh; usually resulting in a term of imprisonment with hard labour.

The harsh conditions in workplaces often resulted in workers absconding. Runaway workers, who were usually young apprentices, were mercilessly pursued. Employers often offered rewards for information as to the whereabouts of fugitive employees. Those aiding a person to flee from employment or break an employment contract could also face legal prosecution. If the absconding employee was tracked down, and if he was an apprentice, he was sometimes given a severe reprimand and the opportunity of returning to his employment. In cases where the deserter was an unskilled labourer the outcome would almost certainly involve a spell in prison. The advert here, from *The Chester Chronicle* of August 1818, is a typical example.

Run-away Apprentice.

ABSCONDED from his Apprenticeship, at Runcorn, on Sunday, the 9th instant, WILLIAM ROBINSON, by Trade a Blacksmith, aged Nineteen Years, of a fair complexion, about Five Feet Seven Inches high, and round-shouldered.

This is to give Public Notice,
That whoever will give such Information as may lead to the Apprehension of the same WILLIAM ROBINSON, shall receive ONE GUINEA REWARD; and any person employing the said Apprentice, after this Notice, will be proceeded against according to Law.
THOMAS TREVETT, BLACKSMITH.

Runcorn, August 17, 1818.

Many of the laws represented a totally unfair use of the legal system as the game laws and employment laws were biased, having been drawn up by the very people they would most benefit. It was most certainly a very prejudiced and unjust set-up. E.P. Thompson in his book*" The Making of the English Working Class"* uses a quote by Oliver Goldsmith which says it all:

> *"Each wanton judge new penal statutes draw,*
> *Laws grind the poor, and rich men rule the law."*

An article in *The Manchester Mercury* in December 1827, relating to the Game Laws, highlights the unfairness of the system, particularly in relation to the implementation of these laws by magistrates.

"It is quite extraordinary to witness the manner in which country gentlemen appear to lose their senses whenever a case comes before them connected with the Game Laws. Whether Whigs or Tories, clergymen or laymen, they all think the preservation of hares, partridges, pheasants and rabbits to be the most important business of life; and when any man is unfortunate enough to be brought before them, on any charge of destroying those precious animals, in any manner contrary to the law in such case made and provided by landed gentlemen, the virtuous indignation of the Justices is immediately roused, and they forthwith proceed – some to commit all manner of injustice, whilst others, like Sir John Stanley, in the present case are satisfied with all manner of nonsense. These men appear to be setting at nought all those scruples which men concerned with the administration of justice ought so tenderly to regard. For instance, in almost any other case other than a charge under the Games Laws, most Magistrates would have felt it highly indecent to sit in judgement on a case in which they were the interested parties. If any man had picked Sir John Stanley`s pocket, the Worthy Baronet would have, or at least should have, been unwilling to act as Chairman at the Sessions when the culprit was tried. But a supposed offence against the Game Laws is quite another matter, and Sir John and Colonel Parker, sit, apparently as a matter of course, to investigate charges of poaching on their own estates. Perhaps they conceive that questions of this sort are those, of all others, in which their judgements are least likely to be warped by prejudices of any kind. If that is their opinion, we can only say, that it is very different to the one entertained on the subject by many others.

Sir John Stanley[106], it will be seen, attributes most of the evils of poaching to the people who purchase the game; but we think there is

---

[106] Lord Derby

one other class of persons upon whom a little of his indignation would not have been thrown away – namely, the landowners and legislators of this country – the men who, to gratify their own absurd vanity, have endeavoured, by savage enactments, to keep to themselves a monopoly of the birds and beasts of the land and the chase; not merely to secure themselves a plentiful supply of these animals, but to appropriate the whole, that the possessions may be a mark of distinction to themselves, and the want of it, a mark of degradation to their fellow subjects. These people, we humbly conceive, might fairly come in for a small share of the Worthy Baronet's censures: and we hope that the next time he undertakes to deliver an address on the evils of poaching, he will not forget the people to whose want of feeling the greater part of it is owing - that is the people who poach from necessity, for food."

Of course the attitudes of all classes of society were deeply embedded at that time, and however unequal this situation may have been, the established social order was generally maintained. Unquestioning loyalty to the Monarchy was part and parcel of this continuance. Alas, after the death of George IV his brother and successor, William IV, also proved to be a man of limited ability and a no less ineffective King. However, when William IV died on 20thJune 1837 England was plunged into a state of national mourning. As a symbol of mourning for the deceased Monarch, who had reigned for barely seven years, black drapes adorned churches and public buildings around the country. In Runcorn, at the beginning of July, a public vestry meeting was held in the Parish Church. The meeting was convened by the churchwardens and was held for the purpose of considering the propriety of putting the Parish Church into mourning for the late King.

During that special meeting a decision was made by the churchwardens that the sum of £20 would be allowed for purchasing the black and purple drapery required to place the church into mourning. It was also agreed that *"after the proper mourning period had passed the mourning drapes would be taken down and kept for future occasions, or given to the deserving poor under the direction of the Vicar and churchwardens"*. However reasonable this proposal may seem, unfortunately when the Vicar, Mr. Gent, heard of the meeting and the decision to spend £20 from the parish funds he was extremely angry. The churchwardens were reprimanded by the irate Vicar who felt that this decision was a violation of his rights and an undermining of his authority. He declared that any cloth or any other item bought with church finances belonged exclusively to him. He would allow them to use the cloth for the mourning period but afterwards he would claim it for his own use, to keep or dispose of as he wished. Needless to say, this caused some controversy in the parish and it is not too surprising to learn that Mr. Gent was not a particularly popular Vicar.

After the country had undergone the period of mourning that normal decency and protocol demanded, there were soon plans afoot to celebrate the accession of the young Princess Victoria. She was just eighteen years of age when she succeeded her uncle, who had been the oldest person to date to come to the throne. He was 64 years old when he succeeded his brother George IV and just short of 72 when he died at Windsor Castle in 1837. Although the country was officially in mourning for him, William had not been a popular King. The fact that he had meddled in political matters had caused some dissatisfaction amongst his subjects. They believed that the King should be impartial in affairs relating to the Government of the country. Some thought that the King's interference was inspired by his even more unpopular German wife, Queen Adelaide. Therefore, despite an outward show of mourning, the forthcoming Coronation of his young niece, Princess Victoria, was eagerly anticipated by the population. They hoped that her reign would bring stability and harmony to the country.

The Coronation of Queen Victoria took place on 28th June the following year. During the first part of that year there were extravagant plans in place to ensure that the event would go off without a hitch. For months beforehand there had been little else talked or thought about but the forthcoming Coronation. Cities, towns and small villages around the country were planning their own celebrations for the big day. Street hawkers were selling sheet music with the words of specially written coronation songs and special coronation medals and ribbons were on sale everywhere. Town worthies around the country were determined that their localities would do justice to the event and that their inhabitants would observe the day with patriotic respect but, at the same time, celebrate the occasion with as much fun as possible. Of course our districts were no different and, when reading about the events of Coronation Day in Runcorn, one can almost feel the excitement of the occasion. The pomp and pageantry which occurred in the town throughout the day was accompanied by genuine joy and a great deal of fun for all the inhabitants, young and old alike. One can only marvel at the planning which went into this event as the festivities, which were almost non-stop, started early in the morning and lasted until night fell. There were even additional events the following evening which ensured that the new Victorian era began in fitting style.

Of course these celebrations were being mirrored in every corner of every town and small village throughout the land.

In London, the dawn of Coronation Day was announced by the firing of guns in St. James's Park and at the Tower. In Runcorn, the big day was also ushered in by the firing of guns and the ringing of bells; at six o'clock in the morning a salute of 19 guns was fired. At the same time, in London, the streets were being lined with streams of eager pedestrians staking their claim to various vantage points along the Coronation route. Whilst events in the capital progressed at a pre-planned pace the timing and organization in Runcorn was no less impressive.

At ten o'clock the inhabitants of the town assembled in large numbers in front of the Town Hall and were joined by the children and teachers from the various schools and Sunday Schools. Each child wore a special coronation medal suspended from a white ribbon and they all carried small flags and banners. The assembled crowd then sang the National Anthem before making their way to The Hill. At eleven o'clock a procession was formed, which included Mr. Harding and his four police constables who were accompanied by the resident of the town who had been chosen to represent *"The Champion of England"*. *"The Champion"* was mounted on a grey charger; he was followed by his *"Squire"* who was also on horseback and carrying a banner; alongside these was a trumpeter on horseback and the Committee of the Town Managers. Joining these were several important gentlemen and the principal inhabitants of the town. Following on in the procession were members of the Independent Order of Odd Fellows in their costumes and regalia, and the Society of Ancient Foresters also in costume and regalia. Accompanying these were three bands playing patriotic music. When the procession reached Doctor's Bridge it was joined by the cannon drawn by horses and attended by the gunners. The procession, accompanied by the lively sound of the bands, moved on through Higher Runcorn to the Beetle Hill, where each group took their allocated positions. The National Anthem was sung again, followed by cheering from the crowd, which numbered around 7000 by this time. Following this a gun salute was fired again. The procession was then reformed and crossed the Heath, then proceeded over Delph Bridge into the town centre en route to the Town Hall.

One can visualise the scene as the procession of townspeople, schoolchildren, and distinguished personages and officials passed through the town. The streets would have been lined with those who did not have a designated place in the procession and the sight of the

Champion of England and his *Squire*, both mounted on horseback and carrying banners, would have raised a hearty cheer or two from the spectators. At the Town Hall[107] a proclamation was made *"calling on all persons who could deny her Majesty's right to the throne to come forward, or ever after hold their peace".* At this point *"The Champion"* gave challenge by throwing down the gauntlet. It was said that *"no traitor was however present, or if present, not bold enough to face the Champion, and peace and harmony was therefore not disturbed".*

After a recital of *The Proclamation* the enormous crowd dispersed to various venues where they continued their own celebrations. The children went to their different schools where small tea parties had been arranged, while the workmen at the soap factories and other establishments were treated to refreshments on the premises by their employers. At three o'clock two contests took place on the river, a rowing match and a sculling match, both events attracted a large crowd of noisy but jubilant spectators. In the meantime, a large party of gentlemen sat down to a meal at the Royal Hotel where Mr. Philip Whiteway presided. In the evening wheelbarrow races, running races and other sporting events took place at various locations. The day's festivities concluded with a brilliant gas illumination near the river bank. The following evening a public ball took place at Wilson's Hotel, where the lovers of dancing tripped the light fantastic till sometime after the peep of dawn. A similar ball also took place at the Royal Hotel the same evening. Overall, the residents of Runcorn must have felt that the start of the new Victorian era had been a day and an evening to remember.

Whilst the events of June 1838 had been a cause for celebration and a way of uniting inhabitants from all walks of life, the social arrangement of classes and the difference of fortunes between them had been an evident fact of life since time immemorial. I have previously drawn attention to the fact that most people had a recognised place in society in relation to those above and below them. There were time honoured attitudes which dictated a deference to those above them and a degree of paternalism to those below. The historian David Roberts, in his studies of early Victorian life, suggests that the average paternalist was an authoritarian who believed in capital punishment, whipping, severe game laws, summary justice for offenders and strict laws defining the duties of servants to their masters. In addition to all these

---

[107] The first Town Hall was in Bridge Street.

things, paternalists also assumed that wealth and power brought with it a right and a duty to rule[108]. In short, paternalists believed that there should be a strong sense of dependency and that those who were dependent should have an unquestioning respect for their betters. In both of our towns, before the inception of significant industrialisation, there existed a small group of social elite who fell into this category. However, the expansion of industry and the development of an industrial economy, rather than an agricultural one, meant that there was a fundamental shift in social attitudes. This brought into being a new industrial middle class which sat side by side with the landowning classes in a new elite category. Nevertheless, paternalism applied as much to the new local industrialists as it did to the ancient landowner. Therefore, even after substantial industrialisation in our area, there was still an elite group who controlled local political and economic power, only now the composition of this group had become more varied.

Social status and displays of wealth were important to the upper classes who put great store in keeping up appearances. In both towns there was a form of social competition among the higher status groups. They took every opportunity available to them to display their wealth and position. This was especially evident when members of local *"society"* threw celebratory parties for birthdays or weddings. These events were reported in the local press for the eager consumption of fellow members of this exclusive set. In April 1817 Runcorn was the scene of an extravagant social gathering to celebrate the birthday of a young man called Thomas Cooper. A report of that event appeared in *The Chester Chronicle*:

"On Wednesday last, the 9th inst., that highly respected young gentleman, Thomas Cooper, Esq., of Runcorn, in this county, attained his majority; on which occasion, an excellent dinner was provided for his tenantry and most of the principal inhabitants of the place and its vicinity. On his health being drunk, he made a very neat and energetic speech; assuring the company that Runcorn and its residents would ever have his best wishes and support. Many loyal and patriotic toasts were drunk, interspersed with some excellent songs. The whole was conducted with a degree of liberality which reflected much credit on the host, every person present being highly delighted with the urbanity of his manners, and the particular attention he paid to each individual. In the course of the day, the bells of the church rang many merry peals;

---

[108] David Roberts – *Paternalism in Early Victorian England* (1979)

and in the evening, the lower orders of society also partook of his bounty."

Employers too, as well as landowners, threw parties to celebrate their family weddings and birthdays. Like landowners, who offered their tenantry an opportunity to share in the festivities by providing a special meal for them, many employers also provided their workmen with a dinner to mark these occasions. Charles Hazlehurst, the son of Mr. Hazlehurst, the soap manufacturer, celebrated his marriage just before Christmas 1842. Although the wedding and official reception took place in Manchester, nevertheless, it was important that the company's employees in Runcorn were allowed to participate in the celebrations in some way. It was remarked at the time that these types of gatherings were important *"To make the workmen interested in the family events and circumstances of their employers, in order to promote that good and wholesome feeling of attachment between masters and servants".*

To mark this auspicious occasion the Hazlehursts' invited their workmen, who numbered almost 120, to a celebratory supper at Hill's Hotel. The invitation said that the occasion was to be held *"In commemoration of the marriage of their young master, Mr. Charles Hazlehurst."* A report of the event said that the *"most grateful workmen sat down to a supper of beautiful roast beef, mutton and other savoury joints and several good fat geese graced the table".* Although the workmen were treated to what appears to have been an excellent meal, I am sure many were disappointed not to have been given the opportunity to raise a glass or two of ale to toast to their generous host. Alas for them it was it was a strictly teetotal affair. The report also tells us that *"After spending a happy evening together the workmen separated without having to reproach themselves for having taken one intemperate draught, and thankful for their plentiful refreshments in meat and drinks."*

Although Thomas Cooper's event was relatively lavish, and the Hazlehurst supper generous, both pale into insignificance when one reads an account of the celebrations which marked the 21st birthday of George Egerton, the eldest son of Lord Francis Egerton who was heir to the Bridgewater Estate. The festivities, which took place in June 1844, began early in the morning in spectacular style, the occasion being akin to a public holiday or a royal event. A field battery of twenty one guns fired a salute which was accompanied by the Parish Church bells ringing out. The church bells continued to peal at regular intervals throughout the day. In the afternoon several steamers arrived from Liverpool carrying hundreds of visitors. Three of the Bridgewater boats, decorated with flags and bunting, also came alongside with their crew raising cheers for the young Mr. Egerton. A report says:

"When the steamers had landed their passengers, the group formed themselves into marching order, headed by Stubbs` splendid band, and proceeded to Cooper's large field, which is the property of Lord Francis Egerton, and adjacent to Bridgewater House, where the amusements of the day commenced with donkey racing for a saddle, bridle and whip, catching the pig with a greasy tail, wheelbarrow racing for a new spade, and climbing the soapy pole for a new hat; there was also a tournament on the water, between two boats` crews of the Duke's men and the Old Quay men – both did their best for the amusement of the many spectators, and it would be impossible to say which had the best of it, for after two and a half hours combating, the parties were withdrawn by Mr. Rippon, the agent. The victors were to have had a new suit of clothes, but it is expected that all the men engaged will receive some token for their heroism and bravery. At four o'clock the whole of the men, with the agents from various places, and the gentlemen of the town, proceeded to the Banquet Hall, a spacious marquee fitted up in the Old Quay yard, by the Trustees` carpenters, and ornamented with festoons, drapery etc., by Mr. Banks of Runcorn, which, considering the little time allowed, reflected the greatest credit on Mr. Banks for the good taste he displayed. Afterwards the invited guests sat down to a sumptuous dinner which included a baron of beef. After dinner the men were again supplied with prime ale and porter and the tee-totallers with lemonade. As night fell the hundreds who wended their way towards the river were treated to a display of fireworks which continued till after eleven o'clock. Unfortunately the end of the day was marred by a tragic accident. Thomas Williams, a porter in the service of the Old Quay Company, fell overboard from one of the ships and was drowned. On the following Tuesday, Mr. Rippon the agent to the Bridgewater Trust, distributed a quantity of bread, a pint of good beer, and a mug to carry it home in, to 220 poor women. The bread and beer were residual from the previous celebrations".

At that time the firing of cannons was a common local occurrence and was generally used to mark events of national importance. Cannon fire was also used at local events such as the launching of ships into our river and, of course, the upper classes used it when celebrating birthdays or weddings or on other important social occasions. Whilst this ritual undoubtedly added to the festive atmosphere of an occasion, the firing of cannons was not without a degree of danger. At the end of

December 1846 a dreadful accident occurred in Runcorn when it was reported that *"a young boy named James Heaton had his head nearly severed from his body by the bursting of a cannon. The cannon was being fired on the occasion of his employer's nuptials"*

The fact that cannons were used on a fairly regular basis prompts me to call attention to the fact that firearms and ammunition were also freely available at that time. Weapons could be purchased quite legitimately on the open market. Gentlemen used rifles and pistols for hunting and target shooting, highway men used them for robbery and, of course, honour duels were often fought using special duelling pistols. Regrettably, the latter use was employed one Wednesday evening in July 1844 when, following a petty disagreement in a Runcorn pub, a rather preposterous event occurred. It is to be regretted that a newspaper report of this incident was so faded that the final paragraph was impossible to decipher. I quote as much of the report as is legible, leaving my readers and I to speculate on what might have been the content of the missing text.

"The inhabitants of Runcorn were much alarmed on Wednesday evening by a report that a duel had taken place, and ended in both combatants being mortally wounded. It appears that Mr. H, of Runcorn, in company with Mr. B, a vinegar merchant from the West of England, were enjoying themselves at the Cholmondeley Arms when their harmony was destroyed by the introduction of a political subject by two other persons who had just entered. Messrs H and B took opposite sides in the argument, and from warm and angry words came at length to blows; but as the combatants were unequal, the friends of Mr. H. insisted that the dispute should be settled by a duel. The necessary weapons were not, however, procurable in a town in which mortal combat had never before been fought; but unfortunately, there was an old horse pistol which had from time immemorial glistened in the hall of the Cholmondeley Arms, and this was taken from its resting place as an instrument wherein to send one or other of the angry disputants to his long rest. The difficulty of there being only one pistol for both was obviated by an agreement that they should use it alternately, and toss for the first fire. Mr. H. was the winner, and twelve paces having been solemnly measured, he took his stand tremblingly, as might be expected, opposite to his adversary, who in full expectation of death, bade farewell to his friends. There was something ludicrous as well as awful in the scene, and the countenances of the antagonists showed that they were fearfully sensible of their situation; but then to retreat was dishonourable. At last the word "fire" was

given; but, from some cause - one party suggested fear, another a tendency to fits, Mr. H. fell upon his knees, instead of firing his pistol, and exclaimed in the agony of the moment "Who would have thought it would come to this?" His second, however, soon caused him to resume his position, if not, his self-possession. The signal was given; the pistol was fired by Mr. H., and singular enough both fell at the same moment to earth. At first it was believed, as blood was visible on the head of Mr. B., that he was shot but upon a minute examination by an unlicensed local practitioner in surgery, it was found that no wound had been inflicted, and the blood had most probably come from a pig which had that day been slaughtered on Cholmondeley Green. Meantime, Mr. H. has lain on the ground in a state of insensibility, and when roused from his stupor, he began to mourn over the day that he was born to be the murderer of his friend.......................... "[109]

At the beginning of the report it is claimed that both combatants were mortally wounded, which means that they both died from their wounds. We must make our own conjectures as to what may or may not have happened during this event, as it was said that no wound had been inflicted on Mr. B. I am afraid this has to be a *"historical cliff-hanger"*.

Throughout this book I offer ample instances of the immense inequalities which were present in our early societies. These examples show that the attitude of the upper and middle classes towards working people tended to be rather unsympathetic. Of course, locally, there were a small number of wealthy men and women who were exceptions to this rule but, generally, the attitude of the upper classes towards their employees was often unsympathetic or cold. In most instances workers were treated with indifference at best and at worst as second-rate versions of humanity. One particularly cruel case came to light during a search of *The Liverpool Mercury*. In a letter, written in 1838 and addressed to the editor, a local lady offers a transcript of a private letter written to her *"servant girl"*. It was stated quite clearly, and without the slightest embarrassment, that the letter was being submitted for the amusement of the newspaper's readers. We should remember that readers of newspapers at that time were mainly from the middle and upper classes as working men and women, if indeed they could read, could not afford to subscribe to a daily newspaper. For those who did read newspapers it was unlikely that *The Liverpool Mercury* would have been their newspaper of choice. In those days newspapers were

---

[109]*The Chester Chronicle* – July 1844

far too expensive for ordinary working people to buy as a tax was levied on each copy. Some papers, such as *The Poor Man's Guardian,* did publish newspapers which could be purchased without paying tax, but these were illegal and the publishers were liable to be prosecuted.

In her correspondence to *The Liverpool Mercury,* the lady claimed that the letter came into her hands accidentally. Nevertheless, after reading it, she decided that it was sufficiently amusing to share with fellow readers of *The Mercury.* I am sure that modern readers will feel shocked by the blatant invasion of the young girl's privacy. To read private correspondence was bad enough, but to then reveal the contents to all and sundry for the purpose of mass entertainment was deplorable. However we should remember that in those days there was an unquestionable assumption on the part of employers that they had special rights over their servants. The strict laws defining the duties of servants to their masters meant that servants had little or no rights, even in matters of a personal nature. In fact, in many cases, female servants were not even allowed to have romantic attachments so I suppose we should regard this employer as being quite liberal and enlightened in her attitude. Actually, this lady would have genuinely believed she was entitled to read her employees letter and share it with whoever she wished. She would not for one moment have considered that in doing so there had been any wrongdoing on her part.

There is some ambiguity as to whether or not this letter was passed on to the servant girl. One would hope it was. There is even the possibility that the readers of *The Liverpool Mercury* were privy to its contents long before the young girl was allowed to cast eyes upon it. When reading it, we cannot fail to feel a great deal of sympathy for the author, Edward, who speaks of having *"a dart in his heart that keeps his eyes from sleep".* He was obviously besotted with Sarah and jealous to the point of distraction. However, poor Edward had no idea that his innocent and rather endearing correspondence would become a source of amusement for the upper class ladies and gentlemen of Merseyside.

Whilst accepting that there is something extremely distasteful in treating another person's private correspondence as a matter for sensational writing, I am sure that there is no harm now, after a space of almost a hundred and eighty years, in printing Edward's correspondence in this work. In sharing this letter with my own readers I hope they will acknowledge the spirit in which it was written. If you raise a smile, I hope it will only be in a kind-hearted and compassionate

GENUINE LOVE LETTER.

To the EDITOR of the LIVERPOOL MERCURY.

SIR,—The inclosed letter having been sent through the medium of the Post to my servant girl, and accidentally falling into my hands, after perusing it I was much amused with its contents. If you think it worthy of a place in your widely-circulated paper, by inserting it you will oblige,   A SUBSCRIBER.

Mi Dear Searh i has thea pleasure of riting a feur words to you this comes from thea bottom of my hart and that i love you most Dearly but it greaves me to see you whith bill Nimrod last night at the end of the street last knight know he had you very snug as I was watchen you motions for a loung time at last you went to the lion there i observed your ways which was hirtful to my feelings te see you so comfortable Now my dear searh if you will promise never te keep bills company again i will buy you one of the finest patterns of a gown piece that can be purchased in the town i have you may believe me or may not been very ill since you was so happy whith bill I could not eat my supper for i went to bed whith a sorrowfel hart Now searh my dear i beg of you not to keep bill company any more as I intend to make you my loving wife as soon as my apprenticeship is out which is only about four months and then we shall be the most loving couple in the town i shall buy crumpets and the beast new butter besides my Dear Sarh i shall clean your shouses every morning before i go to my work and bring your breakfast to bed on saturday night i shall buy you plenty of tripe cow heels sheeps troters and a drop home in the bottle as you know a drop in the morning mixed in our tea is very comfortable but Dear Searh when I think on bill it cuts me to thea hart as i love you all over nay even the ground you walk on and your pritty little dealicate hands shall never no never take up the batting sticks no more but oh when I think on bill when i saw you with him but if ever i see you in the same situation i am Deaterminceh not to put up with it for i will give him a challenge with sword or pistle as i have a little honnor belonging to my family my Dear whereaver i think of you my heart in my belly goes thump again my ribs lov has crept into my heart and it is you alone sweet Searh that can give it ease oh say but that word and i shall then be happy why do you let that nasty fellow bewitch you was he ever half so comely or so handsome as your own Dear edward who can read wright dance and sing and has the blooming cheek the pouting lips the delicas teeth or the handsem leg o your own Dear Edward So remain in tears from happy lover   E D

Dear i must conclude with the folling lines love in my head dispel my rest love in my heart has left a dart and keeps my eyes from sleep and i do a most weep the cause that i write these few lines so kind it is i hope you to a true valentine My distres when well cowed more appear not than thine eyes bright each look i steal affords dlight and tell twas you i prize when squeezing Dishclouts at the sink or washing plates i stand ah me i cry and often think twas you who squeezed my hand sure if you who knowes that i felt you pity me straight say Nor let me thus like dripping melt but fix our wedding day
   No more at prensent
      thea ring his round thea vilants blue and thea kisses
         sweet and soryou

manner. We can see that poor Edward was not the greatest writer, but his desperate declarations of love and jealousy give the letter a naive eloquence which is in a class of its own. I hope the contents of the letter had the desired effect upon Sarah and that she accepted his rather desperate proposal.

This example of the arrogant and dismissive attitude displayed towards a servant only serves to emphasise the wide gulf which existed between the rich and poor at this time. It is not surprising that the grievous social inequalities, as well as the disproportionate circumstances of political representation, created a festering resentment among the working classes. In fact the leading theme throughout the Victorian period seems to have been the advent, either as a threat or a promise, of democracy. However whilst there was a widespread call for universal suffrage from the working classes, the landed classes and social elite put up strong resistance to any sharp or dramatic political change. Following the *"Peterloo Massacre"* demands for social reform continued. In 1836 an organisation was formed in London under the title *The London Working Men's Association*, which was to snowball into a national movement of social protest. The Association's secretary was William Lovett, a quiet, self-educated man who was a radical campaigner for parliamentary and social reform.

Following the failure of the 1832 Reform Act to extend the vote beyond those who owned property, William Lovett drafted a *"People's Charter"* which demanded some specific reforms of the system. Lovett believed that the right to vote seemed to be the only way to change the social order and this was at the heart of his demands for reform. His charter included six main requirements – votes for all men; equal electoral districts; annual elections; payment for Members of Parliament; a secret ballot and the abolition of the requirement that Members of Parliament be property owners.[110] In the years 1839, 1842 and 1848 William Lovett's Chartist Movement petitioned Parliament. Each of these petitions was signed by over a million people and the last petition was reported to have had over six million signatures.[111] The rejection of each petition provoked acts of civil unrest and a number of high profile arrests followed. Earlier, when the 1832 Reform Act failed to be passed, there had been riots around the country and many of the rioters were transported for their protest. Because of the reaction of the authorities, working people around England, especially in the new

---

[110] Today, these requirements are an accepted part of our parliamentary system.
[111] It has been suggested that a large number of the signatures were fake.

manufacturing districts in the north of the country, had become aware of the *"People's Charter"*. When Chartist meetings were organized in their areas large numbers of supporters attended. Consequently, the movement was viewed as a serious threat to the established social system and many property owners believed that the Chartists were planning a violent revolution.

Throughout March and April 1848 Chartist meetings were being organised all around the country. On Good Friday 1848 a huge Chartist meeting was held on Runcorn Hill. As Chartist meetings had sometimes resulted in violence, Mr. Richardson, the Chief Constable of the town and several of his constables were on standby in case of trouble. The Runcorn meeting, which attracted much local publicity, was attended by around 2000 people. It was opened by Mr. H. Reynolds, a surgeon, who asked the assembled crowd to start the meeting by joining him in singing a verse or two of *"Rule Britannia"*. However, the crowd was not in the humour for singing and refused to comply with his request. Perhaps this gives an indication of the anti-establishment feeling which was developing at that time. On the other hand, when Mr. Reynolds proceeded to draw analogies between the Chartists and the ancient prophets who, he said, *"had also struggled for liberty"*, the crowd was more forthcoming and enthusiastic. The other speakers included local Runcorn men such as George Taylor, a shoemaker; William Forrest, a boat-builder; and John Noon, a barber. It was said that all spoke eloquently in favour of the *"People's Charter"*. Despite the presence of such a large and enthusiastic crowd, the Chief Constable and his uniformed support team were not needed as the meeting passed off quite peacefully. It was reported that it was *"a lively but good humoured event"*.

In spite of the obvious unfairness which existed in daily life, it would be quite wrong of me to suggest that all members of the upper classes were unreceptive to the plight of the poor or the troubles of ordinary working men. The Victorian era was marked by some wonderful examples of intense philanthropy and many of our modern day charitable organisations have their roots in this time. Sometimes our more fortunate local residents were moved to acts of mercy when it became obvious that there was real hardship in their midst. In January 1842 members of the District Visiting Society of Holy Trinity Church in Runcorn arranged for the distribution of coal to the poor of the town. It was said that their intention was to:

".. supply the families of the most needy and wretched in the neighbourhood with coals during the severe winter weather. The

visitors of the poor cottages have tickets to give to those families whose circumstances most require relief, and thus the scatterings of benevolence diffuse light, and warmth, and comfort, over many a miserable dwelling, and the abject countenances of numerous families are animated with gratitude for the seasonable aid which protects them from the piercing cold of wintry blasts. Let this plan be adopted in every neighbourhood and many will be saved from the most grinding calamities."

Regardless of any efforts on the part of the more privileged and benevolent members of Runcorn society, poverty and its effects still played a huge part in the lives of ordinary working people. Some twenty years or so after the District Visiting Society had bestowed their bounty on the needy of Holy Trinity Parish we still find examples of extreme hardship and deprivation among the residents of the town. In May 1863 the Registrar General's quarterly returns for *"Births, Deaths & Marriages"* in the Runcorn district highlight some sad facts. As was to be expected, there were a higher proportion of deaths from diseases of various types in the poorer areas of the town. The ages of death were also lower. During the month of January two Runcorn women, the wives of labourers, died; the cause of death in both cases included starvation – one dying from chronic bronchitis and starvation and the other consumption and starvation.

Across the short stretch of the river Mersey, on the Widnes side, things had been much quieter. There are no apparent records of Chartist Meetings or social protest from the small home-grown communities on that side of the river. The indigenous populations in the unremarkable hamlets which comprised the township had pursued the traditional occupations of their fathers in a routine way of life which had not changed for generations. The familiar living and working habits in these small villages, whilst probably mundane and uneventful, offered a quiet security to the inhabitants of these places. In the mid-1840s it would probably have seemed to those native inhabitants that this inconspicuous way of life was permanent and unchangeable. However change was waiting in the wings and by the end of that decade Widnes was on the threshold of an enormous transformation. This environmental, social and economic transformation would be both drastic and irreversible.

Towards the end of 1847 John Hutchinson set up his alkali factory at the south end of the town. This spark of entrepreneurship was to be the catalyst which brought about a rapid and drastic change in the physical and social atmosphere of this small rural part of Lancashire. The influx of workers into the area, who were responding to the needs of the new chemical industry, caused a huge population surge. But as these workers came from the length and breadth of the country, as well as from Wales, Scotland, Ireland and other places, there was an unrefined fusion of customs, backgrounds and personalities. Therefore it is not too surprising to learn that this combination of people with different values and attitudes was destined to create difficulties. The 1851 census[112], which was the first to require details of a person's place of birth, gives an indication of the range of places and the great distances people had travelled to seek employment in Widnes. One wonders how these men came to hear of the demand for labour in the new chemical factories of Widnes.

It is more than likely that news of availability of jobs spread by word of mouth, chain migration or by newspaper adverts. The *Uniform Penny Post,* which had been introduced in 1840, also presented an opportunity to contact people in other parts of the country. This new scheme opened up the postal system to almost every person in Britain. Senders of letters could give their post to a uniformed *"Bellman"* who roamed the streets collecting letters from the public, ringing a bell to attract attention. A penny postage stamp was all that was required, or otherwise the recipient paid a fee of twopence when the letter was delivered. Of course at that time most working people could not read or write so this involved getting someone else to write and read their letters. However, in spite of this drawback, by the early 1860s postal services had become a common means of communication, even for those with limited literacy skills.

Regardless of the great convenience of being able to contact someone in another part of the country by letter, it should be remembered that it was certainly not a quick service. Today one can put a letter in a post-box in full confidence that the correspondence will reach its destination, in whatever part of the country, in a day or two. In the early days it would have taken a significant length of time to deliver a letter which had been posted at the other end of the country. A letter published in *The Liverpool Mercury* in 1864 gives us some idea of the long-winded journey taken to deliver a letter. I should add that this relates to the service from Liverpool to Ditton, so one can only imagine the length of time involved in delivering mail from much further afield.

---

[112] The 1851 census was also the first to show that the majority of the population of England and Wales were now town-dwellers.

> POSTAL DESPATCH.—In reference to the letter of "Progress," inserted a few days ago, "Fair Play" says—"It is true that letters from Liverpool are transmitted to Ditton by way of Warrington. It is not true that the letters for Ditton are taken to Appleton and detained there until a certain number are collected, sufficient to pay for delivery. They are left at Farnworth by a mail cart, which proceeds to Widnes Dock (the postal name of our friend P.'s Woodend). From Farnworth they are taken by a rural messenger, who delivers all letters free along his beat, which runs through the principal part of Ditton, and who travels daily, whether he is the bearer of one letter or of one hundred. The delivery of letters for that portion of Ditton beyond the limits of the rural messenger's walk has been arranged by the residents themselves with the proper authorities."

However, no matter how this novice workforce came to hear about employment opportunities, be it by advertisements, word of mouth or mail, they arrived in Widnes in droves from the length and breadth of the land. Of course this mass influx of workers was not unique to Widnes. This pattern was being replicated in numerous other parts of the land where industry was fast developing. The lure of the new industrial towns meant that a general decline of rural employment was beginning to happen around the whole country. Naturally, no one at that time could have foreseen the extent to which industry would change the environment and social structure of the areas where manufacturing was developing. Neither the masses who came to Widnes as a pioneer workforce, nor the manufacturers who set up their industries, could possibly have envisaged the transformation they were about to create.

The process of urbanisation happened with a speed born out of necessity as a vast new labour force rapidly descended upon the area. The workers came from every corner of this island and also from other lands across the sea. The Irish came here in large numbers and were by far the largest ethnic group in the town, at one time even outnumbering English born workers. With the sudden increase in population there was obviously an urgent need for housing. As there was no local authority at that time to provide the necessary accommodation this void was filled by speculative builders who constructed streets of houses quickly and cheaply. In those days there were no planning regulations to adhere to and no rules regarding density levels, layout of streets, sanitary provisions or other related issues. This allowed builders complete freedom to compress the largest number of homes onto the smallest parcel of land. We can see from early maps that the subsequent arrangement and widths of streets and back entries meant that there was a minimum amount of sunlight and air space. In retrospect, one can immediately see that this was an example of private enterprise at its worst.

The unprecedented rise in population, coupled with such rapid urban growth, inevitably meant that these two factors would create serious social problems. In fact they created a complex, disorderly and very crowded reality where the problems inherent in mass living on a large scale were apparent by a cramped, polluted and ugly environment. In order to visualise what the town was like at that time we can refer to local writings and directories of that era. However most of these sources are only useful in that they give us listings of postal and transport facilities, details of local churches and other notable buildings, as well as the names and addresses of leading citizens and tradesmen. None of these books contain fresh or vivid impressions of the physical and social ambience of the developing town. In spite of this, from what we *do* know, we can envisage the town of that time to be a very noisy and crowded place. We can imagine the sounds of a huge miscellany of people and accents; the ringing of horses' hooves and the trundling of carts on cobblestones; the clattering of clogs; clocks striking and church bells ringing. In addition to all these everyday sounds, the loud incessant drone and unpleasant influences of the chemical industry would have been a persistent and pernicious presence in the background.

We know from a written work by David Lewis,[113] a member of The Local Board that, apart from the noise, the town was a noxious and smelly place. Obnoxious odours emanated from rubbish and dung on the streets and from slops from scavengers' carts, as well as from the midden heaps, privies and ash-pits in back yards. Apart from the abominable smells which were present in the midst of the town and its residential areas, horrible stenches emerged from the local streams due to the industrial and human effluents which polluted them. It was certainly not a pleasant place to live and everything imaginable, from

---

[113] *Widnes– a Review and Forecast*: Councillor David Lewis, J.P. (T.S. Swale, Widnes) 1911

the sights, sounds, smells, and even the after-taste of the noxious air in the lungs became all pervasive. There was also an additional hazard in the expansion of industrial waste which was dumped in areas dangerously close to housing. Like the noxious odours and gases, the dumping of waste became an accepted and routine occurrence. Obviously today this would not be permitted, but at that time there were no clearly developed land-use conventions or effective zoning to move noxious industry away from residential accommodation. Of course the concept of specialised industrial areas did not exist when industry arrived here. When factories were developed it seemed advantageous to site residential housing nearby. One reason for this was to make factories more accessible to workers as there was no reliable public transport available at that time.

It is not surprising to learn that these unwholesome conditions meant that disease was rife in both towns. History shows that diseases such as cholera, typhoid, typhus, smallpox and scarlet fever were endemic during the nineteenth century. It is also evident that the poorer classes were less resistant to contagion because they were underfed and continually exposed to conditions in which infection thrived. Houses were packed tightly together with little space between streets, and the homes themselves were usually overcrowded and often occupied by more than one family. The lack of clean running water in dwellings meant that in many cases personal cleanliness was not easy to achieve or maintain. Wholly inadequate urban sanitary provisions also created opportunities for germs and infections to flourish. In some areas there was no proper drainage, and the lack of facilities to remove sewage meant that during heavy rainfalls noxious waters often ran down the streets, or seeped into backyards, sometimes even penetrating into the houses.

Obviously it would have been extremely difficult to contain infectious diseases under these appalling conditions, especially when people lived in such close proximity to each other. Although the authorities tried to enforce strict controls for preventing the spread of infection this was no easy matter. In the late 1840s there was an epidemic of cholera in the north of England and neither of our towns escaped this terrible scourge. In fact there had already been a serious outbreak of cholera in Runcorn several years earlier[114].Unfortunately doctors of that time were virtually helpless; as the medical profession

---

[114] There was a cholera epidemic in Runcorn in 1832.

did not actually know the cause of some diseases, therefore it was impossible to treat them with any degree of success. It was some time before it was discovered that typhoid was the result of water borne infection or that typhus could be transmitted by lice.

The fear of infection must have been a constant worry to individuals and the dread of mass contagion a worry for the authorities. In September 1849 a female passenger became sick on-board a Bridgewater Packet Boat which was en route from Manchester to Runcorn. By the time the vessel had reached Preston Brook the lady's condition had worsened considerably. The captain of the vessel subsequently decided that she should be taken off the boat and transferred to a flat which would take her to Runcorn. When the flat reached Astmoor Bridge two doctors were waiting to go on-board to attend to the woman and assess her condition. Upon examining her they ordered that she should be wrapped with blankets and taken on to Runcorn as soon as possible. When the flat arrived at Runcorn, around six o'clock in the evening, they had difficulty in landing as no one would come near the flat to help them, for fear of being infected. Eventually around eight o'clock, they managed to get someone to assist and the lady was taken to a house in Halton Lane where she continued to be attended by the medical gentlemen. The house in Halton Lane had been acquired by the Board of Guardians to be used as a temporary isolation hospital. Its purpose was to receive strangers arriving at Runcorn who might be infected with cholera or other diseases. During the night the lady's condition deteriorated and she died at one-thirty the following morning. During the Inquest into her death it was revealed that the captain of the Bridgewater Packet had been ordered by the other passengers to remove the lady from the boat. It was suggested that there had been mass panic on board the vessel as passengers were in fear of being infected. The verdict reached was that the lady, Margaret Nixon, *"Died by visitation of God, from cholera"*. The captain of the Runcorn Packet was criticised for not having brought the lady straight to Runcorn as it was believed that her transfer to the flat and the long delay in bringing her to Halton Lane had accelerated her death.

Smallpox was also responsible for numerous deaths in both towns. In August 1864 a survey of births and deaths in the Runcorn area stated that: *"Smallpox has been very prevalent in this district, especially in Runcorn; it has visited almost every part of the town, and the occupiers of the best class of houses have not escaped this disease any more than those who live in dirty ill-ventilated and overcrowded dwellings. 14 deaths in Runcorn are attributed to this disease and 2 in Halton."* Although outbreaks of the disease abated, it did continue to make dramatic appearances from time to time. In 1876 a spate of cases occurred in Widnes and several people were also infected at Ditton. Another serious outbreak occurred in Widnes in 1883. It had started in June when ten cases were identified in the town centre and afterwards another seven cases developed in John Street, Lugsdale. The Lugsdale cases all involved the residents of two adjoining houses. In October a young man called Thomas Gill, who lived in Gladstone Street, died of smallpox and another case was confirmed on the morning of his death, making over 20 cases in all. The Health Committee feared that there would be a major epidemic in the town and as a precaution a temporary wooden hospital, to isolate and accommodate 12 patients, was erected in the Ditton Gas Yard.

It was an alarming situation and as neighbouring towns were also affected, The Prescot Guardians held an emergency meeting to discuss the possibility of erecting an Infectious Diseases Hospital for the entire Prescot Union. However, our local Medical Officer, Doctor O'Keefe, thought it would be unwise to act in unison with the Prescot Guardians as he feared they would refuse admission to their hospital to any person who was not a pauper. Doctor O'Keefe suggested that a meeting should be arranged with Mr. Shelmerdine, the agent to the Leigh Estate, to request him to grant the temporary use of a piece of land off Moor Lane for the purpose of erecting two temporary infectious diseases tents.

Of course, as stated earlier, minor outbreaks of cholera and smallpox recurred with unwelcome regularity. Scarlet fever and typhoid were also familiar visitors to the district, both of which claimed numerous lives. However we should note that although the poorer classes were far more likely to be victims of these diseases, as contagion spread quicker in areas of dense population, the fact is that disease is no respecter of personage. Even people who lived in better class homes were at risk. In July 1876 one of our major industrialists, Henry Deacon, was struck down with typhoid fever and died. Even more alarming to the general public was the fact that Prince Albert, the Royal Consort, had also fallen victim to this particular disease. If a member of the Royal family could succumb to such a disease it is easy to understand why there was such a fear of epidemics occurring, as most people believed that there was little hope of effective curative treatment.

Doctor O'Keefe, as the Widnes Medical Officer of Health, when referring to cholera and smallpox, was of the opinion that if either of the diseases were to reach epidemic proportions in Widnes it could decimate the population. It would seem that Doctor O'Keefe was not alone in these fears. Because of the number of regular outbreaks of disease in the county the Local Government Board ordered the Widnes Local Board to provide a hospital to isolate infected patients. Surprisingly, the Local Board chose to ignore this order for some considerable time.

It is unclear whether the Local Government order was disregarded for economic reasons or because of the usual conflict of opinions among the Board members. The result was that the Local Government Board issued them with an ultimatum. The Local Board were informed that if they did not provide a hospital the Local Government Board would do so themselves, at the expense of the Widnes ratepayers. It was pointed out that at that present time patients could not be isolated. Because of this, the disease was easily spread from person to person, house to house, and one side of the street to the other. Doctor O'Keefe, when urging the Board to take action, had said that it was impossible to prevent families of patients from mingling with other members of the population. He gave an example of how easy it was to pass the infection on. He said: *"One Saturday night a woman who had been nursing her diseased daughter attended a wake in Oxford Street with her husband. Although they only stayed in the house 15 minutes, that was quite sufficient to dangerously extend the disease and as a consequence several other people were infected"*.

In October 1883 a site was chosen for the erection of an Infectious Diseases Hospital. Mr. T. Ireland agreed to sell the Local Board some land at Crow Wood, Halton View, for a purchase price of £1400. As with most Board decisions there was a lot of disagreement among the members. On this occasion the choice of site and the decision as to who would be a suitable building contractor were causes of conflict. The site which had been selected was not a popular choice, especially among property owners in that district. A deputation of ratepayers headed by the Rev. George Bond, the vicar of Farnworth, presented a petition to the Local Board signed by 128 ratepayers from the district of Halton View. The petition protested against the purchase of any land in Halton View for the purpose of building an infectious diseases hospital. They claimed that Halton View was an improving and rising neighbourhood and the presence of such a hospital would tend to depreciate the value of property in that district. They believed that the chosen site was too near to a public thoroughfare, to St. Ambrose Church, to Albert Road Wesleyan Chapel, Warrington Road Board School and Page Lane Mission Room and School. However, the purchase was completed and the hospital building[115] went ahead. In the intervening period, to provide facilities for the isolation of patients until the hospital was completed, two infectious diseases tents were purchased at a cost of £80 each. They were expected to provide additional accommodation for another 20 patients and were located alongside the existing wooden facility at the Gas Yard in Ditton.

During the nineteenth century the presence of diseases, which recurred with alarming regularity, was a major concern for the Government as well as our local authorities. However there were other important issues which also commanded a great deal of attention in Parliament and among the population at large. The subject of parliamentary reform, which would allow a larger portion of the population to become eligible to vote, was a continuing theme throughout this century. We have seen earlier that Runcorn hosted at least one significant Chartist meeting in the town. However, regardless of its wide popularity amongst working men, the Chartist Movement eventually dwindled out because of disagreements about policy between the leaders. This meant that it was no longer a strong united driving force for reform. Despite the demise of this movement the demand for parliamentary reform did not abate. Changes *did* happen but when they came they were in very small doses. A Reform Bill was introduced in 1832 which granted some small concessions and extended the vote to those who owned some property. Obviously this arrangement made little difference to the general working population of the country.

Prior to the late 1840s the inhabitants of Widnes had seemingly not been sufficiently affected by change, or been militant enough, or large enough in number, to voice concerns relating to social inequality or reform. However, by the mid-1860s Widnes was no longer the sleepy collection of villages it had been at the time of Peterloo. The population was now large and diverse and the occupational structure had changed dramatically. Working men had also become more politically aware and active and had gained the confidence to band together to call for reform. As this new climate of self-belief developed, Widnes became the scene of several lively reform meetings. The first of these meetings was held at the Public Hall in Hutchinson Street in April 1866. The meeting, which was chaired by Henry Deacon, concerned a new Reform Bill which had at that time been set

---

[115] Later to be known as Crow Wood Hospital.

before Parliament for consideration. Joining Mr. Deacon on the platform were several local employers including Mr. McLellan and F.W. Gossage, as well as the inimitable Mr. Shaw Brown and a local GP, Doctor Greenup of Farnworth. Surprisingly, the large audience contained a significant number of women as well as working men.

The Chairman opened the proceedings by saying it was extremely unusual to have a political meeting in Widnes, except on occasions such as elections. He believed it was also the first meeting held in Widnes regarding such an important public matter. It was pointed out that the population of Widnes was between 10,000 and 12,000 and yet the number of voters on the register was only 123. The proportion of votes to population throughout the entire kingdom was about 3½% and therefore, to have an equal and fair voice in the representation, the number of voters in Widnes ought to be 320. Mr. Deacon said:

"...that there had been many slurs cast upon the working classes but, for his own part, he believed that the working classes, if entrusted with the franchise, would not make use of it in furtherance of any of those destructive designs imputed to them, but that one of their first demands would be for the removal of those obstacles which now stood in the way of a plain and practical education of the people, and that by this means a great deal of the difference which now existed between the upper and lower classes of society would be removed, not by the bringing down of the upper but by the raising of the lower."

The second speaker at this lively meeting was a Mr. J.R. Jeffrey whose appearance on the platform was met with lively appreciation by the audience who cheered and applauded as he rose to speak. Mr. Jeffery quoted some of the speeches made by the opponents of the Reform Act of 1832. He endeavoured to show the alarmist views which then prevailed and to demonstrate how subsequent events had falsified the predictions of the enemies of reform. Part of his speech referred to the current system of taxation, which he said was unfair to working men:

"....Did they know that out of every threepenny-worth of tobacco which they bought 2½d went to the Government? Talk about revolution! If Lord Grosvenor and the rest of the peers had imposed upon them the same proportion of taxation upon what they spent, there would be a revolution on the side of the aristocracy tomorrow."

He singled out The Duke of Westminster, who was one of the country's most prominent challengers of reform, for particular attention. He told his audience that:

"The Duke of Westminster, who is vigorously opposed to reform, had an income of more than £1000 a day, and his son Lord Grosvenor thought perhaps that if the franchise were extended to working men the influence and power of his family would be diminished, and possibly their property endangered. If however, he had gained any knowledge by past events Lord Grosvenor should know that exactly the reverse might be anticipated".

During the course of the meeting it was revealed that the Duke of Westminster had been invited to attend that evening in order to give him an opportunity to explain his point of view to the working men of Widnes. Unfortunately the Duke had to decline the invitation as he had an urgent appointment and his son, Lord Grosvenor, was also otherwise engaged. This information was met with a good deal of sniggering and jeering from the audience.

The drinking habits of the population, in relation to crime and antisocial behaviour, have been referred to several times in other chapters. Because alcohol consumption became a huge problem in most industrial towns the middle classes generally believed that alcohol addiction, and what they perceived to be innate moral deficiencies, were responsible for most of the ills in society. Although this opinion, in relation to alcohol, was understandable to a degree some of the underlying factors were ignored. Robert Sherard, in his *White Slaves of England*[116] articles, told us that working men often found that their appetite for food was completely destroyed in the noxious atmosphere of an alkali factory. Arduous labour in sweltering conditions made workers extremely thirsty and, as a consequence, they became accustomed to drinking large amounts of liquid to replace the fluids they had lost through perspiration. As beer was more palatable to them than water, and in those days it was sometimes safer to drink, they consumed large quantities of alcohol. As a result, excessive drinking became an accepted part of daily life for most ordinary working men and drunkenness was common, even amongst children. Beersellers plied their wares from carts outside the factories and a proliferation of pubs, alongside works and housing, were readily available to cater for these needs.

Apart from the act of drinking, the social ambience of pubs provided a relaxing outlet after a gruelling day in the unpleasant and unhealthy

---

[116] Published in *Pearson's Magazine* - 1896

environment of an alkali factory. Although most of the early pubs were small and rough places, later on an increasing number of well-fitted pubs were opened and these provided a more comfortable and pleasant alternative to the cramped miserable hovels they called home. Interestingly, several surveys relating to the consumption of alcohol show that the deeper the poverty of a district the higher the proportion of public houses to population.

Although there was an excessive amount of alcohol addiction in the two towns, and this most certainly contributed to a great deal of public disorder and financial deprivation, perhaps it should be mentioned that there was also a high level of drug-taking during this era. In spite of this habit being relatively common among all sections of society during the nineteenth century, there was little emphasis placed on the evils created by drug addiction. Like alcohol, drugs were affordable as well as being legally accessible. In fact opium and opium derivatives were easily available as were morphine and laudanum. However it is important to point out, that whilst some people took these substances deliberately, others were passive drug-takers as proprietary medicines and sleeping draughts sometimes contained significant amounts of laudanum or morphine. One widely available medicine, called *"Godfrey's Cordial"*, was routinely administered to babies to make them sleep. The soothing qualities of this remedy relied on the amount of laudanum it contained. But apart from laudanum being present in proprietary medicines, some mothers believed laudanum itself to be an acceptable sedative to give to their children. In September 1844 an inquest held at Runcorn into the death of a baby called Elizabeth Evans found that she had been accidentally poisoned by a nurse, Jane Walker. Mrs Walker told the inquest that she had given the child three drops of laudanum in some sugar and water to *"keep it from being cross and to send it to sleep"*. The verdict was *"Died from the effects of laudanum, ignorantly and improperly administered."* The Coroner remarked that this had been the third death from a similar cause in Runcorn in a very short space of time.

Whilst the most common drug-taking of that time involved substances which were mainly used for sedative purposes, alcohol abuse usually created the opposite effect. Drunkenness and related violence were all too apparent and the level of this problem caused general concern. In May 1841 middle class Runcorn residents were saying that *"public immoralities and crime alarmingly prevail on the streets of the town"*. One man remarked that the problem was worse on Sundays and on that day each week upwards of thirty men, *"in a shocking state of drunkenness"* passed his home. He also said that *"the principal inhabitants of the town should be alive to the need for peace, good order and morality in their neighbourhood".* The evils and consequences of intemperance were regular topics in the newspapers, which at that time were read almost entirely by the middle and upper classes. The articles and reports of drunken incidents were often accompanied by moral judgements or biblical quotes. In July 1842 the sudden death of an old man in Runcorn provided another opportunity for the middle classes to preach about the harmful effect of alcohol.

"A few days ago, one Samuel Smith, a lock-tender, at Runcorn, of the Bridgewater Canal Trustees, - an aged man, and, we are sorry to add, an habitual drunkard, joined some drinking companions at the Bridgewater Tavern, and, in a state of excitement from liquor, he undertook the desperate experiment of drinking five or six pints of ale in a few minutes. We believe he succeeded in swallowing five pints in two minutes, and then he died almost instantaneously. Such an occurrence, which seems to bear clear marks of divine judgement, needs no comment. It speaks at once to the understanding and the heart of every drunkard. "Awake ye drunkards, and weep!" The verdict of the inquest was - "Death from excessive drinking".

The evil consequences of becoming addicted to drink were highlighted as often as possible. If there was an unpleasant outcome to an event involving alcohol then this was emphasised as a warning to others. It would seem that the worse the story, the better the readers liked it! A report from 1869, with the headline *"Drink and its Results",* tells us about the unfortunate consequences of alcohol addiction and its sad impact upon a Widnes family.

"William Mason, until recently a respectable draper in Widnes, was brought up before the magistrates and charged with being drunk and disturbing the peace in Waterloo Road. It transpired that within the last two years the prisoner had taken to drink, and had wasted all his substance, some £2000 – now, he and his wife and a family of six children were without anything or anywhere to call a home. He was fined five shillings and ordered to pay costs."

The alarming amount of drunkenness in both towns caused a considerable amount of unease among residents. This concern had led to the forming of local "Temperance Societies" and "Improvement Institutions". The Temperance Movement, which was a major cause of social reform in the nineteenth century, had begun to emerge nationally during the 1830s as industrialisation became more widespread and working habits changed. The movement's main focus was working-class drinking but, interestingly, the upper ranks of the organisation were dominated by middle-class men. These men felt that by fighting intemperance they were helping the working classes. It could also be said that they were creating a more reliable workforce. Publicly, the majority of the upper and middle classes were generally opposed to drink. Despite this public show of disapproval, most of the male members of these social groups were not averse to alcohol themselves. Polite society drank sherry before dinner, wine during their meal and brandy or port afterwards. They usually had well stocked wine cellars and some partook of copious amounts of alcohol behind the closed doors of their comfortable homes and, indeed, some were also drunkards. This was another example of the hypocrisy and double standards that touched nearly all areas of daily life during the nineteenth century.

When looking at the strategies of the Temperance Movement we can see that it focused mainly on the drinking habits of men. One would assume that this was because men drank publicly and because the drinking habits of women were probably unknown. Despite attention being centred mainly on male drinking there was actually a serious problem of alcohol abuse among women also. One Widnes woman appeared before the magistrates, charged with drunkenness and disorderly behaviour, twelve times within the space of a month. However whilst emphasis was put on male drinkers there was no barrier to women becoming members of temperance societies and there were many *"Sisters of Temperance Groups"*.

The number of Temperance Groups in both towns shows that there were significant sections of society who were teetotal. Many of these groups appear to have been allied to religious organisations. These promoters of temperance believed that anyone under the influence of alcohol was no longer in control of himself or herself. Therefore they concluded that alcohol was a pernicious enemy of society in general. In order to encourage personal restraint and discipline, temperance gatherings involved members making pledges representing the ideals of self-control and self-denial. Improvement Societies and Evangelical groups also focused on the evils of drink but, in addition to promoting sobriety, self-help and personal development through religious observance and education was also encouraged.

In an attempt to provide alternatives to the traditional pub as a social gathering place, *"Cocoa Rooms"* and *"Temperance Public*

Houses" began to spring up around the country. These establishments provided tea, coffee and cocoa as well as light snacks. Some even made stoves available for those who wished to cook for themselves, provided they purchased a hot drink. The first Cocoa Rooms in Runcorn were opened just before Christmas in 1877. There were two Cocoa Rooms in Widnes prior to this. These were part of a privately run Company whose establishments were known as *The British Workmen's Public House and Cocoa Rooms.* They had branches in Liverpool and several other places. The Widnes outlets were located in Ann Street and Hutchinson Street. At a meeting of the Directors of this Company, which took place in Liverpool in 1876, it was said that they were offering the working men of the country a substitute for beer. They were providing Public Houses *"where men could enjoy that wholesome and cheap beverage, cocoa, in surroundings suitable to the neighbourhood in which they were placed".* One gentlemen questioned whether working men could be persuaded to go into places so barely furnished, where drink was supplied in mugs and everywhere seemed to be associated with philanthropy and which were generally furnished with nothing but evangelical literature. The Chairman assured the gentleman that the Cocoa Rooms were well attended and the movement was a financial success. He expressed the hope that Cocoa Rooms would soon be established in every town in the country and within the reach of every working man in England.

A TYPICAL COCOA ROOM

In August 1871 the *Independent Order of Good Templars* was established in Widnes. Despite the town's reputation as a haven for drunkards, the group quickly acquired a substantial membership. In 1876 another group of Widnes abstainers decided to provide an alternative establishment to cater for the needs of non-drinkers. They formed a legal "Company" with the intention of building a Temperance Hall on land leased from the trustees of the Hutchinson Estate. It was estimated that the project would cost in the region of £2500 with the sum being raised through the issue of £1 shares. The Company was to be managed by nine directors: John Griffiths, Samuel Hughes, William Hunt, Thomas Jones, James Watterson, David McKay, John Powell, Thomas Reay and Abraham Speakman. The first subscribers to take up shares in the proposed Temperance Hall included John William Coxton, a manufacturing chemist; a local blacksmith called Thomas Reay; Thomas Hulse who was the dockmaster at Widnes Dock; a teacher called Thomas Hughes; Thomas Steele Swale, a printer;[117] Thomas Stanley, a foreman at a local chemical works and James Irvine, a Manchester woollen merchant. They each held one share valued at £1.

Even with a fair amount of interest in the project, and a considerable number of people willing to invest, the Widnes Temperance Hall scheme was officially abandoned in 1881. An extraordinary meeting of the shareholders was held at the Cocoa Rooms in Hutchinson Street in May that year. During the course of that meeting it was decided to wind up the affairs of the Company by voluntary liquidation. It was said that *"despite the Institution having such worthy objectives it was realised that it could not be carried out in Widnes with any commercial success"*. The Chairman of the meeting thanked those who had invested money, especially those members of the working classes who had taken up shares *"in the hope that their investments might not only prove remunerative, but also assist in promoting the comfort and sobriety of the community."*

Regardless of the failure of the Temperance Hall Company, temperance groups and meetings were prolific in both Runcorn and Widnes and, indeed, all around the country. Many of these groups were associated with churches and local clergymen became instrumental in trying to dissuade men from becoming drunkards. In Widnes, the Moss Bank Band of Hope; St. Ambrose Gospel Temperance Mission; The Church of England Temperance Society and the Farnworth Wesleyan

---

[117] In later times the Swale family were the owners and printers of *The Widnes Weekly News*

Band of Hope, together with several Mutual Improvement Societies, offered support to those who were willing to take a pledge of total abstinence. One meeting was reported in *The Widnes Weekly News* in January 1882:

"ENTHUSIASTIC MEETING OF THE TEMPERANCE MISSION IN WIDNES

The local lodges of the Independent Order of Good Templars in conjunction with the Sons of Temperance held their weekly mission at the Lacey Street Wesleyan School when Thomas Horrocks of Darwen, well known throughout the country as "the converted clown", preached two sermons to crowded congregations who listened with rapt attention to the thrilling discourses."

In August 1885, the Widnes *Independent Order of Good Templars* held a parade to mark their 14th anniversary. Around 700 members, including almost 500 juveniles, assembled at the Promenade in West Bank and marched through the streets of the town accompanied by Gossage's Brass Band and the band of the Runcorn Mersey Mission. Several separate temperance lodges took part in the parade, including: *The Star of Widnes; Haste to the Rescue; Hope of Appleton, Sunbeam; Lily; Samaritan* and *Onward.* From the Promenade at West Bank the parade marched to a field off Millbrow, near Millfield Road, where sports and entertainments took place.   Prizes were presented for the sports events and the afternoon was rounded off by the provision of an afternoon tea. In the evening a number of balloon ascents took place from the field.

Most Templar events and meetings seem to have followed the normal well behaved and enjoyable formula.   However, an earlier meeting, which took place just before Christmas in 1876, was marred by a nasty disagreement between some of the members.   The disagreement resulted in an appearance before the local magistrates when one man was summoned for assault.

"At the Widnes Police Court yesterday, Enoch Fowler, the "Grand Worthy Secretary" of the "Haste to the Rescue" Lodge of Good Templars at Widnes, was summoned for violently assaulting Peter Tonkies.   Mr. Swift, Who appeared for the prosecution, said that the complainant, who had been a teetotaller for 16 years, applied to become a member of the Haste to the Rescue Lodge, and, in compliances with the wish of the officials, waited in the ante-room of

the lodge on the night of the 27th ult. The result of the ballot was that Tonkies was rejected through a zealous Good Templar sister stating that he had affirmed that rather than wear the Good Templar regalia he would have his hand chopped off. Tonkies shouted through the keyhole "It's a lie!", whereupon the Grand Worthy Secretary rushed out of the lodge, and with his fist struck Tonkies a violent blow on the temple. In the cross-examination he admitted that when Brother Rogers, a clogger, was sticking up for him he shouted "Go on!" Rogers asked why they would reject an honest man like Tonkies when there were dishonest people in the lodge. After several witnesses had been called on both sides the bench fined the Grand Worthy Secretary £2 and costs, or if in default to go to gaol for three months with hard labour. The money was paid."

Alas, the goodwill and friendliness between Mr. Tonkies and Mr. Rogers, the clogger, did not last. The following year a dispute at another temperance society, of which Tonkies was the Treasurer and Rogers the President, resulted in Tonkies being summoned to appear before Widnes Magistrates. By the time the case came to court the Widnes Temperance Society, of which they were both officials, had become almost defunct. The complaint, in the form of a summons against Peter Tonkies, was brought by the President, Samuel Beckett Rogers. It was alleged that Tonkies had used threatening language to Mr. Rogers. After what appears to have been a fairly trivial altercation, he had called Rogers a *"thief and a swindler"* and had challenged him to a fight. When Rogers refused to fight Tonkies had used threatening language toward him. Tonkies denied all the charges, but the bench held that he had committed a breach of the peace and ordered him to be bound over for six months.

From the above accounts it is evident that abstinence did not always make for entirely peaceful behaviour. One would assume, and hope, that these were exceptions to the rule and that most dealings and events involving temperance societies were carried out in a pleasant and responsible manner. As the objective was to attract members and deter them from the evils of drink, events were usually designed to be enjoyable social occasions in which all the family could be involved. In May 1882 the *Farnworth Church of England Temperance and Total Abstinence Society* had their last meeting of the season. The evening was a fun packed event with light refreshments followed by music, recitations and temperance songs from the Band of Hope. On another occasion, at a meeting of the *Farnworth Wesleyan Band of Hope* in 1884, Mr. John Bray delivered a lecture *"full of sound and wholesome advice. He urged the members to still greater exertions on behalf of the temperance cause, and warned them against the reading of impure literature".* At the end of that meeting five-year old Maud Hollins sang *"Jesus loves the little ones".* The summers brought their own special events for the groups, such as picnics and walking processions accompanied by bands playing temperance songs. In 1889 the Farnworth branch of the *Church of England Temperance Society* held their annual summer demonstration. The members usually walked through Appleton Village, Albert Road and Mill Brow, but unfortunately because of inclement weather the walk had to be abandoned and the members had to continue their celebrations in a school room.

I was to discover that not all temperance outings and events were to pass off without incident. One sunny Sunday afternoon in July 1897 the children from the Sunday school associated with the Runcorn *Camden Wesleyan Band of Hope Society* were en route to Frodsham on their summer excursion when a nasty accident happened. The children and some adult members were being conveyed in two wagonettes containing around 70 people in total. The first vehicle, which contained about 40 children and several adults, was drawn by three horses and driven by a man called Harry Booth, the proprietor of the wagonettes. When travelling down Victoria Road the horses were startled by something and they started to gallop at a furious rate causing the driver to lose control. The speeding animals, by now completely unrestrained, turned over Delph Bridge and began to descend the steep incline and as they did so one of the wagonette poles snapped. The broken wagonette crashed onto the footpath at great speed, colliding with a lamp and smashing a portion of the stone wall. It then tumbled into Canal Street, falling about 25 to 30 feet down the slope. The scene that followed was described as fearsome, with ear-piercing screams and cries from the children and those who were injured. Before the drop into Canal Street some of the passengers, who had been seated on box seats, had managed to jump off and they escaped with just a few minor cuts and bruises. However, those who were trapped in the wagon were quite badly injured owing to the fall onto the pavement below. Although those trapped inside were badly hurt, as the body of the wagonette was covered with a tarpaulin it prevented them from being thrown out. Had they been so, it was believed some may have been more seriously injured. Indeed, it was said that it was a miracle that none of the passengers were killed.

Tenants in the neighbourhood were quick on the scene and carried the injured into their houses. Local doctors, McDougall, McLennan,

Delany and McKenzie arrived at the spot fairly quickly, as did members of St. John Ambulance Association who gave assistance to the wounded. One young lady, Miss Sweetman of Union Street, was unconscious. Many others were suffering from shock and severe concussion. Several children were thought to have internal injuries as well as severe cuts. The names of those who were injured included Miss Littler of Leinster Gardens; Alfred Santley aged 6 and his elder brother. Little Alfred had internal injuries and his brother's spine was seriously damaged. A small boy called Sam Dutton, of Cawley Street, and his three young sisters, Clare, Fanny and Emily were also injured. They all received severe cuts and were suffering from shock. Ruth Rogers of Shaw Street; Robert Davis from Lowlands Road; Miss Bazley of Albert Street and William Walker of Shaw Street were also injured. Although all the occupants of the wagonette were greatly shocked and received varying degrees of injuries, fortunately, only three were serious enough to be hospitalised. Miss Sweetman remained unconscious until around five o'clock the following morning but was thought to have made a full recovery. What a sad end to a day that had promised to be a happy occasion.

When reporting on everyday life in the two towns we cannot overlook the fact that the populations were comprised of a mixture of ethnicities. It has been established that the Irish were by far the largest group in Widnes and therefore they had considerable influence on day to day life in the town. The champion of the Irish population was the peerless Doctor John McNaughten O'Keefe who had enormous clout not only amongst the Irish population but also as a member of various town committees. He served on the Local Board, the School Board, the Library and Technical Institute Committee and he was the town's Medical Officer of Health for a great number of years. He undertook all these civic duties eagerly and diligently whilst at the same time devotedly serving the interests of the underprivileged sections of the community. Although Doctor O'Keefe was the type of man who could inspire great loyalty, he was certainly not an easy man to deal with and probably had as many enemies as friends in the town. However, during his time in Widnes he worked selflessly on behalf of the town and its people. It was through his dogged determination that Widnes got a free public library when it did and, despite resistance from ratepayers, he was extremely vocal in promoting the formation of a School Board. In both these endeavours he faced fierce opposition from other members of the Local Board but he stormed ahead regardless. During one of the countless heated debates in which he was involved he told fellow members of the Board: *"I don't care whether I am a solitary individual or not, I will always do what I can for the benefit of Widnes and its people".*

Doctor O'Keefe, who was a native of Tralee in County Kerry, first came to Widnes in the 1850s and at that time was a young man in his twenties. Prior to coming to Widnes he worked for a short period, as a newly qualified doctor, in Preston.   On his arrival in Widnes he became the assistant of Dr. Greenup at Farnworth before setting up his own practice in Widnes Road. He was a powerful personality, well known for his stubbornness and exactness, not to mention his infamous confrontational manner. He did not suffer fools gladly and therefore, to some people, he was a perpetual thorn in the side or even the devil incarnate. However, most people found him to be a remarkably compassionate and generous man who was known for his many acts of kindness to the sick and the poor of the town.   So, depending on your view, it was a case of love him or loathe him. What is certain is that he was a hugely colourful personality and someone who simply could not be ignored. After his death one contemporary source said *"there was no better-known figure in the town than Doctor O'Keefe[118]."*

Alas, the commanding public persona of Doctor O` Keefe hid a rather sad personal history. In 1872 his young wife, Grace, died at the age of 35. Their 5 month old son, John, had died just four months earlier. These tragic deaths had been preceded by the death of their baby daughter in 1868. So within a space of less than five years Doctor O'Keefe had lost his entire family. Although he had always been involved in community affairs, after the deaths of his wife and children he became even more passionate in his endeavours to improve the lives of the ordinary citizens of the town. From that time on he devoted his working life entirely to the people of Widnes. Although his name is not well-known these days, he made important and lasting contributions to the civic development of the town. Today, there are still a few reminders of this remarkable man; the home he had built, Brendan House, opposite St. Paul's Vicarage in Widnes Road, is still standing. Our public library also serves as a permanent tribute to his hard won achievements on behalf of the citizens of Widnes. The rare photograph reproduced here, although of poor quality, allows us at least a glimpse of this extraordinary man.

118Doctor O'Keeffe died in Preston on 7th April 1898. He was 61 years old

A RARE PHOTOGRAPH OF DOCTOR O`KEEFE

As well as his unstinting civic work for the general population of
Widnes, Doctor O'Keefe was the leader of the local branch of *The Irish
National League* and was always to the fore in promoting local Irish
issues. His political views were by nature Liberal and he was a
prominent and vociferous member of the Widnes branch of the Liberal
Party. Naturally, in the nineteenth century the huge Irish population of
Widnes was concerned with the burning question of Home Rule for
Ireland and Dr. O'Keefe, as an Irishman, was a staunch Home Ruler.
His views on this subject were well known and he repeatedly spoke out
in support of this issue on local political platforms. However, his

involvement in Irish political matters was not confined to Widnes, as he was also a significant figure in Irish organisations in Liverpool and some of our neighbouring towns. In May 1878 a huge meeting was held at the Theatre Royal in St. Helens under the chairmanship of Dr. O'Keefe. Joining him on the stage at that event were some of the foremost Irish political figures of the day. They included the leader of the Irish Nationalist Party, Charles Stewart Parnell MP, along with the well-known Fenian, Michael Davitt, who had recently been released from prison where he had served a sentence for political activities. Incidentally, Davitt was not the only Fenian to visit the area at the invitation of Dr. O'Keefe. In May 1895 the prominent Fenian, Jeremiah O'Donovan Rossa, visited Widnes and gave a lecture to a crowd of around 400 at The Drill Hall.

The Irish population of Widnes was comprised of people from every province of Ireland. Although it is probable that men from Connaught or Ulster may sometimes have found they had little in common with men from Munster or Leinster, nevertheless, their shared nationality bound them together into a very close knit community. The fact that there were so many Irish in the town meant that it was easy for Irish newcomers to blend into the population without too much notice. This meant that sometimes men who were fleeing from the clutches of the law, for whatever reason, found it relatively easy to hide themselves in Widnes or other towns with significant Irish populations.

In those days the exploitative and often brutal landlord system in Ireland was the cause of great social injustice. Small farmers and tenants, with their dependant families, were frequently evicted from their smallholdings and cottages for no good reason. In retaliation, many young men banded together into gangs of raiders who struck in the dead of night and burned down, or blew up, the magnificent homes owned by the offending landowners. They believed that these actions were simply moral reprisals for the numerous injustices that had been committed by the landowning classes and absentee landlords who lived abroad. On the 20th March 1882, Weston House in County Galway, the home of Mr. Rosman a landed proprietor, was blown up and badly damaged. Mr. Rosman, who was a partner in the Dublin brewing firm of Arthur Guinness, had recently instructed his agent to evict three families from their cottages. The cottages were razed to the ground leaving the tenants destitute and homeless.

The men who committed the offence at Weston House were being sought by the police on both sides of the Irish Sea. Six young men had already been detained but the police were still on the lookout for the remaining participants. The following year, in June 1883, one of the wanted men was arrested in Widnes at a house in Elizabeth Street, Newtown. The young man, who had assumed the name of John Smith, was John Rogerson a native of Ballyfoden in County Roscommon. He was 22years of age and had been lodging at the home of a Mrs. Condron in Elizabeth Street for several months. During the whole of this time he had been employed at Pilkington's Chemical works in Moss Bank. It was said that throughout his time in the district he had been a reliable and faultless employee and a quiet, well-behaved lodger. When making the arrest Inspector Barnett of the Widnes police force was accompanied by Sergeant O'Brien of the Royal Irish Constabulary. The sergeant had travelled from Ireland to take Rogerson into custody and return him to Galway to stand trial. It is not known how they managed to track him down but, surprisingly, intelligence and detection appears to have been remarkably good in those days. One has only to read and see the amazingly good descriptions of *"wanted"* people. Sketches of fugitives often included written details regarding posture or manner of speaking, as well as the obvious physical features and any unusual characteristics

It would seem that in the early days both Widnes and Runcorn concealed a number of Fenian activists in their midst. It is a well-known fact that Irishmen from the two towns took part in the ill-fated raid on Chester Castle in February 1867[119]. Michael Davitt, who revisited Widnes some years later at the invitation of Dr. O'Keeffe, took part in that raid and stayed overnight at a house in Caroline Street, Newtown, before leaving for Chester. Later that year a policeman was accidentally killed in Manchester during an attempted rescue of two Fenian prisoners from a prison van which was en route to Bellevue Gaol. Three of the men involved William Phillip Allen, Michael Larkin and Michael O'Brien, were afterwards captured and hanged. However some of those arrested had played absolutely no part at all in the affair but were simply judged to be guilty by association. Two of the men imprisoned had previously lived and worked in Widnes. A young Widnes girl called Mary Flanagan, who at that time was living in Manchester where she worked as a governess, gave evidence against them. She stated that she was the daughter of the landlady of the

[119]Jean. M. Morris, *"Into the Crucible"* (Countyvise 2005);
Peter Beresford Ellis *"A History of the Irish Working Class"* (London 1972);

Foundry Inn near Widnes Dock. She claimed to have regularly seen one of the accused, a man called Jones, in the company of another accused man at her mother's pub in Widnes. Both these young men received long prison sentences although it was generally believed that they had no involvement in the crime.

A week after the incident in Manchester four men appeared before the magistrates in Runcorn, accused of having taken part in the raid on the prison van. The men, Peter Davies, Joseph Beverley, John Gorman, and Frank Avery were charged with *"having been concerned, with others, in the attack on the police van in Hyde Road, Manchester."* It was said that they had all previously resided in Manchester but left the city earlier that week and came by rail to Moore Railway Station. From Moore they walked to Runcorn and from there to Weston where they sought employment at several quarries. During their conversations with some of the quarry workers it emerged that they were looking for temporary work and intended leaving the country shortly afterwards. As the Manchester incident had received a great deal of publicity, and there was a degree of public panic, suspicion was aroused at Weston and the authorities were alerted. The Runcorn Magistrate, Mr. Brundrit, remanded all four men into the custody of the Manchester police who were present in the court. The prisoners were then handcuffed and conveyed in a bus to Runcorn Station accompanied by a large group of police officers, all of whom were armed with revolvers.

As we know, political matters relating to Ireland were a feature not only of earlier centuries but have continued to be an issue right up to the present day. However, in Widnes during the nineteenth century the subject of Home Rule for Ireland was a cause of interest and debate not only among the Irish but also among the general population. In February 1887, Mr. Eustace Carey presided over a huge public meeting in support of William Gladstone's Irish policy. The meeting, which was held at the Baths Assembly Rooms in Widnes, attracted a large audience. Amongst the speakers on the platform was Mr. E.K. Muspratt, in his capacity as President of the Widnes Liberal Association, Messrs. F.H. Gossage; F. Gaskell; J. Goulding; John Davies; C.M. Percy; F. Hartland and J. Dennett as well as several local clergymen. The meeting unanimously supported the principles of Irish Home Rule and the vote was concluded by Mr. E.K. Muspratt making the following statement:

"I move that this meeting desires to record its unabated confidence in our great leader, the Right Hon. W.E. Gladstone, and to express its firm conviction that the only method by which a just, safe, and permanent settlement of the Irish question can be obtained is by passing a measure of self-government for Ireland, based upon the essential principles of Mr. Gladstone's recent Bill; and that, until this settlement is effected, much needed legislation on land matters and other subjects is entirely prevented. I am satisfied that until Ireland is given Home Rule as extensive at least as intended by the Bill of Mr. Gladstone, Ireland was not likely to be content; making it impossible to carry out say English or Welsh legislation."

Mr. Gossage seconded the motion, after which another gentleman on the platform, Mr. C.M. Percy, rose to speak and confirm that he was in full agreement with the Bill and would support it. In conclusion he made the following statement, which was greeted by thunderous applause in the packed hall:

"In supporting this Bill they were upholding the Irish policy of Mr. Gladstone because it was just in itself. When five-sixths of the Irish representation was united in the demand for Home Rule, he thought it was more than sufficient expression of the will of the people. Either the just demands of those people must be conceded, or every vestige and pretence of constitutional government will be swept away. The time had come when a change must take place, and he thought that anyone who had fairly read the provisions of Mr. Gladstone's measure would have seen that, whilst conceding to Ireland all that the Irish people had asked for and all that they wanted, it created no danger to the unity of the Empire. If a just measure, such as he believed Mr. Gladstone's Home Rule measure to be, were conceded to Ireland, we should see the resources of that country developed, and the genius, intellect and ability of Ireland's sons and daughters, which were now directed to the affairs of other nations, directed to their own; we should build up means of employment for thousands and thousands of the people and thus benefit Ireland directly, whilst benefiting England by removing from our labour markets an enormous amount of surplus labour."

Although the politics of Irish nationalism were never far from the minds of the Irish population, there were many other less serious displays of nationalism. The extremely large number of Irish in Widnes meant that the celebration of St. Patrick's Day was a lively occasion in the town. Most years, from noon until late evening on 17th March, the streets and main thoroughfares of the town were packed with throngs of people wearing their shamrocks and green rosettes. Many of the women wore green dresses or some item of green clothing. Indeed, the wearing of green was seen as a symbolic act of unity. No matter how ludicrous it may seem today, several centuries ago it was against the law to wear green in Ireland as this was seen as an act of defiance against the English. The shamrock also had a symbolic significance as this trefoil was used by St. Patrick to represent the Holy Trinity and thus became representative of Ireland's conversion to Christianity. Therefore the wearing of the green and the display of shamrock on St. Patrick's Day were important demonstrations of patriotic pride.

St. Patrick's Day was an important annual event for the Irish of Widnes and Runcorn; indeed it still is for Irish people everywhere. Most people attended Mass to start the day off on a good note. In the afternoon, *St. Mary's (Marie's) Brass Band* paraded around the streets of the town playing Irish tunes. In the evening a concert was usually held in The Volunteer Hall under the auspices of *St. Mary's Young Men's Society*. The concert generally involved renditions of Irish songs and recitations by local amateur entertainers. After the evening's performances had ended, there would be a blessing from the local Parish Priest followed by communal singing of hymns. Although one would generally expect this day to be an occasion for bacchanalian excess, which might result in some disorder, a report of St. Patrick's Day in Widnes in 1884 says *"It is satisfactory to be able to state that no disturbance of any magnitude took place during the day, the atmosphere was joyous and good humoured but there were one or two minor signs of drunkenness"*. It was also said that *"Several bellicose persons had the hardihood to wear an orange lily in honour of King William III."* This final statement highlights the inherent discord which existed between the local Irish and members of the Widnes Orange Order. Of course there was bound to be tension between these two groups and, as this report shows, there was a certain amount of goading between the different factions when either side held a procession or demonstration.

The Widnes branch of *The Loyal Orange Order* had a sizeable membership and their lodge was known as *The Widnes Invincibles*. Although I have no specific details to determine when this particular lodge was founded, I believe it to have been during the 1860s. Prior to that time there were several lodges in St. Helens and, as you would expect, there were several large lodges in Liverpool and its suburbs. It is important to point out, that although there were countless niggles and minor discords between the Widnes Irish and the local Orange Order, any serious disturbances that occurred appear to have been instigated

311

by members of visiting lodges. On one occasion, in July 1867, a Widnes woman was shot by a passenger who was travelling with a trainload of Orangemen on their way home to Liverpool. They were returning from a huge *"12th of July Rally"* in St. Helens. When the train halted for a short time at Widnes Station a crowd of Widnes Irish congregated on the platform to heckle them. In response, the Orangemen waved their flags out of the carriage windows and sang provocative songs. Although it was an ugly scene it was not violent as the two parties were separated, one lot inside the train and the other lot on the platform. However all that was to change when one of the Orangemen, producing a pistol, leaned out of a carriage window and shot an elderly Irishwoman who was standing on the platform. Although she did not die she was quite badly injured. As a crowd gathered round the woman and a doctor was summoned to assist, the train moved out of the station and resumed its journey to Liverpool. The unidentified assailant was never apprehended.

As the population of the town expanded, membership of the Widnes branch of The Orange Lodge grew. The annual celebration of *The Battle of the Boyne* which took place on 12th July each year was a particularly sensitive time in Widnes. Sometimes members of lodges from other towns arrived to augment the local membership in order to form a huge procession for their jubilant march through the town. In July 1883 members from the Kirkdale, Bootle and other Liverpool lodges swelled the local numbers. Because of the large number of Irish in the town the police feared that this event would cause some disturbances. However despite extra police being drafted in, the affair went off peacefully. The 1885 parade also passed off without incident as a report in *The Widnes Weekly News* demonstrates:

"On Sunday morning, the members of the Widnes Orange Lodge assembled in fair number to celebrate the "auspicious 12th of July". Meeting in their Lodge Room in Victoria Road, attired in the insignia of their order, and wearing orange lilies, they walked in procession to Widnes Parish Church. A large number of people assembled in the streets, and although the Orangemen, Nationalists, and Salvation Army were in close contingency to each other, and the former had to walk a considerable distance along streets chiefly peopled by Irish Roman Catholics, there was no evidence of ill feeling, and certainly no indication of a disturbance, which says much for the law abiding and forbearing spirit of the people".

Unfortunately this was not always the case. The following year a huge contingent from the Garston *"True Blues Loyal Orange Lodge"*, wearing their uniforms, insignia and orange lilies, arrived in the town. Apart from their banners and ceremonial regalia, some of them also came armed with spiked sticks and other weapons which they had concealed under their jackets. The disgraceful scenes of violence which erupted in the centre of Widnes on that day were without precedence, and were subsequently to go down in the annals of history amongst the Irish communities of the town. It important to stress that, although they did take part in the parade, no member of the Widnes Lodge was thought to have been involved in this violence. Indeed, reports suggest that the event had been fairly peaceful until later in the day when the *"True Blues"* marched through the south of the town on their way to the Railway Station in Victoria Road to board the train back to Garston. Earlier in the day the procession had made its way to Farnworth Church for a religious service and then adjourned to a field in Farnworth for speeches, social events and refreshments.

Apart from the members of their drum and fife band, which numbered about thirty bandsmen, there were in excess of two hundred Garston men in the parade that day. It was late on a Saturday afternoon and the town was packed with local people. As the procession approached lower Simms Cross, near to the Irish districts, the band and the marchers assumed a different attitude. It was said that the drummers and bandsmen became louder and more enthusiastic in their playing, and the singing and posture of the marchers became more animated and provocative. Several local bystanders were angered by the songs as some referred to the Pope in obscene and derogatory terms. They were also provoked by the some of the Orange supporters who made challenging gestures and shouted insulting remarks. It is believed that the members of the *Widnes Invincibles Lodge* had dispersed some time before this and this procession comprised entirely of members of the Garston Lodge.

Within a short space of time numerous angry people from Newtown and Lugsdale arrived on the scene and a full-blown fight broke out between the marchers and townspeople. A local off-duty policeman, who lived near Simms Cross, was attacked and badly beaten after he had tried to make an arrest. The Policeman, Constable Liptrot, who had been in his home, went to the scene after hearing the sounds of a commotion. He had observed a bandsman and several others striking and kicking a man as he lay on the floor. When he identified himself as a policeman and attempted to arrest the bandsman he was set upon by a group of men and knocked unconscious. A witness, James Fallon from Grenville Street, said he saw seven or eight men assaulting the officer.

A youth named John Tansey gave corroborative evidence. Later in the evening there was more noisy disorder as the remaining stragglers who had remained in the north of the town made their way to Farnworth Station. They had gone through the district shouting and swearing, and they were said to have *"waved their sticks defiantly challenging anyone to come and interfere with them."* The following week fifteen Garston men appeared before the Widnes magistrates charged with assault and causing a breach of the peace. All were given prison sentences. A Widnes man who was summoned for assault was fined. It is believed that representatives of the Garston Lodge never made a return visit to Widnes.

Two years later, on 12th July 1888, a massive gathering of Orange Lodges occurred at Halton Castle in Runcorn. Special excursion trains ran from Liverpool Lime Street to Runcorn Station bringing an estimated 2500 Orange Lodge members and friends to the town. At eleven o'clock in the morning the various lodges formed into groups and marched in procession through the streets of Runcorn en route for Halton Castle. The procession included no less than eight fife and drum bands and the marchers, both male and female, wore orange sashes and emblems of their office or ranking in the Orange Order. As the procession, complete with several large banners, passed through the streets of Runcorn hundreds of townspeople lined the route to watch the colourful display. The procession reached Halton Castle around twelve o' clock and the numbers were then increased by the presence of members of the Widnes and Garston lodges who had arrived earlier.

Despite the large number of attendees at Halton Castle the event was extremely well planned and appeared to go off without the slightest hitch. Entertainment had been organised in the form of dancing and games on the green which had once formed the courtyard of the castle and, in a field below, there were swings and fairground attractions. The Rev. J. Lockwood, the vicar of the parish, opened the church to allow people to view several books which he had put on display. At the same time, a massive catering operation got underway performed by the landlord and staff of the Castle Inn, who dispensed refreshments to the gathering. At two o' clock the chiefs and officials of the Order were entertained to lunch in a Marquee. After lunch a series of speeches were delivered to the massive and appreciative crowd who had assembled on the castle green. The whole event went off without the least hint of trouble and by seven o' clock in the evening the various lodges had made their way down to Runcorn Station and departed for Liverpool. It had been a glorious day weather-wise and it proved to have been a well organised and orderly event.

Although the Irish in Widnes represented a huge section of the population, there was also a significant number of Irish in Runcorn and there were several Irish social and political organisations in that town. In July 1882 the Runcorn branch of *The Irish National Foresters* hosted a huge rally. It was the fifth annual event of this nature and hundreds of delegates arrived in Runcorn to join the local members. The delegates and members arrived at 10 o'clock in the morning and proceeded in a procession to the Public Hall. The local members and visiting delegates wore green and orange regalia and were preceded by huge banners and several bands playing lively Irish tunes. Crowds of enthusiastic spectators lined the streets as the procession passed by. At the Public Hall an address of welcome was given by the Chairman of the Runcorn branch and the proceedings were *"characterised by frequent cheering from the audience"*. The Chairman stated that:

"...they (the Runcorn branch) were full of enthusiasm at the thought of meeting their kindred, who were working with them, in one grand united bond of love and brotherhood, to unite all their fellow countrymen into one powerful association for their own benefit."

Following the official welcome, Mr. James Ryan read an address from the members of the Widnes Catholic Association, he said:

"...that the Foresters, the exiled sons of Erin, should be grateful for establishing branches of the order in Irish populated districts, where the demons of temptation very often existed, and where too often, too, the improvident nature of their countrymen reduced them and their families to such a state of penury that their only means of existence in times of depression of trade was to be found inside the portals of the workhouse, the Foresters were therefore an important organisation who made themselves the benefactors of the whole Irish race".

After an enthusiastic and well attended meeting the delegates and members walked in procession, preceded by the bands, through the streets of Runcorn before travelling on to Widnes where the procession was resumed along the main thoroughfares of the town. In the evening a ball was held in Runcorn Public Hall. Although this jolly affair was typical of the majority of events associated with shows of Irish nationalism, and was representative of the general demeanour of the Irish populations in both towns, there were however several incidents of a not so innocent nature. The covert activities of the Fenian movement that we experienced earlier on had not abated with the passing of time. Throughout most of the nineteenth century there was a significant

Fenian presence in the north of England, particularly in the cities of Liverpool and Manchester. In fact, it was supposed that Fenian cells operated in all of the new manufacturing towns where there were sizeable Irish populations.

In light of continuing Fenian activity it is not too surprising that, from time to time, both Widnes and Runcorn were considered by the police to be places of special interest. Indeed, we have already seen that they were not wrong to assume this. Later on in the century there were several incidents which aroused suspicion and on one occasion a cache of arms was discovered in a house in Market Street, Widnes. In June 1882 alarm was raised by a foreman who claimed that a quantity of explosives had been stolen from a site in Runcorn. The foreman, who had been supervising some tunnel work, claimed that one of his workmen had absconded and taken a quantity of explosives with him. The man had been entrusted with the key of the storeroom and the theft had been discovered when the key was found left in the open door. The man had taken with him a large quantity of nitro-glycerine, gunpowder, fuse and caps. Although the man was not Irish born he was believed to be a Fenian sympathiser, having been brought up in an Irish community. The Runcorn Police were confident that the robbery was connected to Fenian activity. A search was made for the man in Widnes and Staffordshire where he was thought to have connections. It was said that during the previous weeks the police had received several letters drawing their attention to certain suspicious activities in several districts of Lancashire and Cheshire, including Widnes and Runcorn.

The arrival of industry into Widnes in the late 1840s brought employment opportunities for thousands of men. In the early days of our industrialisation such was the demand for labour that the town was a magnet for people responding to the urgent needs of the alkali trade. In Runcorn also there was plentiful employment until the 1860s when the American Civil War had a negative impact upon their soap and alkali industry. Fortunately Runcorn, unlike Widnes, did have additional trades to overcome most of the effects of this downturn. However, apart from trade problems associated with the American War, there was also a serious slump in the alkali trade in the late 1870s. During this time the alkali industry suffered badly due to overproduction and competition from other markets. As Widnes was reliant upon this trade for most of her employment this depression had a huge impact on the town's working communities who formed almost the entire population. By 1878 the trade conditions had caused huge distress in Widnes and most ordinary families were living in abject poverty. Just before Christmas that year a meeting was held in the

Drill Hall to discuss the economic suffering among the townspeople of Widnes. Major James Cross chaired the meeting which was also attended by local religious representatives of all denominations as well as several hundred unemployed men. During the meeting it was unanimously agreed that subscriptions should be sought to help alleviate the distress of the unemployed. A committee was appointed to organise a plan of relief. Messrs. Gossage, soap manufacturers, sent a subscription of £25 for the fund.

Apart from the obvious economic hardship, there were other noticeable signs of a depression in trade. Despite the rapid housing boom which had once taken place, when demand exceeded supply, in October 1876 there was in excess of eight hundred empty houses and numerous empty shops Widnes. One survey reported: *"At this time there are approaching a thousand dwelling houses without a tenant – a state of things too palpably indicative of straitened circumstances to need further demonstration."* It is not certain whether this survey indicates a temporary exodus from the area due to stagnation in the chemical trade, or if it means that multiple occupancy house sharing became an economic necessity. Despite having no doubts concerning the accuracy of this statement, there are several interesting points which give one food for thought. For instance, the population figures show that between the years 1871 and 1881 there was an increase of over 10,000. In addition, local building plans show that the 1870s was a period of prolific house-building. Therefore it is not possible to make a reliable judgement regarding this situation. Happily, several years later, in 1884, things were far rosier following a marked improvement in trade and several local industries were expanding. It was said at that time that there was *"now scarcely a house in Widnes that is empty and owners of property have taken advantage of the great demand to make a general increase in the rents"*. To add to the brighter economic outlook, the town was anticipating an increase in population due to the arrival of the Broughton Copper Company who were planning to open a new works in Ditton Road.

It should be noted, in relation to economic distress and empty houses, that some years later Runcorn also experienced another severe downturn in its trade and population. In February 1895 a spell of wintery weather meant that the Bridgewater Canal was not navigable and much of the town's trade was affected. Several works were laying men off and as a consequence there was severe hardship among the population. Children at the various day schools in the town were supplied with a free meal each day and at the Runcorn branch of *The*

317

Mersey Mission to Seamen over three hundred boatpeople were supplied with dinners. By the end of the year things had not improved much and a continued slackness in trade almost brought several local works to a standstill. In November that year the Ship Canal Company dispensed with the services of over 130 men who had been employed on dredgers, steam-tugs and barges. The reason given was because it was abolishing the double-shift system, meaning that the crafts would only be required during the daytime. Another report, concerning population statistics, claimed that the population of Runcorn had dropped considerably, from around 21,000 in 1891 to about 16,000 in that year, 1895. The cause of this was the state of trade and also the fact that the completion of the Ship Canal had removed a large volume of labour from the town. It was said that there were several hundred properties, both houses and shops, standing empty in the town

Earlier in this chapter we read about the remarkable exploits of a cat belonging to a Halebank blacksmith called Rutter. Returning briefly to the subject of cats, an interesting but frightening incident happened in Widnes in December 1890. This concerned the escape of a lioness from a goods van on the London and North-Western goods line at Widnes. The lioness, which was owned by Wombwell's Travelling Menagerie, had been accidentally left behind in a goods van in the railway yard. If one can actually believe that such a large and dangerous animal could be "accidentally" left behind anywhere! Wombwell's Menagerie had visited the town one Friday night, and on leaving the following morning had sent one of their vans to the Widnes goods yard, marked as empty. The empty van was to be forwarded to Bolton some time later in the week. However when an unsuspecting railway worker opened the van he was stunned to discover that it contained a rather large, vocal and uncaged lioness. The terrified man obviously made a rapid retreat and, in his haste, left the van door wide open allowing the lioness to escape. The lioness was next spotted by two railway workers at Ditton Station, walking along the line. They immediately ran to a nearby signal box and sent word along the line to Halebank for someone to come with a gun. Unfortunately by the time help arrived the lioness had moved on. It was next seen at Halebank railway station where a shocked porter encountered the animal walking along the platform. Naturally, the porter ran as fast as he could in the opposite direction. The stationmaster, hearing the screams and commotion, immediately sent for two neighbouring farmers, Mr. Naylor and Mr. Mercer, who arrived shortly afterwards with their shotguns and managed to lodge a shot in the animal's neck. The shot disabled the animal long enough for one of the farmer's to get close enough to strike it on the head with a hammer. The stunned lioness was then collected by a member of Wombwell's Menagerie who returned the poor frightened animal to its rightful place of residence.

Whilst the smoke, smells and chemical tips must have made the general ambience of the town pretty grim, now and again sparks of enjoyment managed to break through. There were the celebrations of special days such as St. Patrick's Day or the Orange Order's 12th of July commemorations, along with Temperance galas, Whitsun, Easter and Christmas festivities. May Day was another important occasion. Every year around this time crowds gathered for the annual week-long visit of Lord J. Sanger's Circus and Hippodrome shows. Local residents, children and adults alike, thrilled at the sight of Sedgwick's Wild Beast Show and Chippendale's Living Pictures and Menagerie, or the disturbing sight of Marcus, the lion-pawed man. In 1898 when this show made its return visit to the town it also included Gledhill's Living Pictures and Mrs. Carroll's Nautch Girls.

Although visiting circus and fairground attractions caused a great deal of enjoyment and excitement in the district, sometimes these visits were marred by tragedy. In August 1891 a young man was killed after falling from a fairground swing-boat at Runcorn. This accident led the Widnes Local Board to question the wisdom of allowing of this type of attraction to operate in the future. At the inquest into the death of the young man the jury made a recommendation urging the banning of swing-boats. Following this, the District Coroner, Mr. Husband, wrote to both local authorities to advise them to prohibit swing-boats. They were urged to take positive steps to prevent the recurrence of such accidents. The Widnes Local Board were uncertain as to their position legally but agreed that, in the case of attractions such as whirligigs and other steam driven rides, the Board had the power to introduce by-laws.

In addition to the visiting amusements, both towns were lucky enough to have some permanent theatrical venues. Before the building of several theatres, the Public Hall in Hutchinson Street was used as a place for local entertainment, as was the Public Hall in Runcorn[120]. Later on a number of dedicated theatrical establishments were constructed for performance entertainment. *The Theatre Royal* was built in Duke Street, Runcorn in 1869 and the following year a theatre was opened in Widnes. The Widnes theatre, which was

---

[120] The Public Hall in Runcorn was built c.1861

SANGER'S CIRCUS TRAVELLING UP WATERLOO ROAD

owned and run by an actor called Mr. J. B. Preston, was located in Wellington Street adjacent to the Wellington Hotel. This theatre employed a resident company of actors and actresses who performed Shakespearian plays and Victorian melodramas. Mr. Preston himself often took the lead and from time to time groups of travelling players also appeared on the bill. Some of these roving performers, such as Dan Leno, went on to achieve national fame. Being built of wood, Mr. Preston's theatre became known locally as *"the old wooden shed"* but, although primitive in construction, it was immensely popular with the local community. Obviously theatres were important social assets in towns with growing populations and both Runcorn and Widnes were fortunate to have developed such good facilities. In Widnes, Mr. Preston's little wooden theatre was soon eclipsed by other ventures such as the legendary *Alexandra Theatre*. In July 1890 another new theatre opened in Widnes.

WIDNES.

PEOPLE'S NEW THEATRE OF VARIETIES. — Mr D. Cohen, the late manager of the Alexandra Theatre, Widnes, has erected a neat wooden theatre in this town, capable of accommodating about 1,800 people. The stage is 33ft. deep. The opening night is fixed for the 28th inst.

THE ERA – JULY 1890

In spite of the presence of several existing entertainment venues, in February 1894 there was an attempt by Mr. George Mellon to open another Music Hall in Ditton Road. He applied to the Magistrates for a licence to permit music and dancing in a wooden structure which had previously been occupied by a company called *"Ohmy's Circus"*. The application was refused after an objection had been raised by Messrs. Gerrard, Bray and Kiddie, who were the owners of *The Alexandra Theatre*. It seems that the proprietors of *"The Alex"* did not relish the idea of more competition.

Apart from visiting Circus and Hippodrome shows, along with local theatres and pubs, from time to time other types of attractions were provided free. We have seen that employers and landowners often put on grand displays of fireworks and provided meals for their employees and tenantry to celebrate special events. No doubt firework displays were a welcome diversion and the meals were most enjoyable for those fortunate enough to be invited; however, once in a while the general public were entertained to another type of show on the banks of the river. This free mass entertainment took the form of jaw-dropping feats of endurance, or exhibitions of strength and daring, performed in or alongside the river.

In an earlier book, *Into the Crucible*, I described an incident in November 1889 when hundreds of spectators gathered on the shore at West Bank to witness a tremendous feat of daring. A young Widnes man called Tommy Burns thrilled crowds of spectators as he made an audacious dive from the Old Bridge into the Mersey below. At the time of his death in 1897 Burns was being described as the undefeated champion high diver of the world. His remarkable dive from the bridge in 1889 was repeated the followed year, when he was challenged to an amazing contest by an American athlete called Carlisle D. Graham. Graham was a renowned diver who was known as *"The Hero of Niagara Falls"* and at that time he was reputed to be the world champion. The pair dived off Runcorn Bridge into the river, swam ashore and then ran 136 laps around the bowling green at the nearby *"Snig"* (Mersey Hotel). The distance run equated to ten miles. Burns, winning the contest, made a time of eighty-three minutes and received £25.

Nearly all reports describe Tommy Burns as being from Liverpool. In fact, although he was indeed born in Liverpool in January 1868, he spent most of his life in Widnes. The family were Irish and his father was a baker employed in the service of Mr. Wolsencroft in Newtown. The Burns family lived in Midwood Street near Simms Cross and young Tommy and his siblings were educated at St. Bede's School in Appleton. Several years ago, when I first began researching Tommy Burns` career, I was astounded by the things he was alleged to have achieved. If all accounts are to be believed then he was a truly remarkable athlete. I quote from one report:

"Before he had attained his majority he had won over 600 prizes, including prizes for swimming, running, walking, boxing, rowing and diving. He has saved forty-four persons from a watery grave, one of that number being W. Gale, Esq., the well-known steeplechase jockey. He also holds all the Royal Humane Society's medals and certificates for saving life. He was the first and only man to dive from the roof of the Royal Aquarium into a tank six feet deep, in March 1895. He also dived from the roof of a railway car on the Overhead Electric Railway in Liverpool on May 2nd 1895. Dived off Runcorn Bridge, swam to the landing stage at Liverpool, a distance of eighteen miles, then ran to London, dived off London Bridge and ran back to Liverpool inside nine

days, on October 9 1889, thus creating a world record.   Dived from the top of a hansom cab over Putney Bridge in October 1885.   Dived twice from a 90 foot high platform at the Royal National Lifeboat Gala, Reservoir, Birmingham, in July 1895.   He captured a shark, after a desperate fight, while diving off the Pier at New Brighton.   Dived off the largest sailing ship in the world, "The Three Brothers" (150 ft.) at Birkenhead, in 1880   Dived off "The Great Eastern" twenty-six times (75 feet) 1887; Runcorn Bridge six times; London Bridge twice; Suspension and Grosvenor Bridges, at Chester; Tower Bridge and Southwark Bridge in London, in January 1896; Dived off Vauxhall Bridge and then ran to Brighton, dived off West Pier and ran back to London in nineteen hours and four minutes, in January 1896.   Dived off Lambeth, Vauxhall and Chelsea Bridges inside twenty minutes and then ran to Epsom Town Hall inside two hours on Derby Day 1896. Dived off London Bridge and ran to Yarmouth, dived off the pier and ran back to London a distance of two hundred and sixty miles in forty-six hours and fifty-nine minutes, in September 1896.   There are many other daring athletic feats, which space compels us to eliminate."

I think my readers will agree, that if all this is true, it is a really remarkable and unique record. It would seem that Tommy Burns continually pursued more difficult and dangerous ways of exhibiting his athleticism and fearlessness. Apart from the numerous feats listed in the above report he also jumped from the Clifton Suspension Bridge and the Forth Bridge. On one occasion he jumped from a moving train into the docks at Liverpool and on another occasion he leaped from a train while it was crossing the Thames. I am really sorry to say that the intrepid Tommy pushed his luck once too often. He lost his life while attempting to perform a hazardous diving feat at Rhyl in July 1897. He was just twenty-nine years old.

In those days outdoor displays of daring or of extreme physical prowess were quite commonplace and events such as these usually attracted large crowds of spectators. In fact, Tommy Burns was not the first man to perform swimming or diving exhibitions on our stretch of the Mersey. During 1826, and for the next five years or so, there was an ongoing and quite bitter rivalry between two swimmers called Doctor Bedale and a Mr. Vipond. Both men swam from Liverpool to Runcorn on several occasions and also swam in the Thames in London. In their 1826 swimming challenge they both set out from Queen's Dock in Liverpool and swam to Runcorn. Each swimmer claimed that the other had cheated and newspapers of the time took sides as to the merits of each man.   I would assume, from reading many reports of these events, that Dr. Bedale was the less popular. Several newspapers suggested that he was not as good as he professed to be. It was thought that he had been aided by the tides in almost all of his swimming feats. Nevertheless, Doctor Bedale was quite confident in his own ability and challenged several people to beat him. *The Chester Chronicle* of February 1828 printed the following:

Coronets.
SWIMMING.—Dr. Bedale, of Manchester, who swam, or rather floated, from Liverpool to Runcorn in one tide, one day last summer, has challenged Mr. J. H. Smith, of Heaton Norris, near Stockport, to perform a similar feat in the approaching summer for a very considerable sum. Mr. Smith has declined accepting the Doctor's challenge : but, in order to prove the relative powers of the two, a Mr. Street, on behalf of Mr. Smith, has challenged the Doctor to swim any number of strokes not exceeding five hundred, giving him fifteen strokes in every hundred, for twenty pounds —the wager to be decided in still water, on an evening in July, unknown to the public ; the winnings to be given to a public charity either in Stockport, Manchester, or Liverpool.
On the evening of Wedne-

CHESTER CHRONICLE AND NORTH WALES ADVERTISER
(FEBRUARY 15TH 1828)

In August 1832, shortly after Doctor Bedale claimed to have performed another exceptional feat of swimming in London, *The Liverpool Mercury* published this rather caustic opinion of his abilities.

"We never fail to find amusement in the puffing announcements of Dr. Bedale's aquatic feats; but we were particularly diverted with the account of his swimming from London Bridge to Battersea, on Thursday last. We shall copy the paragraph, in order to append to it a few remarks upon the nature of the exploit, and the challenge which the redoubted Doctor has trumpeted forth, to the astonishment of the Cockneys. The following is an extract from the paragraph in the London paper:

"After all was in readiness the Doctor stripped, and threw himself in the river backwards, and disappeared for some seconds. A burst of applause followed the commencement of the feat. Shortly after, the Doctor appeared floating in a most graceful attitude, occasionally performing many singular and unprecedented evolutions in the water, peculiar to this amphibious son of Galen. The artiste arrived at the

Red House in an hour and thirty-five minutes from the time of starting notwithstanding the wind was against him the whole of the distance. The Doctor offers to swim against any person in the world for 500 guineas."

In this account of the marvellous feats of the aquatic son of Galen, we are left quite in the dark as to the real nature and merits of the performance. Battersea is, we believe, only three miles from London Bridge and therefore the distance, if in still water, could not be anything to boast much about. If the Doctor had the tide in his favour, the exploit dwindles down to one of a very ordinary character. There are hundreds of boys who could do the same with the greatest ease.

We have no wish to disparage the Doctor's skill in swimming, but we cannot help laughing outright at his egregious puffing. As we have told him a score of times, his principal merit consists in his capability of remaining a long time in the water, although in this respect, as well as in downright swimming, Mr. Vipond is more than his match; and the friends of that individual would, we have no doubt, back him against Dr. Bedale for any sum, for genuine swimming, though perhaps not for floating on the back, and leaving the tide to do the rest. As far as we have seen of Dr. Bedale's performance, he generally lies face upwards and floats with the current, which is not swimming but drifting. Mr. Vipond, on the contrary, when he performed his wonderful, and, we believe, unparalleled exploit of swimming from the Rock Point to Runcorn, a distance of about twenty-one miles, and which he accomplished in five hours and a half, seldom turned on his back, but was in almost constant action all the time. The greatest distance Doctor Bedale ever swam or drifted was when he passed from one of the south docks to Runcorn, in company with Mr. Vipond; but this distance was at least three miles less than what Mr. Vipond afterwards performed alone: with what face then can the former pretend to challenge all the world, while the latter has done what the Doctor never yet has accomplished?"

In addition to all the free outdoor entertainment, many of the citizens of the two towns were also active in sports themselves. In May 1850 a number of young men obtained a piece of land with the intention of establishing a Cricket Club in Runcorn. It was estimated that at its inception there were to be 35 members. The following year two of the Gossage brothers formed a Cricket Club at Widnes and played their first game at Hill Wood. In 1868 an Athletic Club was also formed in Widnes, although it is believed that there had been an unofficial club in existence long before that date. In September 1868, when the annual Sports Day was held at Farnworth, it was reported that similar forms of entertainment had occurred in various parts of the town in previous years. On this occasion, the inclusion of two novelty races caused considerable amusement:

"The promoters of the Widnes Athletic Sports Festival need not be surprised that their proceedings passed off with great success. After a few races and trials of skill and strength, the majority of the visitors seemed to have had their appetite satisfied. There was no new feature introduced into these sports except two races which some might consider as highly interesting and highly amusing to a country bumpkin, but which would generally be regarded as belonging to that class of vulgar exercises which would prove, if not offensive, at all events uninteresting to a select company of ladies and gentlemen. However, there was nothing which elicited such rounds of applause and uproarious laughter as the sack race and the wheelbarrow race. It may be well to explain that in the latter race young men converted themselves into wheelbarrows by walking on their hands whilst their legs were held up in the air by a comrade. The hurdle race and the steeplechase were spirited competitions, and called forth some of that enthusiasm which had been allowed to flag in the consequence of the repeated delays which occurred during the entertainments."

This small medley of snippets from everyday life in the two towns has shown that the lives of ordinary people were shaped by a variety of fortunes and events. When exploring what life was like for the great majority, the discernible disparity in the fortunes of the upper classes and working people were obvious. The difference in the lifestyle of these two groups had been established since time immemorial but was further influenced by a new system of social relations which emerged after the development of industry in our areas. Changes in daily life were certainly more pronounced for working people than for the upper classes, who preserved their traditional way of life for much longer. Over time the variegated societies in both towns created social clubs and institutions to cater for the needs of their own communities. Many of these organisations were associated with the marked religious or tribal identities which were evident in those early days. These clubs and societies provided valuable benefits as they presented numerous opportunities for social interaction among like-minded individuals.

During this chapter we have seen how poverty, bad housing, disease, crime and alcohol abuse impacted upon everyday life in both towns. The loss of life through work related tragedies also had an effect on communities on both sides of the Gap and became a sad fact of life. Despite these ever present problems and dangers, it is obvious that all was not doom and gloom as many people were able to enjoy the occasional amusements which were on offer. We should also remember, when examining life in those early times that the River Mersey played an important part in the day to day lives of our communities. Apart from contributing to the development of industry, the river provided many opportunities for recreation and for impressive displays of daring. Furthermore, as we will see in the following chapter, it also provided a substantial boost to the local economy by bringing visitors into our area.

JOHN HUTCHINSON – "THE FATHER OF WIDNES"

UP THE MERSEY TO THE SHOWS

I n September 1856 a journalist from *The Liverpool Mercury* was invited to report upon the annual meeting of *The Daresbury and Frodsham Farmers` Club*. That year, for the first time, their agricultural show was being held in Runcorn. Happily, this unnamed reporter was able to furnish us with a brilliant account of an enjoyable action packed day in the town. We can see from his report how important agriculture was to the town and its surrounding area at that time. The descriptions of the show and the cruise up the Mersey are both entertaining and informative. In addition, as this event occurred around the same time as the opening of the new Market Hall, a further report in the same edition included details of the celebratory dinner which took place in the new market after the show. I include the full text of the first article because it provides a contemporary account of life in Runcorn in the mid-1850s.

The first reporter begins by giving us an engaging description of his trip on board *"The Blanche"* from Liverpool up the Mersey to Runcorn, painting a vivid picture of both the coastline and the passengers. The second article reveals the formality of the dinner and the social status of the guests, as well as the sentiments expressed in the numerous appreciative toasts. Both of these accounts provide glimpses of the attitudes and social make-up of the area in the mid nineteenth century, plus an understanding of the importance of crop-growing and farming to the area at that time.

"DARESBURY AND FRODSHAM FARMERS` CLUB;
AGRICULTURAL SHOW AT RUNCORN.

"The good people of Runcorn have been devoting this week to enjoyment. The town has put on quite a holiday garb, and the announcement of the doings there has attracted large numbers of visitors. They had first the great ship launch, then the annual meeting of the Farmers` Club, and the Agricultural Exhibition; next the Bazaar, the proceedings of which are to be devoted to the Church Infant School; and today they will have the opening of the Market Hall. A week of such gaiety has not been witnessed there for a long time, and

329

the importance of the events, as marking the social, commercial and agricultural prosperity of the port and district, require more than a passing notice. It may be that many of our readers have not visited Runcorn, and as it is within an easy sail, and worthy of a visit, it may prove interesting to such as have not been there if we describe what we encountered, what we saw, and how we enjoyed ourselves at the meeting of the Farmers' Club at Runcorn.

We left the George's Pier in the good steamer "Blanche" and on board were several strangers on their way to the show at Runcorn. After the manner of Englishmen, they were seeking for information of all sorts, anxious to get it, and lost no opportunity of obtaining what they sought. The boatmen in the employ of the Bridgewater Trust are civil, and, what is of greater importance, intelligent. They answered all the queries to the objects and places passed on the voyage to Runcorn in a worthy manner and the replies we listened to will bear out what we advance, "That is the Dingle, sir; a very nice place. Don't the houses look comfortable? This first house is Cropper's – Mr. John Cropper's. It was there Mrs. Stowe, the writer of "Tommy's Cabin", stayed when she was in Liverpool. The house to the right is Mr. Lawrence's. He is a great brewer and was once the Mayor. The next house you see is Mr. Edward Cropper's. That's Knott's Hole. There used to be fish nets at that point. There's a good many people bathing. That is Cropper's bathing house, near the shore. There are Rock Ferry and Rock Park. These warehouses higher up are the Price's candle manufactory, at Bromborough. There is the cast-iron church, and those fine houses are in Fulwood Park. Dr. McNeile lives there. Those two white looking vessels are the gunpowder hulks, and higher up you will see Eastham – a nice place to spend a few hours. Those are Garston Docks. Those vessels are getting loaded with salt or coals. Garston will be a great place in a little time. Just above there is Speke Hall. The gentleman that owns it has just got married and taken possession; he is a real Englishman and no mistake, drives his carriage and four, and knows what horses is. That is Ellesmere Port, and there is Ince. That house on the rising ground which looks right down the river is Ince Hall, and there you see Ince Lighthouse. There are the Dungeon Salt works, Hale Hall, and on the point is Hale Lighthouse. The pretty village is Hale. The Child of Hale was a wonderful fellow; he grew six feet high in one night, and is buried in the churchyard, his grave is such a long one. Those fine hills that you are looking at are called Overton Hills; they hide the village, but can just see the church. That is Frodsham, and there's a viaduct which crosses the Weaver, and carries the railway over to Chester; and now you see we are at Weston Point." It is not often that we hear discourse so interesting and instructive, and it struck us as a good feature in those boatmen, and one of which we hope all who feel disposed to have a trip to Runcorn will take advantage of.

The Mersey at Weston Point narrows and takes a sharp turn up to Runcorn. The view here is very pretty, and the expanse of water, flanked by the broad acres of Cheshire, with the Welsh mountains in the distance, has a good effect. The docks at Weston Point are modern and have a substantial appearance. There is a neat red sandstone lighthouse on one side of the pier, and a plain but good-looking church on the other. The position of the church, so close to the pier, has a curious effect. Several "flats" are leaving the harbour, and others are being pulled out, 15 or 20 men having hold of the towline. We landed a few passengers here, and took a good many on – some gaily dressed damsels and smart young men on their way to the enjoyments at Runcorn. There was a meeting of young ladies, who could not have met for some time, and who must have entertained a great affection for each other, if we were to judge from the fervency with which they kissed and shook hands. Here was a mother and her offspring – one a boy about eight years of age, who proved that the progress of the people at Weston Point was not lost sight of, for the child smoked a cigar vigorously, puffing the smoke in the face of his mother and the other passengers, and the lady appeared to enjoy the manly bearing of her promising son. As we left the pier we noticed a very primitive mode of navigation – a vessel, heavily laden, with a line from the masthead attached to a horse on the shore. We could not help contrasting this vessel with the "Royal Charter to Australia in 50 days". We now reach the entrance to the Duke's locks. Here are substantial quays covered with blocks of stone and bales of merchandise ready for shipment. A handsome looking mansion, with neat gardens and beautiful lawn in front, attracted our attention. We were told it was the mansion of the manager, "Where the head men put up when they come down." It seemed a place where the good things of life might be had. That gentleman with his coat off, reclining in the garden chair, with a lady by his side, was no doubt enjoying his cigar very much. He was perhaps one of the head men "putting up". We now discover "The Six Brothers" being towed up to Runcorn by "The Thomas Royden". "The Six Brothers" offered very little resistance to the sturdy, tugging powers of the jolly old "Thomas". Close by this we find the Pilot, with a timber raft and a host of flats in tow. We see the "Snig Pie House" and the boats bringing loads of passengers across from Runcorn Gap. Passing crafts of all shapes and sizes, boats of all sorts of rig, we run swiftly up to the pier at Runcorn. "An hour and 90 minutes, by jingo;

"The Countess" would have done it in half the time!" exclaimed a disappointed passenger.

On landing, we pass through a sort of timber wharf or yard, and come immediately upon the Royal Hotel. Here the bustle began; gigs, dog carts, whitechapels, market carts, shandries, and all sorts of vehicles lined and filled the yard and streets giving a very good indication that somebody had arrived before us. Grooms ran about, beer drinkers laughed loudly inside the hotel, and sounds of mirth and looks of happiness met us in abundance. The place was all astir. Across the streets banners floated proudly, announcing "Success to the Farmers` Club,"; "Welcome to Runcorn"; "'Tis God gives the increase"; "Town and Trade of Runcorn" and other equally expressive sentiments. The shops and shopkeepers were very gay. We walked up Bridge Street. Here is the new Market Hall; it is a plain, substantial edifice of red brick, in good keeping with its use, and will, we have no doubt, prove as serviceable to the community as it exhibits the good sense of the Commissioners. Bills and announcements of all sorts, more particularly those relative to agriculture, meet our gaze. Here we are suddenly pulled up and asked to give a large feed to our animals, at a wonderfully small cost – "one feed for a horse or cow, 1½d; a pig 1d." Then we are told, "If you want a large loaf, a sweet loaf and a white loaf, use Mather's Teetotal Barm!" We pass on. All the hotels are full; jolly farmers, with wives as broad as long, and as happy-looking as they are large, drive into town from all points, and are in a state of great consternation at the crowded state of the stabling. Now we are approaching the show yard, and meet a few Crimean medal men. They say, in reply to the "chuff" of the yokels, "Try to take the change out of us, old fellows, and we'll give you Inkermann," which causes a lusty cheer for the redcoats. We come on a blind begging man, a fancy-toy seller; a few tents, with wheels of fortune and lucky bags, and lottery boxes; lusty country lads, blooming and buxom lasses, rusticity in crowds, risking their money and, with peals of laughter, carrying off a thimble or pincushion for the low charge of eighteen pence. "Never mind," says a good tempered rustic, "If I came to spend my money and enjoy myself, I could not spend it anywhere much faster." That fellow is a philosopher: let men who consider themselves worldly wise think of him.

We now reach the entrance to the show. It was held in a field in Irwell Lane, on the banks of the river, kindly lent for the occasion by Mrs. Cawley, and the Committee have great cause to be grateful, for a more pleasant site could not have been selected. We have a regular crush to reach the entrance gate. Young agriculturalists will bring a lady on *each arm, and they will carry large umbrellas; these will become entangled in the dresses of other couples; bustle is caused thereby, and torn dresses and ruffled tempers are not infrequently the result. The peals of laughter here drowned any manifestations of temper that might have been shown, and as one of a group said when he got inside "We've got in somehow or other." The arrangements made for the accommodation and enjoyment of visitors inside were excellent. Close by the entrance a band of musical performers, in very showy costume, enlivened the proceedings from time to time by the performance of military or popular airs. Here also was erected a spacious marquee, which attracted general attention; here refreshments were to be had; here the trials and sufferings of the farmer` life were talked over. Poor fellows! Here farmers who had not met since last year would have a glass together on strength of meeting, and others who meet daily and weekly would have a glass for the sake of old times, and because they liked it. The place was throng, the sun was hot, and no doubt a good glass of pure Cheshire ale would make the hearts of young and old glad for the time. This is the effect it appeared to have; for merrier men, merrier peals of laughter, or better jokes amongst farmers, we never met with. The rosy-faced old fellow, telling the story of losing a new hat at the first fair he visited, 44 years ago – we will never forget him. His merry tinkling laugh, the tears of joy running down the furrows of his face, and the roars of the youngsters around him – these were worth going to Runcorn to see and hear.*

We now made our way to the spacious marquee under which the poultry was exhibited. The show was good for the place. It was particularly rich in ducks and those truly English birds, geese. The Cochin China fowls were here as ugly in form, as hoarse and ludicrous in voice, as ever. The Polanders, with their top knots giving them such a venerable appearance that you feel disposed to remove your hat in their presence, were here, but not of very excellent character; and there were few game birds. We remarked this to an old farmer. He said "The game birds are not in pens, but there is plenty on `em about the field. Look at those chaps yonder"- pointing to a group of farmers– "there's game birds for you." They certainly were fine-looking men; we never saw finer, and we had no disposition to call their courage or gameness into question, for as the old fellow said "16 stone would not live five minutes `fore `em". In one of the pens the silver prize cups were exhibited. This pen was much admired, anxiously looked on, and judiciously guarded by an old wary-looking agriculturist. We passed from this to another marquee containing what Cheshire is famous for – the cheese.

The cheese in size and appearance excelled all we ever saw. The Cheshire cheeses are generally made very large and when they leave the presses they are not sufficiently solid to keep their shape. Hence it is necessary to wrap linen bands round them. This prevents their bulging out at the sides and cracking, which, if it took place, would injure them in quality and appearance. They require great care, constant turning and examining – once a day, at least – until the bandages are removed. They are then scraped and with a dull-edged knife to rid them of any roughness, and are well rubbed occasionally with a coarse cloth to give them a polish; so we were told by a farmer's wife, who prided herself on her manufacture, and who produced specimens of it that we longed to taste. The prize cheeses were not polished, but in the rough, and many others were still bandaged, to keep them from bursting. A notice on the cheeses irritated us, and seemed to cast a reflection on the visitors – "Persons are requested not to iron the cheese without permission of the owners". Who would have the heartlessness to iron the cheese? Who would dare to touch, leaving the ironing out of the question, either of those three monster prize cheeses, and the proprietor, a man of two and twenty score, looking him in the face. How we longed to live next door to this cheese manufacturer; one would get fat and feel happy in the atmosphere of such a man. The discussions carried on here amongst the fair sex were animated and, would we have understood them, instructive. Butter making, cheese manufacture, bandaging, polishing, colouring, churns and churning, barrel churns, and modern inventions were complimented or condemned with equal vigour; the judge's verdicts, called into question or coincided with; women lusty, loud, vehement, and hearty in praise of their own way and support of cherished opinions. It was a stirring sight: no country but England could produce such women; no county but Cheshire could produce such cheese. This everybody said, so it must be true.

We now go on to the vegetables. Here were wheat, turnips, mangel etc., which had been raised by the aid of superphosphate of lime; and there were testimonials from practical men as to the effect of the substances on their crops. It might be all very well for the land, and, no doubt, was good for the crops, but ground bones and these sort of substances were not pleasant to the olfactory nerves, so we passed on to the agricultural implements. Of these there was a large exhibition. The names of Chivas of Chester, Harris of Lostock, Houghton of Norton, Leathwood of Halton, Watkin of Halton and Gibson of Runcorn, stood most prominently. Every imaginable invention to economise time and labour was to be seen, in most cases in operation. Ploughs, harrows, corn crushers, turnip slicers, cultivators, horse hoes, winnowing machines, cheese making apparatus, poultry troughs, fancy flower pots, and India rubber overshoes. Why the latter should be called agricultural implements we don't know. All these commanded a great share of attention, and some sensible observations were here listened to from the lips of Cheshire farmers. One sturdy fellow, looking at a grubber, observed, "There is not many of these here today." The reply was, "That's just as you think; as for these sort of grubbers, I can do with them, but those lantern-jawed, leather-headed, iron-souled money-grubbers is what I don't like". There's a fellow there, we'll say he's worth £40,000; he won't lay a farthing out on his land, expects the farmer to do it all, and as soon as an improvement is made, up goes the rent; that's what I call a grubber. It would be a good job if there was none of these about". The farmers laughed loudly at the growl, and said he had eaten too much of his own cheese, and it had not agreed with him.

We now strolled out into the field, the crowd had now become great, and the scene was exciting and exhilarating. Young and old, gentle and simple, rich and poor, were here; the glow of rude health upon the cheek, and the total absence of care or anxiety from the features, were remarkable. Young farmers were busy amongst the horses and several were busy bruising each other's hats. Old farmers were chatting with familiar friends, or with their landlords; a few aristocratic-looking people moved about, and a couple of parsons looked extremely pleasant at everybody and everything; cattle were lowing, poultry were crowing, horses were prancing, damsels were dancing, whips were cracking, and lips were smacking over the draughts of good ale. On the river were pleasure boats, containing pleasure parties; on the shore all was mirth and jollity; and this was the Runcorn agricultural show. The bellman now went round and announced a sale, which took place on the ground immediately. The auctioneer began by stating that he was prepared to sell anything, would begin by selling the cart he stood on, and would sell California if he had the chance; as he had not the chance of doing this, he sold a horse; and we left a large audience listening to him and laughing at his good-humoured address.

At two o'clock the public were admitted, and such a gathering, such merry meetings, such shaking hands with lads and lasses, we never saw. The show, on the whole, was most successful. It was the first time the meeting had been held in Runcorn, but we would fain expect it will not be the last. Then, being dinner time, the band struck up "Hail, Smiling Morn!" and with the melody sounding in our ear we left the exhibition field, well pleased, nay, delighted, with all we heard and

335

saw. As we passed towards the new Market Hall we noticed a procession of waiters carrying large dishes from "The Royal", and crowds of hungry children regaling themselves on the smell of the savoury meats such as farmers love. The dinner took place soon after three o'clock, the chair being taken by G. Greenall, Esq. When we say that it was supplied and got up under the direction of Mr. Huxley of the Royal Hotel, I am sure that will be a sufficient guarantee for the quality. Everyone present – and there were about 350 – seemed to enjoy the good things set before him, and the dinner passed off with the same good humour and success which attended the previous proceedings of the day. There was the usual amount of after-dinner speeches, complimentary toasts, responses etc., there was the distribution of prizes, and the usual anxiety was expressed for the welfare of the unsuccessful competitors, all of which is pleasant enough to hear, and can do nobody any harm to listen to. But we would rather leave this in other hands to describe. In conclusion, we were pleased with the trip to Runcorn. We liked the town – liked the people – will venerate the farmers; and most earnestly do hope that whenever they meet again on such an occasion may we be there to see. Until such time we wish success to the Daresbury and Frodsham Farmers` Club."

The second report contained an equally lengthy account of the celebratory dinner which took place in the new Market Hall. We are told that:

"The dinner was held in the New Market which had been decorated and hung with mottoes appropriate to the occasion. The chair was occupied by G. Gilbert Greenall, Esq., M.P; on his right sat Sir Richard Brooke, Bart., and on his left the Rev. J. Barclay, Vicar of Runcorn. There were also at the principal table the Rev. W.F. Attenborough, John and Thomas Johnson, Esqs., Philip Whiteway Esq., Robert Whiteway, Jun. Esq., William and John Brundrit, Esqs., Colonel Brooke, Joseph Stubbs, Esq., J.H. Hayes, Esq., J.A. Patten Esq., Captain Henry Lyon etc.

We were informed that the band of *The 4th Royal Lancashire Militia* was in attendance to provide musical accompaniment to the proceedings. It was said that the band played rousing renditions of the National Anthem before and after the dinner. The rather protracted report gave verbatim descriptions of the numerous toasts which were proposed throughout the evening. These included separate toasts to the Queen; Prince Albert and the rest of the Royal Family; The Emperor and Empress of the French; The Army; The Navy; The Bishop and Clergy of the Diocese; Sir Richard Brooke; The Magistrates of the

County; The Daresbury and Frodsham Farmers' Club; The President of the Farmers' Club; The Runcorn Committees and the Cheshire Dairymaids. Among those proposing toasts were Sir Richard Brooke and Mr. John Johnson:

"Sir Richard Brooke, Bart., next proposed the health of the unsuccessful candidates and was received with cheers. The health of the judges and vice presidents followed, which was responded to by J. Johnson, Esq., who said his words must necessarily be few at that hour of the evening. "Where there were no bees there was no honey" was a good motto. He believed that the people of Runcorn had long been highly industrial; it was looked on by the people of Runcorn as a matter of great pleasure that the market should be opened by the very best men in the county. The greatness of a country was not determined by the breadth of its territory, but by the industry, intelligence, and enterprise of its people. Actuated by such motives, the people must necessarily grow in prosperity, greatness and happiness.

This report provided an interesting example of Victorian values and the pleasantly courteous manner of society at that time. It also offered an interesting picture of the social elite of the town. This is an image of the wealthiest and best educated men of the district supposedly forging a common bond with ordinary people. Some of the individuals mentioned in the above report were men who had the lion's share of wealth and power in the district. I wonder who among their number was the *money-grubber"* referred to by the disgruntled Cheshire farmer?

Across the river, in neighbouring Widnes, the agricultural communities in the northern regions of the town must have watched the success of the Runcorn Show and decided to stage one of their own. Of course by now Widnes was industrialised and had become notorious as a place where nothing could grow because of pollution. Nevertheless, away from the destructive atmosphere in the south of the town, in places like Farnworth, Cronton, Ditton and Appleton, agriculture and rural occupations were still evident. In 1865 the Farnworth Agricultural Society came into existence and subsequently an annual agricultural show was held in a field at Farnworth. Despite the lateness of its establishment as an institute for promoting agriculture in the area, it was no less successful than the Runcorn Show and drew entrants from far and wide. In 1867 the show attracted more than 3000 visitors and offered prizes amounting to £400. Apart from local competitors there were entrants from outlying districts and from distant parts of the counties of Lancashire and Cheshire. As with all gatherings of this nature, it afforded an opportunity for the residents of the neighbourhood to make a jolly day of it. A report of the event tells us that:

".. outside the showground the area was profusely decorated with floral arches which added to the gaiety of the occasion. Within the showground was stationed the band of the 48th Lancashire Volunteers who played in good style a selection of popular music".

The show itself consisted of competitive displays of horned cattle, pigs, sheep, poultry, horses and dogs. The horses included animals used for draught and agricultural purposes as well as hunters and carriage horses. The canine section included pointers, setters, spaniels, greyhounds, newfoundlands, mastiffs and, of course, sheep-dogs. In addition to the awards for animals and livestock, numerous prizes were distributed for a variety of vegetables as well as samples of wheat, oats, clover, and meadow hay. Among those who took home prizes from the various categories on display were Mr. J. Booth of Ditton; Mr. R. Houghton of Cronton; Henry Deacon of Appleton House and Peter Longton of Cronton Hall.

Apart from the obvious thrill of competition, these shows provided an opportunity for local agricultural communities to come together and socialise. Although there was a keen spirit of competitiveness surrounding the event, nevertheless, it was an occasion whereby the remnants of an indigenous lifestyle could be continued and cherished. I am not sure to what extent these events attracted people from the populations at the south end of the town. As, despite their rural origins, I am sure that most of the newcomers would have found little else to draw them to the upper regions of the town at this time.

Farnworth was one of the earliest established communities in the town. It was known as a place where the native populations of pre-industrial times had often gathered for social affairs. One of the oldest events had been connected to Farnworth Wakes, an annual occurrence which was held around the middle of October. It was a three-day event which usually commenced on a Sunday or a Monday and involved a great deal of merrymaking and drinking. "Wakes" were a traditional custom in many Lancashire towns and villages and were originally connected to a religious festival. In fact the whole tradition of Wakes, like many other ancient and modern religious conventions and feast days, had their origin in pre-Christian rituals. However it would seem that, in the latter years of their existence, religion took a minor role in the proceedings. The Wakes came to be viewed mainly as an important episode in the social and commercial life of an area.

In addition to the drinking and carousing which took place at Farnworth Wakes, a programme of entertainment included the barbaric sports of bear-baiting, bull-baiting and cock fighting. As well as these ugly forms of amusement, there was also the pageant connected to the Mock Corporation of Farnworth. This involved a group of residents dressed in bizarre costumes, reminiscent of Morris Dancers, who undertook the duties of a fake Mayor and Corporation. The unfortunate bear was required to play a significant part in this wacky spectacle. Two men were positioned on top of the church tower as lookouts. Their purpose was to warn the crowd below of the impending approach of the bear and its keeper. When the bear was sighted a signal was sent to the bell-ringers and a loud peal of bells warned the waiting crowd of the imminent arrival of the animal. At this point the Mayor and Mock Corporation would form a procession to greet the bear and its keeper. Then, with pseudo ceremony, the Mayor would bestow the honours of the Corporation upon the animal.

After the ceremonial proceedings were over the inhabitants of the village, and large numbers of visitors from outlying districts, were free to enjoy the numerous distractions on offer including stalls, musicians, hawkers, card-sharps as well as the ubiquitous broadsheet and ballad-mongers. The unfortunate bear, which had played its part in the opening ceremony, was subsequently led to a field north of the church (which now forms part of Farnworth graveyard) and tethered to a wooden stake where he was "baited" by a horde of savage dogs. The bear was fastened in such a way as to allow it a degree of movement which enabled it to retaliate. This meant that, apart from the horrific injuries inflicted on the bear, many of the dogs were either killed or maimed in the process. Bulls were baited in a similar manner, tied to a post and then attacked by a pack of bull-dogs. Cock-fighting also took place nearby, and there was the customary betting on the outcome of all these events.

Along with the various entertainments on offer, the event was also an occasion for buying and selling cattle and horses which were usually tethered, for appraisal by potential buyers, on either side of Church Street[121]. There were also numerous opportunities to purchase alcohol which generally resulted in a great deal of drunkenness, fighting and

[121] Now known as Farnworth Street

riotous behaviour. Unfortunately, as this sort of conduct was prevalent, it became one of the more commonly associated aspects of the event. It is worth saying that although industrial Widnes gained a reputation for violent behaviour, we should be aware that social problems of this nature were not new, nor were they limited to the population which arrived with the onset of industry. The old communities of traditional social structure were generally no better behaved. Although the vast majority probably enjoyed the celebration of Farnworth Wakes without problem, the event was more often than not accompanied by some form of public disorder and violence. In reality, it was usually a bawdy and brutal event involving blood, beer and betting. Nevertheless, despite its unpleasant reputation, Farnworth Wakes was an important event in the life of the village. In addition, it had a magnetic appeal for people from outlying districts and the wider countryside around.

We should remember that Runcorn also had a "Wakes Celebration" which, like those in other towns and villages, had its origin in religious ritual. In much the same way as Farnworth Wakes had become notorious for drunken and boorish behaviour, Runcorn "Wakes" also appears to have descended into an occasion more concerned with dissipation than religion. One Runcorn resident clearly lamented the change of tone. In this indignant offering of November 1841 he says:

"When we consider that our country wakes or feasts had their origin in the piety of antiquity, and were designed as religious observances, to preserve in memory the dedication of the parish church, it is indeed grievous to witness the present prevailing perversion of a laudable and interesting institution to sensuality and vicious indulgences. This week the annual holiday of the Wakes has occurred in Runcorn; but instead of the season being celebrated according to its primitive intention, we are concerned to say that it commenced by the most scandalous profanations of the Sabbath, and has continued, day after day, in scenes of such brutalizing intemperance, rioting, brawling, outrages, dissoluteness, and the demoralisation of youths of both sexes, as to make the heart of every good man mourn, and loudly call upon the magistrates, gentry, and clergy, to adopt strong measures for the suppression of such abominations, immoralities and crimes"

RELIGIOUS MATTERS

Throughout this book I make numerous references to the Industrial Revolution and its potent effects on society. I particularly highlight the part its aftermath played in the development of our two towns. It was a period synonymous with the rise of a middle class who grew both wealthy and powerful through an expanding capitalist trade market. This rise had a huge effect on all areas of life including the long established religion of the nation. In earlier times, the Church of England had mainly adopted an aristocratic set of ethics but these values were abandoned by some of the new bourgeoisie in favour of the new tenets of Protestant belief, designated Nonconformist or Dissenting. The new industrialist class, the nouveau riche, wanted a system of morals and conduct that would incorporate both Christian virtue and business values. This desire to harmonise Christian values with a middle class work ethic led to the formation of a variety of new sects of Protestant faith in England. The principal non-conformist denominations of nineteenth century England were Methodist, Baptist, Congregationalist, Unitarian, Quaker and Roman Catholic.

A bout of church building occurred in most industrial towns during the nineteenth century. New churches were being constructed in order to meet the demands of the various denominations within the rapidly growing urban populations. Both Widnes and Runcorn offered a variety of churches of different non-conformist affiliations, as well as churches belonging to the Established Church and the Church of Rome. Both towns also housed several churches and chapels which were built specifically for their sizeable Welsh communities. Obviously religious establishments, of all denominations, played an important role in both towns. These institutions were able to navigate the shock of urban society and, indeed, transcend the class and social barriers that existed among the new populations. For example, church or chapel could play an important part in the assimilation of new arrivals in the towns. This was particularly effective and cohesive among the Roman Catholic Irish, Lithuanian and Polish immigrants and, of course, the Welsh churches and chapels united the Welsh arrivals in much the same way.

Although we would like to believe that there was a fair amount of religious tolerance between the faiths, unfortunately, this was not always the case. There was extreme mistrust and fear of those who promoted unorthodox doctrines. In July 1842 a strange preacher appeared on the streets of Runcorn. His arrival in the town caused considerable consternation and was remarkable enough to be reported in several newspapers. One report appeared under the headline *"Fanatics and Mormonites"*.

"As we were passing up the streets of our little town of Runcorn on Saturday evening, we observed a number of idlers and children collected near the Town Hall, surrounding a strange looking creature, apparently from the wilds of America or the banks of the Mississippi, with lanky hair and shaggy beard; and this deformed piece of humanity was affecting to preach or prophecy to the curiosity gazers around him. We believe these fanatic impostors are intruding themselves into our country villages and hamlets, and they may be useful in terrifying naughty children – or if the farmers would take and plant them in their corn fields to frighten the crows away, some good purpose might be answered by them; but we cannot believe that any sensible men and women will patiently listen to the hideous bawling and false prophecies of such poor crazy, ignorant, or else wicked and designing men."

It is clear that the presence of Mormons in the district caused concern among some sections of the community. On 25th August 1853 the incomparable Mr. Samuel Shaw Brown delivered the second in a series of lectures in The Foresters` Hall in Runcorn. The theme of the lectures centred round the *"social, moral and religious dangers of Mormonism"*. On this occasion the meeting was chaired by The Rev. William Roberts and the room was crowded to excess with an extremely enthusiastic audience. Proceedings were interrupted from time to time by two Mormon gentlemen who heckled Mr. Brown and the Rev. Mr. Roberts. There were also a number of counter-hecklers who shouted down the Mormons. At the end of what appears to have been a rather lively lecture, the Mormon gentlemen were invited onto the platform to make an official reply to Mr. Shaw Brown's criticisms of their religion, but they declined to do so.

Despite vocal opposition from some Runcorn residents it seems that the followers of Mormonism were not driven away from the area completely. In July 1854 a number of Mormons held a meeting on Runcorn Hill. As might be expected, this meeting created some disquiet among the local community and a group of residents arrived on the scene to protest and heckle the speakers. The Mormons were ridiculed and taunted and their founder was described as an adulterous impostor. A lot of name calling and threats were issued from both groups but, fortunately, the event fizzled out without any violent incidents occurring.

On a more tranquil note, in January 1849 *The Manchester Courier* provided their readers with some information on the origins of the Christian church in Runcorn. The article was written on the occasion of the consecration of the new Runcorn Parish Church. The article makes some speculations as to the date of the first church in the area.

"The person responsible for the first erection of a church on the site on which stands the new church for the parish of Runcorn, was most probably Ethelfleda, the noble daughter of the patriot king, Alfred, to whom the government of the earldom of Mercia was entrusted by her brother, Edward the Elder. This lady founded the town of Runcorn, and one so pious would not leave it without a church. There are no authentic documents to bear out this theory, but it is quite maintainable, at all events, the church was in existence prior to The Conquest. It was annexed to the Abbey of Canons Regular, or Augustines, founded by William, the son of Nigel, the first Baron of Halton. Since the days of Ethelfleda it must have been twice re-constructed, as the most ancient part of the late edifice was of the early English style of the latest period of the 12th century; and in taking down the tower the hiatus was supplied, for in the rubbish were found Norman capitals of the eleventh century, clearly indicating the intermediate structure. The church has at intervals been supported, and in one instance enlarged, under a faculty granted by the Bishop of the diocese, but on being taken down the strength of the structure was found to be in an inverse ratio to the periods of alteration, the enlargement under the faculty referred to, not of fifty years standing being the most faulty. The original structure would have stood for centuries to come."

As we can see from the above account, a church had stood on this site for several hundred years and over time there had been considerable re-building or extending of previous structures. In 1802, because of a growing congregation, the church was considerably extended by enlarging the south aisle. However, because the original structure was in such a poor condition this extension did nothing to enhance or improve the space as the congregation continued to grow. Unfortunately, the poor quality of the alterations, repairs, and building work which had occurred over the previous centuries meant that the

343

strength of the building had been compromised. In December 1843 a committee had been appointed to review the state of the building. Some financial assistance was offered by Lord Francis Egerton and Sir Richard Brooke. They both gave £300 to the Church repair fund under the precondition that the money was given on the understanding that it should be repaired efficiently and not undergo mere patch-up repairs. Mr. Loch, the MP, was also involved in the discussion as how best to preserve and renovate the church for the future. Sometime later it was decided that the most prudent course of action would be to demolish the building and replace it with a new church on the same site. The last service in the old church was held in September 1846 and the new church was opened in January 1849. The new church could accommodate in excess of 1000 and was built at a cost of £8052.

At the time of the opening of the new All Saints Parish Church, in 1849, Canon John Barclay was the Vicar of Runcorn. He had come to the town in 1845 and remained until his retirement over forty years later. Some years earlier the congregation had expressed disapproval and a lack of confidence in their vicar, the Rev. Mr. Masters, but with the subsequent arrival of Canon Barclay the parishioners were once again united and confident in the virtue of their vicar. Canon Barclay was an exceptional man who was liked and respected by all the townspeople, rich and poor alike. He was also known for his diligence in advancing Christian values. During his tenure he was responsible for overseeing the establishment of St. Peter's Mission in Dukesfield and the building of St. Michael's Church in Greenway Road as well as the school in Shaw Street.

The industrialists who developed our towns also played a significant part in promoting religion of varying persuasions by financing churches and chapels in the area. The Runcorn soap-makers, the Hazlehursts, who were Methodists, were particularly benevolent. By 1858 Thomas Hazlehurst had already made generous financial contributions towards the building of Methodist chapels at Helsby, Farnworth, Widnes Dock, Runcorn and Weston. When the old All Saints Church was demolished in 1846 the pulpit was bought by Thomas Hazlehurst who presented it to the Methodist Chapel in Beaconsfield Road across the river in Widnes. When the new Farnworth Methodist Chapel was built in Derby Road the pulpit was moved into the new building.

ST. PAUL'S METHODIST CHURCH, RUNCORN

One cannot help but be impressed by the progress that Methodism made in the area in such a relatively short space of time. However, this advancement was not without the occasional man-made hindrance or misunderstanding. A slight storm in a teacup occurred in the early days of Runcorn Methodism when, in February 1834, a controversy arose regarding a musical instrument. An article appeared in *The Liverpool Mercury* which claimed that a workman had been unfairly dismissed from his employment because he had refused to contribute towards an instrument for a Methodist Band. The article caused a great deal of

345

indignation and resulted in an angry letter to the newspaper from another correspondent, thought to be Methodist Minister from Runcorn.

Music and Methodism:

Under this heading we inserted, some weeks ago, a communication from a correspondent to the effect that at a certain town "on the banks of the Mersey", no place being mentioned, a man had been dismissed from his employment in consequence of his refusal to contribute a shilling towards the purchase of a musical instrument. This statement, it appears, has given great offence at Runcorn, which happens to be one of the many places situated "on the banks of the Mersey"; and in "The Albion" of Monday last we find a letter on the subject, under the signature of "Veritas". The writer is exceedingly indignant at the statement inserted in The Liverpool Mercury, which he describes as "a palpable and most gross falsehood, written with the malicious intention of injuring our (that is, the Methodists) character". Now, we can assure "Veritas" that neither we nor our correspondent had any such intention, the object of the paragraph being simply to point out what appeared to be a gross instance of oppression; and we have further to inform Veritas that, in consequence of that exposure, the man who was dismissed has been restored to his employment. It appears that the cap did not fit anyone at Runcorn. It is, therefore, somewhat strange that "Veritas" and others should be so anxious to try it on; stranger still that there should have been a subscription at Runcorn for the very same purpose as that mentioned by our informant; and, strangest of all, that "Veritas" should have got into such a towering passion about it. We advise him to keep his temper more under control in future – especially, if he be a clergyman; and in order to show him that we should have been impartial enough to insert his exculpation, so far as the inhabitants of Runcorn are concerned, had he thought proper to direct it to us, we shall allow him to tell his own story as to what occurred at that place "on the banks of the Mersey". He says: "In justice to the public, and for our own character, allow me to state the facts. At a Methodist chapel, "on the banks of the Mersey"; it has lately been thought necessary to add to the instrumental music of the orchestra, and for this purpose a voluntary subscription amongst their own sect was proposed, to purchase a double-bass and violin; I need scarcely add, but to vindicate the truth, that the money was readily raised by voluntary means, and that neither force nor intimidation was used, either by direct or indirect means, and the trumped up story of the man being dismissed without the least foundation in truth, and has emanated from the writer's pen through spleen or malice."

In August 1858 the foundation stone was laid for another chapel at Five Crosses near Frodsham.   Once again the financial benevolence of Thomas Hazlehurst was responsible for making this possible. In fact, apart from the land, he financed the entire building project.   On that occasion his wife was given the honour of laying the stone and, following the official ceremony, Mrs. Hazlehurst was presented with a miniature silver trowel to commemorate the event.   As a historical exercise, during the stone laying ceremony a small glass time capsule containing a parchment was placed beneath the foundation stone.   The parchment contained the following information:

Presented to
Mrs Thomas Hazlehurst,
by friends at Five Crosses and vicinity,
on laying the foundation stone
of the
Wesleyan Methodist Chapel,
at that place,
the erection being at the sole cost
of
Thomas Hazlehurst, Esquire.
30th August, 1858.
A bottle, containing a parchment document, as follows, was placed beneath the stone.
Wesleyan Chapel, Five Crosses.
Presented to the Wesleyan Methodist Connexion by Thomas Hazlehurst, Esquire, of Runcorn.
The Foundation Stone of this Chapel was laid on Monday, August 30th, 1858, in the 21st year of the reign of Her Majesty Queen Victoria, by Mrs Thomas Hazlehurst.
President of the Conference—The Rev John Bowers.
Secretary of the Conference—The Rev John Hannah, D D.
Ministers of the Runcorn Circuit—Rev Joseph Hollis, Rev Joseph B. West.
Trustees of the Chapel—Messrs Thomas Hazlehurst, Charles Hazlehurst, and John Simpson, Runcorn; William Church, John Guest Williams, John Rimmer, George Sharrock, Samuel Walker, William Maddock, and Samuel Smith, Frodsham; William Hulse, Samuel Bassnett, and George Carter, Five Crosses; Joseph Challoner, Kingsley; Henry Lowe, Sutton.
Architect—Mr Winn. Builder—Mr Davies.

WIDNES METHODIST CHAPEL, VICTORIA ROAD

In July 1864 the Rev. Marmaduke C. Osborn opened an impressive Methodist Chapel in Victoria Road, Widnes. The construction of this imposing building had, once again, been made viable by the benefactions of Thomas Hazlehurst. Although Hazlehurst's business interests were largely in Runcorn, where he also resided, we can see that his generosity in support of Methodism was certainly not confined to that town. Hazlehurst had offered to fund the cost of building the Widnes church if the Methodist Society would pay for the land. As a result, the Victoria Road site was bought for £500 and a splendid building was erected at a cost of £3,354. The building costs were wholly financed by Thomas Hazlehurst.

The other Runcorn soap-makers, the Johnson brothers, who were Anglicans, were also extremely benevolent in their religious patronage. They were among the main contributors when donations were sought for the building of Holy Trinity Church in Runcorn. Finances for the building of this church, which was completed and consecrated in 1838, were raised by subscription and with the assistance of a grant from the Church Building Society. John and Thomas Johnson contributed largely to the building costs and supplied the endowment and the Curate's living of £200 per year. Afterwards an Infant School was constructed at the sole expense of The Countess of Ellesmere. Mr. John Wilson was subsequently engaged as the schoolmaster.

Following the success of the Infant School, the incumbent, the Rev. James Cox, sought to have a larger school built which would accommodate 150 boys and 150 girls. The building costs of £1,400 were raised with the aid of grants from The Council of Education and The National Society, as well as a large financial contribution from the patrons of the church, John and Thomas Johnson. Donations for the school were also received from Sir Richard Brooke and the Marquis of Cholmondeley. Some years later, as the congregation expanded, the Johnson's provided financial support for the enlargement and improvement of Holy Trinity Church. They also donated the decorative Minton tiles which were used to cover the three steps in the newly extended eastern apse.

Of course, when writing of the various religious groups, I should not neglect to mention the Salvation Army who had a significant presence in both towns later on. In fact, the founder of the movement, General Booth, came to Runcorn in July 1886 to open their new barracks, which was to be known as *"The Citadel"*. The building, erected on the site of the *"Old Hall"* in High Street, was expected to accommodate about 1200 people. It was constructed at a cost of £1500 and on its completion there was only £250 debt remaining. A local chemist, George Marshall, who was the Treasurer, contributed £50 and a Mrs. and Mrs. Richardson made a joint contribution of £20 to reduce this debt. The Salvation Army had a substantial following in Widnes also and their Widnes barracks were located in Hibbert Street, near Simms Cross. Army members were a familiar sight in both towns as they staged their impromptu hymn-singing gatherings in local streets and open spaces. These open-air services, with lively music accompanied by lots of tambourine shaking, usually attracted a sizeable assembly. Victoria Square in Widnes was a regular venue for this type of service and they also held well-attended dinnertime services in some of the local factories. Most people felt no religious enmity towards the members of the Salvation Army as they were known to practice their Christianity in a practical as well as spiritual manner, and their support was always to the fore in times of local distress.

Across the river in Widnes religious edifices were no less impressive. It is believed that there had been at church at Farnworth from at least the 12th century. There was certainly a church in existence prior to 1431 as, at that date, there is evidence to suggest that the church was already quite old and in need of repair.[122] The chapelry at Farnworth was originally a subordinate part of the parish of Prescot. It was a *"chapel of ease"* to Prescot and was built to serve the early settlement which existed at Farnworth. Although the religious district was secondary to the main parish of Prescot, in fact, in early times Farnworth was a place of considerable importance. It was once a Borough and from the 14th century it was the seat of a Manorial Court.

The historic parish of Prescot was split into two sections each consisting of a number of townships. One section was the Prescot side and the other the Farnworth side. The Farnworth side included the townships of Bold, Cronton, Cuerdley, Ditton, Sankey, Penketh and Widnes. The beautiful and ancient church at Farnworth, which served the communities of these townships, was originally dedicated to the Anglo-Saxon St. Wilfrid and it contains two chapels. The Bold Chapel was founded in the 15th century and the Cuerdley Chapel was founded by William Smyth, the Bishop of Lincoln, in the early 16th century. Unfortunately, on Christmas Eve 1854 the roof of the chantry and north aisle were badly damaged during a violent storm. The following year Henry Bold Hoghton, of Bold Hall, provided a substantial financial

---

[122] Charles Poole: *"Old Widnes and Its Neighbourhood"*

donation to enable extensive repairs to the roof and rebuilding work to be carried out on the church.

In 1859 the Farnworth *"chapel of ease"* was created a separate parish from Prescot and the church was re-dedicated to St. Luke. At that time the title and status of *"minister in charge"* was upgraded to that of Vicar. Up until that time St. Luke's was the only church of the Established Faith in the area but, as the town expanded, so too did the congregation. It became obvious that another place of worship was needed at the south end of the town to serve the growing population in that district. Towards the end of 1858 a new church was built to provide for the growing Anglican community in the area around Widnes Dock. Although the new church and churchyard was not officially consecrated until Thursday 23rd December, St. Mary's Church, Widnes Dock, had opened for Divine Service some months before. The building had been placed under licence from the Bishop until a formal consecration could take place.

The new St. Mary's Church contained seating for 424 persons of which 144 would be free. It was constructed with a view to enlargement if a further increase in population warranted it. The church was erected with the aid of voluntary subscriptions and it was planned to build a parsonage on a plot of land adjoining the churchyard, by the same means. In addition to this, a generous endowment of £40 per annum was provided by William Wright of West Bank. As well as this endowment, and to supplement any income from other sources, the Incumbent was also entitled to the rents of those pews which were not set aside as free.

Although the Mother Parish was Farnworth, the Widnes Dock district was assigned to the new St. Mary's Church. This meant that it became a separate parish for ecclesiastical purposes and the Incumbent was given authority to solemnize marriages and perform all other Divine offices. Moreover, the fees received for these services would go to the Incumbent for his own use. In spite of the initial excitement of having a lovely new church at Widnes Dock, this structure had been built upon a base of chemical waste which caused the foundations to shrink and crumble. The use of chemical waste for this purpose had become common in the district and several other buildings experienced problems with their foundations. In the case of St. Mary's Church the problem was severe, causing the structure to become unstable. This resulted in the building eventually having to be knocked down. A new site, near to West Bank Promenade and Victoria Gardens, was chosen for a replacement church and around 40 houses were demolished to make way for the new structure. The official dedication service of this new St. Mary's Church took place in 1910.

Another Anglican Church, St. Michael's at Hough Green, was opened in 1870. The church was opened under licence from the Bishop in February that year although it would not be officially consecrated until some considerable time later. The building was designed to accommodate about 350 initially, but was constructed in a way which would allow enlargement to take place at a future date to make room for upwards of 500. The structure was of a neo-Gothic design which was the work of a Liverpool architect called Mr. E. Grayson. The building work was carried out by a St. Helens contractor named Mr. W. Middlehurst. One rather interesting and heartening feature of the building work was that the whole of the building materials had been *"carted gratuitously by the farmers of the neighbourhood."*[123] The land was donated by Thomas Shaw, Esq., and was considered at that time to be worth at least £300; it also included sufficient room to build a vicarage and school.

The opening service of St. Michael's, Hough Green, was conducted by the Rev. Canon Warr of St. Saviour's Church in Liverpool. He told the congregation that the official consecration would not take place until an endowment fund of £1000 had been raised, towards which about £300 had already been promised. Although there was still a considerable amount of money to be found, there was no shortage of practical gifts offered for the new church. Mr. Shaw, who had donated the land, also presented the communion plate. The altar cloth was the gift of Mrs. Newton of Mossbrook Park; the chancel chairs were presented by G. Newton Esq., of Liverpool; a set of collecting boxes by Mrs. Longton of Ditchfield Hall; the altar desks were given by Mr. T. Smith of Cronton; and the ladies of the district presented the harmonium. At the close of the service a collection was made and the contributions amounted to nearly £50 – a considerable sum for a collection plate at that time.

By 1879 it was estimated that there were around 9000 members of the Church of England resident in the town. Although St. Michael's Church at Hough Green had been opened under licence early in 1870, the two existing "Widnes" churches at that time, St. Luke's in Farnworth and the original St. Mary's Church, in West Bank, could

---

[123]*The Liverpool Mercury* – February 1870

only accommodate around 1900 worshipers. Therefore, a committee was formed in the hope that funding could be raised to build another two churches, one in Halton View and another at Simms Cross. The Committee's resolve was boosted by the fact that two local residents were prepared to donate land on which to build these churches. Mr. Bibby was willing to give an acre of land for one church and Mrs. Lee offered an acre of land for the other. Although the offers were genuine, there was a worry that if these offers were not taken up quickly the land might otherwise be sold for building purposes and other suitable sites might not be available in the future. Therefore the Committee immediately set about obtaining subscriptions in the hope of raising £10,000 to build the two churches. Unfortunately they were only able to raise £7,000 so they had to adapt their plans accordingly. It was decided to use £3000 to build a church at Halton View, which was to be dedicated to St. Ambrose, and the remaining sum would be spent on building a church at Simms Cross, which was the most populous area. This latter church was to become known as St. Paul's.

The foundation stone for St. Ambrose Church was laid by the Home Secretary, Mr. R. A. Cross[124], in October 1879. The second church, St. Paul's in Victoria Square, was dedicated in 1884. At the time of building, St. Paul's did not have the tower which we see today; this was added later and completed in 1907. Interestingly, despite the church being dedicated in 1884, the first marriage to be solemnised in St. Paul's did not occur until the beginning of October 1895 when Caroline, the daughter of Henry Deacon, married the Rev. W. Hodgson. At the end of this ceremony Gossage's Prize Band played Mendelssohn's *"Wedding March"*. Afterwards the happy couple were presented with a bible by the churchwarden, Mr. Lowe, in recognition of the fact that they were the first people to be married in the church.

As we have seen, Thomas Hazlehurst, the Runcorn soap-maker, was instrumental in funding the building of several Wesleyan Methodist churches in Runcorn and Widnes. Despite the fairly rapid growth of this religious group it is worth mentioning that the Wesleyan religion in Widnes had developed from fairly small beginnings. In 1835 Mr. Palin, who was the dock-master at Widnes Dock, opened up his house for the religious instruction of boatmen and dock labourers. However, as the congregation increased, it became necessary for the services to be moved to a large room over a sail-makers establishment at Widnes

---

[124] Mr. Cross was appointed Home Secretary by the Prime Minister, Benjamin Disraeli, in 1874.

Dock. This room was used for many years until, by the determined efforts of William Hartland[125], a dedicated chapel was built in Sutton's Lane in 1850. By 1885 there were no less than eight Wesleyan chapels and schools in Widnes, all virtually free from debt. The Mother Church was the handsome edifice in Victoria Road which was built with the generous help of Thomas Hazlehurst. This impressive church was constructed almost fifty years after the first small Methodist group was established by Mr. Palin at Widnes Dock.

As the Irish made up a great portion of the population there was naturally a large Catholic presence in the town. The Catholic Mission in Widnes was established sometime around 1750. Although there was no dedicated chapel at that time, a room in Lower House was used to celebrate Mass. The Rev. Marmaduke Wilson was the priest in charge at that time and afterwards served the mission of Appleton. A church, dedicated to St. Bede, was built in 1847[126] and at the time of its construction was thought perhaps too large for the congregation. Father Wilson died in 1882, by which time he was an octogenarian. His successors were the Rev. T. Pinnington, the Rev. J. Rigby and Rev. H. Gillow. Like most churches of that time the Appleton Mission relied on the generosity of individuals to fund their living and help with the financial cost of building churches and schools. The Dennett family were the great benefactors to the mission at Appleton in its early days. The land on which the first chapel and presbytery was built was given by Mr. W. Dennett and his daughter, Miss Dennett, contributed liberally to the support of the Mission. In 1823 a schoolhouse, which was later demolished, was erected on the site of what was later the Girls` School. Mr. John Glover was the first schoolmaster; afterwards he became a priest at Whitby where he died.

On the death of the Rev. Father Gillow, the Rev. Father George Fisher was appointed to St. Bede's. During Father Fisher's pastorate he erected the handsome Girls` School which was opened in 1852. Father Fisher also laboured zealously in establishing the Mission of St. Mary of the Assumption (later known as St. Marie's) in Newtown, and a church was built there in 1865. After 27years service in Widnes Father Fisher was created a Dean and transferred by the Bishop to the historic mission of Hornby, near Lancaster. The Rev. Father Finnegan succeeded Father Fisher in 1875 and he received the title of Dean in 1886. In 1884 the Rev. Father Fennelly was the pastor, and it was

---

[125] William Hartland, known as *"The Father of Widnes Wesleyanism"*

[126] The church was formally opened in September 1847. The Rev. Dr. Brown officiated at the opening service with the Rev. James Shepherd of Liverpool preaching the dedication sermon.

during his tenure that the Boys' School was opened in October that year. Obviously, as the district expanded the religious needs of the growing Catholic communities needed to be addressed. The two existing churches were adequate for specific districts, namely Appleton, Simms Cross, Newtown and Lugsdale; however the growing Catholic communities at Widnes Dock and Ditton were left wanting. These needs were furnished at later dates by the building of St. Patrick's in an area near Widnes Dock and St. Michael's at Ditton. All of these churches were built with the aid of subscription or the benefactions of generous individuals. Interestingly, St. Patrick's Church was partly paid for by liberal donations from Roman Catholics in Ireland.

We have previously seen wonderful examples of the generous patronage of the Hazlehurst family of Runcorn, who were instrumental in funding the construction of several Methodist chapels in Runcorn and Widnes. Widnes Catholics too also gained greatly from the benefactions of several exceptional individuals who gave land and funds to provide places of worship for their co-religionists. The Dennett family have already been referred to in relation to St. Bede's parish, but another person who deserves special mention is The Hon. Mrs. Stapleton Bretherton of Rainhill, also known as the Marchioness Stapleton Bretherton, or Lady Stapleton Bretherton. Her title, *Marchesa Romana*, was a papal honour which had been conferred upon her by Pope Pius IX in recognition of her services to the Roman Catholic Church.

Lady Stapleton Bretherton was the daughter of Bartholomew Bretherton, a well-known Liverpool mail coach proprietor who managed to amass a huge fortune before the railways became the more preferred form of transport. With his fortune he bought several estates in Lancashire and had numerous land and mining interests in the county. However, being a devout Roman Catholic, he also made more altruistic use of some of his money by building and endowing St. Bartholomew's Church at Rainhill. After his death his daughter inherited his entire estate and spent much of her fortune on religious and charitable works. She married firstly, William Gerard the brother of Sir John Gerard of Garswood, St. Helens, but was widowed quite young. Some years later she married the Hon. Gilbert Stapleton who was the brother of Lord Beaumont.

Her charitable work for the Roman Catholic Church in Widnes commenced in the early 1870s when she donated her Ditton Estate, Ditton Hall, to a group of German Jesuits. This religious order had

355

been expelled from their homeland in 1871 as a result of the May Laws which had been brought in by the German Chancellor. After their expulsion from Germany a large number came to England. On hearing of their plight, Lady Stapleton Bretherton donated Ditton Hall to a group of Jesuit refugees in order that they might carry on their educational and missionary work. It was said at the time that the mansion and extensive grounds were worth almost £60,000 – a generous gift indeed! At Ditton, the exiled German priests continued the work of the college they had been forced to leave, and devoted themselves almost exclusively to the study of theology. In May 1879 a new church dedicated to St. Michael was opened in the grounds of Ditton Hall, most of the building costs being borne by Lady Stapleton Bretherton. The Right Rev. Dr. O'Reilly, the Bishop of Liverpool, officiated at the opening Mass. Just before the sermon Father Clare, of St. Francis Xavier's in Liverpool, who was assisting in the service, read a telegram which had just been received from Rome. In the telegram Pope Leo XIII sent his blessing to Lady Stapleton Bretherton and all who were present at the opening of the church. Two years later sixteen students of the Jesuit College, Ditton Hall, were ordained in St. Michael's Church.

Catholic Academy.
APPLETON IN WIDNES, near WARRINGTON.

Another Roman Catholic establishment, Appleton Academy, in Highfield Road, was set up in 1830 by Mr. James Eccles. Mr. Eccles' tenure was fairly short with the school being taken over in 1834 by Mr. Richard Bradshaw, who was originally from Chorley in Lancashire. As an additional point of interest, in June 1848 Mr. Bradshaw married the daughter of the previous owner, Margaret Eccles, at St. Marie's-on-the-Sands, Southport. Although it has been widely believed that Appleton Academy provided education specifically for young men who were studying to be priests, in fact, the Academy offered a broad sphere of education for all young boys. The average age of pupils was between 11 and 13 years of age but it also received students as young as 8 years, hardly an age to train for the priesthood. Despite the long held supposition that this was a seminary, it would seem that the Academy was simply a private school with a strong Roman Catholic ethos. However this fact does not dismiss the possibility that some of its pupils may have eventually gone into the priesthood.

In 1865 the Roman Catholic Academy at Appleton was providing a wide variety of lessons including Drawing; Dancing; French; Latin etc. for a fee of £35 per term. Along with Mr. Bradshaw and his wife, other members of the Academy staff included his brother-in-law Robert Eccles who was an assistant teacher; and his sister Elizabeth Bradshaw who was responsible for domestic care. Apart from his primary work at Appleton Academy, Richard Bradshaw was actively involved in other aspects of education in the district. He was the manager of St. Bede's School and a member of the Widnes School Board.

Although the Academy was owned by Richard Bradshaw up until the time of his death in 1890, in the years prior to this there had been several unsuccessful attempts to sell the school. An advert placed in *The Liverpool Mercury* in 1883, reproduced overleaf, suggests that the building was still in use as a functioning educational establishment at that time. However, one might assume that by this time Mr. Bradshaw was well into retirement age and no doubt ready to leave his business interests behind. It would seem that, in disposing of the property, he had no great ambition to see the building maintained as a school. It is even suggested in the advert that the property would lend itself to being converted into residential dwellings; which is precisely what happened some time later.

THE LIVERPOOL MERCURY – SEPTEMBER 1883

Regardless of the fact that Widnes industrials were not nearly so generous in subsidising churches and chapels as the Runcorn manufacturers, John Hutchinson did donate the land in Lugsdale Road on which St. Marie's Roman Catholic Church was built. However, at the time the building was constructed this land was only being leased to the Church. It would seem that sometime later John Hutchinson was persuaded by his great friend, Father Fisher the curate from St. Bede's, to donate the land to the parish. In view of the fact that Hutchinson was not a Roman Catholic, nor was he a regular attendant at any church of any denomination, this benevolence was somewhat unexpected. Despite his non-attendance at religious services, Hutchinson was born and raised as a member of the Anglican Church and in his *"Last Will and Testament"* he expressed a desire that his sons would follow in that faith. Regardless of this, there was a huge Roman Catholic influence both in his life and in his household. Mrs. Hutchinson was a Roman Catholic and, although his sons were Anglican, his daughters were baptised into the Catholic faith. His close friend, Father Fisher, also had a significant impact on the lives of the whole Hutchinson family. As well as being father confessor to Mrs. Hutchinson, Father Fisher acted as a spiritual tutor to the Hutchinson children at Appleton Lodge. However as the eldest son, John (Jack), got older, a special tutor was brought in to prepare him for his planned education at Harrow Public School.[127] Concerning this, one would assume that Hutchinson had chosen Harrow for his son's education as it was one of the few public schools of that time which included science and chemistry in their syllabus.

Even though industrialists played a major role in the public affairs of Widnes and Runcorn, ministers of religion also formed an influential group in both towns and were viewed as important members of society. Although there were enormous disparities in income and status between some clergymen, nevertheless, all were viewed as being pious, conscientious and virtuous. Unfortunately, in reality, some were less moral and dutiful than others. The behaviour of a few clergymen fell well below the standards expected from men of the cloth. Indeed, in the case of one cleric, his behaviour would have been considered equally shocking and immoral had he been simply a layperson. The outcome of his scandalous actions resulted in a prison sentence with hard labour. It should be said that in view of further revelations, and historical hindsight, I believe he got away lightly.

It goes without saying that most of the clergy of Runcorn and Widnes were men of impeccable character who were devout and hardworking. In most cases there had never ever been the slightest whiff of scandal attached to their names. On the other hand, there were a few isolated cases where one or two clergymen behaved in a manner which

---

[127] Jack Hutchinson went to Harrow shortly after his Father's death but his time there was short-lived due to his unacceptable and erratic behaviour. He built up huge debts when he was barely out of his teens, mainly due to excessive drinking and gambling. His wayward conduct created huge problems for the Trustees of the Hutchinson Estate.

was unbecoming to their station in life. Their inappropriate and, in some cases, criminal activities brought enormous disgrace upon their religious office. In January 1837 a young girl, who was a servant in the home of the Vicar of Runcorn, the Rev. Mr. Masters, gave birth to an illegitimate child. Shortly after its birth the baby was found dead in a bedroom at the Vicar's home. As there were marks around the baby's throat, indicating that it had died by strangulation, the young girl was arrested and removed to Chester Castle to await trial. She was subsequently charged and found guilty of infanticide and served a prison term. Throughout the court proceedings the girl refused to name the father of the child but it was widely believed in the town that the Vicar was the father.

Mr. Masters had been appointed Vicar of Runcorn in 1816 and was at that time a married man. His wife died in 1824 and afterwards he remained a widower, although there were rumours of him having had several relationships. One rumour, which the gossip mongers relished, involved his supposed liaison with his young servant. The rumours surrounding the Vicar were so persistant that his congregation had dwindled down to a very small number. It was reported that on one Sunday there were only eleven faithful followers at his service. This seemed to be all the more concerning when it was remarked upon that the "Dissenting Chapels" were crowded to capacity. As the gossip escalated, the general feeling in the town was that if such a claim had been brought against a "Dissenting Clergyman" he would have been removed from office immediately, until a formal ecclesiastical inquiry had been carried out. It was regretted that the Established Church was not behaving in the same way and that the Vicar was being allowed to continue his duties. The feelings of indignation amongst his parishioners was so strong that, in order to secure his ecclesiastical punishment, they decided to file a suit against the Vicar with the Bishop. At this point, no doubt alarmed by the turn of events, the Vicar wrote a personal letter to the Bishop in which he emphatically asserted his innocence. Nevertheless, the complaint from his parishioners resulted in the Vicar being tried by a Judge of the Consistory Court of the Diocese

The verdict of the Ecclesiastical Court was that Mr. Masters was *"not guilty"*. This judgement was unsurprising as there was no tangible evidence to substantiate the charges against him. It was simply a case of him saying he was innocent and, as there was no evidence to demonstrate otherwise, the charge against him was unproven and he was found not guilty. Encouraged by the *"not guilty"* ruling of the Consistory Court, the Vicar decided to sue several newspapers for libel.

His main target was *The Chester Courier* from whom he sought substantial damages. Unfortunately for him, the official Civil Court which heard his lawsuit was less trusting of his innocence than the Diocese Court. This resulted in a long drawn-out legal case in which the Vicar's personal life was laid bare for the avid consumption of the scandal hungry public.

The young girl at the centre of the case was asked to make a sworn statement and was told that she could be charged with perjury if any details of her statement were untrue. She was told that a frank and truthful declaration was essential. The frightened young girl gave a brief description of the circumstances surrounding her employment in the home of the Vicar. A report of the case informs us that the young girl had been a servant in the Masters' home since she was thirteen years of age when she was first engaged to help Mrs. Masters. After the death of the Vicar's wife, the girl continued her work in the house and acted as a maid to the Vicar's sister, Miss Masters. No concerns had been raised or complaints made about the girl during the years she was employed by Mr. Masters. Although she had refused to name the father of her child during her own trial, she later confided in Miss Masters to whom she had grown close. During later legal proceedings it came to light that, following the girl's disclosure, Miss Masters had confronted her brother with this accusation and he had not denied it. The girl's sworn statement included the following information:

"The affidavit went on to state that after the death of his wife Mr. Masters continued a widower: that he was in the habit of taking toast and water into his bedroom, where she frequently washed his feet; that about four years ago, or early in 1834, Mr. Masters first began to kiss and take liberties with her, and on one occasion threw her on the bed and endeavoured to have intimate relations with her, and that on several occasions he solicited her for that purpose, but that she resisted all his endeavours in importunities, until one evening in the autumn of 1834, having as usual taken warm water into his bedroom, he attacked her and threw her on the bed and succeeded in accomplishing his object, and that he frequently acted in a similar manner afterwards, but always showed the greatest affection for her. The affidavit then stated Miss Masters had asked whose child it was, and when she said it was her master's, Miss Masters said "May God forgive you both".

Unfortunately for Mr. Masters, his attempt to claim damages from *The Chester Courier* backfired when the newspaper hired a highly competent lawyer to fight their corner. The court case received a great

361

deal of publicity and *The Chester Courier* took full advantage of their media position to take the moral high ground. There was wide coverage of the case in both national and local newspapers. Therefore, instead of allowing the previous rumours to die down, the publicity only served to resurrect the earlier gossip, causing irreparable damage to Mr. Masters' already tarnished reputation.

It was not only the Church of England who were disgraced by the scandalous behaviour of a clergyman. At the beginning of January 1877 the Roman Catholic residents of Runcorn were horrified to learn that their priest, the Rev. Joseph Daly[128], would appear at the Cheshire Quarter Sessions charged with theft. His distraught and disbelieving parishioners were even more stunned when they read reports of the proceedings in the national and local press. For, not only had the popular Priest been accused of stealing a sum of money, amounting to £12, from a local grocer, it was also alleged that he had been conducting an illicit affair with the grocer's eighteen year old daughter. One newspaper headline included the sub-heading *"Shocking Revelations of Immorality"*. Most parishioners refused to believe the scandalous accusations levelled against their priest and continued to support him. However the outcome of the trial, and the subsequent exposure of previous shameful charges relating to an earlier scandal, left even his staunchest supporters shocked and disappointed by his mendacity and outrageous behaviour.

Although the 37year old priest was fairly new to the district he had become extremely popular with his parishioners. Father Daly had come to Runcorn from Stockport near Manchester a little over six months earlier. In view of his popularity, it would seem that he had settled into his role as pastor to the Roman Catholic community quite well and quite quickly. Some months earlier, on his arrival in Runcorn, not yet having the luxury of a presbytery, he had been offered temporary accommodation with the grocer and his family. The grocer, Mr. H[129] lived behind his shop in High Street and also owned another shop in Church Street. He was a very successful businessman who was well known and respected in the community. As an act of generosity he had invited the priest into his home as a guest and not as a paying lodger. This made the ensuing events all the more contemptible and treacherous. The Priest enjoyed the hospitality of the grocer and his family for a little over six weeks after which time he was able to move into his own accommodation.

---

[128] The surname is spelt *Daley* in other reports.

[129] For various reasons I have withheld surnames relating to this case..

Whilst he was living at Mr. H's house, and enjoying his hospitality, Father Daly's struck up a friendship with the grocer's daughter which afterwards, allegedly, led to an intimate and improper relationship. Some weeks after the priest had moved into his own house, the grocer's son, William, who was the Manager of a chemical works in Widnes, heard rumours to this effect and told his father. The father subsequently confronted the priest and warned him not to visit the house again unless either he or his son was at home. It seems that Father Daly had assured Mr. H. that the rumours were completely untrue but he agreed that, in order to prevent further tongue wagging, it would be unwise to visit the house if Miss H was alone. However, despite this promise, the priest did not keep his word. At the trial it was revealed that the priest had slipped into the house on several occasions and spent the night with the grocer's daughter. Furthermore, his presence was witnessed by two servants who were employed in the house.

At his trial the priest denied all the charges against him. He was outraged and insisted that he was totally innocent of any crime or, indeed, of any improper behaviour with the young woman. At this point it should be noted that during Father Daly's trial all the main prosecuting evidence presented to the Court was given by the grocer's daughter. Even though there was no doubt that a theft had occurred, and the daughter had confessed to her role in the robbery, there was no firm evidence to incriminate the priest. His implication in the crime was simply based on the testimony of the grocer's daughter. She was the chief witness for the prosecution. Furthermore, the truth of her evidence was unsupported. Today one would say that the evidence against him was open to doubt as it was simply his word against hers. Incidentally, there were no witnesses called for the defence, as the indignant Father Daly believed that his word should be good enough.

Below is an edited transcript of a report which appeared in *The Liverpool Mercury* in mid-January 1877. This gives a summary of the case, the trial, and the subsequent verdict:

"Mr. H's family, which consists of a son and daughter approaching maturity, and two other sons of tender age, are Roman Catholics, and the prisoner had been brought into close contact with them in the capacity of Father Confessor. Mr. H said that owing to suspicions of his (Rev. Daly's) misconduct with his daughter, he was required some weeks ago to ask him to give an undertaking that he would not again come to the house unless he (the father) or her brother was in, and he

appeared to have kept the promise he then made, except on two occasions, one of which was Thursday the 5th December. On that day he dined and supped with Miss H, the father being away on a journey and the brother at Widnes, at his daily occupation. The shop, which is approached from the house through a door in the passage was, as usual, closed and locked at night and the following morning the drawers were found to have been forced and money taken.

The chief testimony against the prisoner (Rev. Daly) was that of Miss H, a handsome and accomplished young person of about eighteen years of age, and this was of the most extraordinary kind. She stated that the prisoner used to visit her father's house and that she confessed to him once. He lodged at her father's house after he came to Runcorn for six weeks. Two days after he left, he succeeded in seducing her and on several occasions since he had slept with her at the house. He would remain playing cards with her Papa and would then ask to be permitted to sleep in his old room and then come into hers. On 5th December he came to the house a little after noon and dined with her, having been with her on the previous night. With the exception of two children, who occasionally came in and out, and the servants, they were alone. The prisoner left the house at three o'clock and returned at a quarter to nine, and supped alone with her in the dining room. Before or during supper the prisoner asked her if she thought the man had left the money in the shop, and she said she would go and see. After supper she told Father Daly that the servants had asked to go to the Public Hall to a ball, and he said "let them go". When they had gone and the children had been put to bed, she procured the key of the drawing room door, which fitted the shop door, and went down into the lobby with the prisoner (Rev. Daly) and got inside the shop. He asked her where the money drawer was and she showed it to him. He endeavoured to open the drawer with a bread-knife which was on the counter, but it was not strong enough, and she went to another drawer and produced a nail and gave it to the prisoner. He forced the drawer while she pulled it for him, and it came open. There were two paper parcels in the drawer. Father Daly opened them, and she saw they contained gold and silver. He abstracted the money and told her to put the papers on the fire, which she did. There was a key in this drawer to the one containing coppers, and he requested her to open it to see how much money was in it. When she did so, he told her to carry the drawer into the sitting room. Father Daly brought a paper bag out of the shop, which she held open, and he poured the coppers into it. All the afternoon before that the prisoner had asked her if she could not get some money for him, and she said she did not know. On Saturday evening, December 2nd, the prisoner had been in her Papa's bedroom *looking at the safe, which he said was very strong. After returning the copper drawer to its place, Father Daly went into the sitting room with her and had some brandy and water. He remained with her until the servants came home and she let him out. Before he left he told her to leave the back door open, as someone would be suspected of coming in by that entrance. She was unable to do so in consequence of her brother coming home so late, but she threw the scullery window open. She confessed the whole affair to her brother, as she heard he would get into trouble over it. Several witnesses were called, who in part, corroborated this statement. Mr. McIntyre, (representing the defendant, Fr. Daly) rested his defence mainly upon the circumstance that "Miss H's evidence was entirely uncorroborated" pointing out several discrepancies in her evidence now and that given before the Magistrates. The Chairman summed up at length and the jury returned a verdict of guilty, after a few minutes deliberation. The Chairman said the Bench entirely concurred in the verdict. A worst case could not be conceived and the sentence, which would be a severe one, would be eighteen months imprisonment with hard labour."*

At the beginning of the trial, Mr. Swetenham, the Prosecuting Counsellor, had made his opening statement to the jury. Mr. Swetenham was careful to emphasis the possibility of religious bias. He advised the jury to put aside any prejudice they may have towards Roman Catholicism. He urged them to act in an honourable and impartial manner when reaching their verdict. Below is a further edited transcript from a report of the trial:

Mr. Swetenham, in opening the case for the prosecution, said it was his duty to lay before the Court the details of an exceedingly distressing case – distressing, because it could not be otherwise than distressing to any person of right mind to see a person who had occupied the position of a minister of religion standing at the bar of an English court of justice, to take his trial for larceny such as that laid out in the indictment; and it was distressing also because he would have of necessity to call a young lady who, he believed, had been virtuously and tenderly brought up, and she would be obliged to give in evidence circumstances tending not only to her own shame, but also to proclaim substantially her own dishonesty, and, in point of fact, to show that she was only not quite so dishonest as the Prosecution said the prisoner at the bar was. Unquestionably, the interest of the prisoner in the matter was paramount, for, although he might possibly be of a different persuasion, so far as religion was concerned, to some of them, he (the learned counsel) felt perfectly certain he had only to bespeak on that

365

latter account a more than usual consideration – and tenderness he might say – as to the prisoner at the bar. He had only to say that on the part of the Prosecution they expected a degree of perfect dispassionateness and candour, and at the same time such a feeling of duty in their minds as, when they had fully heard out the case and had given their verdict, they, one and all, would be able to say to themselves when they went home that they were certain it was the verdict of an honest British jury".

The main crux of the case was based on the evidence of Miss Winifred H, the grocer's daughter. It has to be said that representation for the Defendant was very weak. Father Daly's solicitor appeared to think it inconceivable that a jury would take the word of a young woman rather than believe a 37year old clergyman. He seemed confident to rely on that assumption and called not a single witness for the defence. On the other hand, the Prosecution took full advantage of their star witness and emphasised her youth and naivety. There was a clear inference that she had been an innocent and honourable young girl until she came into contact with Father Daly. She had been educated in a convent in Manchester before being sent to another convent in Boulogne to finish her education. She had returned from her *"Finishing School"* in France only three years before. It was stressed that she had been *"tenderly and virtuously brought up"*. Naturally the case caused a sensation throughout the country. Each morning, as the trial progressed, newspapers gave their readers a description of the previous day's proceedings. Most newspapers described the moment when Miss H. first took the stand, saying: *"Miss Winifred H was then called; she was well dressed and presented the appearance of a highly respectable and well educated young lady"*. Miss H. began her testimony by giving a brief description of her personal circumstances. She said:

"I am the daughter of William H, who lives at Runcorn. I have a brother named William. He is older than me. My age is 18. I have three sisters away from home, and two little brothers at home. I was educated at a convent in Salford first, and afterwards I was sent to Boulogne and finished my education there, returning home about three years ago. Since then I have acted as my father's housekeeper and he allowed me a sum of money, but not for dresses.

I remember Father Daly coming to be a priest at Runcorn. He came the first Sunday in July, and stayed at our house as a guest for five weeks. My father is a member of the Roman Catholic congregation in Runcorn. All the family have been brought up in the same religion and the prisoner acted as Father Confessor to us all. I have only confessed to him once. When he lived with us during those five weeks no improper familiarity took place between us. It was after he left that the first improper intimacy begun. I think it was in the month of August. I recollect a letter being given to me by one of the servants. It was on the Thursday before the 5th December, after the return of myself and my father from Buxton. In consequence of the receipt of that letter, I went upstairs to my bedroom and went into the adjoining room and found Father Daly. I did not stay more than a minute with him and I left him there. Later in the evening, about half past eight, I went to my own bedroom and saw that Father Daly was there. He told me to lock the door and go downstairs. I did so, and remained down until a little after nine. My father was in the sitting-room and I went to the drawing-room. Shortly after nine o'clock I went upstairs again, unlocked the door, and joined Father Daly. I slept that night in the same bed with him (Sensation in the Court). I rose the next morning shortly after eight o'clock. Before I left the room Father Daly went back to the adjoining room in which I found him in the first instance on the previous evening. That is a room we do not use except when my sisters are at home. He remained in the house until my father had gone to his business".

Miss H went on to tell the Court that Father Daly had spent the night with her on six or seven occasions after that. On one occasion when they were alone in the house he had gone into her father's bedroom to inspect the safe. He mentioned to her that it appeared to be remarkably secure. From her evidence it would certainly seem that he had pre-planned the robbery and had, at that time, been pondering on how to open the safe. In the days prior to the robbery Father Daly had repeatedly asked her if she could get him some money as he had some urgent bills to pay. As she could not, he put another plan into action which involved staging a robbery. When reading accounts of the girl's testimony it is obvious that this impressionable young woman was swept along under the priest's manipulative influence. The robbery was the culmination of his power over her. The following day, when the robbery was discovered by the shop manager, the police were called in. They saw no signs of a forced entry and therefore quite rightly assumed it was an *"inside job"*. Later she became worried when she realised that her brother would be wrongly suspected of leaving the door to the house, or the scullery window, unlocked. She feared that her father would be angry with him. She was clearly distraught and riddled with guilt and subsequently decided to confide in her cousin, Miss I. Miss I. urged her to tell the police what had actually happened and persuaded her to confess her own part in the affair. At that point she confessed the whole thing to her brother and as a result Father Daly was immediately arrested.

Once she had made her official statement to the police, and her role in the robbery was disclosed, her father immediately threw her out of the house and disowned her. His anger and disgust was so strong that even when her uncle offered to take her in the father tried to dissuade him from doing so. He was completely opposed to anyone in the family giving her shelter, instead, he thought she should be ostracised. He believed that because of her disloyalty and immoral behaviour she had disgraced the whole family. He suggested they should sever all ties with her. He forbade her siblings from making contact with her and said she should be shunned and banished forever from the family circle. However, as she was close to her cousin, Miss I, the uncle took pity on her and took her in. During the trial Miss H was asked why she was now residing at the home of her uncle. She told the court:

"My father said he was very angry with me, and would not have me at home until I told all about it. When I told him he compelled me to leave his house after ten o'clock on Wednesday night. Since this has happened, bills have come in to me for dresses and drapery that my father did not know about. The bills have been sent to my father's house. There are five or six of them. I don't know the amount of them. I don't think they would amount to more than £20. I have not seen my father since this was found out. He has been to my cousin's house but I have not seen him as he has refused to speak to me".

No doubt this sensational trial caused great stirs of excitement and disgust in equal measures. The case involved many of the salacious elements which generally titillated the Victorian public; religious scandal, crime and immorality. The court was packed to capacity every day, mainly with Runcorn ladies hoping to be both shocked and outraged as further lurid details were revealed. A hint of the atmosphere surrounding the case can be gained from this short report:

"Intense interest was manifested in the case and the Court and its approaches were crowded by people desirous of listening to the details. It had been rumoured that additional evidence to that given before the Magistrates at Runcorn would be forthcoming, and that Miss H had confessed that the prisoner had seduced her. On the Magistrates bench, and in other parts of the Court, were a number of ladies, and they appeared much interested in the extraordinary evidence given by the young lady. The prisoner, who was dressed in the ordinary garb of a Roman Catholic priest, when placed in the dock seemed to be somewhat nervous and to feel his position acutely. He handed a written

statement to his counsel, and then asked the warder to be allowed to sit down at a table for the purpose of writing. He was doing this when the case was about to be opened by the Prosecuting Counsel and the Chairman said that he must stand at the bar. He immediately rose from his seat and did so, but a short time afterwards Mr. McIntyre (the Defence Solicitor) applied that he might be obliged with a seat. The Chairman said he was informed that the prisoner had not been in good health and therefore gave him permission to be seated; otherwise no difference would have been made between him and any other prisoner. After this he remained seated and listened attentively to the evidence given by Miss H in particular. As the trial progressed, the agitation he had first exhibited became less, and he appeared to treat the matter with a considerable degree of calmness.

Miss H is a young lady possessing considerable attractions, and gave her evidence with remarkable firmness and apparent candour. After she had completed her evidence, Mr. Swetenham intimated that, as Miss I, her cousin, had been mentioned during the progress of the case, he would put her into the witness box, not for the purpose of questioning her himself, but in order that Mr. McIntyre, if he desired to do so, might put any question to her. Mr. Swetenham then called upon her to go into the witness box. Miss I was occupying a seat on the Magistrates` bench, and on rising she fainted away and would have fallen on the floor had not a lady who was close to her caught her in her arms. She was taken out of court into an adjoining room but in a few minutes returned into the Court and said she had recovered. She was not, however, called as a witness. The father of Miss H. was not present in the Court, but her uncle, in whose charge she is at present, occupied a seat near the witness box".

In his final summing up, Mr. Swetenham said;

"....Miss H was the principal witness, and he was bound to tell them that he could look upon her evidence as nothing else but the evidence of an accomplice and, of course, in dealing with the case it would be the bounden duty of the jury to consider carefully the evidence which she had given, and particularly the manner in which she gave it, for the reason that the evidence of an accomplice was always, and most properly, to be looked upon with the gravest suspicion. It was perfectly competent for the jury to act, if they thought proper, upon the uncorroborated evidence of an accomplice, but the judges and those who presided in courts of justice always warned juries that they should look carefully for some corroboration, and that it generally was a

dangerous thing to act upon uncorroborated evidence. The manner and demeanour of Miss H in the witness box would be a great guide to them as to whether she was the witness of truth. Father Daly was the Father Confessor to the family and she had said that on one occasion she confessed to him. She had also told them that Father Daly had seduced her. It might be said that this young lady had stolen the money herself and was now trying to lay it upon her Father Confessor, but he (Mr. Swetenham) thought that would not bear argument. In conclusion, he had to say that he was sure the jury would give the case their most careful consideration and, in the result, he was sure that their verdict would be such a one as would be satisfactory not only to their country but to their own conscience".

In the end, the jury accepted the version given my Miss H. Father Daly was given an eighteen month jail sentence, with hard labour. No charges were brought against Miss H for her part in the robbery. I do not know whether or not she was ever reconciled with her father, although one would hope that she was. I believe that she was just a young and impressionable girl who was ill-used by a dishonourable and devious older man. It would be sad to think that her whole life may have been blighted by the folly of her youthful behaviour.

Naturally the case against Father Daly had caused a great deal of shock, alarm and unrest in Runcorn, particularly among the Roman Catholic population. A large section of his congregation simply refused to believe the accusations levelled against him, even after such compelling evidence was presented in court. To them it seemed beyond belief that he could have behaved in such a dreadful manner. In those times, it was almost inconceivable that a man of God could conduct himself in anything less than a moral and law-abiding way. Most were of the opinion that the charges against him were total fabrications. They believed that Miss H had stolen the money herself and put the blame upon their priest to deflect suspicion from her to him. They were outraged and angry that the reputation of their popular clergyman had been tarnished by her accusations.

When the eagerly awaited result of the trial was announced, and news of Father Daly's guilt reached the population, there was a seething atmosphere of anger in the town. The feeling was so strong that the Runcorn police were put on over-time. There was a real fear that an attempt would be made to rescue the Priest as he was being escorted to prison. Because of this threat, the prisoner was transported to Knutsford Gaol in a closed carriage just before six o clock on a Sunday morning. The normal method for transferring a prisoner was by rail at mid-day. When this subterfuge was subsequently revealed, a large and vociferous crowd surrounded Runcorn Police Station and expressed their displeasure at their priest's clandestine removal. At the same time, in another part of the town, an angry crowd congregated near the shop and house of Mr. H., the grocer. Mr. H and his premises had to be guarded by the police as there were serious fears that he would be attacked or his shop vandalised. Even his servant was heckled by a group of irate people as she made her way to church. The servant was so frightened she had to be escorted to and from the chapel by a policeman. During that weekend several fights broke out between overwrought partisans of Father Daly. This resulted in a number of people being brought before the Magistrates on the following Monday morning. However, all this commotion was to no avail as Father Daly was beginning his well-deserved prison term. There is no record of what became of him after his release — let us hope he was a reformed character!

Of course it is quite understandable that the supporters of Father Daly were convinced of his innocence. It seemed unthinkable that, as a priest, he could behave in anything but an honest and virtuous manner. To those who knew him he had obviously come across as a likeable and pious man. They firmly believed that the evidence against him was unproven, especially as his conviction was based entirely upon the unsubstantiated evidence of Miss H. Some thought that, because of his religious persuasion, he had not received a fair and unbiased trial. I suppose, in the circumstances, one could reasonably give him the benefit of the doubt as the whole case against him was unsupported. It was basically a case of his word against that of Miss H and it could be claimed that the girl was simply a fantasist. However I am sure that readers of this book will be reluctant to give him the benefit of doubt after I reveal some additional facts.

As Father Daly was 37years of age when he was arrested and tried for his criminal behaviour in Runcorn, I began to question his personal and previous history. If he was indeed guilty, was his behaviour at Runcorn completely out of character or were there any previous indiscretions which might have sounded alarm bells? Surely someone wouldn't suddenly embark upon an immoral or criminal career at that age, without some previous hint of a character flaw. I knew that Father Daly had come to Runcorn from Stockport so that seemed the most likely place to begin. However, as I began to look into his time in Manchester I was totally unprepared for what my search would eventually throw up.   I was to discover something far more shocking and sinister than his immoral and illegal activities in Runcorn.

During the course of my research I learned that, only a few months before coming to Runcorn, Father Daly had been involved in a rather sordid murder case in Stockport.   In this instance a young woman, thought to be a prostitute, had been poisoned by a person, or persons, unknown.   Father Daly was the chief suspect and was only cleared when three Runcorn men came forward to give him an alibi for the day of the murder.   However, despite the evidence of these men, I think a huge question mark still hangs over this case.   I include below several reports from the Stockport case and I leave you to draw your own conclusions.   In view of his Runcorn congregation's apparent trust and devotion, I wondered if the men who provided the alibi may possibly have done so because of a misguided sense of loyalty to the priest.   This first report, dated October 1876, which is rather sympathetic towards Father Daly, attempts to explain why the priest often visited the murdered woman.

"In this Manchester case a "gay woman" was found, suffocated by chloroform under suspicious circumstances and all the evidence points to murder, since the bottle containing the poison was removed, thus clearly establishing the fact that it could not be a case of suicide. At the inquest suspicion was set up against a Roman Catholic clergyman, who had been seen occasionally in the girl's company. However, it will be a terrible thing for doctors and clergymen if their acts of mercy are construed into acts of depravity. A doctor has to save bodies from death, and a clergyman has to save souls from perdition, and it is clear that both must enter curious places. Unless prostitutes are to go out of the world uncured and unshriven it is clear that their medical and spiritual advisers must occasionally be in their company. No doubt the Catholic clergyman was often in the girl's presence; no doubt he was constantly with her if he, in the exercise of his duty and the wideness of his faith, desired to lead the unfortunate woman away from a horribly depraved and abominable life."

During the Inquest several female witnesses were called to give evidence; two of these lived in the same building as the deceased woman and another lived in the house opposite. All were friends of the dead woman and it was intimated in some reports that one of them, who shared accommodation with the deceased, was also a prostitute.   An account of the Inquest, which appeared in *The Liverpool Mercury*, referred to the evidence of one of the female witnesses. The witness had stated, when talking of the deceased, that:

"They were simply friends in the same position in life as each other. There had been no gentlemen callers in the house on the Saturday, Sunday or Monday. When she (the witness) was informed by the deceased that a gentleman was coming to stay with her, she asked if she was not afraid of getting into trouble, and the deceased replied that she was not, she would take care of that. The deceased had been away from the house from the Wednesday prior to her death until the Monday afternoon. She said she was going to Runcorn, and on her return she said she had been there. She also said that the gentleman she expected to come and see her lived at Runcorn. The deceased had a child about two years ago, but witness understood that it was not born alive – the deceased told her she had seen the gentleman at Runcorn and that he had given her a sovereign: also that she expected to receive £2 more from him when he came on Monday evening. Witness always regarded the deceased as a respectable woman with the exception of the misfortune she had had."

The Manchester Courier also included a report of the Inquest and quoted the evidence of another female neighbour. Father Daly's involvement with the deceased woman and his response to suggestions of impropriety is also mentioned:

"The witness said that Winifred Markland Walton was a respectable woman; but she did speak to her of visits to her of several gentlemen, and on the 2nd October she said she expected a friend, and a gentleman was seen to enter the house that night. A medical man gave it as his opinion that the deceased had died from poisoning by chloroform. Several visits to the deceased, on the part of Mr. Daly, a Roman Catholic Priest living in Runcorn, were alluded to in the evidence, and that gentleman during the enquiry, after being cautioned by the Coroner, emphatically denied that there was any foundation for the scandal which had been circulated about the deceased and himself, and said that if the Coroner thought there was any case against him he could call witnesses to prove that he was at Runcorn on the night in question. The Coroner said he thought there was some evidence against Father Daly, and that gentleman should call witnesses. He subsequently called a witness who swore that Father Daly was in Runcorn on the night in question."

Over the following days, as more witnesses were questioned, the newspapers continued their reports:

"Mary Ann Ogden, on being asked if she had seen any gentlemen go to the deceased house, answering (pointing to the Rev. Father Daly of Stockport) that she had "seen that gentleman go several times;" she had also seen other gentlemen go too. She lived opposite the house of the deceased and could plainly see when anyone called. After Father Daly had been there on one occasion, deceased asked her if she had seen him, and, on her replying in the affirmative, the deceased said it was "Father Daly, from Stockport."

John Markland; (who was the father of the deceased), stated that he was an overlooker at the mill and resided at Edgeley, Stockport. His daughter, the deceased, had been a respectable, dutiful, young woman but left his house two years ago on becoming pregnant. He had before that spoken to her frequently respecting her imprudence and thoughtlessness, and on one occasion, hearing that she and Father Daly had been seen in a fly carriage together, and had acted somewhat familiarly towards each other, he went to Father Daly's house and remonstrated with him on the fact. That was twelve months before his daughter left home. Prior to her death the deceased spent between two and three weeks at his house, leaving it on the Wednesday that she said she went to Runcorn.

Father Daly, who has charge of a Roman Catholic Chapel at Runcorn, was then sworn in at his own request. The Coroner then cautioned him that what he said might be used against him, and he then asked if, in the Coroner's opinion, there was any evidence against him so far. The Coroner said he believed that there was. He did not say there was direct evidence. Father Daly then declared he was not near the house on the day in question; that he was in Runcorn, and did not leave there until the Wednesday, as he was prepared to prove. He was in the most painful position. For himself he did not care, but there were his parents, his bishop, his fellow priests and the great scandal that had been caused to be considered. He denied that he was the father of the child, as the deceased had claimed, to say so was a calumny. He avowed his entire innocence of any improper connection with the deceased and asked that witnesses might be called.

Mr. Peter Peters, booking-clerk, of Runcorn Railway Station and Mr. J. L. Jones, hotel-keeper; and Mr. J.H. Meadowcroft, auctioneer, all residing at Runcorn, deposed to seeing Father Daly in the town on the evening of Monday 2nd October. The Coroner, in summing up, observed that there was no doubt that the deceased met her death by being administered chloroform and it was a significant circumstance that no bottle was found in the house. This showed that the poison was

probably taken into the place by the person who called. A verdict of
"Wilful Murder by Person Unknown" was given."

It would be quite wrong of me to say that Father Daly was guilty of this crime. Three independent witnesses placed him in Runcorn at the time the murder was said to have been committed. Despite this, there are still a number of uncertainties connected to this case. One does wonder, as post-mortem sciences were not so sophisticated in those days, if the time of death could have been miscalculated. Other serious accusations which emerged during the course of the Inquest give plenty of food for thought. From evidence given by the father of the deceased, it is obvious that his daughter and the priest had been in some form of relationship for a number of years. The murdered woman had also claimed that the priest was the father of her dead child, although the priest had emphatically denied this allegation.

From the evidence presented at the Inquest we can see that in the days immediately prior to her murder Winifred Markland Walton had turned up in Runcorn. She told her neighbour that while she was in Runcorn Father Daly had given her a sovereign. She also told the neighbour that Father Daly would be coming to the house in Stockport on the Monday (the day of her death) and would then give her £2. Is it possible that Winifred was blackmailing Father Daly? Or had her arrival in Runcorn been an acute embarrassment, causing him to devise a plan to be rid of her? Unfortunately we will never know the true circumstances of her death, or the identity of the perpetrator of this crime. What *is* certain is that Father Joseph Daly was a calculating and incurable womaniser. It seems quite incredible that, after being embroiled in such a serious scandal in Stockport, he immediately resumed his wayward behaviour and started a new relationship with another innocent and impressionable young girl in Runcorn.

Another strange link to this case occurred at Runcorn Police Station at the beginning of December 1876 when a local publican was summoned for permitting unlawful gaming to take place in his establishment. The publican, John Longshaw Jones, claimed that he had not appeared at an earlier hearing as he had lost his summons and couldn't remember the date or details. Superintendent Steen of the Runcorn Police said he had found the summons issued to Mr. Jones whilst searching the home of Father Daly. It was hidden in Father Daly's wardrobe. There was no explanation as to how or why it came to be concealed in the priest's wardrobe, but it will be remembered that

Mr. Jones was a key defence witness for Father Daly in the Manchester murder case.

The charges against Father Daly almost certainly created a renewed surge of anti-Catholic feeling in Runcorn. At that time religions other than the Established Church, though tolerated, were still viewed with a degree of distrust. Roman Catholicism was treated with particular suspicion and anti-Catholic sentiments were not unusual among the general population of the country. Most historians claim that anti-Catholicism in England effectively began when Henry VIII broke with Rome and established his own English national church. Even today there are still constitutional laws which discriminate against Catholics. For instance, there is an edict which states that a Roman Catholic cannot inherit the English throne. It should be pointed out that this ruling does not discriminate against persons of any other specific faith or creed. Therefore, the despicable actions of Father Daly only added fuel to an already smouldering fire.

The Roman Catholic community in Runcorn, although still relatively small, had grown considerably since the arrival of industry. In earlier years a substantial number of Irish labourers had arrived into the area to work on local farms and on the canals. Their presence contributed greatly to an increase in the Catholic populace. Prior to this minor influx, in the early years of the 1800s there was probably only a handful of Catholics in Runcorn. In that early period there was no church or other building available for this small group to allow them to attend Mass. As a result they were obliged to cross the river to Widnes where, although there was no church, Mass was regularly celebrated in several houses, including Lower House and a house at Appleton.

With the arrival of Irish labourers who came to work on the farms, docks and waterways of Runcorn, as well as the existing local Catholic inhabitants, by the mid 1840s the Catholic population in Runcorn had noticeably increased. It soon became obvious that there was a need to institute a Catholic Mission in Runcorn and this was subsequently established by Father Edmund Carter in 1842. At that time the Catholics of Runcorn still had no church, so it was necessary for services to be conducted in a number of lay-buildings. It is believed that Mass was celebrated in several places including Stenhill House in Saxon Road and even a hay-loft situated in the Heath Road area. In May 1842 more than 300 Catholics assembled in Runcorn to attend a service conducted by Father Carter. The gathering included a large number of young men and women who had travelled from Father

Carter`s previous parish in Manchester. A report of the event appeared in *The Chester Chronicle*:

RUNCORN.—On Sunday last, a meeting of Roman Catholics was held in the town of Runcorn, when upwards of 300 persons attended divine service. At an early hour of the day there arrived from Manchester about 180 Catholics, consisting of young men and women, beautifully dressed, who came hither for the purpose of testifying their respect for their much revered pastor, who has been lately removed from them to the Runcorn mission. They walked in excellent order to the place of worship, carrying a large tablet with the following inscription on it:—" Cookson-street Catholic Sunday School. Established by the Rev. E. Carter." In consequence of its being the first meeting of the sort held in this neighbourhood during the last 300 years, it has no doubt excited some curiosity, but, much to the credit of the good folks of Runcorn, there was not the least interruption offered on the occasion.—*Correspondent*.

It is interesting to read the final comment in this correspondence. The writer thought it necessary to draw attention to the fact that there had been no disruption to the proceedings by local inhabitants. Father Carter, who had obviously been well loved in his previous parish, spent only a short time in Runcorn. He was succeeded by Father Gerald Ward. In June 1844 a correspondent from the Catholic newspaper, *"The Tablet"*, reported on the state of Catholicism in Runcorn:

"It is gratifying to notice that after a lapse of nearly three centuries, the true religion begins to dawn again at Runcorn. The number of Catholics is already about 300. They belong, for the most part, to the working classes; and although the zealous pastor, the Rev. Gerald Ward, has not yet had the happiness of satisying his desires by erecting a suitable church for their accommodate, he, I understand entertains a hope that ere long that want will be supplied. The Rev. Ward has established a night school at his own house, at which from fifty to sixty children attend. He and his sister are the sole teachers. The children are dismissed at eight o`clock, night prayers being previously said for them by the Rev. gentleman. Many Protestant children also attend."[130]

---

[130]*The Tablet* – 14th June 1844

Two years later, in 1846, the first St. Edward's Church was constructed, using local stone, in Windmill Street. Father Gerald Ward was still the priest in charge at this date, so happily his ambition had been realised.

The relatively swift expansion of the Catholic population in Runcorn, and other local towns, can be mainly attributed to the dreadful effects of the Irish Famine which resulted in thousands of destitute Irish coming to England. The poor unfortunate souls who swamped the towns and cities of northern England had appeared on these shores impoverished, demoralised and often close to death. Their arrival here placed an abnormal burden upon the English Poor Law system and, consequently, this created a great deal of anti-Irish and anti-Catholic reaction among the native English population. This attitude became ingrained and, although it gradually diluted, the unpleasant circumstances surrounding Father Daly's scandalous behaviour would certainly have resurrected strong anti-Catholic feelings in the town.

Widnes too was not without its clerical scandals, although it should be said that the behaviour of the Vicar of Farnworth pales into insignificance when compared to the actions of the dastardly Father Daly. At the beginning of 1888, the parishioners of St. Luke's Church in Farnworth had become alarmed by the intemperance of their vicar, the Rev. George Bond. It was said that on many occasions he delivered his Sunday sermon while under the influence of drink. On some Sundays he was so drunk that his sermons were totally incomprehensible to the congregation. It was also alleged that he had been drunk while officiating at a marriage, a funeral and several baptisms. Such was the problem that in March that year charges of inebriety were brought against him by his parishioners and a formal complaint was made to the Bishop of Liverpool. As was the custom, the Rev. Bond could choose for the charges against him to be tried by a jury of his clerical peers at a Consistory Court of the Diocese, or the case could be adjudicated upon by the Bishop alone. He chose to be judged by his Bishop.

In April 1888 the Bishop of Liverpool, the Right Rev. Dr. Ryle, gave a ruling that the Rev. George Bond was guilty of drunkenness and conduct unbecoming a clergyman. The result of this judgement was that the Bishop suspended the vicar from his office for three years. Obviously, the Rev. Bond was greatly distressed by the decision to deprive him of his living for such a considerable length of time. He decided to go abroad and remain out of the country until the end of his suspension. On his return to England at the end of the three years he was reported to be unwell and unfit to resume his duties. It was widely rumoured that he was still battling his drink problem and therefore unable to recommence his clerical responsibilities. He spent the following eight months recuperating at his temporary residence in Roby but, sadly, he died in February 1892 before he could return to his former parish. His remains were conveyed to Farnworth for burial. The service was conducted by the Rev. J.R. Jones who had been acting curate in the Rev. Bond's enforced absence. He was assisted at the service by the Rev. R. Bond, the brother of the deceased vicar. It was a sad story, as the Rev. Bond had at one time been very popular with his parishioners. Unfortunately, his drink problem made his position as vicar untenable. Of course he was an alcoholic and regretably, try as he might, the poor man was unable to beat his addiction. It was a rather sad end for everyone concerned.

After the death of the Rev. Bond the benefice of Farnworth was offered to the Rev. J. Wright Williams, the Vicar of Rainford. The value of the living was said at that time to be £364 per annum with the use of the Vicarage. Interestingly, the Rev. Mr. Williams was no stranger to Farnworth Church. He had previously served there as vicar from 1879 until his appointment to Rainford early in 1888. It was after his departure for Rainford that the Rev. George Bond had arrived. But, as we have seen, the Rev. Bond was only in office at Farnworth for a short while before being suspended by the Bishop. As the Rev. Mr. Williams had previously been at Widnes for almost ten years, and had been away for barely four, it must have seemed like a return home for him.

Whilst these past pages have told the story of the misbehaviour of some of our local clergymen, most of our religious representatives were beyond reproach and they were as virtuous and honourable as we would expect them to be. In the summer of 1914 one such upright and praiseworthy Roman Catholic priest fell foul of the law through no fault of his own. This poor priest was arrested and thrown into a prison cell like a common criminal. In July that year this well-known Widnes Roman Catholic Priest had a rather upsetting experience whilst on a trip to London. He had travelled down to the city to meet his brother, also a priest, who was returning from missionary work in West Africa. They had arranged to meet at the house of mutual friends. Upon arriving in London much earlier than expected, the priest made his way to his friends' house to await the arrival of his brother. On reaching the house the door was opened by a well-spoken gentleman who informed the priest that his friends were out but were expected home shortly. He was invited into the house and shown to the parlour where he was told to make himself comfortable. He passed the time away by browsing through several books which were on a shelf in the room and by helping himself to a glass of sherry. After a relatively short space of time the parlour door was flung open and several policemen and plain clothes officers stormed into the room. Before the astonished priest knew what was happening, he was forcibly manhandled, handcuffed, and taken to the nearest police station. After some intense questioning, and despite his loud protestations of innocence, he was put into a police cell where he was detained for almost five hours. It was only when his friends arrived home, and his brother arrived at the house, that news of the arrest reached them.

It would appear that in the previous weeks the house had been broken into several times, and there had been a spate of other burglaries in the area. As a consequence, the neighbours and the police were on the lookout for any unusual activity. A vigilant neighbour had informed a local policeman, who was on beat nearby, that a strange man was in the house. When the priest arrived it was assumed that he was an accomplice. It took well over four hours for the shocked and worried Widnes priest to convince the authorities of his innocence. When they eventually made enquiries of the house owner they were able to verify his story. It was only then, and after some grovelling apologies from the police, that the priest was eventually released. It transpired that the man who had let him in was actually the burglar. It was certainly an eventful and memorable trip to London for the poor priest and one which he would not wish to repeat.   .

POLICE, CRIME AND DISTURBANCE

W hen studying the history of the two towns we find that the degree of crime in both places was relatively high. However our towns were by no means exceptional in this respect as crime was fairly widespread, particularly in new industrial areas. During the nineteenth century Widnes had a particularly bad reputation not only as a place of pollution and dense development but also as a crime ridden location. Whilst this reputation was well earned, when taken in relation and comparison to the population figures it is evident that Runcorn also had a comparatively large amount of crime. Both towns had at different times experienced increases in population and with this expansion came an increase in crime. Considering the varied composition of the growing populations in both towns it is perhaps not too surprising that these melting-pots of human life inevitably created social difficulties and forms of civil disobedience. However when studying crime statistics of the period it is important to re-emphasise that both towns were probably no worse than other places where similar patterns of development had occurred. If we examine the social histories of our neighbouring towns of St. Helens and Warrington, and other places, we can see that similar levels of crime were present; therefore this was not a trend unique to our own area.

The instances of law-breaking, of all types, which occurred in both Widnes and Runcorn, could fill several books and more. The criminal proceedings in our local Magistrates Courts and in the higher courts of law, such as the County Assizes, offer us a glimpse of the types of crime which were common in the two towns. We can see that most offenders were young males and generally the offences were related to drunkenness, fighting, vagrancy or petty theft. The most common crimes committed by women were surprisingly similar to their male counterparts with drunkenness, disorderly behaviour and petty theft being among the main offences. Domestic violence did occasionally come before the Courts but this was not as frequent as one might expect. This type of cowardly violence tended to be committed in the privacy of the home and, although it was usually obvious when a woman had been the victim of abuse, wives did not often make formal complaints.   Among some working-class communities domestic violence was tolerated, while amongst other classes the publicising of such behaviour, especially in a court of law, would have been regarded as bringing a family's reputation into disrepute.

When reading reports and records of various types of crime we should bear in mind that this information cannot be viewed simply as bland confirmation of an abundance of criminal activity, but rather as a pointer to the overall social atmosphere of those times. Whilst it is patently clear that most of the defendants brought before the local courts came from the working classes, we should remember that this section of society comprised the largest portion of the population. Therefore, it is not too surprising that they contained the largest group of lawbreakers. In addition, when one takes into consideration their collective despondency, deprivation and surroundings, one can see how these factors may have contributed to their general misconduct.

A comparative study of nineteenth century crime throws up some interesting features regarding certain types of offences. It would appear that some crimes were prevalent during particular situations and less dominant at other times.[131]   For instance, when there was full employment the main type of crime brought before the local magistrates involved drunkenness and fighting. In times of economic and industrial depression the main offences related to stealing and poaching. Of course, in those times the middle class assessment of criminal offenders was linked closely with their perception of the social order. They would certainly not have acknowledged the fact that crime was most likely to be connected to poverty or other forms of social deprivation. The widely held view was that an offender usually came from the lower reaches of the working class who were reluctant to do an honest day's work and who preferred idleness and drink. In fact, it was generally believed that the problem was an ingrained moral deficiency among the "lower" classes. They also blamed any decline in an individual's religious observance to be a reason for law and order problems. Of course there were also plenty of middle class criminals, but the view taken of this type of offender was simply that this person was a black sheep, or a rotten apple, in the midst of an otherwise law abiding society.

In Runcorn, the docks, river and canal traffic brought in a transient workforce of mariners, navigators and dock workers who sought out entertainment during their time in the town. Their trade was very

---

[131] See *"Victorian Crime and Criminals"* Edward Sutton (London 1986)

welcome in the pubs and inns along the river and dock areas, but their presence often led to drunkenness and fighting which, in turn, kept the local magistrates busy. In Widnes also, a proliferation of pubs and inns contributed to a great deal of drunkenness and disorderly behaviour among the new industrial inhabitants of the town. Although industrial development and improved transport facilities were a boon to the local economies on both sides of the river, widespread crime and social problems soon became unwelcome by-products of these things. Whilst drunkenness was a major problem and cause of crime, employment on the river and canals also provided numerous opportunities to engage in another source of criminal activity.   Theft from boats was a very common occurrence and usually involved a member of the crew or a land based canal or dock worker.   Sometimes the culprit was discovered, not through any brilliant detection work, but because of some silly error or occasionally by the brazen display or use of the stolen items

Evidence shows that punishment did not always fit the crime, nor was it even handed. We can see that the penalties imposed were often extremely harsh and disproportionate. Working class men and women could be imprisoned for trifling misdemeanours while their so called *"betters"* caused incomparably greater damage and received much lighter sentences, or in some cases escaped scot-free. Working class women and children were often severely punished for stealing small items of food and yet serious fraud on a large scale, committed by middle-class offenders, was sometimes treated quite leniently. Records show that, generally, middle-class lawbreakers were less likely to receive a sentence of *"hard labour"* while the working classes, sometimes even young children, regularly had this proviso added to their prison sentence.   The fact that this state of affairs went unchallenged tells us as much about society in general as it does about the criminal justice system of those times.

Although we can clearly see that the nineteenth century legal system was prejudiced and extremely unfair, it is worth noting that in earlier periods, in the eighteenth century for example, the criminal justice system was even worse.   Local officials, such as Parish Constables and Justices of the Peace, oversaw a tradition which assumed deference to their *"betters"*, namely the aristocracy or wealthy local landowners, and most criminal law reflected this attitude. There are several local cases which demonstrate the severity of sentencing for relatively minor crimes. In 1848 a 26year old Widnes man called Titus Slater was given a sentence of eighteen months imprisonment with hard labour – his crime, stealing a block of cheese from the home of Robert Sutton at Widnes.

As we saw in a previous chapter, in earlier times transportation to Botany Bay or Van Dieman's Land (Australia) might have been the destiny of young Titus Slater. In July 1828 this was the fate of a Runcorn man called James Dumbavand who was found guilty of stealing a quantity of rum out of a puncheon which had been put on board a ship in Liverpool. The ship, which was called *"Success"*, belonged to the Trustees of the Duke of Bridgewater. When the puncheon arrived at Preston Brook it was weighed and found to be much heavier than expected. The authorities, suspecting some illicit activity, analysed the rum and discovered that it had been diluted with water. On searching Mr.Dumbavand's home in Runcorn, two bottles of rum were found which tallied exactly with the quality of the rum which had been despatched from Liverpool. Dumbavand could not account for the rum which was found in the house and he was immediately arrested. He was subsequently found guilty of stealing and sentenced to seven years transportation. Another Runcorn man, called John West, was also involved in the theft and was indicted for receiving stolen goods - he too received a sentence of transportation.

Transportation was officially abolished in 1857 although by that date it had already trickled down to a relatively small number due to mounting protests from Australia. Nevertheless, as it had been a common punishment since 1718, it was the fate of many of our local men and women. At the outset, the Americas rather than Australia had been the original destination for convicts who were found guilty of varying degrees of crimes. It has been estimated that over 50,000 were sent to the Americas between 1718 and 1775. It is interesting, but perhaps not too surprising, to learn that in port cities such as Liverpool the local Court Judges were often wealthy merchants who had trade or personal interests in American plantations. While the main labour-force for their cotton plantations was usually African slaves, they thought nothing of sentencing petty criminals to years of hard labour on their own property. This was a devious way of supplementing their workforce without having to buy additional slaves. Although the American War of Independence put a stop to British transportation, penal colonies were continued in Jamaica and other Caribbean islands before being given a new lease of life in Australia. During the "transportation era" numerous local people were transported for crimes of one sort or another to all these places.

Prior to its abolition in 1857 transportation had been a common and accepted form of legal punishment. However there was also another way in which a man could be imprisoned and transported by sea against his wishes, even if he was completely innocent of any wrongdoing. Press gangs operated in nearly all the major ports in Britain and were used by both the Royal and Merchant navies to staff their ships when they were short of sailors. Liverpool was notorious for the press gangs that lay in wait in city pubs to *"impress"* some poor unsuspecting individual who may be the worse for drink. One pub, famous for its press gang operation, was *The Baltic Fleet* opposite the Wapping Dock. This well-known pub, which reputedly had a series of caverns and cellars beneath it, was so named because of Liverpool's strong trade link with the Baltic countries. There are a number of interesting stories relating to *The Baltic Fleet*, one concerns a tunnel linking the pub's cellar with the docks. This tunnel was supposedly used by the press gangs to take the impressed men to the ships. According to legend, the gangs would encourage the men to get drunk in the pub above after which they would be captured and taken through the tunnel to the waiting ships. For the unsuspecting drunkard the hangover next morning would have seemed trivial when compared to the realisation that he was out on the open sea and destined for several years away from home. Of course the story of *The Baltic Fleet* tunnel is renowned, but whether it is fact or myth I really can't say.

Naturally, being so close to Liverpool, it is perhaps inevitable that some of our local residents were impressed into service whilst taking a drink in the city. We know of at least two instances where local men suffered this fate. One man, James Heyes of Appleton, was first impressed into service in 1806. He was initially taken on board *The Elephant* which sailed under the command of Captain Dundas, then again taken to serve on *The Bulwark* under Captain Elphinstone Fleming. He was a member of the crew that conveyed cannons to the foot of Matagorda, whilst under bombardment, to replace those that had been dismounted by French fire. When speaking of this event in later years he claimed to have seen *"the heroine of Matagorda carrying water to the English artillery men."* It would seem that Mr. Heyes' time in the navy was both dangerous and adventurous, but extremely interesting from a historical point of view. Whilst on board a ship in the Bay of Roses he was involved in the capture of a fleet of French merchantmen. This was an important gain for the English as these ships were laden with supplies for the French army in Spain. Having served five long years as an impressed sailor, he came home to Widnes in 1811 and never again returned to sea. He was so fearful of being taken back to sea that he never claimed the £70 in wages that was owed to him. He had given a false name when he was impressed so there was

385

no way he could be traced. He served the whole five years under the name of James Hughes. Happily Mr. Hayes lived well into his eighties and was able to tell his tale. He died at his home in Halton View on 28th October 1873.

A similar case involved a Widnes man called Thomas Ford who was the captain of a local schooner called *"The Elizabeth"* which sailed a route between Widnes and Liverpool. One night, when his ship was berthed in St. George's Dock in Liverpool discharging its cargo for foreign ports, Captain Ford went ashore to buy provisions for himself and his crew. Whilst shopping in the city he was waylaid at the bottom of Shaw's Brow and *"arrested"* by a press gang who were on the lookout for likely recruits for the war against Napoleon. Captain Ford was *"drafted"* straight away to take his place on the famous *"HMS Bellerophon"* where he was employed as a sharpshooter in the topmast. During Mr. Ford's time on the vessel it was engaged in numerous battles with the French fleet. He was still on board the ship on 15th July 1815, about a month after the Battle of Waterloo, when Napoleon, seeing that further action was useless, surrendered to the Commander of *"HMS Bellerophon"*. Napoleon was received on board from his jolly boat, to which a gang-plank had been lowered, and handed over his sword to Captain Maitland who was in command. Afterwards he was taken to Plymouth where he remained on board the ship for two weeks while the authorities decided what to do with him. He was subsequently transferred to *"HMS Northumberland"* and taken to St. Helena where he remained in exile for the rest of his life. When relating his escapades to his family, Mr. Ford told them that before leaving *"The Bellerophon"* Napoleon had personally thanked Captain Maitland and all the crew for their consideration and hospitality.

Both James Heyes and Thomas Ford had been unfortunate enough to encounter the infamous press gangs in Liverpool. Interestingly though, their enforced service into the navy made them unwilling participants in some of the most momentous events in British and French history. Thomas Heyes, though obviously not unscathed by his experiences, managed to return home and spend the next sixty odd years in Widnes with his family. Sadly, Thomas Ford was not so lucky and the outcome was not a happy one. During his service he had been shot and badly wounded. After the wars were over he was drafted home wounded and eventually died from his injuries. He is buried in Sankey Churchyard. All the wages and prize money owing to him were lost due to the family not putting in a proper claim. The money was held in Chancery where it will, allegedly, remain until doomsday.[132]

As we have seen, transportation for stealing was a common penalty up until the mid-1800s. It was the second most common serious punishment after hanging. Alas, the death penalty was no stranger to some of our inhabitants either, as there were several local cases in which capital punishment was the sentence. In September 1817 three Runcorn men were hanged at Lancaster Castle for the violent rape of a young woman. Across the river in Widnes the shocking murder of Patrick Treacy in 1879 resulted in two men being hanged at Kirkdale Gaol. A third person, the victim's wife, was also convicted but had her sentence commuted to life because she was pregnant and about to give birth. In this shocking murder case one of the men strenuously denied any participation in the crime. He went to his death still proclaiming his innocence. On the eve of the executions the other man confessed to his own part in the murder and also confirmed that his co-accused was entirely innocent of any wrongdoing. Unfortunately, both men went to the gallows despite the overwhelming likelihood that one was quite innocent. The wife, who had been having an affair with one of her co-defendants, was most probably the instigator of the crime. She escaped the hangman's noose and, instead, was sentenced to life imprisonment for her part in the murder. After serving several decades in Woking Prison and Holloway she was eventually released on licence when she was in her 70s and died shortly afterwards.[133] In the Runcorn rape case, despite being found guilty of this heinous and brutal crime, the three men persistently declared their innocence but the law took its course and all three were hanged. A newspaper of the time included the following statement about the executed men:

"We give in our last page, some very sensible remarks on the late executions at Lancaster, extracted from The Courier. Of the guilt of the three wretched men, we think there can be no doubt. The crime was brought home to them on clear circumstantial evidence – on such evidence as no rational Jury could for a moment hesitate upon. Of the declarations of innocence as to the crime, made by the parties on the scaffold, we think little. It is one part of a system which, thanks to these enlightened days, and to our new religious and political Guardians, great offenders act upon, and unhappily for morality, is getting into pretty general practice. The executions of Messrs. W; Y and B, for a

---

[132] From: The correspondence of his grandson, the late Arthur Ford.

[133] *"Yesterday's People"* – Jean M. Morris (Springfield-Farrihy 2012)

rape in the neighbourhood of Runcorn, is too recent to have escaped our recollection. These miserable men, under the fatal tree, persisted to the last in declaring that they were being murdered, and one of these men asserted, "they were brought there like a bullock to be slaughtered" – and, yet no doubt of their guilt was entertained by any one."

Although drunkenness and fighting were high on the list of offences dealt with by the local magistrates, there was also an extremely high number of robberies in the towns. Many of these were violent and the robbers were sometimes armed and prepared to use their weapons. In December 1827 four thugs broke into the house of the Rev. Mr. Thompson, the Vicar of Farnworth, robbing him and badly injuring a female servant. A report of the incident in *The Chester Chronicle* tells us that on Thursday 13th December 1827:

"A gang of four robbers broke into the house of the curate of Farnworth and demanded his money. A servant girl, who was equally stout of heart and arm, being roused from sleep by a man opening the door of her room, and thinking her master in danger, sprang out of bed and knocked the foremost robber down with her fist. The others, however, soon overpowered the Amazon, and cruelly beat her on the head with an iron poker. The Reverend gentleman, who is advanced in years, hearing the noise, came out of his room and entreated the villains not to murder the girl, promising to give them his money. He then went to a box in which there was £31, chiefly in gold, and the robbers, following him, took away the box and its contents together. They also got some plate, and then made off. We have not heard that the villains have been discovered. The girl, though seriously wounded in the head, is recovering"

Instances of petty pilfering from boats on the local river and the canals reached almost epidemic proportions in the 1820s. As we read earlier, transportation for some of these crimes was not unusual. In September 1829 another robbery on the canal was solved through the keen observation of a Manchester cotton printer. The discovery of the culprits was a sheer stroke of good luck and a case of being in the right place at the right time or, in the case of the culprit, in the wrong place at the wrong time. A report of this incident tells us:

"For a long time past complaints have been made of the plunder of packages of goods, on their passage by canal from Manchester to Liverpool, for exportation, which, in many cases, has not been discovered until the arrival of the packages at their foreign destination, and the perpetrators of which have hitherto successfully eluded all

endeavours to trace them. Yesterday week, however, a clue was obtained which led them to the apprehension of John Burrows, the master of a flat belonging to the Old Quay Company at Runcorn, and Alice Burrows, his wife; John Rose, the master of a flat belonging to the New Quay Company, and his wife Ann Rose. They were apprehended in consequence of Mr. Butterworth, a calico-printer, in Manchester, seeing Alice Burrows in James Street in Liverpool wearing a gown of printed cotton, of a peculiar type of cotton of his own manufacture, none of which had ever been sold in England. Some printed cottons of a similar character were found in John Rose's cottage, which is situated on the banks of the canal at Latchford, close by where the flats pass between Manchester and Liverpool."

Drunkenness and debauchery appeared to be a major problem in Runcorn in the early 1840s. Several residents were moved to write to the local newspapers voicing their concern about the worrying state of affairs. In response, a journalist penned the following article in April 1841:

"Wishing, as we really do, to promote the welfare of Runcorn in every possible way, we hope that our friendly hints, from time to time, will not be received amiss, indeed, we have the satisfaction of knowing that they have been favourably regarded in the past. In a country town, of increasing population, like Runcorn, where the police establishment is so insufficient, public acts, immoralities, and crimes, will be sure to make a fearful and rapid progress. We lament to say that the beer-houses of Runcorn are generally supported by indulgences too vicious to be described, outraging all morality and destroying all public decency and good order. Without they are immediately restrained and placed under different regulations, the consequences will ere long be very serious, and especially upon the youthful population of both sexes, who are attracted to these haunts of iniquity, night after night, by the sounds of music and singing, and the levities of dancing. We know that these irregularities would not be allowed, and many others that we might mention, if Runcorn possessed a resident magistrate, and we now must call the serious attention of our Runcorn friends in the imperative necessity of an intelligent, vigilant and highly principled resident magistrate being appointed from their resident gentry. The town has around 10,000 inhabitants and not a magistrate, for what reason? Cannot a suitable gentleman be found, of standing, character, and intelligence sufficient to fill the office with honour and efficiency? This can never be said while such men reside in Runcorn as Mr. John Johnson, Mr. Whiteway, Mr. Brundrit, Mr. Hazlehurst and the clergy of

this town. We hope something will be done in a matter so important to Runcorn and the neighbourhood."

At this time the role of Mr. Harding, Runcorn's Chief Constable, was also coming under scrutiny and his competence was in question. Mr. Harding had first been appointed to this position sometime around 1825 when the population of the town had been considerably less and therefore policing had been far easier. However as the community had increased, so too had instances of drunkenness and crime. By the early 1840s there was mounting concern about the state of law and order in the town. In May 1844 a committee of Local Ratepayers met to discuss the duties of their Chief Constable with a view to improving local law enforcement. At that meeting it was revealed that Mr. Harding had a wide ranging list of responsibilities. Apart from his duties as Chief Constable he also held the offices of Deputy Constable; Assistant Overseer; Assistant Highways Surveyor; Collector of Poor Rates; Assessor of Land and other Taxes; Collector of Church Rates; Assistant Overseer of the township of Weston; Collector of Assessed Taxes; Collector of Income Tax under Schedules A, B, and D; Keeper of the Town Hall; and Keeper of Lock-Ups. In fact it was claimed that eleven different roles were being filled by Mr. Harding. Poor Mr. Harding, this was an enormous list of duties to be undertaken by one individual. Therefore, in view of this overwhelming workload, it must have been rather galling to be the subject of criticism and dissatisfaction.

Fortunately for Mr. Harding the outcome of the meeting was beneficial to him. It was agreed that the Bench of Magistrates would be asked to bring the town under the auspices of the County Police Act. This meant that responsibility for the police force would be taken away from Mr. Harding and he would be allowed to devote more time to collecting rates and his various other duties. Although it was probably a very satisfactory result for Mr. Harding, unfortunately, this was not before he had endured a considerable amount of public criticism. A well-known local man, who I now believe was Samuel Shaw Brown, had written a series of fault-finding letters to local newspapers. The author of these letters made disparaging claims regarding the efficiency of Mr. Harding and his small team of policemen. These written attacks were extremely unpleasant and personal, so much so that the subject was raised during a meeting of ratepayers. A newspaper report of that meeting ended with the following statement:

"Thus ended the meeting for which preparations have so long made, to the prejudice of Mr. Harding, by personal attacks upon him through the columns of The Liverpool Mercury and Liverpool Times. The conduct

of the individual who first addressed the meeting has excited almost universally (out of his own clique) feelings of deep and undisguised disgust. Let his professions in his first address be compared with his subsequent remarks. The question is asked in all circles, why should this individual, a comparative stranger, without stake or interest in the town, be put forward as mouth-piece universal and accuser general? No satisfactory answer has yet been given. Before his advent there were fewer displays of dangerous oratory, but more unanimity – less excitement, but greater satisfaction – less talk, but more work. We pray for a return of the good old times."

Three years later the situation in Runcorn had not improved much and local residents were still complaining of violence on their streets. It should be pointed out that not all of this unwelcome aggression was the result of personal antagonism but rather pugilistic rivalry in the form of organised street fights. Of course this kind of activity, which also involved betting, was illegal. It was also very unpleasant for those who lived in close proximity to the districts where these fights were being organised. In August 1847 a large horde of men gathered in the vicinity of Hatton Garden near to a place called Martin's Garden. It was said that the mob filled the entire street down to the Nelson Tavern and also blocked part of the main road in High Street. Amid this throng were several groups of pugilists challenging and being challenged, as well as men taking bets on the outcome of the fights. It would seem that, despite numerous prosecutions, this had become a fairly regular and quite open occurrence in that neighbourhood. Surprisingly, most of those involved were repeat offenders but despite this they were only fined and bound over to keep the peace. Among those summoned to appear before the magistrates on this occasion were: William Ellis, George Waterhouse, John Foster and Thomas Phillips. A week earlier another group of men, including Richard Footall, Henry Hunt Taylor, Joseph Elsby and William Rose appeared on a similar charge.

Prize fighting, as it was called, was a common occurrence in many northern towns but most particularly in areas where there were large numbers of working men. Both Warrington and St. Helens had problems with prize fighting incidents and there were countless arrests associated with these illegal events. However at the time Runcorn was experiencing these incidents, Widnes, still being a relatively quiet place, was not yet affected by this type of activity. Nevertheless it was inevitable that, as the area became more heavily populated, prize fighting would make an appearance in and around Widnes. There were several early cases of men fighting at Bold Heath for a purse of £5 a side. Huge gangs of men assembled for these events but almost all of those involved and prosecuted were from neighbouring St. Helens. Although prize fights were illegal they occurred with amazing regularity and by the 1870s this activity had become a major problem for the Widnes authorities. Despite being secretly organised they managed to attract relatively large crowds of spectators.

Although prize fighting was viewed as sport by the onlookers, and a way of earning money for the participants, the events were usually rowdy and violent due to quarrelling among spectators who were betting on the results. Sometimes these events had unhappy results arising not only from the brutal injuries inflicted upon the contestants but also from other incidents involving bystanders. On one occasion, as the police put in an appearance at Fiddler's Ferry, the combatants and spectators were forced to make a rapid exit. Many had arrived at the event in boats, coming across the river from Runcorn or down from Warrington. Their hasty departure by the same method was somewhat frantic and some men were obliged to jump in the river in an attempt to reach the boats. One young man, Edward Maude, attempted to swim across the river although, being late autumn, it was freezing cold and a strong tide was flowing at the time. Unfortunately he did not make it across the river and was drowned. He was a young married man with several children. As a point of interest, a report of the two fights which had occurred that evening tells us that one contest lasted 1 hour and 45 minutes and the second was broken up after 55 minutes due to the arrival of the police.

A report, transcribed below, from *The Warrington Evening Post* of September 1879 shows how much attention these clandestine events attracted.

"Prize Fight at Fidler's Ferry: With an apparent revival of prize fighting, the neighbourhood of Fidler's Ferry near Widnes and Warrington, seems to have been chosen as a battle ground by reason of its proximity to Cheshire, the Mersey only dividing at this point the two counties. On Friday last, whilst an inquest was being held in The Ferry Inn, on the bodies of two persons who were drowned nearby, a large number of persons arrived by train from Warrington and Widnes. The fact of one party coming by way of Warrington was done as a ruse to throw the police off their guard. At Fidler's Ferry it was announced to be a pigeon shooting match, and a number of the party carried guns. Owing to a previous arrangement, boats had been provided and were in readiness to convey the "fancy" across the river. The inquest to

which allusion has been made had just been concluded when the noise and shouting occasioned by the fight was remarked upon. The fight was between a man from Widnes and another from St. Helens, but their names have not transpired, and the amount staked was, we are informed, £50 a side. The very bloody fight lasted for nearly an hour. "

Fidler's[134] Ferry and Cuerdley Marsh were thought to be the most popular venues for Widnes events as they were quiet areas which offered a degree of privacy. The fact that these locations could be reached by boat for those crossing the Mersey from Cheshire was also an advantage. Despite the secretive nature of these events they were highly organised. Many of the fights occurred on the days when the Local Petty Sessions were taking place, meaning that most of the police officers would be otherwise engaged. The common practice was to take possession of a field adjacent to the river and, without any regard to the farmer's crops, form a ring with ropes and stakes. It is perhaps interesting to note that many of these fights were organised by Manchester men and in these cases the prize fighters were also from Manchester. One such fight, between *"Bill Brown and Jack Miller"* for a purse of £50, was broken up by the police and resulted in the participants being summoned to appear in court. At the hearing, the Magistrates denounced the *"disreputable practice of men coming from Manchester to disturb a quiet neighbourhood".* The combatants were both Manchester men. Bill Brown was the landlord of the Railway Inn at Salford and Miller was the proprietor of the Original Pink Tavern in Bury Street, also in Salford. It appears that Brown was the victor, the fight having gone to twenty-one rounds before the arrival of the police.

Although Runcorn residents complained bitterly to the police and local authorities about antisocial behaviour on the streets of the town, it was often hard to control the situation. Almost a decade after Mr. Harding had been removed from office as Chief Constable it seems that things had not improved. Several frustrated ratepayers resorted to writing to local newspapers to voice their anger and air their grievances. No doubt this was a way of getting it off their chest whilst at the same time provoking some public reaction. One resident wrote to *The Liverpool Mercury* in August 1852. When publishing the letter, part of which is quoted below, the newspaper stated that this was just one of countless correspondence they had received on the same subject:

---

[134] Earlier spelling is Fidler's

"...it is outrageous that disorderly persons are allowed to congregate in considerable numbers at several parts of the town, to the great annoyance of the well-disposed inhabitants. The practice prevails mostly at the bottom of Mersey Street and at Delph Bridge. Here the parapet is often covered and the passage obstructed. In attempting to pass, respectable females are frequently insulted; and it often occurs that when they are under the protection of a father, husband, or brother, they meet with the same fate. On Sundays the evil takes a more aggravated form still. Now, I would ask if our police regulations are so lax as to be unable to grapple with such detestable exhibitions. Cannot these outrages upon decency, order and propriety be restrained? Is there no silencing the volleys of obscene language which fall upon the ears of our wives and daughters as they pace the streets? To such questions I would answer "Yes"; and in confirmation thereof offer two facts:- First, there are certain spots in the town where no such scenes as I have described are witnessed; and secondly, when we had less than half our present police establishment there was little cause for complaint. I think, therefore, that I am right in assuming that the law, under the County Police Act, supplies a remedy. Let me then urge upon our inspectory to accept this exposé as a motive to undertake the removal of this abomination as soon as possible, and thus rise to the full dignity and usefulness of their office. To do this might involve inquiry into the general efficiency of our police force, which certainly cannot be very great, when a whole neighbourhood can be disturbed by a series of rows extending over an entire day without any legal interference.

Signed: A Ratepayer – Runcorn, August 24th 1852."

When looking at crime in both towns we can see that alcohol abuse and its effect was a common theme. The vast majority of crimes were fuelled by drink and although much of this criminal conduct was petty, such as disorderly behaviour, there were several instances of a more serious nature. In February 1847 a man named Richard Edwards, a Runcorn carpenter, appeared before the Magistrates charged with the murder of his wife, Betty Edwards. Mrs. Edwards was described as a quiet, peaceable woman and the loving mother of several children. On the day of the murder Mr. Edwards, who was portrayed as a man overly fond of alcohol, had stayed away from work and spent the day out drinking. During the afternoon Mrs Edwards had sent one of her children to her husbands workplace to collect what wages were due to him. When Edwards eventually came home from the pub, in a state of extreme intoxication, he wanted money but his wife refused to give it to him. She told him that everything she had was owed to the local shopkeeper for provisions. Edwards lost his temper and physically attacked her in the presence of their children. It was alleged that he grabbed her by the hair and struck her several times around the head and neck, knocking her to the ground and kicking her severely. The eldest son, who was a young apprentice, attempted to intervene and protect his mother but the father threatened him. The frightened boy ran to fetch the neighbours but by the time he returned with help his mother was already dead. At that point the son attempted to go for a doctor, but the father prevented him from doing so and threatened him again. He told the boy that if he brought a doctor he would kill him as well. When neighbours examined Mrs. Edwards and told her husband that she was dead he replied *"Good! – To hell with her!"* The police arrived in due course and Edwards was taken into custody. An inquest was held on the body at The Royal Hotel in Runcorn, and the jury returning a verdict of *"Wilful Murder"*. Mr. Edwards was taken to Chester Castle and was subsequently to stand trial for murder at Chester Assizes.

Crimes of domestic violence were quite commonplace, although these rarely reached the law courts as society generally ignored them. Some women accepted this situation as a routine part of life and children were exposed to this form of violent behaviour from an early age. Despite this unpleasant side of married life, some women were not deterred from entering into wedlock several times during their lifetimes. In fact there are countless cases of bigamy committed by local females. One interesting and rather comical case occurred in Runcorn in August 1864. A lady called Hannah Green was charged with entering into a bigamous marriage not once but twice! It appears that Ms. Green was no great catch though, as one of her *"husbands"* became so fed up with her that he attempted to sell her at a fair for a shilling.

Hannah Green`s case caused a great deal of interest and amusement when she appeared in court at Runcorn. The charges brought against her were that she married a man called Samuel Thompson on 7th March 1861 whilst her legal husband, Thomas Sparkes, was still alive. There was also a second charge of marrying a man called Henry New in October 1859. Henry New died shortly after the wedding and there was nothing to suggest that he had been a knowing participant in the bigamous relationship. When one of the witnesses, Rachael Woodward, a Runcorn boat-woman, gave evidence there was a great deal of laughter in the courtroom. Mrs Woodward told the court that:

"Hannah Sparkes had lived with Thompson for several years and had married him in 1861. Thompson started to ill-treat her shortly after the wedding and the couple fought continuously. He often threatened to sell her, and did so for a shilling at "Brummagem Fair", some years ago, selling her with a halter around her neck".

It was claimed that Thompson had *"bought"* her himself some years previous to this. In her defence Hannah Green said that she had not been legally married to Sparkes, a Runcorn boatman, but had only lived with him as his wife and called him *"her husband"* for convenience – His Lordship, in his summing up, said that:

"the notion that a man could rid himself of an uncomfortable helpmate by taking her to a market with a rope round her neck was formerly very prevalent, but he though it had fallen out of fashion before now, It was important that the minds of ignorant people should be, by all means, disabused of such an impression". The jury returned a verdict of *"Not guilty"*.

In spite of this Judge assuming that the practice of *"selling wives for a shilling"* had died out, this did not appear to be the case. Several years later, in the autumn of 1876, a married couple from Widnes called Jackson, who had gone to reside at Prescot, were said to have found married life so difficult they were advised to separate. The husband remained at Prescot but the wife and family moved back to Widnes. Shortly afterwards the husband was summoned to appear before the Magistrates for neglecting to support his family and as a result he received a term of imprisonment. The wife subsequently took in a lodger who, it was said, *"became so enamoured of his hostess that he offered to purchase her for a shilling".* The offer was communicated to the husband who expressed his willingness to close the deal. The result was that the husband placed an advert in a local newspaper to inform all interested parties that he had willingly agreed to sell his wife for the sum named. He also included a formal promise *"never to molest her or injure her by any word or act from that day forward".* It was subsequently reported, that on the following Saturday afternoon the woman and her new partner were seen, arm in arm, promenading the principal streets of Widnes *"intent on purchasing the necessary domestic articles wherewith to begin their new sphere of life".* I presume that all parties lived happily ever after!

By the 1840s and early 1850s Runcorn already had an increased and growing population due to the development of industry in the town. Across the river in Widnes the population was still relatively modest, comprising mainly of the indigenous communities and the newer residents of the small neighbourhood around Widnes Dock. Although the town had not yet reached the high levels of crime it would later achieve, nonetheless, comparable instances of lawbreaking and violence were present among the indigenous communities. At one sitting of the local Petty Sessions in 1845 seventeen persons were fined 5shillings each for drunkenness and disorderly behaviour. Thomas Ashton, a local weaver, received a fine of 10 shillings for assaulting another weaver by the name of Robert Piercey. At a later session the licensee of a pub, Ann Heyes, was fined for permitting drunkenness on the premises, as was another beer-seller called Elizabeth Brown. A local watchmaker, Peter Walton, and a labourer called Abraham Millington were both summoned for fighting in the streets. And, of course, the celebration of Farnworth Wakes had gained an unfavourable reputation for drunkenness and violence.

Despite there being numerous reports of appearances before the local magistrates, the official Charge Book for the Prescot Division of the Lancashire Constabulary for the period 1849-1852 [135] shows just 131 arrests in Widnes. This seems to be an especially low figure for a three year period but we should remember that the town and its industries were still in their infancies. The population was still relatively small as the area had not yet been swamped by an influx of new workers. It is clear that most of the 131 arrests during this three year period were alcohol related, as were the majority of crimes in later periods. From this information we can easily see that this type of crime was not the sole domain of the new industrial populations who came into the town later. The conduct of the later inhabitants was only exceptional due to the sheer numbers of offenders and any increase in crime was in line with the extraordinary rise in population figures.

Reports on the administration of Lancashire for the period 1838-1889 [136] tell us that a large building programme was carried out throughout the whole county during this time. This included three new county asylums, new county offices at Preston, new assize courts, eight militia storehouses and one hundred and fifteen new police stations. In 1851 a new Police Station was built in Widnes. At that time the police force for the town consisted of one married sergeant, three married constables and two single constables. As the population then was only

---

[135] County Record Office - Preston

[136] Ibid.

3217 this level of staffing was thought to be sufficient for the needs of the town. However, an application in March 1859 to lease further parcels of land in both Widnes and Rainhill for possible future expansion was approved by the Magistrates of the Prescot Division. By 1866 the population of Widnes was around 12,000 and the original Police Station had become inadequate for the requirements of the developing community. The staffing levels had increased to one sergeant and nine constables and it was recognised that this number was likely to rise because of the growing population. This meant that, from an accommodation point of view, the size and condition of the Police Station were a cause for concern. In December 1866 it was proposed that £1200 be borrowed against the police-rates for the purpose of extending the existing Police Station to provide an office, a magistrates' room, a larger kitchen and two other rooms to accommodate any additional constables that may be needed.

In April 1869 a leading Lancashire Judge was asked to make a study of criminal offences in the county. His report and his personal analysis of crime in Lancashire, and its causes, was duly submitted and his findings published in *The Police Gazette*. Using as his basis the annual police returns for the county, which showed a great increase in cases of drunkenness, he concluded that almost all criminal activity had originated, to a greater or lesser extent, in drink. He attributed most of the crime, as well as the poverty and lunacy which existed in the county, to the drunken habits of the people. He claimed that nine-tenths of the prisoners in the county gaol could trace their fall, directly or indirectly, to the use of strong drink. With regard to *"lunatics"*, although he was not able to validate his claim with any analytical evidence, he said that:

"His experience as a visiting Justice for many years past led him to believe that drink had very much to do with it. The annual cost of the maintenance of lunatics was upwards of £100,000; and the number under confinement was constantly increasing, more from the cause which he had pointed out – namely drunkenness – than from any natural cause."

His comprehensive, though debateable, report continued in the same vein. Whilst there is no doubt that alcohol was a contributing factor in petty crime, it was certainly not the chief feature in cases of poverty or mental health. The inmates of asylums may have been, in some cases, confined because of alcohol related illness but we should remember that people could be incarcerated in these institutions for a variety of reasons. Sometimes young unmarried mothers or post-natal depressive women, or people suffering from minor breakdowns, could be locked away in asylums for an indefinite period. In 1869 there were three Lancashire County Asylums, these were based at Lancaster, Prestwich and Rainhill. The total number of inmates for that year was 2340. In addition to these official institutions there were a number of private asylums where people of means could confine their family members in a less grim environment. It was estimated that there were about 160 people in private asylums at Haydock and other places.

It is quite clear that petty crimes committed by children could not be put down to alcohol abuse. My research shows that most of their misdemeanours were related to the childish opportunistic theft of small objects or items of food. The punishments were unusually harsh by todays standards and in most cases seem to be totally disproportionate to the crimes they had committed. In August 1860, Mary Bazley, a little girl of twelve, appeared before the Magistrates in Runcorn for stealing a florin from Mr. John Brierley`s shop. She was described as *"a quiet respectably dressed little girl"*. She was sentenced to one month's imprisonment and afterwards to four years in a reformatory. Her father was ordered to pay one shilling a week towards her maintenance in the reformatory. Over in Widnes, in October 1869, eleven year old James O'Neill was charged with stealing the tap off a brass oil lamp, the property of Edward Crump, a builder. Young James was committed to the workhouse for a week and afterwards was sent to St. George's Industrial School for five years. Another case, in December 1876, involved a group of small boys accused of breaking into two shops in Newtown and stealing sundry items including eggs, tobacco and toys. When they appeared at Widnes Police Court one boy was so small he had to stand on a chair so he could see over the dock. It was said that the other boys, with the exception of one, were no higher than the dock. One can only imagine how intimidating these proceedings must have been for such small children. I could find no report of the sentences they received; one would assume that this would most probably have involved being sent to a reformatory for several years. I include here a report of their *"crime"* and their appearance in court.

"Boy Burglars at Widnes: At the Widnes Police Court yesterday seven boys named respectively, Thomas Smith aged 10; Patrick M'Grace aged 12; Thomas Gilhooley aged 13; George Holden aged 12; Edward Newman aged 13 and John Arthur Cavanagh aged 8; were each charged with breaking into two lock-up shops on Sunday last, tenanted by Mr. Gould, grocer and Mr. Mckinlay, toy merchant. Cavanagh, against whom the charge was withdrawn, was put into the witness box

399

to give *"Queen's evidence"* and on being asked if he knew where boys went to who told lies, he replied *"I don't know".* Subsequently on being pressed, he boldly affirmed that that class of individuals *"went to hell",* and the Bench deeming the answer satisfactory allowed the boy to proceed, and accepted his evidence. None of the prisoners, with one exception, were higher than the dock; Cavanagh had to be placed on a chair while giving his evidence. From the statements of the various witnesses it appeared that Smith gained admission to Mr. Gould's shop through breaking a pane of glass, and after getting into the shop he let the other prisoners in. They lit a fire, boiled eggs, partook plentifully of potted salmon, buns, preserves and biscuits and after having eaten their fill broke about 30shillings worth of eggs and took away 10lbs to 12lbs of tobacco. The thieves then proceeded to Mr. McKinlay's toy shop, where Smith, after climbing up the spout, got on the roof, and after taking off some slates let himself in and then opened the shop door for his companions. In the toy shop the prisoners made a general onslaught on the articles, and took away about £10 worth of goods – including two concertinas, six clarinets, four boxes of rings, a quantity of good purses etc. Drawers were upset and the shop was found to be in general confusion. The property was discovered at the prisoners` residences. Superintendent Brindle said some more boys were still wanted and being sought, and the prisoners were remanded in custody for a week to await trial.

The drastic increase in population in Widnes brought with it an inevitable increase in crime. It should be said that even though Runcorn's population was not as large there was still a significant level of crime. The Police Court in Runcorn was probably every bit as busy as that of its neighbouring town. Cases of assault and robbery, as well as drunkenness and vagrancy, were just as common in Runcorn as they were in Widnes. Some police and court reports give us an idea of what life was like in the town. For instance, in July 1887 Thomas Jannion, described as a man *"of bad character"*, was sentenced to three months hard labour for assisting in the management of a *"house of ill-repute"* in Cooper Street. In addition he was sentenced to a further month for assaulting an old woman named Emma Jones. At the same session Ellis Davies, who was coachman to Mr. Shaw of The Highlands, Higher Runcorn, was fined five shillings and costs of sixteen shillings for assaulting John Crichton who was the son of an actor, by striking him on the head with a whip. A young man called Alfred Armstrong was fined two pounds and five shillings for being drunk and disorderly and for assaulting Police Constable May. If he did not pay the fine he would be imprisoned for six weeks.

Physical assaults upon members of the Police Force were a common occurrence and countless cases were reported in both towns. There are numerous cases too in which the Police were summoned for assault upon members of the public. When studying these statistics it is interesting to consider the attitudes of those times with regard to the Police Force. Generally, the working class stance towards the law and its agents was a complex one that reflected the unequal structure of society. Initially, when the Police Force was started in London in 1829 to fight lawlessness in the Capital, it was made up of ex-military men. However when various Acts of Parliament (1829-1856) enabled the Force to develop nationally it attracted men from other walks of life.

Although one would have hoped that the police service offered a high degree of professionalism and efficiency, in reality, policing in the early years of the nineteenth century was rather ineffective and often vulnerable to corruption. Because of this, the working classes had little respect or confidence in the impartiality of the Police Force. In fact they had good reason for this lack of trust. There were a number of incidents in which men were arrested and imprisoned on some minor pretext. When some of these cases came to court it became obvious that they had been the victim of some personal grudge by the arresting officer. Fortunately, in many instances the charges were dismissed by the Court. One interesting case took place in Widnes in 1869 and involved two men from Newtown called Thomas Tansey and Thomas Smith. The men were charged with having assaulted and resisted Sergeant Graves and Constable John Alsop in the execution of their duty. Tansey was also charged with being drunk and riotous. In addition to the charges against the two men there were also cross summonses against some of the Police. Inspector Peters was summoned for assaulting Mr. Tansey and Sergeant Graves and Constable Alsop for assaulting Mrs. Tansey. When the case came to court the courtroom was overflowing with noisy spectators and the proceedings lasted about seven hours, which was a relatively long session in those days.

It seems that on the previous Saturday evening around 6pm Constable Alsop and another Constable were on duty in Ann Street in the Newtown neighbourhood. At around 7pm Inspector Peters arrived to visit his officers and, about the same time, Thomas Tansey passed down Ann Street on his way home to Caroline Street. The police claimed that as Tansey was drunk they decided to take him into custody. However, it was said, that on the suggestion of Inspector Peters they let him off with a warning and advised him to go home. It

401

was alleged by the police that from this time, up until around 11 p.m., Tansey was constantly turning up in the streets making threatening and offensive remarks to them. It was said that Tansey eventually went home but when the officers came into Caroline Street he was stood on his doorstep. The police officers claimed that Tansey continued to create a disturbance and, because of this, they attempted to arrest him. During the scuffle that followed Constable Alsop was dragged into the house and pushed into the coal cellar where Tansey attempted to attack him with a poker. Sergeant Graves then arrived and Tansey was pulled out of the house into the backyard and handcuffed. During this time a large crowd had gathered outside in the street, among them was Thomas Smith, who allegedly hit one of the constables with a poker. As events developed, the crowd grew considerably and there was some attempt by them to rescue Tansey from the clutches of the police. The crowd's angry determination was so great that the police and their unwilling prisoner were forced to seek refuge in a pawnshop owned by a Mr. Jameson in Ann Street. During the commotion that followed the windows of Mr. Jameson's shop were smashed. From that time until almost one o'clock in the morning the police and their prisoner were barricaded in the pawnshop waiting for the angry crowd to disperse.

During the court case that followed numerous witnesses were called in support of Mr. Tansey's claim that he had been assaulted and falsely arrested. Several witnesses said that Mr. Tansey was certainly not drunk, nor was he creating trouble. Among the witnesses was Mr. Jameson, who was described as a respectable businessman. Mr. Jameson claimed that he had seen Tansey earlier that evening on his way home and he was, without doubt, quite sober. He was also quite sober when he was under arrest and sheltering in his shop with the police. He said that earlier in the evening when he had first seen Tansey he heard Constable Alsop make several provocative comments to him. He believed that the remarks were deliberately intended to incite a reaction from Tansey. Mr. Jameson's view was that Constable Alsop was trying to find an excuse to arrest Tansy and was doing his utmost to goad Tansey into action so that he could apprehend him.

Of course, on the face of it, this could be viewed as a typical drunken Saturday night affray. The instances of drunkenness, particularly at weekends, were alarmingly regular and some men and women were habitual offenders. For instance, in just two weeks during the summer of 1865 thirty seven residents of Widnes Dock appeared before the Petty Sessions charged with drunkenness. In January 1869 a man called Patrick Goulden made his thirty-third appearance at Widnes Police Court on a charge of having been drunk and behaving riotously.

However, in the Tansey case, there is compelling evidence to suggest that all is not as it seems. It could be said that some of the witnesses were biased in favour of their neighbours. However, Mr. Jameson's evidence has a ring of truth. It would certainly be more beneficial for him to be on good terms with the police so it is unlikely that he would side with Tansey unless he was just being absolutely truthful. It is also improbable that the police would have allowed Mr. Tansey to create a public nuisance for a whole four hours, from 7pm until 11pm as they claimed, without arresting him. The result of the case was that both Tansey and Smith were fined and bound over to keep the peace. The cases against the police were dismissed. As the verdicts were announced there was angry uproar in the crowded courtroom. Of course, cases like this only served to alienate the local residents and did nothing to inspire feelings of confidence in the integrity of the Police Force or the legal system.

Throughout this chapter I have cited several instances of violent behaviour. Although violence was usually a crime associated with male residents there was certainly no lack of violent female offenders in both towns. In January 1877 a woman named Elizabeth Hesmond was committed for trial, charged with wounding James Leonard, a labourer. The prisoner and the victim's sister-in-law were fighting on Widnes Marsh one Sunday night. Their husbands were standing by watching. At some stage Mr. Leonard and Mr. Hesmond had an altercation which resulted in another fight taking place. During the fight between the men, Mrs. Hesmond left the scene and returned with a large axe which she used to strike Mr. Leonard on the forehead, causing serious injury. That same week another woman, Elizabeth Pendlebury, appeared before the Runcorn Petty Sessions charged with drunkenness and violent behaviour. She was charged with behaving in a threatening manner towards the servant who gave evidence against the Runcorn priest, Father Daly. The bench sent Elizabeth Pendlebury to gaol for a month, with hard labour.

Other forms of violent and unpleasant behaviour involved the treatment of animals. In earlier times the cruel acts of bear-baiting, bull-baiting and cock-fighting were accepted forms of entertainment. Ordinary people once looked upon these barbaric activities as forms of sport and saw nothing wrong in them. However, by the 1870s the Society for the Prevention of Cruelty to Animals had come into existence and many people were beginning to question the morality of some sports. In November 1871 an action was brought against three Widnes men, William Hunt, a cooper; James Lewis, a labourer; and

403

George Cooper, a publican. The action had been instigated by the Liverpool branch of The Society for the Prevention of Cruelty to Animals. The case involved alleged cruelty to a rabbit, causing it to be worried by dogs. A complaint had been made to Inspector Fowler of the Widnes Police who, after ordering his officers to investigate the complaint, had subsequently brought the action to court. A description of the event in question, whilst providing a distressing account, also gives us an idea of how popular this type of activity was. The court case was reported thus:

"Police constable No. 401 said that on the 18th of the present month, about four o'clock in the afternoon, he was in company with Inspector Brown near the race ground at Widnes, when he was attracted to a crowd of 150 men and boys assembled on some ground enclosed by a brick wall. There were among them several dogs; Cooper and Lewis each held a dog in slips, and Hunt had a bag containing wild rabbits. He took a rabbit from the bag, and after showing it to the dogs ran some distance with it, shaking it the whole time. He then put the animal on the ground, and the dogs were slipped by Cooper and Lewis. The rabbit reached the wall and climbed halfway up, when it fell and the dogs seized it, pulling it in different ways. The badly injured rabbit was taken alive from the dogs and replaced in the bag. In his (the Constable's) opinion it was great cruelty to treat the rabbit in that way: - Mr. Bretherton, the Defence Counsel, said that the witness had been at a coursing meeting and seen the greyhounds pull the hare different ways, he had also been at foxhunts. There were many such coursing meetings in the neighbourhood of Widnes. Mr. Bretherton also said that they had the present advantage of having on the Magistrates Bench an English sportsman; and he would therefore know the customs and manners of sportsmen. He contended that the summons had not been supported by the evidence adduced, no cruelty having been shown. There did not appear to have been little more cruelty than there was in running a hare. It was quite true that the ground was enclosed, but that fact did not alter the case. It was an everyday matter to train greyhounds in the way that the defendants had been doing. Furthermore, the Act stipulated that the cruelty must extend to a number of animals. The rabbit was not included on that list, and the wild rabbit was certainly not a domestic animal. He referred also to similar cases tried at Birmingham, Manchester and Sheffield, in all of which it was decided that the rabbit was not within the provision of the Act of Parliament. The Magistrates dismissed the summons".

In the crowded urban atmosphere of our industrial towns, where huge multitudes of people from diverse backgrounds were thrown together in an unnatural mix, there were bound to be episodes of tension or discord. We have seen in this chapter that crime, of all degrees of seriousness, was rife in both towns. Violence, theft, drunkenness, scandal, intrigue, gossip, petty quarrels, sharp practice, fraud and immoral behaviour – all these transgressions were present in day to day events in both Runcorn and Widnes. Another type of crime which was also prevalent during this era and deserves special mention was poaching. Because of the poverty associated with low wages or unemployment, the temptation to catch rabbits or shoot game for the pot was extremely tempting; therefore, poaching was fairly widespread. Apart from the benefit of bringing food to the table, some habitual poachers also enjoyed the battle of wits against the police and gamekeepers. However, for those who were caught the penalties were extremely severe. The Game Laws were stringently enforced and the police had powers to stop and search suspected poachers or those trespassing on land.

It would be quite impossible to include more than a brief example of the numerous poaching prosecutions which occurred in both towns. In February 1839 a man named John Higginson was charged with trespassing in the grounds belonging to William Hurst at West Bank. David Corns, who was servant to a Mr. Kidd, claimed that on the day in question he was driving his master's gig at West Bank when he saw Higginson shoot a hare in one of Mr. Hurst's fields, which was at that time tenanted by a Mr. Rimmer. Higginson was fined forty shillings and sent to a House of Correction for three months. Poaching was endemic in all places where there were expanses of land with rabbits, hares or other game available for the dinner table. Two men were given huge fines for trespassing on land belonging to a Mr. Gawsworth at Farnworth in August 1845. The men, Charles Barlow and James Thornhill, had both been summoned for poaching together on the same land several times before. Barlow had been caught trespassing at least eight times and Thornhill at been summoned for poaching at least three times. The total fines inflicted upon Barlow had amounted to £8.3s. However, both men had up to that time been lucky enough to avoid a custodial sentence.

Whilst, on the face of it, poaching and trespassing may seem fairly innocuous crimes there was a more serious element to many of these incidents. Assaults by poachers on gamekeepers and vice versa were regular occurrences and some of these assaults were of a serious nature. In November 1862 two Widnes men, William Locket and Michael

Knockton, both known poachers, were summoned for trespassing with ferrets and nets in search of game on land at Cuerdley. They were also charged with assaulting the gamekeeper, Mr. Lightfoot. It was alleged that when the gamekeeper caught them in the act of poaching the two men attacked him and gave him a violent beating. It was said that Knockton was armed with a long bladed knife and would, in all probability, have stabbed Lightfoot but for the sudden appearance of another gamekeeper. Of course Knockton would have brought the knife with him as part of his routine poaching tackle and there is no evidence to suggest he had intended to use it on the gamekeeper. Knockton was fined £5 and imprisoned for the assault. Lockett received a lesser sentence and a fine of £2.10s.

The old question of *"who polices the police?"* was raised in 1890 when an Inquiry into allegations of irregularity in the administration of the Cheshire Police Force took place at Chester Castle. The Inquiry concerned an allegation brought against the Runcorn Police by Mr. Slater-Lewis, a member of Cheshire County Council. Mr. Slater-Lewis claimed that there was an unacceptable level of drunkenness among the police in and around the town of Runcorn. He also said that their Superintendent, Superintendent Hollingworth, was the worst offender. The chief witness called to support Mr. Slater-Lewis's claim was ex-Inspector O`Donnell who had spent several years at Runcorn before his retirement.

The allegations referred to the period 1886-1889. It was stated that during that period 7 out of the 15 policemen who were stationed at Runcorn had been reported for drunkenness. It was also stated that the Wilson Hotel was the regular drinking place, till all hours of the night, of the Magistrates` clerks and assistants. Mr. O`Donnell told the Inquiry that when he was first sent to Runcorn he had been given to understand that there was a great deal of rollicking and drunkenness going on among the public generally. He had no idea that the police would be as bad. He said that Sergeant Gosling's laxity was noted on many occasions. He had also seen Superintendent Hollingworth under the influence of liquor on a number of occasions.

During the course of the Inquiry, which lasted several months and cost the local taxpayers £600, Superintendent Hollingworth called several character witnesses to vouch for his sobriety. Doctor McDougall, the Medical Officer of Health for the district, told the panel that:

"During that period he had had many opportunities of judging Hollingworth's character, and certainly had no suspicion that he was a drunkard. As Medical Officer of Health, he wished to take exception to a statement by Superintendent O'Donnell that he had had great difficulty in regard to brothels; that the town was in a very immoral state; and that the police had great difficulty in dealing with them in consequence. That was not a true statement, for to his knowledge there was now not a single brothel left in Runcorn. Since the Criminal Law Amendment Act was passed in 1887, lodging house inspectors were appointed, who brought home to the owners of the houses the fact that the penalties would be enforced, with the result that they were now done away with. In this work he had had the valuable support of Superintendent Hollingworth. It was not due to the exertions of ex-Inspector O'Donnell that the diminution of these houses occurred. He was mischievous and interfering and created an unfavourable environment."

As an additional note of interest, it was not accurate to claim that all brothels in Runcorn, and in Widnes too for that matter, had been done away with. There are numerous cases in both towns where lodging-house keepers had been fined *" for permitting persons of opposite sexes to occupy the same sleeping apartment"* One does not need to be Sherlock Holmes to deduce what sort of lodging houses these referred to. Around this time too, a case was brought before the Magistrates claiming that two women had committed a robbery at a house of ill-repute in Runcorn. The women, Catherine Matthews who was from Widnes and Elizabeth Abbott the keeper of a house of ill-fame at Runcorn, were charged with robbing a German sailor in Runcorn. They were both imprisoned and received sentences of six months and twelve months respectively, both sentences were to be served with hard labour.

Although the main focus of the Inquiry seems to have been centred on the drunkenness of the Runcorn police, a further accusation concerned the unprofessional and dubious conduct of deploying large numbers of policemen to assist gamekeepers in pursuit of poachers. An extract from the proceedings tells us more about these accusations:

"(1)That the police have from time to time, especially within the last 14 years, been employed, to the neglect of their proper duty, in aiding gamekeepers at nights, sometimes on private land, therefore their beats being meanwhile totally unprotected from crime.

(2)That it is part of the police system generally to conceal this fact of so doing by entries in their journals, misleading the Government Inspector of Police.

(3)Specific charge – that on the 24th day of September, 1889, the town of Runcorn was cleared of all police on duty (except office clerk) from eleven p.m. until four a.m. or thereabouts, for the purpose of aiding gamekeepers on Sir Richard Brooke's estate at Norton, several miles from their ordinary beats, with the consent or knowledge of their Superintendent, and that their beats in Runcorn were meanwhile totally unguarded"

The result of the Inquiry found that at least 16% of the whole Cheshire Police Force were considered to be drunken and unreliable. The charges against Superintendent Hollingworth were upheld and he was transferred to Stockport, although he was not demoted. At the conclusion of the Inquiry the Chairman of the panel, Doctor Hodgson, made the following statement:

"Coming to that part of the report dealing with game and poachers, he strongly condemned the entry of poachers in the police journals as being described as "suspicious characters". He believed in calling a spade a spade, and that there was something radically wrong in this practice of keeping a proper entry out of the journals; and substituting a phrase that might indicate any other class of offender. Such a practice tended to make the police crooked instead of straight."

It is quite clear that the journal entries which describe poachers as suspicious characters were meant to mislead. The reason for doing so was that they were working for a private individual, Sir Richard Brooke, on his private land, instead of carrying out their official duties. If they were pursing *"suspicious characters"* then it could be construed that they were on official business. It was an outrageous state of affairs but no action seems to have been taken against the Officer in charge. From the report we are led to believe that this was a long standing arrangement, something that had happened regularly over a period of fourteen years. I should like to remind readers that Sir Richard Brooke was a Runcorn Magistrate.

BABIES AND CHILDREN

The sailcloth industry in the northern end of Widnes offered employment to whole families of weavers; fathers, mothers and children. Of course children, until they were old enough to become fully fledged weavers, were usually only given menial tasks to perform. These tasks mainly involved bobbin winding and tidying up. However, even this minor work provided a welcome and necessary contribution to the family income. Although the employment of children under 9 years of age was illegal after 1833, it continued unofficially in many of the sailcloth factories in our area. Because it was mainly an industry where whole families were employed on a semi-formal basis, employers often flouted the employment laws, especially as parents were willing and often keen to allow their children to work to supplement the family economy.

Both men and women worked in the local weaving sheds, but for those women of child bearing age there was no such thing as maternity leave before or after the birth of a child. Most women worked well into their pregnancy and some were compelled, for financial reasons, to continue working almost up until the birth. One astonishing example of this occurred in mid-February 1841 when a lady called Mrs. Bradshaw gave birth to three bouncing sons. The triplets were born within three hours of her leaving her work at the sailcloth factory of Thomas Kidd in Farnworth. The following report appeared in *The Liverpool Mercury* on 20th February.

> **BIRTH.**
> On Tuesday last, as Dr. Kidd, of Farnworth, was passing over Lunt's-heath, in Widnes, he was called into a cottage to see Mrs. William Bradshaw, a midwifery patient. She had been at work in the factory of Thomas Kidd, Esq. at three o'clock, and at six she was delivered of three fine male children, all alive and hearty. The mother is doing well, and the trio have been baptized William, Samuel, and John.

I would suppose that the birth of triplets came as a huge shock to Mr and Mrs. Bradshaw. It is almost certain that medical science would not have been advanced enough at that time to predict a triple birth. Anyway, it is reassuring to know that they were all delivered safely and the mother was doing well. She must have been a tough woman to have been doing strenuous factory work just three hours before giving birth to three bouncing babies. It is hard to imagine but that was the norm in those days. Women were expected to take childbirth in their stride and working right up until the onset of labour, in no matter what capacity, was not an unusual occurrence. It has been said that industrialisation had a huge impact on women's place in society and that this was the beginning of their participation in the labour force. But this is not quite true, as women were always expected to work. Some worked in domestic service or in agriculture, labouring alongside their husbands on farms, or in cottage industries or factory trades like Mrs. Bradshaw. They did this while giving birth, raising children and looking after the house. In fact, at that time women's role in society was seen as the drudge rather than the companion to the man.

If Mrs. Bradshaw was surprised by the unexpected birth of three babies, then the lady who lived at the Hanging Birches Farm near the Black Horse had experienced an even greater surprise just a few weeks earlier. In this unfortunate case there was no celebration or delight but, instead, a great deal of heartbreak and tragedy. A newspaper report of 2nd January 1841 gives this account of a rather sad and shocking event.

"On Tuesday week an occurrence of an extraordinary nature came to the knowledge of the inhabitants of Widnes. In the course of the day a plain-looking woman, with a child in her arms, walked into the "Hanging Birch", a small beer-shop at Widnes, and called for a glass of ale. This request was addressed to the female who kept the house, who, at the time, was busily employed preparing a batch of bread for the oven. She immediately abandoned her then occupation to wait upon her customer, and went down stairs to draw the beer, leaving her own infant in the cradle fast asleep. On her return from the cellar the landlady's surprise may be conceived at finding her customer had vanished, without waiting for the liquor she had been put to the trouble of drawing. The abrupt departure of her guest caused no suspicion at the moment of anything being wrong, as everything, on her return from below stairs, appeared just as she had left them. In a little while, however, a discovery took place which nearly deprived the poor woman of her reason, and might have led to consequences not easily foreseen. The child in the cradle having become restless, and notifying, by loud screams, that the attention of a parent would be desirable, the mother

stooped to take it in her arms, when, who can describe the state of her feelings, she found the infant quite black in the face. Thinking it was labouring under strong convulsions, she posted off for medical assistance, in a state of mind bordering on distraction. The medical man, on being consulted, declared that nothing on earth was the matter with the child, it being as healthy a babe as had lately come under his inspection; and as for the darkness of its face, it was produced by natural causes, the fact being that the child was born black, for no other reason than because its progenitor must have been of the same colour. The truth of the matter instantly crossed the mind of the unhappy woman, and the conclusion was that her own "sweet babe" had been carried off by the stranger woman, who had substituted this precious child of ebony hue – a black child, on the principle that "exchange is no robbery". The hue and cry was instantly raised, but without leading to the discovery of the perpetrator of this wanton and cruel outrage. The child was immediately packed off to the workhouse where, we believe it still remains, but with slender hopes of paternity[137]".

Parts of this article have been ommitted as I feel it would be offensive and distasteful to quote the racial terminology used in the original newspaper report. However this extremely sad case is an example of the dreadful prejudice which existed at that time. Obviously the mother of the child was white and the baby was black. It is also likely that the child was illegitimate, which in itself would have presented huge problems for the mother. To bear a child of mixed race, in what was then a hugely bigoted society, would have been an added difficulty. In spite of these fears, it seems beyond belief that any mother would willingly part with her own baby because of the colour of its skin. This action in itself is an indication of the level of intolerance and racial discrimination of those times. There were no winners in this tragic story. The lady from The Hanging Birches had lost her own beloved child and so had the mother of the black child. This mother had probably hoped that her child would be well cared for by the landlady, unfortunately, the outcome was terrible. The landlady and authorities packed the black child off to the workhouse and its fate is unknown. It is heartbreaking to contemplate the life which lay ahead of this poor abandoned baby, unwanted and unloved, and sent to a place known for its cruel and harsh regime. The poor landlady was naturally inconsolable, and the fate of her baby unknown. One would hope that

---

[137] Liverpool Mercury – 2nd January 1841

its substitute mother loved and cared for it as her own. This was a tragic and cruel deed which was clearly motivated by the odious attitude of society at that time

Of course intolerance towards other races was quite obnoxious, so too was the attitude of society towards illegitimate children. During the 17th and the 18th centuries the negativity displayed toward illegitimate children and their mothers was evident in legislation which denied them assistance from the Poor Rates. When the Poor Laws were reformed in 1834 a *"Bastardy Clause"* absolved the alleged father of any responsibility for his illegitimate child. At that time it was generally believed that both poverty and illegitimacy were due to the moral failings of the individual. Therefore the New Poor Law was designed to restore virtue and stimulate a thrifty, industrious mind-set among *"the lower classes"*. As a consequence of this widely held view, the law was deliberately intended to victimize the unmarried mother both socially and economically in an effort to restore female morality.

In those days there was no financial support or other social care for young girls who *"got into trouble"*. If an unmarried mother was unable to support her child it was almost impossible to place it in an orphanage. Most orphanages accepted only *"lawfully begotten"* children and denied entry to those born out of wedlock, despite the fact that the largest number of orphans were illegitimate. Because of this situation many young unwed mothers, unable to deal with the desolation and shame, placed their infants in workhouses where their survival was questionable. The workhouse was often the last resort for pregnant girls who had been abandoned by their families. Unmarried pregnant girls were given shelter in the workhouse but in order to earn their keep they were required to work, often scrubbing floors and doing similar heavy work right up until the time of their confinement. This type of drudgery was the expected compensation for their board. For the children who were born within the precincts of the workhouse their future was tarnished by the disgrace of having their place of birth recorded on their birth certificates. This meant that not only were unmarried mothers ostracised by society, the innocent children were also stigmatised by the circumstances of their birth.

Of course there were limited employment opportunities for single girls who were pregnant or had illegitimate children in tow. Most girls worked in domestic service and were under the close scrutiny of their employers. It was almost impossible to conceal their condition in the latter stages of pregnancy and they were usually dismissed from their post if a pregnancy was suspected. This form of childbirth brought not only censure from society, but often the stigma also meant alienation from family and friends. Often the family of the girl would coerce the father of the unborn child to make an honest woman of her and forced marriages of this type, known as *"shotgun weddings"*, were a common occurrence. However, for those girls who did not make it to the altar, the future was bleak.

It is patently clear that unwed mothers and their infants were spurned and ostracised not only by society but also by charitable institutions. In 1842 the Poor Law Commissioner issued orders that *"loose women"* ought to be separated from women and girls of good character in the workhouses. So, even in the grim confines of that unpleasant institution, they were considered an affront to morality. The inference was that they would contaminate the minds and morals of those they came into contact with. As a result of this humiliation many unwed mothers, unable to cope with the shame of their situation, committed infanticide. I must say that during the course of my research I found it both distressing and shocking to discover how widespread this practice was. There can be no doubt that society's attitude to illegitimacy was mainly responsible for the growth of this abominable crime. Many young girls, who were incapable of carrying out such heinous acts themselves, turned to baby farmers who specialized in the premeditated and systematic murder of illegitimate infants. Although these evil baby farmers preyed on the infants of humiliated and alienated mothers, society in general was partly responsible for enabling the growth of a fresh and murderous form of an old system.

One can scan the columns of many provincial newspapers of those times and find seemingly innocuous advertisments which offer to care for, or adopt, a child for a specific sum of money. These adverts were aimed at mothers of illegitimate babies. They would have been intended to appeal to mothers who were having difficulties coping or finding employment with the added liability of a child. This is one example of numerous similar adverts I found in *The Liverpool Mercury* and other northern newspapers.

NURSE: Child Wanted, or to Adopt: -- The Advertiser, a Widow with a little family of her own, and moderate allowance from her late husband's friends, would be glad to accept the charge of a young child. Age no object. If sickly would receive a parent's care. Terms, Fifteen Shillings a month; or would adopt entirely if under two months for the small sum of Twelve pounds.

HUNDREDS OF VICTIMS.

Amelia Dyer,
Baby Farmer
and Strangler.

EVELINA EDITH MARNON.

AMELIA DYER.

Reading, England
Executed: June 10, 1896

THE PRACTICE OF BABY FARMING WAS SO WIDESPREAD IN VICTORIAN TIMES THAT
IMAGES, SUCH AS THE ABOVE, WERE REGULAR FEATURES IN NEWSPAPERS AND
POPULAR MAGAZINES OF THE TIMES.

Although innocently misleading to the general public, adverts of this type were a veiled message to unmarried mothers. At first glance the information about the character and financial condition of the person soliciting for work, caring for a child, appears to be genuine. However, no name and no address were given and no references were asked for or offered. The sum of 15 shillings a month to keep an infant or a sickly child was obviously inadequate. This sentence was included to make it more convincing. In fact the object was to take the child for the sum of £12. Obviously a sickly child or an infant under two months were the least likely to survive and would also be the cheapest to bury. For the sum of £12 the child would be taken and no questions asked. No personal information was exchanged and the transaction between the mother and the baby farmer would usually take place in a public place. Once the money and the baby were handed over the mother knew she would never see the child again. £12 was a great deal of money for a young girl on her own, but paying this was preferable to the exposure of having an unwanted child. £12 released her from a shameful burden, but the innocent infant was condemned to death.

During the course of my research into this distressing subject I came across a report which told me a little about the way in which baby farmers operated. I quote from one small section:

"The primary objective of professional Baby Farmers was to solicit as many sickly infants or infants under the age of two months, as possible, because life was precarious for them and their deaths would appear more natural. They would adopt the infants for a set fee and get rid of them as quickly as possible in order to maximize their profits. The infants were kept drugged on laudanum, paregoric, and other poisons, and fed watered down milk laced with lime. They quickly died of thrush induced by malnutrition and fluid on the brain due to excessive doses of strong narcotics. The cost of burial was avoided by wrapping the naked bodies of the dead infants in old newspapers and dumping them in a deserted area, or by throwing them in rivers."[138]

Of course most girls could not afford to pay for the services of a baby farmer and therefore many took matters into their own hands. I found a disturbing number of cases of young women being convicted of *"infanticide and concealment of birth"* in both Runcorn and Widnes. In almost all these cases the women were young and unmarried. In court, after pleading temporary insanity, most of the cases received a sympathetic response from the Judge. Most were dealt with quite leniently although they usually resulted in a prison sentence. Despite the fact that there was a significant number of local cases, it should be said that our area was no worse than most other places in that respect. Throughout the nineteenth century this hideous crime was widespread all over the country and, at one point in time, it was said to have reached almost epidemic proportions. We have previously seen the extract from a report on baby farming which states that the bodies of babies were usually dumped in rivers or deserted places. In fact, over

---

[138] *"Victorian Society and Morality"* - J. A. Sampson (London 1954)

the years, the bodies of several dead babies were found in Ditton Brook and other local sites.

One of the more sensational local cases occurred in 1837 and has been discussed in more detail in an earlier chapter. This case involved a young girl who was a servant in the home of the Vicar of Runcorn. There is no information to indicate if the baby was *"full-term"* but, from all accounts, there was no suspicion that the girl was pregnant until she gave birth. A few days before the birth she had complained of feeling unwell and her condition seemed to worsen. On the day she gave birth she had been asked to fold some curtains but as she appeared to be in some pain, her mistress, Miss Masters, urged her to get some medical assistance. Soon afterwards she went into another room and a short while later Miss Masters heard the cries of a baby. Miss Masters at once called for a doctor and when he arrived he could find no sign of a baby. After a search of the room the dead baby was discovered concealed in a corner covered with a dirty cloth. After a post-mortem examination it was said that the marks of a finger and a thumb were discernable on the baby`s neck. The terrified girl was immediately arrested and committed to Chester Castle, after which she stood trial and was convicted of wilful murder. The girl was sentenced to a significant term in prison for the crime.

One feels a degree of sadness and sympathy in cases such as the above, where one can plainly see that an innocent young girl had been taken advantage of. Her actions were probably the spontaneous result of fear and panic, rather than evil intent. Although one cannot know the real circumstances of any case, nevertheless, some reports do provoke some feelings of compassion for the accused. In December 1855 a respectable young Widnes girl called Emily Craggs was arrested for concealing the birth of a female child. She was released on bail as she was unwell. When she appeared in court she wore a heavy veil and was so weak and delicate that she had to be given a chair. Although she entered a not guilty plea, the Jury, after a very short deliberation returned a verdict of guilty. The Judge, obviously moved by the demeanour of the young prisoner, said he would need to make an example of her so would sentence her to the minimum of two months imprisonment. During her trial the girl, who appeared to be distraught and quite frail, was accompanied by her elderly father who seemed most concerned for her welfare. One wonders how she survived two months in prison.

Over the years there were countless cases of infanticide in both towns. Usually there had been some attempt to conceal the birth by *"dumping"* the dead child in some place far removed from the home of the mother. Often this was a ditch, a stream, a dustbin or ashpan. In some cases the mothers were assisted in the murder of their baby by a third party. The accomplice was frequently the father of the child and in some cases it was a friend or close family member. There were several local cases where it was not the mother who was responsible for the murder and concealment of the baby, but someone else. In June 1861 an elderly woman named Mary Harney from Widnes was charged with the murder of her daughter's newly-born illegitimate child. In this instance, although the grandmother of the child was the person responsible, the daughter was also implicated. However, the daughter had suffered serious complications after the birth and it was said that she was too ill to appear in court. The grandmother was sentenced to six months imprisonment with hard labour.

The extent of the crime of infanticide throughout the country was a serious cause of concern to officers of the Justice System. A great deal of time was taken up by the Assize Courts in prosecuting young women. A jail term did not seem to be much of a deterrant as instances of infanticide continued to increase at an alarming rate. In Chester, at the Cheshire Summer Assizes in August 1865, Lord Chief Justice Cockburn made a statement to the Court concerning the number of cases of infanticide on the list. He said to the Jury who were about to try a number of these cases:

"Now, gentlemen, it is a matter of common knowledge that the crime of infanticide has been of late very much on the increase, and the public mind has been shocked and startled lately in a trial from which it appears that in some parts of the country infanticide is practiced as a trade. This, therefore, is not a time when it would be excusable to speak lightly of any of the offences – either the offence of concealment of birth, or the more serious offence – which indeed no one can speak lightly of – child murder.

The extent of this crime reached a peak in the 1870s when it attained an almost rampant scale. The problem was so acute in London that in 1870 alone 276 dead infants were found in the streets and alleyways of the city. Although this extremely sad type of social problem did not reach the scale seen in the 1870s it did continue to occur with an unwelcome regularity in both towns. In Widnes, in July 1890, the body of a newly-born male child was found discarded in an ashpit of a house in Waterloo Road. After a post-mortem examination it was decided that the baby had been born alive. In September 1892 a

417

17year old unmarried girl from Farnworth surrendered herself to the police and confessed to having concealed the birth of her child. In her confession she admitted that she had hidden the body in an ashpit at Farnworth. The dead child, which had been wrapped in brown paper, was found in the ashpit shortly afterwards. The young mother was subsequently charged and sent for trial at the Liverpool Assizes where she received a prison sentence.

Naturally we all find the crime of infanticide quite shocking. One cannot imagine the desperation which would drive a mother to commit such an act. The accompanying charge of *"concealment of birth"* suggests that the shame of having an illegitimate child was a driving factor. No doubt economics would also have played a significant role. An unmarried mother, with no means of support for herself or her child, would find it hard to cope financially. In those days there was no welfare system to rely on; there was no child benefit payment or subsidised housing for unmarried mothers. Instead, the burden of support would be placed upon the family. However we should remember that in many cases young unmarried mothers were disowned by their families for bringing disgrace upon them, so there would be no help from that source.

In lots of cases there was an attempt to get support from the father of the child. Unfortunately in those days, prior to the the discovery of genetic profiling, DNA tests were not available to help with paternity claims. Therefore, in cases of children born outside of wedlock, it was very difficult to prove the parentage of the child if the suspected father denied his responsibility. It was not uncommon for a girl to bring a claim case against the alleged father and, in these cases, the legal proceedings were usually reported in the local press. The newspapers were generally quite uninhibited in their reporting and often gave a candid and embarrassing account of the relationship between the two parties. Countless cases of this nature were brought before our local magistrates. One Runcorn case appeared in *The Liverpool Mercury* in 1868. This was was particularly interesting for the fact that one of the witnesses for the defence was a well-known local woman named Ruth Roberts.

In this report Ruth Roberts is described as a charwoman but one wonders if this was the same Ruth Roberts who, in previous times, had made a living carrying water around the town and selling it by the canful. That Ruth Roberts had developed a lucrative business catering to people who were too proud to walk down to get their water from the

Sprinch Brook or the several other wells which the Runcorn townspeople relied on for their water supply.

> THE RUNCORN BASTARDY CASE AGAIN.—
> SHAMEFUL REVELATIONS.—At the Widnes petty
> sessions, yesterday, John Blundell, master ship-
> wright, of Runcorn, was again summoned by his
> cousin, Mary Wright, to show cause why he
> should not contribute to the support of her illegiti-
> mate child, of which she said he was the father.
> It will be remembered that the case was before the
> bench at the last petty sessions, when it was dis-
> missed for the want of corroborative evidence.
> Since then other evidence had been found in the
> person of the sister of the complainant, who
> deposed yesterday that during the early part of
> this year she slept with her sister Mary, and that
> the defendant was in the habit of going to bed
> to her sister. For the defence, Ruth Roberts, a
> charwoman, was examined, and she said that she
> had seen indecent tricks take place between the
> complainant and a young man named Wrench, and
> that the complainant had given her £1 not to
> mention what she had seen, as she intended to
> father the child on James Blundell. Mr. Swift,
> for the complainant, and Mr. Day, for the defend-
> ant, having addressed the bench, the magistrates
> consulted and decided again not to make any order.

As readers will probably realise, most cases of infanticide were connected to illegitmate births, however, not all cases fall into that category. The advent of the insurance business brought a further motive for murder. The most notorious local case of the times, where insurance was the incentive, occurred in Widnes in 1879 when the wife of Patrick Treacy and their two lodgers were indicted for his murder. They were all found guilty and sentenced to death by hanging. Mrs. Treacy, who was pregnant at the time, had her sentence commuted to life imprisonment but the lodgers were subsequently hanged at Kirkdale Goal in Liverpool. This was a callously premeditated murder in which the motive was the insurance money. Mrs. Treacy had previously taken out several insurance policies on the life of her husband. [139] Each policy was for a substantial amount of money. Unfortunately, murder for insurance money was also the motivation behind numerous crimes of infanticide during the nineteenth century, and there were several infamous cases of this nature which shocked the nation. Although Patrick Treacey had been shot dead, the most common method of murder for insurance was by poisoning. It was common knowledge that arsenic poisoning was particularly difficult to detect, as its symptoms were similar to those of dysentery and other gastric causes of natural death.

During the nineteenth century it was common practice for families to enrol their children in a *"burial club"* for a halfpenny per week. If the child died the club would pay out as much as £5 towards funeral expenses. Since a cheap funeral would cost around £1 this would leave a considerable surplus for feeding and clothing the remaining children. Some familes enrolled their children in several clubs to increase the payout. Unfortunately this meant that the appeal of life insurance payouts became a potent cause of infanticide. So widespread was the burial club scandal believed to be, that questions were asked in Parliament. Because of this mounting concern, legislation was passed in 1850 prohibiting insuring children under the age of 10 for more than £3. One of the most infamous cases of this type was that of Mary Ann Cotton from County Durham who murdered most of her 15 children and step-children, as well as her mother, three husbands and a lodger. She was hanged in 1873.

One alleged case of infanticide, which received extensive nationwide publicity, occurred in Runcorn in 1846. This case involved the death of two young children and the alleged attempted murder of a third child. The deaths were thought to be connected to insurance claims. The 31year old father, who I shall refer to as Mr. P,[140] was employed as a ship-carpenter in Runcorn. He had recently enrolled as a member of the *Weaverham New Friendly Society* and could expect to receive substantial payouts from them on the deaths of his children. In addition to this, the mother who was 27years old, had recently entered the children in the *Liverpool Victoria Legal Burial Society*. Subscriptions to this society were 1d (one penny) per week for children of 5years and above, and ½d (halfpenny) per week for children under 5. The payout for children over 5 was £5 for funeral expenses, for children under 5 this amounted to £2.10s. (Two pounds and ten shillings).

---

[139] *"Yesterday's People"* – Jean M. Morris 2012 (Springfield-Farrihy Publishing)
[140] I think it would be wrong, for a number of reasons, to include this surname.

On the 6th of March that year the couple's youngest child, a ten month old infant called James, was reported to have been found dead in his bed. An Inquest was held and the principal witness examined was the mother of the child. The mother gave a detailed account of the symptoms and illness the child had experienced in the days prior to his death. Such was her evidence that the Coroner was led to believe that the death was the result of one of the various childhood diseases that was common among children at that time. A verdict was returned which simply stated *"found dead"*. Ten days later, on the 16th March, another child, Richard, was taken ill. This child was taken to a see a local medical gentleman, Dr. Edward Pye, who precribed a medicine. A day or two afterwards the mother returned to Dr. Pye and told him that the child was no better and begged him to give her alternative medication. Dr. Pye gave her two lots of powdered medicine for the child. Unfortunately, this child died on 21st March. The powdered medication, given to the mother by Dr. Pye, was later found unopened in the home of the parents.

The deaths of little James and Richard did not cause any immediate misgivings as infant mortality from a variety of ailments was fairly common at that time. Obviously there was nothing about their deaths which gave Dr. Pye any reason to suspect that anything improper had occurred. Although, as is often the case in such matters, in hindsight many people could remember incidents which in retrospect might be viewed as suspicious. It later emerged, during the subsequent court case, that prior to the burial of the second child the father had given orders to the Sexton of the church that the body of the first dead child should be taken out of the grave. He requested that the grave be made deeper and the new coffin placed under the body of the previously buried child. At the time, although the Sexton thought the request rather strange, it did not arouse any undue suspicions.

Just over a month after the death of the second child, on Monday 27th April, the mother took a third child, Thomas, to the surgery of Dr. Pye. Young Thomas was three years and two months old. His symptoms appeared to be common childhood ailments which, at the time, produced no alarm in the mind of Dr. Pye. However as the child's condition worsened considerably over a period of days, Dr. Pye developed serious reservations about the situation. As a result of his grave doubts he contacted the local Magistrates and also the County Coroner and voiced his concerns. In the meantime, the child's condition had rapidly deteriorated and he was dangerously ill. Dr. Pye ordered the mother to preserve the child's vomit for examination and emphasised the importance of this request. However despite his explicit instructions, she did not do so. As a result of this, Dr. Pye came to the conclusion that the mother was being deliberately uncooperative and he became concerned for the life of the child. After further consultation with the Magistrates the child was removed from its parent and both she and her husband were taken into custody.

Subsequent inquiries led to a suspicion that arsenic had been administered to the child. The Coroner then issued a warrant for the exhumation of the bodies of James and Richard and ordered Dr. Pye to make a post mortem examination of them. On the coffins being opened, both bodies were found to be remarkably fresh considering the period of time which had elapsed since their deaths. This strengthened the belief that arsenic had been given to them, as it has the effect of preserving dead bodies. The bodies of both childen were removed and taken for official post-mortem examination. Samples were removed from several organs and analysed. The body of Richard was examined by Dr. Brett, who was a Professor of Chemistry in Liverpool, assisted by a Mr. Page. Arsenic was found in the brain, kidneys, spleen and liver. Grains of white arsenic were also found in the contents of Richard`s stomach. It was stated that this amount was enough to kill several persons. Arsenic was also clearly detected in the viscera of the body of young James.

When the parents appeared before the local magistrates, charged with the murder of their children, a great deal of circumstantial evidence was presented to the Jury. This evidence mainly concerned the mother and there was nothing more than suspicion against the father. As a consequnce, he was discharged but the Jury returned a verdict of *Willful Murder* against the mother in both cases. The mother, on hearing the verdict, burst into tears and loudly declared her innocence. She was subsequently committed for trial at Chester Assizes.

When the 27year old mother appeared at Chester Assizes in August 1846 she was indicted for the murder of her two children. During her trial several witnesses came forward to speak in her defence. All these people gave wonderful character references for both the mother and the father. Of the father it was said that *"..amongst those who knew him he was considered a respectable, industrious, sober and humane man."* The mother was described as having *"an excellent character for kindness and humanity"*. It would seem that the witness statements had a significant bearing on the result of this case. The father had previously been discharged and no charges were brought against him.

The mother was found to be *"not guilty"* and was subsequently aquitted.

It was certainly a strange case and one which created a great deal of public discussion and differing opinions. In spite of the damning findings of the post-mortem examination, as well as a huge amount of circumstantial evidence, the mother was exonerated. Of course the law requires that a crime be proven *"beyond reasonable doubt"*. In this case the legal defence argued that whilst there was no doubt that arsenic was present in the bodies of two of the children, there was considerable doubt as to whether or not the children might have taken the poison by accident. It was claimed that the poison was in the house as it had been purchased to kill rats. It was alleged that all three children may have consumed quantities of arsenic by mistake. Nevertheless this begs the question as to why, after the deaths of two of their children, these parents did not become ultra mindful of the dangers of having arsenic in their home.

Whatever the truth of this situation, for several months these parents were featured in all the national and local newspapers and branded as child killers. In fact it is quite amazing to me that a Jury exonerated the mother as the pre-trial publicity was extremely prejudicial. The newspaper reports which appeared prior to her trial were, without exception, predisposed to a guilty verdict. There was not one single report of these awful events which raised a hint of doubt over the parents' guilt. Furthermore, I could not find even the slightest suggestion of a possibility of innocence in any report. Several headlines were quite specific in their belief in the parents' guilt and the motive for the crimes. One example was *"Children Poisoned to Obtain Funeral Club Money"*. It does seem incredible that the Jurors were not influenced by such a vast amount of negative reporting. Of course the sad fact is that Mr. and Mrs. P. may just have been innocent parents who, through some ill-fated coincidence, lost two of their three children in the same manner.

A similar case, which happened in 1856, involved a 43year old man and his 31year old wife who lived in Nelson Street, Runcorn. The couple were arrested for the murder of their newborn baby daughter and, as usual, local and national newspapers ran a series of sensational headlines about the case. *"Child Murder at Runcorn"* was the damaging caption used by several northern publications. The body of the child had been examined by a local surgeon, Dr. Wilson, and a preliminary post-mortem indicated that the child had been poisoned with sulphuric acid. A further and more detailed examination by a Professor of Chemistry from Liverpool confirmed the previous findings. His report said that *"analysis of the internal organs and stomach found sulphuric acid in a very strong form, more than sufficient to cause death"*. Despite this detrimental report, the parents were found not guilty of murder and were acquitted due to lack of evidence.

Both these cases highlight the sensationalist nature of the Victorian press. When looking at the general standard of journalism in those times it is clear that, in newspaper coverage, there was usually a presumption of guilt rather than innocence. This attitude appeared to be prevalent when reporting crime of any nature. The principle that one is considered innocent until proven guilty was generally disregarded in order to create a melodramatic or sensational story. It would seem that the grimmer and more lurid the story the more the press and their readers enjoyed it. The Victorian public, like their predecessors, enjoyed the sensation-horror of murder and scandal but, perhaps more importantly, they were reassured by the belief that wrongdoers would get their comeuppance. Reports of trials were lengthy with each detail being consumed with an avid hunger by readers who ultimately wished to be comforted by the conviction of the villains.

We should remember that the presumption of innocence is the bedrock of our legal system. This hypothesis is a legal right and the burden of proof should always be on the accuser and not the accused. Unfortunately, as the Victorian Press enjoyed unprecedented influence, *"trial by newspaper"* was a fact of life in those days. Newspapers were allowed to speculate on a suspect's guilt and sometimes unproven hearsay, or unfavourable opinions regarding the character of the accused, were printed during trials. The Runcorn child deaths were prime examples of the Victorian Press at its worst. In view of the amount of negative and harmful publicity I am absolutely astonished that both sets of parents were eventually acquitted. These days, in cases where a jury is involved, there is an obligation on behalf of the press to refrain from publishing anything which may prejudice a fair trial. It is clear that this type of regulation did not exist in earlier times.

It is with some relief that we leave behind the grim circumstances surrounding child deaths. On a much lighter note, the birth of a baby is generally a joyful occasion and the christening is usually a time for celebration and thanksgiving. As we have seen in these pages, babies and children can bring both joy and heartache in abundance. The lady in Lunts Heath who gave birth to three bouncing babies, after a long and arduous day in Mr. Kidd's sailcloth factory, was no doubt feeling elated once she had got over the shock! On the other hand, the unfortunate lady from the Hanging Birches near the Black Horse was left broken hearted when her baby was callously stolen. For the next "Baby" story we stay in the north end of Widnes, not too far from the scenes of some previous incidents.

In September 1861 another mother was becoming concerned about the survival of her child. In the village of Farnworth a lady called Mrs. Hill, the wife of William Hill, had just given birth to a baby. As was the custom those days, a friendly female relative or neighbour had acted as midwife for the confinement. In this case the lady assisting at the birth was an anxious neighbour. Despite a fairly normal pregnancy it would seem that immediately upon entering this world Mrs Hill's baby displayed little sign of life. There were none of the expected instantaneous yells or movements from the newborn babe and the neighbour feared that the child was unlikely to survive. As the mother was still weak and incapacitated, the neighbour, being a good Christian woman, at once hastened with the child to nearby St. Luke's Church where she asked the the Vicar, the Rev. Jeffs, to baptise the child without delay.

The neighbour knew that Mr. and Mrs. Hill had previously decided that if the child was a boy he would be called *"William"*. Therefore, acting upon the neighbour's specific instructions, the Vicar proceeded to christen the child *"William"*. On returning to the house the neighbour was questioned by the mother, who had now regained some of her strength, as to the gender and condition of her child. Happily the baby had now revived slightly and upon closer examination it was discovered that the baby was female and not male. The neighbour returned at once to the Church to explain the mistake to the Vicar. Unfortunately the name had already been recorded in the register and the Vicar informed her that no alteration could be made. One wonders what happened to little *"William"* Hill, did she survive to become known by some female derivative of the male name *"William"*, maybe Wilhelmina?

THE PLAIN OF BALACLAVA

The position of the armies before the Charge
of the Light Brigade, 25th October 1854

Russian troops ■
British troops □
French troops ◇

⊕ The Redoubts
✱ The position of
   Lord Raglan

Area of charge of Heavy Brigade
and area of Light Brigade camp

CAUSEWAY HEIGHTS

The Woronzoff Road

Tchernaya River

Traktir Bridge

FEDIOUKINE HILLS

The North Valley

The South Valley

The Heavy Brigade

93rd Highlanders

Kadikoi

Royal Martines

BALACLAVA

1 MILE
2000 Yards

0   500   1000   1500

THE NOBLE SIX HUNDRED

I think most readers will be familiar with the story of the ill-fated Charge of the Light Brigade, immortalised by Lord Tennyson in his famous work which was once a staple poem in classrooms across Britain. The events which took place during the Battle of Balaclava caused a sensation in Victorian Britain and soon became the stuff of legends. Since that calamitous event all those years ago, controversy has raged over the mistake which sent the Light Brigade down the valley instead of up onto the Causeway Heights. Although Lord Lucan was to receive most of the blame, an ambiguous message from Lord Raglan was said to be at the heart of a mistake which caused the death of hundreds of men. Another theory was that a trumpet call was sounded which led the men into battle, however no-one knows if this was fact and, if so, who sounded it. The controversies which surrounded the event were numerous and blame was thrown in all directions. In addition to these debates, the extraordinary clash of personalities between Lord Lucan, Raglan and Nolan was thought to have played a major part in the unfortunate saga in which so many young men were sent to inevitable slaughter.

When reading about famous historical events, the major players in these actions have become well-known names. We know who they were and what they did, or rather what historians tell us they did. Those who played less significant roles are usually consigned to history, unknown and forgotten. They are generally regarded as merely bit players in a bygone drama. Yet each man or woman involved in these historical events was a person of importance in their own right. They were sons or daughters, brothers or sisters, husbands or wives, or the fathers or mothers of someone. Their life was unimaginably precious to those who loved or knew them. Some of these nameless players paid the ultimate price by giving their lives for their country and although they belonged to an anonymous mass they were each, in their own way, a vital part of the events which they were caught up in. Widnes author, Harry Jones, in his wonderful book *"I don't want to be a Sunbeam"* gave us a moving reminder of this fact. In this book, the

427

potted biographies of First World War soldiers from Widnes, while often distressing to read, are also in a strange way uplifting. Through his painstaking research Harry Jones has shown us that before that dreadful War these men had lived fairly unremarkable existences. They had come from our own communities, lived in our streets, gone to our local schools and churches and worked in local industries. They were just like us in so many ways, until they were required as cannon fodder for a ruthless war machine. We owe a great debt of gratitude to Harry Jones for shedding a more personal light on these men and their lives, the ordinariness of which is all the more poignant.

Unlike the local dead of the two World Wars, whose names appear on cenotaphs in both towns, there are few acknowledgements of those who fought in earlier historical combats like the Battle of Balaclava. However, we do know that men from both sides of our river were involved in this, as well as some other key events in the Crimean and Boer Wars. In a previous book, *"Into the Crucible"*, I gave an account of how the Widnes Volunteers made an offer to serve overseas at the outbreak of the Boer War. They subsequently joined with the 1st Battalion of the South Lancashire Regiment at Ladysmith in March 1900 and were heavily involved in the sieges of Ladysmith, Mafeking and Kimberley. Naturally, the Boer War being the more recent means that there are numerous sources of information concerning that conflict. We have many letters from local men, written to their families back home, which give us first-hand accounts of some of the fighting.

Unfortunately there appears to be a dearth of specific material about local veterans of The Charge of the Light Brigade, although it is believed that quite a few local men took part in this tragic event. Nevertheless, despite this apparent lack of information, I am sure there is probably a mound of interesting material in local family possessions or other sources to which I am not privy. Whilst acknowledging that there is limited data about early veterans to draw upon, I am fortunate to be able to share a small amount of information on two Widnes veterans of the infamous Battle of Balaclava. These men were Thomas Wright, who lived in Major Cross Street and George McGregor who traded as a herbalist in Hutchinson Street.

Thomas Wright was actually born in Warrington but spent most of his long life in Widnes. When he was young he lived for a short while in Cholmondeley Street before moving to Major Cross Street where he resided for a large part of his life. His military career began when he enlisted into the 17th Lancers known as the *"Death or Glory Boys"* in the early 1850s. He served in the Indian Mutiny and all through the

Crimean War and, of course, he was a survivor of the famous Charge of the Light Brigade at Balaclava. In later life he was employed as a labourer at the Gaskell Deacon works in Widnes. Mr. Wright was a popular and well-known figure in the town and because of his role at Balaclava he was something of a *"local hero"*. When he died it was suggested that he should be given a full military funeral but this did not happen. In April 1903 a memorial stone, paid for entirely by public subscription, was erected over his grave at Widnes cemetery. After a public ceremony, the grave and memorial stone were officially handed over to Widnes Town Council who, as the representative body of the Widnes townspeople, was charged with maintaining both the grave and memorial. Also donated to the town at the same time was a *"large carbon portrait of the great hero, which was handsomely framed"* This portrait, also purchased by public subscription, was donated on the explicit understanding that it would be placed on permanent display in the Public Library in Victoria Square[141].

George McGregor, another veteran of Balaclava, also had an extremely eventful military career. He served in the Punjab and Kaffir Wars and went all through the Crimea. He subsequently took part in the quelling of the Indian Mutiny and the Chinese War. He was discharged on full pension in 1862 after 20years service. However, he was not content to finish with military action and when the American Civil War broke out he decided to join in the fray, but lost his right arm in the process. Fortunately, from a historical perspective, George McGregor was a prolific letter writer. Like Thomas Wright, he was also a participant in the ill-fated Charge of the Light Brigade and it was in respect of that event that he was prompted to take up his pen on several occasions. He wrote numerous letters of complaint about the treatment of the survivors of that infamous event.

Mr. McGregor's letters provide an interesting historical account of the shoddy behaviour of the British Government towards veterans who had been part of that blood-soaked battle. It is interesting to note that despite his palpable outrage he manages to retain an inherent sense of loyalty to his Queen and country. His first letter concerns an article published in *The Liverpool Mercury*. The newspaper had stated that a British Government agent was searching for a man called John Levick who served with the British Army throughout the Crimean War. The article suggested that the Government had had some difficulty in tracing survivors from the War, particularly those associated with The

---

[141] Numerous enquiries have failed to locate the present whereabouts of this picture.

Charge of the Light Brigade. Mr. McGregor was quite cynical of this claim. In May 1889, as one of the survivors of *"The Noble Six Hundred"* he wrote the following response to the article.

"In last Saturday's issue you refer to an agent of the British Government searching for the whereabouts of John Levick, whom you say served all through the Crimean War. With your permission I wish to give you and your readers a little insight into the doings of the aforesaid British Government respecting the noble 600. John Levick was well known to me. He was a sergeant for some time in the 8th Hussars. I am rather surprised to hear that the British Government are so anxious to make "some substantial return to any survivors of that famous charge." If they intend to do anything, they had better do it quickly, for up to the present they have shown to such survivors nothing but studied neglect. Let them begin with poor Thomas Rodgers, of the 4th Hussars, now an inmate of the Withington Workhouse in Manchester. If they want the names of the survivors they can be supplied to the amount of seventy-six very quickly. Sixty-four of these sat down to a banquet in London on October 25th 1888. And ten sat down on the same date in Manchester at Mr. Flood's Crosby Hotel. I myself am one of the survivors of the noble 600. My regimental number was 1382, 4th Light Dragoons, now named the 4th Hussars, and up to the present time the British Government has entirely lost sight of me. From the tender mercies of such a Government I say "May the Good Lord deliver us." There is not one of the noble 600 alive today that would not fight for the Royal ensign of Old England, but I fear they all will agree with me when I state that England is the richest and meanest nation under the sun. Many of the poor survivors are in great need of some "substantial return". This I know for a fact, and I for one would be extremely gratified if the British Government, in what you say they intend to do, would do so speedily, and thus in a small measure wipe off the great reproach that lies at their door. " God Save the Queen".

Several months later, in October 1889, Mr. McGregor wrote a follow-up letter to *The Liverpool Mercury*. It appears that the intervening months had brought no further action by the Government to remedy these terrible injustices.

"May I again trouble you about the Charge of the Light Brigade, and the late festivities commemorating Balaclava Day. I see in a late issue of your dear little paper that you refer to the 196 men who returned to the British lines on that eventful day, and you add "of these but a few are now known at the War Office to be still living." I ask why is this? Is it that they are all dead and being dead are completely forgotten?

Or is it that the War Office, in the exercise of its tender and manifold mercies, has ignored them? Sir, with shame and regret I must confer to the latter belief. All the survivors of that glorious charge are not yet dead. If called upon I could give the names of eighty, among who must be reckoned your very humble servant. No – the stern fact remains that if the survivors are not known to the War Office, it is because the said office does not care to look after them or recognise them. The old accusation still remains that a man may fight for his country, may lose a limb, be crippled for life, be reduced to the lowest edge of poverty, and the country won't acknowledge him. I am not speaking for myself just now. Providence has placed me above the cringing posture of begging bread from my countrymen. But I am writing on behalf of many a poor fellow, survivor of those inglorious days, who would be glad of a little help from the War Office. What should be done? At once let the authorities bestir themselves. Let them – and the task would be easy – let them find out the names and abodes of all the survivors and grant at once the necessary and substantial recognition of their services. If required, I will assist the War Office in this honourable task, and do so most cheerfully. Surely, the time is gone by when the bravest nation under the sun will hesitate to perform such a noble act, and thus wipe away one terrible blot which bids fair to eternally besmear her escutcheon.
I trust that you will insert this letter in your columns, as I thank you for doing with my previous contribution. God Save the Queen".

George McGregor, One of the Six Hundred.
10 Hutchinson Street, Widnes October 30ᵗʰ 1889"

I think most people reading this today will share George McGregor's sense of outrage that these gallant men were treated in such a cavalier and shoddy manner. The fact is, that those who survived were lucky to have escaped with their lives because of a calamitous mistake by their commanding officers.[142] One can only hope that Mr. McGregor's campaign to get reparation for his fellow veterans had a successful outcome.

---

[142]On its return The Light Brigade had a mounted strength of 195 officers and men from an original strength of 673. 247 men were killed and wounded. 475 horses were killed and 42 wounded. The 13th Light Dragoons mustered 10 mounted men.

In reality, at that time there were hundreds of old military and naval veterans living in conditions of profound poverty. At the beginning of December 1899 the plight of old soldiers was discussed at a meeting of the Runcorn Board of Guardians. The Runcorn Board and several other Local Boards had received a letter from the Union Guardians in the London Borough of Poplar requesting that all local Poor Law Unions should petition the Chancellor of the Exchequer. The petition should request that some provision be made from national sources to provide money for the maintenance of the wives and children of soldiers and sailors. Because of a complete lack of support from the Government most of these destitute families were being supported solely by charities. The Poplar Union also suggested that petitions be submitted for adequate maintenance for disabled soldiers and sailors and for the widows and orphans of all soldiers and sailors. Mr. A.R. Norman, a local J.P. and member of the Runcorn Board of Guardians, agreed that something needed to be done. He told the meeting that there was at that very time a man of good character, a Crimean veteran, residing in the Runcorn Workhouse. Speaking of this man he said;

"He was not a man who had spent his money in drink, but had always been willing to work. It was a scandal that such a man should be in the workhouse, and he thought some of the money now being raised ought to be earmarked for the benefit of those who were in such circumstances. The Patriotic Commissioners had £800,000 and yet they allowed men who had fought for their country to end their days in the workhouse."

Mr. Norman informed the Runcorn Board of Guardians that the Crimean veteran was over 70years of age and was a very decent old man. The Board agreed to act upon the suggestion of the Poplar Union. The Clerk was also instructed to make inquiries as to whether the Patriotic Commissioners' Funds could not be applied to the case of the elderly veteran in the Runcorn Workhouse.

EPILOGUE

The county of Lancashire has often been credited with creating the first industrial society in the world. The county was certainly the birthplace of the factory system, a place where anything and everything was made and where coal was mined. Lancashire was also home to the first artificial inland waterway in Britain, a canal, which was built to cater for the transportation needs of the growing industries. Perhaps I should also point out that during the period of time covered in this book Widnes was an integral part of the county of Lancashire rather than a part of Cheshire. Of course that fact had no significant bearing on Widnes's development as an industrial town, for although Lancashire could claim to be the first industrial society, the effects of the Industrial Revolution spread quickly. As a consequence, industrial areas swiftly developed in many other places around the country.

The towns of Widnes and Runcorn played important roles in the development of industrial Britain, both contributing through the production of vital commodities to serve the growing needs of a manufacturing country. Alkali, the core product of the Widnes chemical industry, was an essential element of production for numerous manufacturing industries; and the stone quarried at Runcorn contributed greatly to the physical development of Britain by providing the material to construct docks, bridges and magnificent buildings. Soap as well as alkali was also an essential article of trade, with Runcorn being the first of the two towns to manufacture this commodity on a large scale. However, Widnes, the latecomer, was subsequently to develop this industry into a considerable enterprise. In addition, local transport links, whilst providing huge benefits to our own local industries, also contributed greatly to the development of both Liverpool and Manchester as important trade centres.

As industrialisation developed around the country the general population was changed from a mainly agrarian society into an industrial one. The rapid development of industry locally meant that the indigenous populations were insufficient in number to supply the needs of these growing industries. As a result it became necessary to attract labour from other areas around Britain as well as from other countries. The new workers and their families, those migrant men, women and children who were drawn by the hope of a better life, swarmed into the area in their thousands. In the main they had come from rural areas which had offered fresh air, space, and the emotional comfort of long established rural communities. They arrived into places where they were required to live huddled together in tightly packed urban developments, with little thought having been given to comfort, space or wellbeing. The reassuring support of their traditional communities was replaced by an unfamiliar mass of people with few common bonds to unite them. Apart from the unpleasant living arrangements, they were also thrust into an alien working environment. They soon discovered that factory work was regulated by rules and timekeeping and involved labouring for long hours in hazardous and appalling conditions. The fresh air and green fields which they had enjoyed in their country homes became a distant memory as they became engulfed in smoke, gas and the noxious odours of the alkali process. They were also deprived of the natural pleasure of the green spaces and vegetation they had once taken for granted, as their new homes were in the immediate vicinity of the chemicals works where nothing could grow because of atmospheric pollution.

The new workforces in both towns were comprised of an irregular mix of people. The Runcorn quarries attracted many workmen from Wales, while the building of canals brought workers into the area from Ireland and other parts of Britain. In Widnes the population surge was rapid and the mix was more varied. The arrival of industry into Widnes brought migrants from all corners of Britain and Ireland and later in the century these numbers were supplemented by the arrival of migrants from the Baltic regions and other countries. Although the populations of both towns increased dramatically it should be said that there was also a transient aspect to this working population. Almost every facet of this new urban society was affected by the flow of migration inward and outward as some workers moved on to new horizons, while others stayed and settled.

The coming of industry into the area altered the social composition of Widnes irrevocably. The multicultural mix of people meant that Widnes became a vibrant melting-pot that contained a colourful and pulsating assortment of human life. Some of the immigrants, such as those from Ireland and the Baltic regions, had been driven from their homes by starvation, hardship or tyranny. Nevertheless, no matter where they came from, the common factor was that all had been attracted by the prospect of self-improvement and opportunity.

The rural backgrounds of almost all the newcomers made them especially ill-fitted for the ordeals of urban life, which involved mass living in unhealthy and overcrowded dwellings. Many sought escape from their appalling surroundings and working conditions by over-indulging in alcohol and this became a major cause of crime. The blend of ethnic nationalities and religions was sometimes a source of conflict and varying degrees of discrimination were present in all aspects of daily life. The Irish and Baltic immigrants were the main targets of intolerance but this was not necessarily a local phenomenon. These two groups faced discrimination in all the areas of Britain in which they had settled. Many of the Irish had arrived on these shores as destitute and half-starved migrants who were fleeing from almost certain death in their own country. Unfortunately they arrived at a time when this country was struggling to deal with its own levels of poverty. Therefore the influx of destitute Irish placed an impossible burden upon an already overstretched economy. This situation, coupled with the fact that they were of a different religion to the established church in England, created a lasting animosity towards the Irish. The migrants from the Baltic regions fared no better, as they were thought to have undermined the labour market by working for lower wages, although this was proved to be untrue in most cases.

In the early days, despite the obvious intolerance displayed against people of different nationalities, it is probable that all ethnic groups had their own sets of prejudices. In all societies there is a natural fear of anything unfamiliar which may bring about a drastic change in their way of life. The arrival of foreign immigrants into the mix caused these fears to develop into powerful feelings of resentment. This was a prime example of the unpleasant side of human nature whereby people feel threatened or fearful of anything, or anyone, who does not fall into a traditional social or ethnic mould. Unfortunately people who are different, for whatever reason, are often an easy and obvious target for discrimination. The Lithuanians and Poles faced particular and undeserved hostility as their language, dress and culture isolated them from other social groups

The unprecedented surge in population, particularly in Widnes, brought forth a massive boom in house building and, as demand often exceeded supply, this meant that there was a high level of overcrowding. The homes were built quickly and cheaply with little consideration given to the provision of services to make them healthy places to live. Most streets were unpaved and the drainage was wholly inadequate and incapable of dealing with heavy rain and human waste.

In fact, the living conditions of town dwellers in both towns were deplorable. In the early days, in both Runcorn and Widnes, the official administration and responsibility for services had been carried out by *"Surveyors and Highways Committees"*. However as the towns developed and expanded, it was obvious that more responsible governing bodies needed to be established to oversee the provision of vital facilities for their growing populations. Runcorn, who had developed as a centre of industry much earlier than Widnes, formed their *Runcorn Improvement Commission* in 1852. Thirteen years later, in 1865, the *Widnes Highways Committee* was replaced by the *Widnes Local Board of Health.*

Apart from the business of providing essential services to the two towns, the Managers and Ratepayers had the problem of dealing with the difficulties related to urban poverty. Although the influx of workers into the area would suggest that plentiful work was available, in fact, employment was often dependent upon fluctuating trade markets. This meant that work was sometimes irregular and poorly paid. As a result of the uncertain labour market, and the social problems associated with unemployment and poverty, another vital element of daily life was the subject of Poor Relief. The old Poor Law, which dated from Tudor times, had initially been a method of relieving rural poverty. Over a period of time several minor changes had occurred in its operation. In 1834 a *Poor Law Amendment Act* was passed which reformed the whole system. The revised Poor Law was designed to be far more stringent in its application. New eligibility rules were introduced which were intended as a deterrent in the hope that only those who were truly desperate would apply for relief. Despite the new rules there was still a considerable and sustained demand upon the system and the financial cost to local ratepayers became a cause for grave concern.

Over the following years the bodies responsible for the management of both towns continued to work towards making them agreeable places to live, whilst at the same time trying to balance the books and satisfy the local ratepayers. The problems they faced at that time were numerous and fairly unique, especially in Widnes with its hasty development and unprecedented increase in population. The special material difficulties associated with urban expansion were a major challenge, particularly as uncontrolled jerry-built housing had sprung up rapidly and were cheek by jowl with the new factories.

Besides the difficulties associated with unrestrained building development, which created bad living conditions, there were serious problems associated with the behaviour of a new and evolving population. The great economic and social transformation which occurred in our area produced a chaotic situation whereby a totally new social order struggled to deal with a variety of previously unknown problems. The migrants from the countryside, who became our first truly industrial society, had to learn how to live a new urban way of life. Naturally they took time to adopt urban attitudes but, as they did so, their values and urban horizons were influenced by the physical and mental limits of each working-class neighbourhood they occupied. As a result many of these neighbourhoods became self-contained communities with distinct identities which were shaped by the dominant ethnic group in that area.

The crowding together of thousands of human beings, from diverse environments, religions and cultures meant that there was bound to be a degree of tension and conflict. Throw into that mix an abundance of public houses with long opening hours, providing copious amounts of alcohol, and the result was inevitable. It is no secret that in those early days the two towns were often lawless and brutal places. Cases of drunkenness, fighting, alcohol related crime, poaching, theft and violence of all kinds became common occurrences in the Magistrates Courts of Widnes and Runcorn. Unfortunately murder was also a familiar visitor to our streets. It was all a very long way from the idyllic pictures of Widnes and Runcorn which had been painted by previous generations.

In addition to an unprecedented surge in population and the problems of social integration, the physical landscape of both Runcorn and Widnes were radically changed by the development of industry. As we have seen, both towns were once places renowned for the beauty of their landscapes. They were recognised destinations for those seeking recuperation or for those who simply wished to spend some quality time in healthy and picturesque surroundings. Widnes, once just a collection of small rural villages, was to experience the most radical change. As industry developed on an unparalleled scale the verdant terrain in the south of the town was decimated. Where once had been majestic trees, lush pastures and cattle leys, those vistas had been replaced by a forest of smoking chimneys and dense unhealthy housing. Of course Runcorn did not escape lightly either. There were increases in population on that side of the river as well and, alas, the disreputable behaviour of some led to unease among the native inhabitants. The topography and atmosphere of that area was also altered extensively. We have already seen how the Bridgwater Canal cut into the Runcorn landscape and gobbled up acres of fertile pastureland. The noxious pollution brought about by the expanding

Runcorn soap and alkali industries was also a considerable cause of complaint. Needless to say all these changes, in both towns, were a consequence of the Industrial Revolution. Alterations in society, working habits and lifestyle as well as the landscape and environment were put down to *"progress"*. However once this march of *"progress"* had been set in motion it was unstoppable and irreversible. I think it is fair to say that, despite the advancements and achievements of this age, the drastic transformations in both society and the environment were probably a cause of great lamentation among the indigenous populations of both towns.

In conclusion, we can see that from their relatively small beginnings by the turn of the century both Widnes and Runcorn had developed into thriving urban centres. Widnes, once the slowcoach, had rapidly overtaken her neighbour as a centre of industrial enterprise and urbanisation. The population of Widnes had increased dramatically and the social composition of its society had become diverse both culturally and spiritually. Apart from population surges, the physical landscape of both places had also changed beyond recognition as urbanisation and industry expanded in equal measures. So we can see quite clearly that even though the Industrial Revolution had come fairly late to our areas it was a catalyst for change. The effect on our two towns was both extreme and irreparable as our area and its people became an integral part of one of history's greatest social and economic transformations.

When reflecting on all the past negatives of industrial pollution and the social ills of harsh living and working conditions, in retrospect, we still have a lot to thank John Hutchinson for. Over the past 150 years or so we have been fortunate in having had in our midst several great men who endeavoured to improve the lives of ordinary residents. Some names spring readily to mind, the indomitable Doctor John O` Keeffe who was the champion of the underprivileged in Widnes; Thomas Hazlehurst the great patron of Methodism in both towns; David Lewis, Dan Garghan and a very young Jack Ashley who all served selflessly on Widnes Borough Council to improve the lot of their fellow townspeople. They were all men of vision who strove to instil in our citizens a sense of self belief and pride in their respective towns.

The town that John Hutchinson created has developed extensively over the years. It is now a far cry from the collection of small rural hamlets with a modest population of just over two thousand people. Today Widnes is still growing and thriving, although most of our manufacturing base has disappeared along with the unpleasant sights and smells of the chemical industry. In the past few decades the new incomers attracted to Runcorn and Widnes were mainly migrants from Liverpool, barely a dozen miles away. However, more recent times have brought a small wave of Polish workers into the town. Hopefully these days we are far more tolerant than the Widnesians and Runcornians of the past. In the Widnes of today the grass is green and trees grow and flourish, the homes have gardens, and the town has several lovely parks and green recreational spaces. Although we can never reclaim the idyllic pre-industrial scenes of the past, nevertheless, all in all, Hutchinson's town is not a bad place to be.

Author`s Note:

Unfortunately the poor print quality and condition of some original old newspapers has made them difficult to read and reproduce. Despite that fact, I have included them wherever possible in order to provide readers with an authentic historical record. .

BIBLIOGRAPHY AND SOURCES

Commoners: Common Right, Enclosure and Social Change in England
Neeson, J. M., *1700–1820* (Cambridge, 1993).

The Great Reform Bill in the Boroughs: English Electoral Behaviour
1818–1841 Phillips, J. (Oxford, 1992).

Labour in British Society: An Interpretative History
Price, R., (London, 1986).

Social Classes and Social Relations in Britain, 1850–1914
Reid, A. J., (Basingstoke, 1992).

The Eclipse of a Great Power: Modern Britain 1870–1975
Robbins, K., (London, 1994).

Cholera, Fever and English Medicine, 1825–1865
Pelling, M., (Oxford, 1978).

British Historical Statistics
Mitchell, B. R., (Cambridge, 1988).

Directory and Gazetteer of the County of Lancashire, 1824 (Vol 2)
E. Baines

The Victoria History of the County of Lancaster vol III
W. Farrer and J. Brownbill (1907)

A History of the Chemical Industry in Widnes
D.W.F. Hardie (1950)

The Place Names of Lancashire
E. Ekwall (1922)

British Economic Growth during the Industrial Revolution
Crafts, N. F. R (Oxford University Press, 1985)

The idea of poverty: England in the early industrial age
(London: Faber, 1984)

Crime and English Society 1750-1900
Clive Emsley - 2nd edition (Longman, 1996)

The English Police: A Political and Social History
Clive Emsley - 2nd edition (Longman, 1996)

White-Collar Crime in Modern England: Financial Fraud and Business Morality 1845-1929
George Robb (Cambridge University Press)

Street Violence in the Nineteenth Century: Media Panic or Real Danger? Rob Sindall (Leicester University Press, 1990)

Reconstructing the Criminal: Culture, Law, and Policy in England 1830-1914
Martin J Wiener (Cambridge University Press)

A History of Modern Political Thought
Iain Hampsher-Monk (Oxford University Press – 1992)

Problems of Social Policy
R.M. Titmuss (HMSO 1950)

Documents in English Economic History since 1760
W.B. Clapp (Bell – London 1976)

The Workshop of the World
J.D. Chambers (Oxford University Press 1961)

Population and Society 1750-1940
N.L. Tranter (London – Longman 1985)

The Age of Reform (1815 -1870)
E.I. *Wood*ward (Clarendon Press, Oxford 1958)

The Population History of England (1571-1870)
E.A. Wrigley (Cambridge University Press 1981)

The Workhouse System (1834-1935)
M.A. Crowther (London – Batsford 1981)

Paternalism in Early Victorian England
D. Roberts (London 1979)

The Making of the New Poor Law
A. Brundage (London 1978)

Class in English History (1680-1850)
R.S. Neale (London – Blackwell 1981)

Enterprise and Trade in Victorian Britain: Essays in Historical Economics McCloskey, D., (London, 1981).

History of Irish Labour in Nineteenth Century America
Jean M. Morris (Springfield Farrihy - New York –2007)

Yesterday's People
Jean M. Morris (Springfield Farrihy – England 2013)

Into the Crucible
Jean M. Morris (Countyvise 2005 and Arima Publishing 2009)

An Economic History of Ireland since 1660
L.M. Cullen (Dublin – Lyons 1971)

Early British Steamships
Nigel W. Kennedy (London 1933)

Medieval Cheshire
H. Hewitt (Manchester University Press 1929)

History of Merchant Shipping and Ancient Commerce
W. S. Lindsay (London 1874)

An 18th Century Industrialist – Peter Stubs of Warrington
T. S. Ashton (1939)

The History of the Irish Working Classes
P. Beresford Ellis (London 1972)

Victorian Society and Morality
J.A. Sampson (London 1954)

Victorian Paternalism
J. J. Eade (London 1979)

NEWSPAPERS, PERIODICALS AND OTHER SOURCE MATERIAL

Gore's Liverpool Directories, 1813-1825
Slater's Directories of Lancashire
Pearson's Magazine (1896)
The Tablet (1844)
The Chester Courier and North Wales Advertiser
The Chester Chronicle
The Courant
The Liverpool Mercury
The Manchester Times
The Leeds Mercury
Leamington Spa Courier
The Glasgow Herald
The Motherwell Times
Historical Society of Lancashire & Cheshire (transactions)
Notes by Albert Constable (The Catalyst)

SOURCES - LOCATIONS

The National Archives, Kew, London
The British Library, London
Lancashire Archives and Record Office, Preston
Chetham's Library, Manchester
Cheshire and Chester Archives, Chester
The Catalyst, Widnes
Public Record Office of Scotland, Edinburgh
National Library of Ireland, Dublin
Liverpool Central Library
Warrington Central Library
St. Helens Central Library
Widnes and Runcorn Central Libraries

INDEX

Q

R

S

Lightning Source UK Ltd.
Milton Keynes UK
UKOW06f0748170317
296857UK00007B/84/P

9 781326 865252